Women Writers
of Yiddish Literature

ALSO EDITED BY ROSEMARY HOROWITZ

*Memorial Books of Eastern European Jewry:
Essays on the History and Meanings of Yizker Volumes*
(McFarland, 2011)

*Elie Wiesel and the Art of Storytelling*
(McFarland, 2006)

# Women Writers of Yiddish Literature
## Critical Essays

Edited by
ROSEMARY HOROWITZ

McFarland & Company, Inc., Publishers
*Jefferson, North Carolina*

LIBRARY OF CONGRESS CATALOGUING-IN-PUBLICATION DATA

Women writers of Yiddish literature : critical essays / edited by Rosemary Horowitz.
       p.    cm.
Includes bibliographical references and index.

**ISBN 978-0-7864-6881-2** (softcover : acid free paper) ∞
**ISBN 978-1-4766-1990-3** (ebook)

1. Yiddish literature—Women authors—History and criticsm.
2. Women authors, Yiddish—Biography.   I. Horowitz, Rosemary, editor.

PJ5121.5.W66 2015
839'.1099287—dc23                                   2015005873

BRITISH LIBRARY CATALOGUING DATA ARE AVAILABLE

© 2015 Rosemary Horowitz. All rights reserved

*No part of this book may be reproduced or transmitted in any form or by any means, electronic or mechanical, including photocopying or recording, or by any information storage and retrieval system, without permission in writing from the publisher.*

On the cover: Esther Dominitz (author's collection)

Printed in the United States of America

*McFarland & Company, Inc., Publishers*
   *Box 611, Jefferson, North Carolina 28640*
   *www.mcfarlandpub.com*

# Table of Contents

*Preface by Rosemary Horowitz* ............... 1

Lost and Found: Yiddish Women Writers
    IRENA KLEPFISZ ............... 5

A Review of Yiddish Women Writers in English-Language Anthologies
    ROSEMARY HOROWITZ ............... 11

Still Waiting for Tomorrow: Lily Bes and Her Contemporaries in the 1920s
    HINDE ENA BURSTIN ............... 26

The Red Flower: Rebellion and Guilt in the Poetry of Celia Dropkin
    SHEVA ZUCKER ............... 51

Borrowed Shoes: Shira Gorshman's Politics of Literature
    FAITH JONES ............... 70

From Diamond Cutters to Dog Races: Antwerp and London in the Work of Esther Kreitman
    DAFNA CLIFFORD ............... 88

To Dive into the Self: The *Svive* of Blume Lempel
    ELLEN CASSEDY *and* YERMIYAHU AHRON TAUB ............... 103

"Of all the men I am the most manly": Aspects of Gender in the Poetry of Khane Levin
    JOANNA LISEK ............... 126

The Iron Rod of Desire: Imagism and Modernism in Anna Margolin's *Drunk from the Bitter Truth*
    PAULA HAYES ............... 157

Forgotten Playwright: Kadya Molodowsky and the Yiddish Theater
    DEBRA CAPLAN    180

Gender and Nation in the 1945 Poems of Kadya Molodowsky and Malka Heifetz Tussman
    KATHRYN HELLERSTEIN    195

Gendered Experience in Chava Rosenfarb's *The Tree of Life: A Trilogy of Life in the Łódź Ghetto*
    JULIE SPERGEL    208

The Earth Hurts Me: On the Poetry of Hadasa Rubin
    MAGDALENA RUTA    230

Remembering Two of Montreal's Yiddish Women Poets: Esther Segal and Ida Maza
    REBECCA MARGOLIS    248

Rajzel Zychlinski's Poetical Trajectories in the Shadow of the Holocaust
    ELVIRA GROEZINGER    270

*Bibliography*    295
*About the Contributors*    308
*Index*    311

# Preface

ROSEMARY HOROWITZ

Taking stock of the state of Yiddish literature in 1939, the critic Shmuel Niger concludes that after World War I more women were writing Yiddish literature than ever before.[1] He specifically points to Ezra Korman's 1928 anthology *Yidishe dikhterins* as an indication of the increasing number and importance of women writers.[2] Of the almost seventy women included in the collection, Niger estimates that about fifty became prominent after the war. Biographical dictionaries of modern Yiddish literature published after 1928 reference even more women. For example, the volumes of the *Leksikon fun der nayer yidisher literatur* contain entries for approximately 300 women.[3] However, over the years, knowledge about women Yiddish writers has diminished despite their previous numbers and importance.

The origin of the present collection of essays may be traced to Northampton, Massachusetts, where in the late 1980s a group of friends wanted to learn about Yiddish literature written by women.[4] Our first task was to develop lists of names and titles of works. Although we never finished our project, groups in other places finished theirs. So now besides having more Yiddish works by women included in English-language anthologies, we have several collections of short stories by women—*Found Treasures: Stories by Yiddish Women Writers*; *Arguing with the Storm: Stories by Yiddish Women Writers*; and *The Exile Book of Yiddish Women Writers*.[5] We also have translations of a few Yiddish novels by women—Esther Kreitman's *Deborah*, Esther Kreitman's *Diamonds*, Rokhl Faygenberg's *Strange Ways*, and Chava Rosenfarb's *The Tree of Life*.[6] We have collections of poems too, including Rajzel Zychlinski's in *God Hid His Face*, Anna Margolin's in *Drunk from the Bitter Truth*, Malka Heifetz Tussman's in *With Teeth in the Earth*, Rokhl Korn's in *Paper*

## 2   Preface by Rosemary Horowitz

*Roses*, and Celia Dropkin's *The Acrobat: The Selected Poems of Celia Dropkin*.[7] Additionally, translations of Yiddish literature by women may be found in various journals and magazines, such as *Bridges* and *Pakn Treger*, as well as on websites and blogs, for example, Nora Gold's "JewishFiction.net," Sheva Zucker's "Candles of Songs," and Andrew Firestone's "Yiddishpoetry.org." Even though the corpus in translation is modest, today's readers have greater access to works in English by women who wrote in Yiddish than previous ones.

Along with accessibility to texts, readers need access to literary history and criticism. For example, Zelda Kahn Newman's analysis of the letters between Kadya Molodowsky and Rokhl Korn gives insights into the life and times of the writers; Kathryn Hellerstein's study of literary history reveals the contributions made by women poets over four hundred years.[8] Works like those serve to deepen the appreciation of literature. Yet, while essays on women's literature in Yiddish by critics such as Ethel Raicus, Shirley Kumove, Janet Hadda, Kathryn Hellerstein, Norma Fain Pratt, Naomi Brenner, Barbara Mann, Abraham Novershtern, and others may be found scattered throughout books and periodicals,[9] no collection of criticism devoted to the range of genres used by women writing in Yiddish is currently available, although the volume *Jewish Women Writers in the Soviet Union*, a study by Rina Lapidus of eleven Jewish women who wrote in Russian, may be considered a parallel one.[10] Thus, one goal of my volume is to fill the gap in the Yiddish scholarship by highlighting the diversity of women's genres. Since the range of women's writings is still neither widely known among scholars nor among general readers, the volume also aims to introduce a new audience of English readers to the writers. In Yiddish, "*hemshekh*" means continuation, and so ultimately, the overarching goal of this volume is the continuation of our *yerushe*, our inheritance—Yiddish culture in general and women's literature in particular.

## Notes

1. Shmuel Niger, "New Trends in Post-War Yiddish Literature," *Jewish Social Studies* 1:3 (July 1939): 337–358.

2. Ezra Korman, *Yidishe dikhterins: antologye* (Shikago: L. M. Shtayn, 1928). Besides poems, the anthology contains biographies, bibliographies, drawings, and photographs.

3. Samuel Niger and Jacob Shatzky, *Leksikon fun der nayer yidisher literatur* (Nyu York: Alveltlekhn yidishn kultur-kongres, 1956). The number is an estimate since at least one writer, Rachel Auerbach, refused to include her bio-bibliography in the post-war volumes funded by German reparations money.

4. Over the years, members of the group included Chana Pollack, Leslie Morris, Nina Dabek, Rena Fisher, Kol Goodstein, Rebecca Lillian, Eileen Rutman, and Rosemary Horowitz. Irena Klepfisz, Rakhmiel Peltz, and Hannah Kliger inspired us.

5. Frieda Forman, Ethel Raicus, Sarah Silberstein Swartz, and Margie Wolf, eds., *Found Treasures: Stories by Yiddish Women Writers* (Toronto: Second Story Press, 1994); Rhea Tregebov, ed., *Arguing with the Storm: Stories by Yiddish Women Writers* (New York: Feminist Press, 2007); and Frieda Forman and Sam Blatt, eds., *The Exile Book of Yiddish Women Writers* (Holstein, Ontario: Exile Editions, 2013).

6. Esther Kreitman, *Deborah* (New York: Feminist Press at the City University of New York, 2004); Esther Kreitman, *Diamonds* (London: David Paul, 2010); Rokhl Faygenberg, *Strange Ways* (Jerusalem: Gefen, 2007); and Chava Rosenfarb, *The Tree of Life: A Novel About Life in the Lodz Ghetto* (Melbourne: Scribe, 1985).

7. Rajzel Zychlinsky, Barnett Zumoff, Aaron Kramer, and Marek Kanter, *God Hid His Face* (Santa Rosa, CA: Word & Quill Press, 1997); Anna Margolin and Shirley Kumove, *Drunk from the Bitter Truth: The Poems of Anna Margolin* (Albany: State University of New York Press, 2005); Malka Heifetz Tussman and Marcia Falk, *With Teeth in the Earth: Selected Poems of Malka Heifetz Tussman* (Detroit: Wayne State University Press, 1992); Rokhl Korn and Seymour Levitan, *Paper Roses: Selected Poems of Rachel Korn* (Toronto: Aya Press, 1985); and Celia Dropkin, *The Acrobat: The Selected Poems of Celia Dropkin,* translated from the Yiddish by Faith Jones, Jennifer Kronovet, and Samuel Solomon (Huntington Beach, CA: Tebot Bach, 2014).

8. Zelda Kahn Newman, "The Correspondence Between Kadya Molodowsky and Rokhl Korn," *Women in Judaism: A Multidisciplinary Journal* 8:1 (Spring 2011): 1–26, http://wjudaism.library.utoronto.ca; and Kathryn Hellerstein, *A Question of Tradition: Women Poets in Yiddish, 1586–1987* (Stanford: Stanford University Press, 2014).

9. Some examples of literary criticism published in books are Ethel Raicus, "Women's Voices in the Stories of Yiddish Writer Rokhl Brokhes," in *From Memory to Transformation: Jewish Women's Voices*, ed. Sarah Silberstein Swartz and Margie Wolfe (Toronto: Second Story Press, 1998), 25–34; Shirley Kumove, "Drunk from the Bitter Truth: The Life, Times and Poetry of Anna Margolin," in *From Memory to Transformation: Jewish Women's Voices*, ed. Sarah Silberstein Swartz and Margie Wolfe (Toronto: Second Story Press, 1998), 35–48; Janet Hadda, "The Eyes Have It: Celia Dropkin's Love Poetry," in *Gender and Text in Modern Hebrew and Yiddish Literature*, ed. Naomi B. Sokoloff, Anne Lapidus Lerner, and Anita Norich (New York: Jewish Theological Seminary of America, 1992), 93–112; and Kathryn Hellerstein, "From 'ikh' to 'zikh': A Journey from 'I' to 'Self' in Yiddish Poems by Women," in *Gender and Text in Modern Hebrew and Yiddish Literature*, ed. Naomi B. Sokoloff, Anne Lapidus Lerner, and Anita Norich (New York: Jewish Theological Seminary of America, 1992), 113–143. Some examples of criticism published in journals are Norma Fain Pratt, "Anna Margolin's *Lider*: A Study in Women's History, Autobiography, and Poetry," *Studies in American Jewish Literature* 3 (1983):11–25; Naomi Brenner, "Slippery Selves: Rachel Bluvstein and Anna Margolin in Poetry and in Public," *Nashim: A Journal of Jewish Women's Studies & Gender Issues* 19 (2010):100–133; Barbara Mann, "Picturing the Poetry of Anna Margolin," *MLQ: Modern Language Quarterly* 63:4 (2002): 501–536; and Abraham Novershtern, "'Who Would Have Believed That a Bronze Statue Can Weep': The Poetry of Anna Margolin," *Prooftexts* 10:3 (September 1990): 435–467.

10. Rina Lapidus, *Jewish Women Writers in the Soviet Union* (Abingdon, Oxon: Routledge, 2012).

# Lost and Found
*Yiddish Women Writers*

Irena Klepfisz

Some of the most successful projects of second-wave feminism in the United States were rooted in the work of academic and activist feminists engaged in researching and (re)discovering women leaders and intellectuals in historical, literary, and scientific fields. One result was the establishment of women and gender studies throughout the United States. Feminists specifically concerned with literature and the arts focused on "a room of one's own" and began to identify dozens of women fiction writers, intellectuals, and poets never mentioned, much less included, in the traditional American literary canon. Thus, women writers who had once been best sellers and were unknown and invisible in the 1970s and 1980s, suddenly re-emerged and had their work in print again. Minority and ethnic feminists also started to examine their own cultures, searching for women who had been erased and forgotten. Among those newly found were major figures such as Zora Neale Hurston and Anzia Yezierska, whose visibility was due to the work of dedicated feminists Alice Walker and Alice Kessler-Harris.

It is, therefore, not surprising that those of us who grew up in the cultural and intellectual Yiddish *svive*, that is environment, also cast a critical feminist eye on the Yiddish literary canon expecting to find Yiddish women writers who had been dismissed or written out of history. Yiddish culture, as it had been passed down to us, was devoid of work by women artists, but our feminist instincts told us that somewhere there existed works by women writers other than Rokhl Korn and Kadya Molodowsky. We knew that these two poets were exceptions and that they should be sharing our attention with many other women artists who deserved to be read, studied, and incorporated, not simply into the Yiddish literary canon but into our Yiddish worldview.

Until the early 1980s, English translations of Yiddish women's writing consisted almost exclusively of poetry, in keeping with the accepted assumption that women's more emotional nature was better suited to poetry than to prose, which required an intellectual muscle that women lacked.[1] Rosemary Horowitz, editor of the present collection, outlines in her contributory essay how this assumption is magnified in English-language anthologies of Yiddish literature. The resulting view of Yiddish literature makes women's contributions barely visible in many collections. It was a desire to counter this assumption and to make available in English the work of Yiddish women prose writers that I translated and tried to bring to public attention two (very short) stories by Mclodowsky and Fradel Shtok in *The Tribe of Dina: A Jewish Women's Anthology* (1986, 1989),[2] a collection I co-edited. It was a modest beginning.

But my two translations were hardly a voice in the wilderness. In the next three decades, there were many feminists with my Yiddishist background and other feminists just learning Yiddish and learning of Yiddish culture who dedicated themselves to bringing to the forefront Yiddish women artists—poets, novelists, short story writers, and intellectuals. They did this in two ways.

Given that most English anthologies of Yiddish literature barely, if at all, acknowledged the existence of Yiddish women writers, translation of Yiddish women writers became an important aspect in broadening the field. Beginning in 1990, the feminist magazine *Bridges* became committed to publishing Yiddish women writers in the original and in translation and did so for the next eleven years, inspiring both translators and scholars.[3] As a result, it made more accessible the legacy of Yiddish women's culture to many Jewish and non–Jewish women who did not speak or read Yiddish.

Also, as of now, four anthologies of Yiddish women's prose in translation have been published: *Found Treasures: Stories by Yiddish Women Writers* (1994); *Beautiful as the Moon, Radiant as the Stars: Jewish Women in Yiddish Stories* (2003); *Arguing with the Storm: Stories by Yiddish Women Writers* (2008); and *The Exile Book of Yiddish Women Writers: An Anthology of Stories that Looks to the Past So We Might See the Future* (2013).[4] The online magazine *Jewish Fiction*, started in 2010, includes Yiddish women's writing in translation, along with women's writing in other Jewish and non–Jewish languages.[5] It has made a valuable contribution by expanding the list of Yiddish women writers—past and present. At the same time, recognition of the scope and range of some Yiddish women poets has increased with individual volumes in

English translation devoted to the work of a single poet, for example Kadya Molodowsky, Chava Rosenfarb, Rajzel Zychlinski, Anna Margolin, Malke Heifetz Tussman, and Rokhl Korn. All these translations—prose and poetry—cannot as yet be characterized as an explosion, but they certainly have made a significant contribution to filling in the void that feminists had identified in the Yiddish literary canon.

If translation is a first step in acquainting non–Yiddish readers with the Yiddish women's writing, the second is gaining critical understanding, stimulating critical interpretations, and providing perspectives so that these rediscovered writers are not left hanging in limbo. A common view of Yiddish women artists—when they were/are recognized—was/remains as "other." Nothing illustrates this sense of otherness more than Joseph Leftwich's revised and expanded anthology *The Golden Peacock: A Worldwide Treasury of Yiddish Poetry* published in 1961. The anthology included twelve women poets, the largest representation of women's poetry before, and in many cases since, in English translation. But Leftwich's sense of the woman poet as "other" is clearly evident in the organization of his anthology. In *The Golden Peacock*, Leftwich grouped the poets according to where they were born and/or published. But after the final sections, "Romania" and "England," he appended two more sections, ostensibly to fulfill the geographic "worldwide" promise of his title. These sections are "Women Poets" and "Hassidic Poets." Hassidic religious traditions and conscious separation from secular literature lend logic to their segregation. However, the wrenching of Yiddish women writers from their male counterparts and from the shared geographic and collective historical roots of Ashkenazi Jews is telling. The women's "otherness" is stark. As Leftwich presents it, Yiddish "Women Poets" is a country unlike any other: without borders or history and without connections to Jewish religious/literary traditions or communal life. Here is the paradox: Yiddish women writers *do* exist at the same time that they *do not* occupy any space or belong in any Yiddish literary context or Jewish history.

Not surprisingly, the essays in this volume, *Women Writers of Yiddish Literature: Critical Essays*, unequivocally disproves the existence of an unrooted, isolated "Yiddish women's country." Each of the writers discussed is contextualized in relation to her birth and Jewish upbringing and her relation to the Jewish and non–Jewish environment in which she was creative. For example, there are examinations of Kadya Molodowsky's relationship to the Yiddish theatre of her time; Shira Gorshman's and Khane Levin's struggles with communism and art ideology; Blume Lempel's and Rajzel Zychlinski's connections or lack thereof to their contemporaries; Celia Dropkin's and

8   Women Writers of Yiddish Literature

Anna Margolin's relationship to various Yiddish poetry movements; Esther Segal's and Ida Maza's commitment to encouraging creative environments through salons; and Molodowsky's, Malka Heifetz Tussman's, and Chava Rosenfarb's diverse responses to the Holocaust as survivors and witnesses analyzed from a gender perspective. In addition, there is analysis of some of these women's awareness of issues related to women's equality as seen in the writings of Lily Bes and Hadasa Rubin. Throughout, we are made aware of the endless migrations some of these women endured while they tried to write in each new place of settlement: pre-war Eastern Europe, post-war Poland and the U.S.S.R., the United States, Israel, France, and Canada. *Women Writers of Yiddish Literature* demonstrates what should be obvious to all critics, namely that Yiddish women writers were/are writing from the *same* Jewish experience and the *same* Jewish history as their male contemporaries, though their perspectives remain individual and original, deserving of scholarly analysis and interpretation.

*Women Writers of Yiddish Literature* is the first collection of criticism focused entirely on women who wrote in Yiddish. As the scholars themselves indicate, there is still much work to be done. Indeed, there are probably more than three dozen writers referenced in these articles who await translation and critical attention. More research is needed; more texts need to be identified and recovered. That a great deal of material has been lost as a result of the Holocaust and the scattering of the surviving Yiddish speakers to different parts of the globe cannot be denied. As a result, even if we were able to identify all that was written and published, some women and their work will be recovered in part only, if at all.

Nor can it be denied that during the height of creativity, during most of the first half of the twentieth century and immediately after World War II, many Jewish women simply did not have the support—culturally, socially, or personally—that would have enabled them to become artists. A number of published writers allude to this in their fiction. Rokhl Brokhes in "Di zogerin" [The Sayer], Fradel Shtok in "Opgeshnitene hor" [The Shorn Head], and Celia Dropkin in "Di tentserin" [The Dancer], all focus on Jewish women who are frustrated creatively. They are artists manqué, who often do not even have the vocabulary to express their artistic yearnings.[6] We read of Gnesye in "Di zogerin" who is aware of the craft of her prayers, but is completely frustrated by the community's trivialization of her art; of Sheyndl, the young window in "Opgeshnitene hor" who expresses her artistic impulses through needlework and interior decoration; and of Gysia in "Di tentserin," who is clear about her desire to become a dancer, but whose gender and prescribed obligations preclude her from ever becoming one. All three try to ignore the men in their constricting environments and the social and religious duties imposed on Jewish women. None succeed. Gnesye and Gysia are deemed mad by their neighbors and family, while Sheyndl is humiliated and, the reader may project, ultimately ostracized by her *shtetl*.

These fictional characters represent the lost Yiddish women artists of past generations; they are mirror images of lost women artists of other ethnic and religious communities. Their Yiddish stories are universal. They remind us of a truism: in the past and today, women in many societies are prohibited from fulfilling artistic and intellectual dreams. We may be living in a post-feminist age, but patriarchy and sexism still need to be addressed.

Why and how this happened and continues to happen, however, is not the subject of this collection. *Women Writers of Yiddish Literature* documents the persistence and perseverance of thirteen women who were able to produce art, have it published, and are lucky enough to have it survive and become accessible to us today. It enriches our understanding of dynamic individual writers who were determined to give expression to their visions through poetry, fiction, and drama. It does so by dealing directly with the texts in the original Yiddish, and thereby, increasing the desire, for those who cannot read Yiddish, for more translations (and sometimes even, for learning the language). Some of the writers are well known; others are entirely new. Certainly the former have work that needs further examination. And the latter provide us with the opportunity to expand our knowledge of Yiddish women writers by identifying work to be translated and read and included in anthologies or collected in individual volumes. All of us look forward to new assessments, critiques, and contextualizations. This volume emphatically proves their value in providing us with a deeper and more complex understanding of women's contributions to Yiddish literature, culture, and politics.

## Notes

1. See my "*Di mames, dos loshn*/The Mothers, the Language: Feminism, *Yidishkayt*, and the Politics of Memory," *Bridges* 4:1 (Winter-Summer 1994/5754): 12–47. In this article, I demonstrate how contemporary Jewish male intellectuals who often profess to support feminist goals, never use women's writing—either in Yiddish or English—in their research and analysis of Jewish issues and history.

2. Melanie Kaye/Kantrowitz and Irena Klepfisz, eds., *The Tribe of Dina: A Jewish Women's Anthology* (Montpelier, VT: Sinister Wisdom, 1986); and Melanie Kaye/Kantrowitz, Irena Klepfisz, and Esther F. Hyneman, eds., *The Tribe of Dina: A Jewish Women's Anthology* (Boston: Beacon Press, 1989).

3. See *Bridges: A Journal for Jewish Feminists and Our Friends* (1988–2011). *Bridges* also published Jewish women's work in translation and in the original Ladino, Hebrew,

and Spanish. All single articles are available on JSTOR.com, and all available issues are for sale on Abebooks.com. Single pdfs may be obtained by contacting the former editor Clare Kinberg at ckinberg@gmail.com.

4. Frieda Forman, Ethel Raicus, Sarah Silberstein Swartz, and Margie Wolf, eds., *Found Treasures: Stories by Yiddish Women Writers* (Toronto: Second Story Press, 1994); Sandra Bark, *Beautiful as the Moon, Radiant as the Stars: Jewish Women in Yiddish Stories: An Anthology* (New York: Warner Books, 2003); Rhea Tregebov, ed., *Arguing with the Storm: Stories by Yiddish Women Writers* (New York: Feminist Press, 2007); and Frieda Forman and Sam Blatt, eds., *The Exile Book of Yiddish Women Writers* (Holstein, Ontario: Exile Editions, 2013). Although *Beautiful as the Moon* includes writing by male writers, the selections are predominately by women.

5. See JewishFiction.net, www.jewishfiction.net. Nora Gold is the editor of the website.

6. See Brokhes's "Di zogerin" [The Sayer] and Dropkin's "Di tentserin" [The Dancer], translated by Shirley Kumove and published in *Found Treasures*; and Shtok's "Opgeshnitene hor" [The Shorn Head] translated by Irena Klepfisz and published in *The Tribe of Dina*.

# A Review of Yiddish Women Writers in English-Language Anthologies

ROSEMARY HOROWITZ

Tragically, the near destruction of Jews in Eastern Europe during the 1940s and the purges in the Soviet Union during the 1950s, combined with a series of less calamitous events, decimated the Yiddish-speaking communities in the regions. Consequently, the need to translate Yiddish literature became an imperative for the continuity of one aspect of Jewish secular life. However, translation is not a neutral practice; rather it is driven by ideology.[1] Thus, decisions about what to translate into which languages fundamentally affect the transmission and preservation of culture. The translation of Yiddish literature in English, in particular, raises questions such as these: what do English readers know about the literature; what should they know; and which writers should be translated and why? Even more specifically, what do and what should English readers know about women writers given that at the start of the twentieth century, writing by women regularly appeared in Yiddish magazines, newspapers, and books, but that since then, awareness of the extent of women's contribution to the source literature has diminished? One way to study continuity and change in literature is to focus on the anthology as a literary form. Examining the inclusion and exclusion of writers in anthologies from synchronic and diachronic perspectives provides one way to gauge the transmission of literature. This approach is more than a counting exercise, because the anthology occupies a key place in literary history.

The value of studying anthologies has been well-established by David Stern. Not only does Stern provide exemplary studies of various anthologies, he presents a critical framework for examining the genre.² Of course, a complete assessment of Yiddish literature in translation requires studies of anthologies, as well as critiques of the literature and other types of analyses. While much still needs to be done, the essays in this volume take a step in that direction. This particular essay builds on Kathryn Hellerstein's analysis of Yiddish women poets in Yiddish-language anthologies and Jeffrey Shandler's analysis of Yiddish writers in English-language anthologies.³ Shandler sums up one reason for studying English-language anthologies when he writes that the "collections are of interest not only as literary works of translation and canonization, but also as agents of cultural transmission."⁴ With that as my starting point, this chapter explores the dynamics of canon formation and cultural transmission by examining women's Yiddish-language writing included in selected English-language anthologies. At least as reflected in the anthologies, what becomes evident from a historical perspective using gender as a unit of analysis is that the presupposition that Yiddish women authors primarily wrote poetry has been corrected by second-wave feminists who argue for the recognition of women as writers of novels, essays, short stories, plays, memoirs, and diaries, as well as poems. Basically, second-wave feminists challenge the assumption that women were primarily poets because they were temperamentally suited to that form. While the Yiddish women themselves might reject the definition of feminist or even the category of woman writer, nevertheless, given that the anthology is a significant literary genre, the increasing attention to Yiddish women writers among contemporary English readers as a matter of course will impact literary history.

English-language translations of Yiddish writers are not a recent phenomenon. Even before the vast proportion of the Yiddish reading public was annihilated, English-language anthologies of Yiddish writers were in circulation. One early example is Helena Frank's 1912 *Yiddish Tales*, a compilation of forty-eight short stories by twenty writers. Despite her goal of introducing non–Yiddish readers to Yiddish literature, Frank did not include any women writers in the volume, although she could have included Yente Serdatsky, whose stories appeared in 1905 in the literary journal *Veg* published in Warsaw by I. L. Peretz. While fame came to other Yiddish women writers about a decade later, Serdatsky already had an established reputation as a writer by 1908.⁵ *Yiddish Tales* has an extensive publication history, with reprints issued by the Jewish Publication Society (JPS) in 1938, 1943, and 1945. The mission of the Jewish Publication Society, which was founded in 1888 in America, is to print the great books of Judaism for the English-reading world. Thus, the stature of *Yiddish Tales* was enhanced by its association with the JPS. Currently, *Yiddish*

*Tales* is available in editions issued by numerous publishers. The volume is also now in the public domain, so readers have access to an electronic version uploaded in 2010 by Project Gutenberg, as well as print-on-demand versions by General Books and BiblioBazaar. Editors at BiblioBazaar, for example, hold that the "work is culturally important, and despite the imperfections, have elected to bring it back into print as part of our continuing commitment to the preservation of printed works worldwide."[6] Also, believing that the volume is significant, Kessinger Publishing issued the book as part of its Legacy Reprint Series.

Another figure who introduced Yiddish writers to English readers was the journalist, author, critic, translator, editor, publisher, and lecturer Isaac Goldberg. Among Goldberg's publications are more than forty booklets written, edited, introduced, or translated for the Haldeman-Julius Publishing Company as part of its Little Blue Book series. Emanuel Haldeman-Julius was newspaper publisher and a socialist reformer who believed in the transformative power of reading.[7] Given his political leanings, Haldeman-Julius wanted to make works available to working class readers. To that end, he published a series of inexpensive booklets on hundreds of topics. The Yiddish titles in the series are *The God of Vengeance*, *Yiddish Short Stories*, *The Spirit of Yiddish Literature*, and *Great Yiddish Poetry*. For *Yiddish Short Stories* (1923), Goldberg gathered short stories by I. L. Peretz, David Pinsky, Sholem Asch, Abraham Reisen, Lamed Shapiro, and Joseph Opatoshu. In his introduction, Goldberg makes no mention of any woman writers. About *Great Yiddish Poetry* (1923), Goldberg writes that the collection "is a very modest sample case, and so to be considered."[8] The only woman represented among the fifteen poets is Fradel Shtok, who continued to be widely anthologized over the years. Even though Haldeman-Julius Publishing Company is no longer in business, the Little Blue Book series has collectors and fans who are interested in the booklets and make information about the books available in print and electronic sources. Ongoing interest in the booklets perpetuates Goldberg's restricted view of women writers. Samuel Imber's *Modern Yiddish Poetry* (1927) does the same.

Leo Schwarz was another important early anthologist. His *The Jewish Caravan* was issued in 1935, revised and enlarged in 1965, and reprinted fourteen times. The first edition contains no Yiddish women, whereas the 1976 edition features eighty-one authors, three women. With an entry on the Warsaw ghetto, Vladka Meed is the only Yiddish woman writer. Schwarz's *A Golden Treasury of Jewish Literature* (1937) was first published by the Jewish Publication Society of America and then reprinted by Kessinger Publishing in 2005. The volume contains the work of one hundred thirty-one authors, including the Yiddish writers I. J. Singer and Sholem Asch. Of the nine women writers in the volume, none writes in Yiddish. Although his influence has been reduced because "[a]mong other factors, shifting literary tastes and the migration of writers from the margins to the American literary mainstream, Schwarz's literary conservatism diminished his influence as a critic and historian of the Jewish American literary scene."[9] Despite that, assumptions about women writers that guided Schwarz continue to guide later anthologists.

Joseph Leftwich, considered an ambassador of Yiddish literature to the English-speaking world,[10] also foregrounded women's poetry rather than other genres His *The Golden Peacock* (1939) contains works by two hundred and seventy-nine poets arranged in the following order: The Great Figures, Soviet Poets, Galicia, America, South America, Poland, Romania, Palestine, France, England, Women Poets, The Older Poets, and Folk Songs. Except for Rikudah Potash, who is identified as a Palestinian poet, all the other women, namely Kadya Molodowsky, Chana Levin, Shifre Cholodenko, Rokhl Korn, Fradel Shtok, Malka Lee, Malke Locker, Miriam Ulinover, Anna Margolin, Celia Dropkin, Sarah Reisen, Esther Shumiatcher, Rajzel Zychlinski, Rosa Peretz-Laks, Deborah Fogel, Rosa Guttman, Ida Maza, Rebecca Gallin, Bertha Kling, Miriam Wohlman-Czervaczek, Rachel Cohen, Katie Brown, Sarah Eisen, and Lottie Malach, are classified under the label of women poets. While aware of the participation of women in various literary movements, specifically mentioning Fradel Shtok and *Di yunge*, Leftwich nonetheless places her with the women rather than with the American poets. So, although most of the volume is organized by geography and includes numerous women, Leftwich separated the women from their regional, historical, social, and literary context.

The 1961 revision of *The Golden Peacock* has fewer authors and a different structure. Specifically, Holocaust poems are interspersed throughout various sections; French poets are omitted; Palestine is changed to Israel; and the number of women is halved. Removed from the volume are Shifre Cholodenko, Sarah Reisen, Rosa Peretz-Laks, Deborah Fogel, Rosa Guttman, Ida Maza, Rebecca Gallin, Bertha Kling, Miriam Wohlman-Czervaczek, Rachel Cohen, Katie Brown, Sarah Eisen, and Lottie Malach. Except for Ida Maza, the others in the collection seem to have been excluded by future anthologists. One other change is that Rikudah Potash is included with the women and not with the Israeli writers.

Leftwich's *Great Yiddish Writers of the Twentieth Century* gives prominence to the essay form. The volume published in 1969 and 1987 by Jason Aronson contains entries by eighty-one writers; the essayist and short story writer Lili Berger is the only women included. *An Anthology of Modern Yiddish Literature* (1974), another Leftwich collection, published as part of the International PEN Books, contains works by forty writers. In his foreword, Leftwich notes that he was the PEN representative for the Yiddish division for more than thirty years. Yet, despite his vast knowledge of Yiddish literature, Leftwich's decision to include only Kadya Molodowsky and Rokhl Korn diminishes the accomplishments of many other women.

The editorial choices made by the anthologists in the first-half of the twentieth century depended upon the assumptions of the time about women writers, and as a result, the Yiddish writing published in English translation was predominately by male authors and the breadth of writing by women was generally unknown to the majority of English readers. This portrayal of the Yiddish canon in English translation continued into the second-half of the twentieth century, especially with the postwar partnership of Irving Howe and Eliezer Greenberg. Their anthologies dominated the market of English-language anthologies of Yiddish literature for decades and strengthened the perception that Yiddish women primarily wrote poetry. The collaboration between Howe, Greenberg, and Schocken Books is significant because Salman Schocken was an influential bibliophile, printer, and publisher and because one goal of his company, which started in 1931 in Berlin, was to issue important titles on Jewish themes.[11]

Howe and Greenberg's first volume, *A Treasury of Yiddish Stories*, published in 1953 by Meridian Press, contains short stories by twenty-three writers. Its publication history is extensive. Viking Press reprinted the volume in 1954, 1968, and 1989; Schocken Books reprinted an edition in 1954, 1973, and 1985; Meridian Books reprinted an edition in 1958; World Publishing Company reprinted an edition in 1954, 1960, and 1961; and Penguin issued an edition in 1954 and 1990. The volume has also been digitized. Even though the introduction says that the goal of the collection is "a rounded sampling of Yiddish prose fiction,"[12] no women are included. By contrast, the companion volume, *A Treasury of Yiddish Poetry* (1969), reinforces the image of woman as poet. Reprinted in 1976 by Holt, Rinehart, and Winston and in 1976 and 1985 by Schocken Books, the volume includes the work of fifty-eight poets. Contained in the volume are poems by Rashelle Vepinski, Anna Margolin, Celia Dropkin, Rajzel Zychlinski, Dvora Fogel, Kadya Molodowsky, Rokhl Korn, Rikudah Potash, and Rosa Gutman-Jasny. Relevant to the history of Yiddish women writers in the English-language anthology is that the essayist and poet Adrienne Rich, who translated a number of poems by women writers for Howe and Greenberg, was at the forefront of the movement to reclaim Yiddish women's literature. She was also a founding editor of *Bridges, A Journal for Jewish Feminists and Our Friends*, a magazine that premiered in 1990.

Howe and Greenberg's *Voices from the Yiddish: Essays, Memoirs, Dairies*, issued in 1972 by the University of Michigan Press and reprinted in 1975 by Schocken Books, contains works by twenty-six authors. No women are included in the collection, even though Howe and Greenberg could have included Bella Chagall's *Burning Lights*, originally published in 1946 by Schocken Press. The omission of any women authors from *Voices from the Yiddish* suggests that women were neither writing essays or memoirs nor keeping diaries, further stereotyping their lack of generic diversity. Similarly, *Ashes Out of Hope: Fiction by Soviet-Yiddish Writers*, compiled by Howe and Greenberg and published in 1977 and 1978 by Schocken Books, includes no women, not even Shira Gorshman. In 1977, Howe compiled the volume *Jewish American Stories*, which contains twenty-six short stories. Again, while several Yiddish male writers, namely Sholem Aleichem, Isaac Babel, and Isaac Bashevis Singer are represented in the collection, there are no entries by women.

While women are represented as poets in other volumes from the 1960s and 1970s, such as Leonard Opotov's *Five Yiddish Poets: Gross, Greenberg, Sutzkever, Zichlinsky, Glantz* (1962) and Joanna Bankier's *The Other Voice: Twentieth-Century Women's Poetry in Translation* (1976), the volumes of short stories from the period exclude them. A volume with no women writers is Henry Goodman's *The New Country: Stories from the Yiddish About Life in America*, printed in 1961 and reprinted in 2001. Also containing no stories by women is Max Rosenfeld's *Pushcarts and Dreamers: Stories of Jewish Life in America* (1967), with ten male authors; it was reprinted in 1969 and 1993. Still another is Saul Bellow's *Great Jewish Short Stories* (1963), which includes the work of twenty authors. Of that total are nineteen men; six are Yiddish writers. Grace Paley is the sole woman. The volume was reprinted at least seven times by various presses and is important given Bellow's stature as a writer and intellectual.

Regarding multi-genre collections, some, like Abraham Chapman's *Jewish-American Literature* (1974), only feature men's fiction, poetry, autobiography, criticism, and essays; whereas others, such as Jacob Glatstein, Israel Knox, and Samuel Margoshes's *The Anthology of Holocaust Literature* (1968), include women's writings. With entries by sixty-two authors and with seven reprints between 1973 and 1982, Glatstein, Knox, and Margoshes's volume emphasizes first-hand accounts of the catastrophe. For their collection, the editors gathered excerpts from diaries, memoirs, and letters. Fourteen women are represented. One notable entry is a two-page translation from

Rachel Auerbach's *Der yidisher oyfshtand: varshe 1943* [The Jewish Uprising in Warsaw, 1943]. Auerbach was an activist before, during, and after the war. In addition to publishing numerous books and articles of her own, she worked with Emanuel Ringelblum's underground documentation group, the Central Jewish Historical Commission, the Jewish Historical Institute, the Central Commission for Investigation of German Crimes in Poland, and Yad Vashem. Another notable entry is by Feigele Peltel Miedzyrzecki, known as Vladka Meed. The entry, taken from her memoir *On Both Sides of the Wall,* describes the underground resistance in Warsaw. Postwar, Meed was active in Holocaust commemoration and education. While not adequately underscoring Auerbach's or Meed's importance, the two entries do hint at their role in history and their writing.

Taken together, Howe, Greenberg, Glatstein, Leftwich, and Bellow, the important anthologists of the 1950s, 1960s, and 1970s, tended to overlook the variety of genres used by women. The female anthologists of the period showed the same tendency.[13] Thus, the existing image of women writers was reinforced during that period. Until 1980, readers of English-language anthologies of Yiddish-language translations might have concluded that the alignment between Yiddish women and poetry was unassailable and that women only wrote poems. However that year, Norma Fain Pratt drew attention to the need to reassess the contribution of Yiddish women writers in the Yiddish canon, and by extension to the canon in English translation, by purposefully naming fifty-three Yiddish women writers in the appendix to her article "Culture and Radical Politics: Yiddish Women Writers, 1890–1940."[14] Even though she lists well-known writers, such as Kadya Molodowsky and Fradel Shtok, Pratt's primary goal was to introduce the work of Yiddish women writers to a new generation of readers. She presents her readers with this request:

> Every effort must be made to rescue this literature from oblivion, not only for its intrinsic value, but also because it and the lives of those who created it provide us with a much broader insight and deeper understanding of the cultural transformation of East European Jewry in America.[15]

Thus, for the sake of literature and culture, the works of Yiddish women writers need to be recovered. Predictably, the article generated a variety of responses from scholars, activists, translators, and others. Irena Klepfisz and Melanie Kaye/Kantrowitz responded with *The Tribe of Dina: A Jewish Woman's Anthology* (1986), a collection edited and published as an issue of the journal *Sinister Wisdom*. Foregrounding the place of Yiddish in Jewish women's history, the editors included a short story by Fradel Shtok, several poems by Kadya Molodowsky, and several poems by Anna Margolin, along with a brief biography of each woman. Three years after its initial publication, a revised and expanded edition of *The Tribe of Dina* was issued by Beacon Press, making the anthology more commercially available.

Following that, there were other volumes directly challenging the long-standing impression that Yiddish women's writing was limited to poetry. Significant texts are *Found Treasures: Stories by Yiddish Women Writers* (1994); *Arguing with the Storm: Stories by Yiddish Women Writers* (2007); and *The Exile Book of Yiddish Women Writers* (2013). For instance, the compilers and translators of *Found Treasures* are members of a study group in Canada who set out to intentionally promote Yiddish women writers. The members of the group identify as feminists wanting to reclaim the works of their foremothers. At some point, the members decided to make their translations accessible by publishing a volume of their work. The volume features stories by Sarah Hamer-Jacklyn, Esther Singer Kreitman, Rokhl Brokhes, Dora Schuler, Miriam Raskin, Fradel Shtok, Ida Maze, Shira Gorshman, Malke Lee, Yente Serdatsky, Celia Dropkin, Rokhl Korn, Lili Berger, Blume Lempel, Chava Rosenfarb, Kadya Molodowsky, Chava Slucka-Kestin, and Rikudah Potash. About the group's goals, the editors write, "Without remembrance there is no continuity."[16] Thus by forging a link between writing and memory, group members connect Yiddish literature to ethnic identity. Klepfisz's introduction to the volume further reveals the impetus behind the book project:

> What is evident is that women's prose contributions to modern Yiddish literature are now being recovered only because of feminist efforts. The work is motivated by scholarly interest, but also by Jewish women's needs to reconstruct and claim an authentic past in which women were included. Without it, most of us feel uprooted and incomplete.[17]

Klepfisz goes on to suggest that the publication of *Found Treasures* is a major step toward that reconstruction.

The publication history of *Arguing with the Storm* parallels that of *Found Treasures*. The compilers and translators of *Arguing with the Storm* were members of another Canadian group who wanted to promote the works of Yiddish women writers. After finding and reading works in Yiddish, the group also decided to make their material accessible. Like *Found Treasures*, the volume *Arguing with the Storm* contains fiction and non-fiction, with selections by Sarah Hamer-Jacklyn, Bryna Bercovitch, Anne Viderman, Malke Lee, Frume Halpern, Rokhl Brokhes, Paula Frankel-Zaltzman, Chava Rosenfarb, and Rikudah Potash. The editor of the volume, Rhea Tregebov, remembers that her "group felt frustrated that these works were largely unfamiliar, and that the literary achievements of their writers had been lost."[18] As Kathryn Hellerstein emphasizes in her introduction, the aim of the book is to halt future attempts to diminish the work of Yiddish women writers or silence them.

*The Exile Book of Yiddish Women Writers* (2013) took a similar path to publication. Besides debuting the works of a number of writers, the volume showcases the diversity of genres by featuring novelists and diarists, along with storytellers and memoirists. Thirteen authors are included in that work: Lili Berger, Rokhl Brokhes, Sheindl Franzus-Garfinkle, Shira Gorshman, Chayele Grober, Sarah Hamer-Jacklyn, Blume Lempel, Rikudah Potash, Rokhl Korn, Miriam Krant, Ida Maze, Chava Rosenfarb, and Mirl Erdberg Shatan. The goal of *The Exile Book* was similar to the other Canadian volumes; some members of *The Exile Book* group were active in the *Found Treasures* project too.

Taken together, *Found Treasures*, *Arguing with the Storm*, and *The Exile Book* introduce contemporary English readers to the diverse genres used by Yiddish women writers. The cultural and historical influences of the second-wave women's movement form the backdrop to the publication of those volumes. The three volumes were made possible in part because of the establishment of feminist-oriented publishers. Second Story Press, which issued *Found Treasures*, is a Canadian company committed to promoting works that feature girls and women. Margie Wolfe, one of the women in the translation group is the founder of the press. Started in 1988, the company "is dedicated to publishing feminist-inspired books for adults and young readers" and to issuing books "that entertain, educate, and empower."[19] The Feminist Press at the City University of New York, the publisher of *Arguing with the Storm*, has a comparable mission. According to The Feminist Press at the City University of New York, the company:

> is an independent nonprofit literary publisher that promotes freedom of expression and social justice. We publish exciting authors who share an activist spirit and a belief in choice and equality. Founded in 1970, we began by rescuing "lost" works by writers such as Zora Neale Hurston and Charlotte Perkins Gilman, and established our publishing program with books by American writers of diverse racial and class backgrounds. Since then we have also been bringing works from around the world to North American readers. We seek out innovative, often surprising books that tell a different story.[20]

Thus, the goal of Second Story Press and The Feminist Press at the City University of New York is to promote the work of forgotten writers and highlight the work of multi-cultural current ones. Exile Editions is also an outlet for non-mainstream authors.

A number of other post–1980 anthologies may have been influenced by the growing interest in women's literature. An example is *Here We Are: An Anthology* (1989), a volume containing short stories and poems in English, Greek, Hebrew, and Yiddish by sixteen women. Its editor notes that her group wanted to highlight the writings of women from different cultures. Towards that end, several Yiddish language poems in English by Tova Grosman are included. Other volumes from the period emphasize short stories. One example is Joachim Neugroschel's *No Star Too Beautiful: Yiddish Stories from 1382 to the Present* (2002). Besides Glukl of Hameln, included in the Old Yiddish section, the rest of the women in Neugroschel's collection are from the modern period. Included among the thirty-eight modernists are Fradel Shtok, Sarah Smith, Bertha Lelchuk, Sarah Hamer-Jacklyn, Rokhl Korn, Frume Halpern, and Chava Rosenfarb. Another collection highlighting women as short story writers is Sandra Bark's *Beautiful as the Moon, Radiant as the Stars: Jewish Women in Yiddish Stories* (2003), which contains sixteen stories by women and six by men. An interesting aspect of the collection is that women writers, such as Celia Dropkin, Dvora Baron, and Blume Lempel, are juxtaposed with classical men writers, such as Sholem Aleichem, I. L. Peretz, and I. B. Singer. However, even women-oriented anthologies like Robert and Roberta Kalechofky's *The Global Anthology of Jewish Women Writers* (1990) do not necessarily contain works by women who wrote in Yiddish.

The decisions of compilers not influenced by feminist concerns continued to be influenced by traditional anthologizing practices that gloss over the range of women's genres. One example is Ilan Stavan's *The Oxford Book of Jewish Stories* (1998), with works by thirty-nine male and thirteen female writers. Nine selections are from Yiddish male writers, none from Yiddish women. Another example is *The Soul of the Text: An Anthology of Jewish Literature* (2000), which features Sholem Aleichem, I. L. Peretz, and I. B. Singer, but no women. Likewise, none are in Miriam Weinstein's *Prophets & Dreamers: A Selection of Great Yiddish Literature* (2002), even though Weinstein notes that "Yiddish has always had a female association."[21] Nevertheless, she limits that association to the *tkhines* and *tsene urene*. Similarly, with sixty-nine stories by eight writers, Albert Waldinger's *Shining and Shadow: An Anthology of Early Yiddish Stories from the Lower East Side* (2006) contains no women writers. Seemingly unaware of this omission, Waldinger states:

> The translation of Yiddish into English is the only way that such love mixed with distance can be communicated to English-speaking readers throughout the world—especially to the writers' heirs in the United States, sons and grandsons who are encouraged to see themselves as contemporaries of their fathers.[22]

His use of the family motif of sons and grandsons ignores the possibility that daughters and granddaughters are also reading the literature of their fathers and mothers.

Even as they were overlooked as fiction writers, women continued to be regularly anthologized as poets. This is the case in Howard Schwartz and Anthony Rudolf's *Voices Within the Ark* (1980), as well as in Irving Howe, Ruth R. Wisse, and Khone Shmeruk's *The Penguin Book of Modern Yiddish Verse* (1987). For example, *The Penguin Book of Modern Yiddish Verse* contains works by thirty-nine poets, including Anna Margolin, Celia Dropkin, Kadya Molodowsky, Malka Heifetz Tussman, and Rokhl Korn. Likewise, Benjamin and Barbara Harshav's *American Yiddish Poetry* (1986) contains poems by seven poets, including Malka Heifetz Tussman. Another collection, Aaron Kramer's *The Last Lullaby: Poetry from the Holocaust* (1998) contains entries by eighty-four authors, seventeen women. Quite exceptionally, the collection contains twenty-six poems by Rajzel Zychlinski, more than any single writer in the collection, including Avrom Sutzkever. Using the organizing principle of American leftist politics, Amelia Glaser, David Weintraub, and Dana Craft compiled *Proletpen: America's Rebel Yiddish Poets* (2005). Among the thirty-nine authors are Esther Shumyatshe, Dora Teitelman, Sarah Barkan, Malke Lee, Sarah Fell-Yellin, Sarah Kindman, and Shifre Weiss. As he states in his introduction to *Proletpen*, Dovid Katz hopes to integrate left-leaning Yiddish men and women writers into the canon, arguing that the literature from that time is "an important chapter in the history of this era in Yiddish literature."[23] He specifically acknowledges the contribution of women poets to that history. Richard Fein's *With Everything We've Got: A Personal Anthology of Yiddish Poetry* (2008) highlights poetry too. In his introduction to Fein's volume, Seth Wolitz notes that Yiddish women poets "were perhaps fifty years ahead of their times in terms of women's liberation."[24] He names Miriam Ulinover, Celia Dropkin, Anna Margolin, Kadya Molodowsky, Dvora Fogel, Rokhl Korn, and Rajzel Zychlinski as writers whose poetry reached remarkable aesthetic and intellectual levels. Surprisingly, of all the women who Wolitz mentions, the only one Fein included among the sixteen authors is Anna Margolin. And, lastly regarding poetry, Emanuel S. Goldsmith and Barnett Zumoff worked on *Songs to a Moonstruck Lady: Women in Yiddish Poetry* (2005) and *Yiddish Literature in America, 1870–2000* (2009). The first collection contains poems about women and poems by women. Alongside entries from some regularly anthologized writers, for instance, Fradel Shtok, Anna Margolin, Celia Dropkin, and Kadya Molodowsky, there are entries from some rarely anthologized ones, namely Soreh Birnbaum and Shoshana Balaban-Wolkowitz. The second,

*Yiddish Literature in America, 1870–2000* comprised of works by seventy-one authors, includes Fradel Shtok, Anna Margolin, Celia Dropkin, Kadya Molodowsky, Rajzel Zychlinski, Rashel Veprinski, Dora Teitleman, Malka Heifetz Tussman, Rokhl Korn, Chava Rosenfarb, and Bella Schechter Gottesman. Although some of these women wrote short stories, Goldsmith and Barnett Zumoff's collections continue the conventions regarding women as primarily poets.

*Jewish American Literature: A Norton Anthology* (2001), compiled by Jules Chametzky, John Felstiner, Helene Flanzbaum, and Kathryn Hellerstein, deserves special consideration because of its publisher, as well as its contents. W. W. Norton is an important textbook publishing company, and its anthologies exert a major influence on educational curricula. The Norton anthology may have even changed the teaching of literature.[25] Regarding the contents of *Jewish American Literature*, the section "The Great Tide 1881–1924" contains entries by twenty-six writers, including Yente Serdatsky, Celia Dropkin, Anna Margolin, and Fradel Shtok; the section "Achievement and Ambivalence 1945–1973" contains entries by thirty-two writers, including Malka Heifetz Tussman and Kadya Molodowsky. Although the generic diversity of women's writings in Yiddish is not spotlighted in *Jewish American Literature*, the collection may likely secure a place within the canon of Yiddish literature in English translation for the Yiddish women writers in the volume given the widespread adoption of Norton anthologies in the classroom. This may be the case especially for Dropkin, Margolin, and Molodowsky, who each have an essay in the Dictionary of Literary Biography's *Writers in Yiddish*.[26] About textbooks more generally, perhaps other publishers of educational materials, such as Longman or Heath, might issue a compilation in the future and solidify the reputation of other women writers.

Clearly, a growing number of anthologists are recognizing the multiple genres used by women who wrote in Yiddish. This increasing recognition of women as novelists, essayists, short stories writers, playwrights, memoirists, and diarists not only enlarges the Yiddish canon in translation, but also affects the history of the literature. As facility with Yiddish decreases among secular speakers, the availability of English-language works becomes more critical for those contemporary readers who want to access the literature. Along with the expansion of the canon, the widening acknowledgment by anthologists of women writers helps to correct the history of Yiddish literature in translation insofar as the exclusion of the full scope of women writings distorts literary history. As the contributions of women who wrote in Yiddish become harder to overlook, a reconsideration of Yiddish literary history in English translation is in order. In the source language, as well as in the target language, the canon becomes more complete when all of its writers are included.[27]

In addition to their role in canon formation and literary history, anthologies impact cultural transmission. With regard to Yiddish literature, there are important overarching issues regarding the attraction to the language. Bennett Muraskin suggests that left-leaning publishers and anthologists, such as Emanuel Haldeman-Julius, Irving Howe, and Eliezer Greenberg, were drawn to the literature because they perceived Yiddish as progressive. Even today, Muraskin observes that that Yiddish continues to attract "Jewish rebels and outsiders."[28] However, the role of Yiddish in modern Jewish history is more complex. As David Fishman argues, the assumption that modern Yiddish culture was "proletarian based and Socialist oriented" is far too simplistic.[29] That assumption, he points out, is based on the awareness that the Bund promoted Yiddish for political purposes, but on a lack of awareness that Yiddish was championed by other groups for other purposes. Similarly, feminists are drawn to Yiddish for a variety of scholarly, communal, and personal reasons. One might be looking for a secular Jewish model for life, a foundation for activism, a basis for artistic work, a women's lineage, a family connection, or something else. Regardless, Jewish cultural heritage overall is enriched by those anthologies inspired or produced by feminists. Ultimately, all readers may benefit from the discovery and availability of Yiddish writings by women, which in turn may lead to an increasing appreciation of women's contribution to history.

## Notes

1. About translation as an ideological practice, see Itamar Even-Zohar, "The Position of Translated Literature within the Literary Polysystem," in *Literature and Translation: New Perspectives in Literary Studies*, ed. James Holmes, Jose Lambert, and Raymond van den Broeck (Leuven: ACCO, 1978), 117–127; Itamar Even-Zohar, "Polysystem Theory," *Poetics Today* 1 (1979): 287–310; and Andre Lefevere, *Rewriting, Manipulation of Literary Fame* (London: Routledge, 1992).

2. See David Stern, ed., *The Anthology in Jewish Literature* (New York: Oxford University Press, 2004). Stern's framework has five parts. The first analyzes the literary form, which refers to the way that the anthology is organized; a volume may be arranged by time period, historical event, genre, gender, language, region, theme, or some other organizing principle. The second examines the history of an anthology, which covers publishers, reprints, reputations of its compilers and translators, and other matters. The third relates to the role of the anthology in building a literary canon. The fourth foregrounds the role of the anthology in transmitting tradition; and the fifth concentrates on the role of the anthology in transmitting culture and community.

3. See Kathryn Hellerstein, "Gender and the Anthological Tradition in Modern Yiddish Poetry," in *The Anthology in Jewish Literature*, ed. David Stern (New York: Oxford University Press, 2004), 259–280; and Jeffrey Shandler, "Anthologizing the Vernacular:

Collections of Yiddish Literature in English Translation," in *The Anthology in Jewish Literature*, ed. David Stern (New York: Oxford University Press, 2004), 304–323.

4. Chandler, "Anthologizing the Vernacular," 305.

5. Dorothy Bilik, "Yente Serdatsky," *Jewish Women: A Comprehensive Historical Encyclopedia*, 1 March 2009, Jewish Women's Archive (assessed July 2, 2013), http://jwa.org/encyclopedia/article/serdatzky-yente.

6. Review of Helena Frank, *Yiddish Tales*, Google book review, books.google.com.

7. For more information, see Albert Mordell, *The World of Haldeman-Julius* (New York: Twayne, 1960).

8. Isaac Goldberg, ed., *Great Yiddish Poetry* (Girard, KS: Haldeman-Julius, 1923), 12.

9. Jeremy Shere, "Collective Portraits: The Anthological Imagination of Leo W. Schwarz," *Shofar: An Interdisciplinary Journal of Jewish Studies* 23:3 (Spring 2005): 47.

10. Jewish Telegraphic Agency, *The Global Jewish News Service*, "Joseph Leftwich obituary," March 7, 1983.

11. For a review of the anthologies, see David Roskies, "The Treasures of Howe and Greenberg," *Prooftexts* 3 (January 1983): 109–114. For more information about Schocken's publishing enterprises, see Anthony David, *The Patron: A Life of Salman Schocken, 1877–1959* (New York: Metropolitan Books, 2003).

12. Irving Howe and Eliezer Greenberg, *A Treasury of Yiddish Stories* (New York: Schocken Books, 1973), 2.

13. An example is Ruth Whitman's *An Anthology of Modern Yiddish Poetry* (New York: Workman's Circle, Education Department, 1979).

14. Norma Fain Pratt, "Culture and Radical Politics: Yiddish Women Writers, 1890–1940," *American Jewish History* 70:1 (September 1980): 68–90.

15. Ibid., 88.

16. Frieda Forman, Ethel Raicus, Sarah Silberstein Swartz, and Margie Wolf, "Preface," in *Found Treasures: Stories by Yiddish Women Writers*, ed. Frieda Forman, Ethel Raicus, Sarah Silberstein Swartz, and Margie Wolf (Toronto: Second Story Press, 1994), 17.

17. Irena Klepfisz, "Queens of Contradiction: A Feminist Introduction to Yiddish Women Writers," in *Found Treasures: Stories by Yiddish Women Writers*, ed. Frieda Forman, Ethel Raicus, Sarah Silberstein Swartz, and Margie Wolf (Toronto: Second Story Press, 1994), 56–57.

18. Rhea Tregebov, "Preface and Acknowledgments," in *Arguing with the Storm: Stories by Yiddish Women Writers*, ed. Rhea Tregebov (New York: Feminist Press, 2007), x.

19. "About Second Story," *Second Story Press*, secondstorypress.ca, website.

20. "About FP," *The Feminist Press*, feministpress.org, website.

21. Miriam Weinstein, *Prophets & Dreamers: A Selection of Great Yiddish Literature* (South Royalton, VT: Steerforth Press, 2002), 3

22. Albert Waldinger, *Shining and Shadow: An Anthology of Early Yiddish Stories from the Lower East Side* (Selingsgrove, PA: Susquehanna University Press, 2006), 24.

23. Dovid Katz, "Introduction," in *Proletpen: America's Rebel Yiddish Poets,* ed. Amelia Glaser and David Weintraub (Madison: University of Wisconsin Press, 2005), 22.

24. Seth L. Wolitz, "An Exilic Homeland: Yiddish Poetry," in *With Everything We've Got: A Personal Anthology of Yiddish Poetry*, ed. Richard Fein (New York: Host Publications, 2009), xvii.

25. "Norton History," W. W. Norton & Company, wwnorton.com, website.

26. Joseph Sherman, ed., *Writers in Yiddish* (Detroit: Thomson Gale, 2007). Rokhl Korn and Chava Rosenfarb each have an entry in Sherman's volume too.

27. See Michael Gluzman, "The Exclusion of Women from Hebrew Literary History," *Prooftexts* 11: 3 (September 1991): 259–278 for a similar point about Hebrew literature.

28. Bennett Muraskin, "Introduction," *The Association of Jewish Libraries Guide to Yiddish Short Stories* (Teaneck, NJ: Ben Yehuda Press, 2011), xvi.

29. David Fishman, *The Rise of Modern Yiddish Culture* (Pittsburgh: University of Pittsburgh Press, 2005), viii.

# Still Waiting for Tomorrow
*Lily Bes and Her
Contemporaries in the 1920s*

## Hinde Ena Burstin

Little is known about Lily Bes's life or the circumstances under which she wrote. No entries on Bes appear in the lexicons of Yiddish literature or in Berl Kagan's comprehensive listing of Yiddish writers' pseudonyms, and despite my extensive searches, no biographical information on Lily Bes has come to light.[1] Bes published the poems "Tsu a kolege" [To a (Male) Colleague] and "Fun eynge vent" [From Cramped Walls] in the New York communist newspaper *Di frayhayt* in 1929.[2] She had previously published a number of poems in the newspaper. "Tsu a kolege" and "Fun eynge vent," along with some of her other poems, merit exploration because they capture the conditions and convictions of many Yiddish women writers of the 1920s.[3]

Implicit in discussing the work of an unfamiliar writer is the recognition that publication has been a difficult endeavor for women. This does not diminish the value or significance of what they wrote. As novelist and literary theorist Tillie Olsen asserts, "We must not speak of women writers in our century ... without speaking also of the invisible, of the as-innately capable: the born to the wrong circumstances—diminished, excluded, foundered, silenced."[4] These silences are amplified in the understudied field of Yiddish writing by women. Yet as "Tsu a kolege" and "Fun eynge vent" demonstrate, the fact a woman was unknown did not prevent her from writing poems that encapsulate the significant themes in women's lives. Exploring such poems broadens literary knowledge and provides a more comprehensive picture of the field of Yiddish writing by women.

Even in the absence of personal data on Lily Bes, much may be gleaned from the historical, social, and cultural contexts in which "Tsu a kolege" and "Fun eynge vent" were published. Bes's poems appear working-class in tone and content. The two poems, along with at least seven others, were published in New York following a substantial wave of Jewish immigration to the United States from Eastern Europe and during a time of significant upheaval in Jewish communal life. Given the mass immigration to the United States during this period and the publication of Bes's poems in New York, it seems probable that Bes lived in the United States. Notably, the feminist researcher Norma Fain Pratt includes an extract from "Fun eynge vent" in her pioneering essay on immigrant American Yiddish women writers.[5] Furthermore, Rokhl Holtman, editor of the Sunday women's page of *Di frayhayt*, implies that she is acquainted with Bes.[6] This reinforces the likelihood that Bes lived in America. Bes's poem "A land aza," published in *Di frayhayt* on December 23, 1928, is critical of a land that appears to have everything, but is filled with gold dust that chokes the people.[7] This is in keeping with the way many Jewish immigrants of the time viewed America, further suggesting that Bes lived in the United States at the time of publication. However, the international nature of Yiddish publishing meant that Yiddish writers living on one continent often published on another.[8] It is possible Lily Bes wrote her poems in Eastern Europe, where the largest proportion of Jews lived at that time.[9] The circumstances that Bes depicts in these two poems are relevant for both American and Eastern European contexts. Therefore, the Eastern European and American contexts each facilitate a reading of the texts within the historical and cultural circumstances in which Yiddish women poets produced and published their work in the 1920s.

## *"Tsu a kolege"*

The poem "Tsu a kolege" functions as a magnifying glass through which common conditions confronting Yiddish women poets are identified and represented, capturing an important time when Yiddish women were on the brink of greater social, cultural, and literary agency and illuminating the challenges that many Yiddish women writers faced. The poem depicts the social, cultural, and literary contexts for Yiddish women poets in the 1920s. The words, so full of passion and hope, were written by a Yiddish writer who is unknown to contemporary readers. Bes's invisibility juxtaposes poignantly with the optimism she expressed about the future for Yiddish women writers. Her words are an outcry of the silenced. As indicated in the title, the speaker addresses her poem to her colleague. Nouns are gendered in Yiddish. Thus it is clear in the original Yiddish that the speaker is addressing a man.[10] This is significant because gendered expectations determine the divergent writing conditions of the female speaker and her male colleague.

The opening lines of the poem immediately locate the poem and the speaker in the domestic sphere, where Jewish women's lives were largely lived.[11] The speaker depicts her world through daily objects and work tools. Thus, she describes her day in terms of the cradle, not the child; the oven and pot, not the food; and the broom, not the home. This emphasizes function over affection, creating a sense of objectification and emotional detachment. Given the large number of working-class women employed in domestic service and childcare,[12] it is possible that the oven, the cradle, the pot, and the broom are not located in the speaker's home. Whether carrying out these duties at her own home or for a boss, the speaker appears here as both trapped in, and alienated from, an enclosing environment. This highlights the numbing nature of domestic work. Bes expands on this issue in a letter to Holtman, writing, "Heavy human worries enchained my hands. I had no courage to take a pen in my hands. The will to do so had been extinguished."[13]

Yet, even when creative fires are burning, lack of time enchains creativity. The poem dramatizes this message through incremental repetition of the word "*baym*" [by the], emphasizing both the repetitive nature of the speaker's tasks and the many places where she creates. This alerts the reader that the speaker is constantly and simultaneously working and writing. The plosive "b" adds a tone of disdain at the amount of work that the speaker must undertake.

The opening lines of Bes's poem reflect the restrictive reality for many Yiddish women writers.[14] In the early part of the twentieth century, Jewish women were overburdened with responsibility. Most Jewish women married young and bore many children. Many also had the financial responsibility for their families. Yiddish writer and political activist Gina Medem portrays a typical Jewish woman, stating, "She wants to stop for a moment to gather her thoughts—but she does not have any time."[15] Domestic obstacles and lack of time are issues that Yiddish women writers have in common with other women writers. Tillie Olsen depicts these same barriers in her description of writing while standing on a bus, ironing clothes, or snatching a moment deep in the night when all her chores were completed.[16] Feminist literary researchers and theorists have highlighted the conflict between creativity and traditionally undervalued nurturing roles such as motherhood and domestic work.[17] Inequitable gendered expectations restrict the time, space, and freedom for women writers to focus fully on their creativity. These socially-imposed silences have significant bearing on the quality and availability of literature, as Olsen asserts:

> The cost to literature of its sporadic, occasional, week-end or sabbatical writers ... *is* unfinished work, minor effort and accomplishment, silences—where there might be a great flowering. And some writers are grated to pieces by the constant attrition. Lost forever.[18]

Perhaps this is what occurred to Lily Bes. Caught up in the incessant demands of the oven, the cradle, the pot, and the broom, her words may have floundered—unfinished, forgotten. In that regard, she is not alone.

Lack of time is an important theme for Bes, both the daily lack of time of women overburdened with too much work and the lack of time that has passed since women gained the education and agency to enable them to develop their writing skills. In her letter to Holtman, Bes asserts that women have only recently liberated themselves from their cages, and so have not yet had time to create something great. She argues that men did not create great works in their earliest writings either.

Furthermore, compared with men, time-poor and overburdened Yiddish women writers had little support. Major Yiddish novelist and poet Chava Rosenfarb articulates this gender imbalance and lack of support, stating:

> The male writer usually had a wife, who revered him in much the same way as the religious Jewish woman revered her husband, the talmudic scholar. She acted as his pillar of support, his guardian angel, his kindly critic, his faithful servant who walked around on tiptoe whenever he was at work writing and admonished the children to be quiet.... Such a godsend, such a wife, the Yiddish woman writer never had and badly needed.[19]

Bes was aware of this imbalance and the impact that it had on Yiddish women writers. The privileging of men's work and lack of support for women contributed to a rupture in some Yiddish women poets' writing careers. As Pratt states, "The common pattern was to write before marriage and after widowhood."[20] Domestic and familial burdens also meant that Jewish women's path in life was often severely constrained. Bes depicts this constraint, writing in the poem, "*Mayn veg iz gelegn fun shtub bizn kleytl / Un mer hot far mir nit geklekt*" [My path only led from my home to the store / Not a thing more existed for me]. These lines portray a world that is limited to a single path. It is not clear whether the speaker goes to the store to shop or to work. In keeping this interpretation open, the poem speaks to women tied to the home and to those who also work outside the home. *Mayn veg* is used idiomatically in Yiddish as "my path in life." Thus, the speaker's use of *mayn veg* suggests a sense of resignation that her path in life consists of family and work to the exclusion of all else. This seems underscored by an ingrained and unquestioned assumption that this was Jewish women's lot in life. The line that follows "*un mer hot far mir nisht geklekt*" [nothing else existed for me] could be read as employing irony that this single path in life is sufficient. However, it suggests a defeated tone, in which the speaker seems to consciously and passively accept her situation. The second stanza signifies a shift in tone and consciousness as the speaker's sense of self grows, along with her indignation. She asks, "*Haynt vilstu gor, khaver, mit mir zikh farmestn?*" [Today, you want to compete with me, my friend?]. The stanza begins with the word *haynt*, locating the poem in the present and giving it a context in the then-current time.

It is worthwhile to explore the "today" of the poem. Bes's poems were published at the height of Yiddish women's publishing, several months after the release of Korman's groundbreaking *Yidishe dikhterins: antologye* [Anthology of Yiddish Women Poets], which features over three hundred pages of poems by sixty-nine Yiddish women poets and one male masking as a female.[21] A considerable number of Yiddish women writers, including Leah K. Hoffman, Miriam Ulinover, Anna Bloch, Ida Glasser-Andrews, Khane Leye Khveydanski, Yudika, Sarah Reisen, Rosa Yakubivitsh, Rosa Gutman, Rashel Veprinski, Pesi Hershfeld, Kadya Molodowsky, Khane Vurtsel, Rokhl Korn, and Esther Segal, published collections of their own poetry in the 1920s.[22] It was a significant breakthrough for these women to be published in book form, because for the most part, Yiddish poetry by women was dispersed throughout journals, newspapers, and other regional publications.[23] With the exception of Anna Bloch, Khane Leye Khveydanski, and Khane Vurtsel, the other women went on to have long careers as Yiddish writers.

During the 1920s, Yiddish women writers published their work in numerous daily and weekly Yiddish newspapers, journals, and collections.[24] There were also a number of Yiddish women's journals, such as *Di froy* [The Woman] (Vilna, 1925–1933) and *Froyen-shtim* [Women's Voice] (Warsaw, 1925). On the surface, the time appeared full of promise. However, a comparison of publishing of Yiddish writing by men and women at that time is revealing. In 1927, *Kletskin farlag* published 77 books. Only one—Kadya Molodowsky's *Kheshvendike nekht* [Nights of Kheshvan]—was by a woman.[25] Molodowsky eventually became the best-known of the Yiddish women writers and a respected Yiddish editor and literary commentator. *Farlag gezelshaft* (Warsaw) published at least 59 books in 1927. All were written by men, with the exception of Rokhl Faygenberg's *A pinkes fun a toyter shtot: Khurbn-Dubova* [A Record Book of a Dead City: The Destruction of Dubova].[26] Faygenberg was not new to publishing. Her groundbreaking novel, *Oyf fremde vegn* [Strange

Ways], had been published in 1925. This novel chronicles the impact of urbanization and patriarchy through exploring the relationship between a Jewish woman and a married man. *Farlag gezelshaft* (Warsaw) also published one book *about* women in 1927, *Barimte yidishe froyen* [Famous Jewish Women], compiled by the Yiddish writer Sh. L. Tsitron.[27] Tsitron does not include any of the modern Yiddish women writers in his book. Comparable publication data for Yiddish publishing houses in the United States is unavailable.[28]

Underrepresentation of women is also evident in Yiddish journals and newspapers. In 1928, the year when *Yidishe dikhterins* appeared, *Literarishe bleter* [Literary Pages], the most prestigious Yiddish literary journal of its day, devoted more space to publishing male English writer Thomas Hardy and German male writer Alfred Henschke[29] in translation than to publishing Yiddish women writers. Even articles about Francis of Assisi were allocated more space than Yiddish women writers, in the primary Yiddish literary journal of 1928. Of the sixty pages of poetry published in *Literarishe bleter* in 1928, only nine contained *some* writing by women. This is significant, given that there was no shortage of Yiddish material by women, as evidenced by Korman's anthology and the numerous published collections of women's poetry at that time.

In 1928, *Froyen: literarishe zamlung* [Women: Literary Collection] was published by *Tsentraln felker farlag* in Moscow.[30] This volume, compiled by I. Rabinovitsh, aimed to "depict the artistic representation of women's lives from the distant past to today."[31] However, the 181-page collection includes only nine pages of writing by a woman, Lydia Seyfulin, and one page by an unknown author, R. Fish, who *may* have been a woman. This represents less than six percent of the volume. While the volume's preface includes laudatory declarations about the liberation of Soviet women,[32] as low as four percent and as high as eight percent of the authors, were women. That a collection about women contains only one or possibly two women contributors highlights the sexism and cultural asymmetry that existed even in radical Jewish circles and accentuates the marginalized position of women in the Yiddish literary world.

Accessible information regarding publication of Yiddish women writers in the United States suggests a similar situation. Morris Bassin's *500 yor yidishe poezye* [Five Hundred Years of Yiddish Poetry], published in New York in 1917, includes ninety-five Yiddish poets, only eight of whom are women: Zelda Knizhnik, Yehudis (Rokhl Bernshteyn), Rosa Goldshteyn, Anna Rapaport (Zif), Roza Y. (Yakubovitsh), Paola R. (Prilutski), Soreh Reyzin, and Fradl Shtok.[33] These women all made significant contributions to Yiddish literature. However, at that time, many other women were producing poems that also merited inclusion in the anthology. The meager selection of only eight women poets severely undermines women's role in Yiddish poetry over the five hundred-year period. Even less representative is Zishe Landau's 1919 *Antologye: di yidishe dikhtung in amerike biz yor 1919* [Anthology: Yiddish Poetry in America Until the Year 1919].[34] Only three poems by two women, Celia Dropkin and Fradl Shtok, are included in the volume, comprising a total of three pages of the 172 in the collection.

Critical responses to *Yidishe dikhterins* round out the picture. Korman's anthology received few reviews in the Yiddish press. Some were vitriolic, vilifying both the compiler of the anthology and the women poets.[35] The objectification and sexualization of the poets is notable, for example, in Melech Ravitch's review, where he accuses Korman of being a love-struck polygamist and describes one of the poets as having "a beautiful face, and therefore, can't be expected to also be a good poet."[36] Trivialization also took other forms. Literary critic Shmuel Niger comments in his review that while the number of women publishing Yiddish poetry has increased significantly, what has increased even more is the number of women "writing verse, although they could be doing possibly more useful things."[37] Indeed, it was Niger's dismissive attitude towards Yiddish women poets that inspired "Tsu a kolege."[38] The outright hostility that Yiddish women poets confronted has a long history, with male writers and editors seeking to undermine and discredit talented female writers.[39]

The male literary establishment marginalized Yiddish women writers, while seeming to support them. Bes highlights this contradictory response, stating that women's creativity is "extremely underappreciated, even by those from whom we could have expected a different approach."[40] As Irena Klepfisz states, "Yiddish women writers were trapped by the conflicting motives of the men who exercised power and control over Yiddish journals, newspapers and presses."[41] Thus, while the 1920s represented a transitional period of growth in Yiddish women poets' creativity, innovation, and publication, women continued to be underrepresented in Yiddish publications. This underlines and accounts for Bes's accent on *haynt* and the speaker's incredulity at her colleague's desire to compare himself with her.

Within this publishing scenario, the speaker's use of the multilayered word *khaver* is powerful. Depending on context, *khaver* may mean a male friend or a male comrade. Given that Bes's poem was published in the communist journal *Di frayhayt*, it is possible that the poet consciously chose the politically nuanced *khaver* as opposed to the more neutral term, *fraynd*. Bes appears to express leftist leanings in her poem "A land aza," yet this is suggestive rather than conclusive.[42] It cannot be assumed that Bes identified as a communist since Yiddish writers of all political inclinations published in *Di frayhayt* because of the paper's commitment to Yiddish literature.[43] Notably, of the radical Yiddish papers of the time, *Di frayhayt* was considered the most supportive of the struggle for women's rights.[44] Further, the term *khaver* is not as overtly communist as the term comrade.[45] *Khaver* is widely used by Bundists and other socialists, but it is also used apolitically. In recognition of this and in deference to the rhyme scheme, *khaver* is translated as friend.

Whether interpreted as friend or comrade, *khaver* implies an equal relationship, as does *kolege*. Yet, in social terms, the speaker is clearly not her colleague's equal, for he is not bound by the many duties that keep her from writing. He is able to develop his creativity and have it reviewed on its own merits. Thus, the use of *khaver* may be read as a critique of the inequality and competitiveness between men and women who were ostensibly comrades, given that Yiddish women poets experienced "the profound contradiction faced by most other radical women in the early twentieth century of living within a pattern of seeming acceptance combined with implicit exclusion."[46] The speaker in Bes's poem accentuates this contradiction with her use of *khaver*. In choosing *khaver*, Bes also emphasizes the intimacy of their shared goals as writers and stresses her sense of herself as equal to him, despite social inequities and literary exclusion. The speaker's tone may be read as ironic or even bitter, mocking their unequal social status and his desire to compete with her.

In a letter to Holtman, Bes writes that her poems tore themselves out of her as a response to literary critic Shmuel Niger trivializing Yiddish women poets in his review of Korman's anthology, where "he dissects the book so smoothly and genteelly, before concluding that it was not worth the effort to publish the book."[47] Thus, the *khaver/kolege* may be read as Niger, the catalyst for Bes's poems. Notably, Niger was a Socialist Zionist.

The irony of Bes calling Niger a *khaver* and a *kolege* is evident, given their unequal social status. The impact of this unequal status is further emphasized when the speaker in the poem adds, "*Du konst es mit virde yetst ton*" [You can die with dignity now]. The privileging of men's work and the conditions in which men produce their work underscores a position of power that enables men to compete and win. These cultural asymmetries and social inequities ensured that men maintained significant control of the Yiddish press.[48] No women held a permanent editorial position on any of the radical papers at this time.[49] The dominance of male editors and publishers has been widely recognized as easing male poets' path to publication.[50] The underrepresentation of women in publishing further ensures that men can retain their dignity in comparing themselves with women. Yet, Bes's poem also hints at the lack of dignity exercised by editors and critics, who sought to humiliate women poets in a number of ways. This unequal status also prevented women from challenging male editors and critics. Bes highlights the issue of power in her correspondence, conceding that it would be considered the greatest impudence for her to say something directly to Niger. "Who dares to even begin with such authorities?" she asks.[51]

The Yiddish literati maintained an authoritarian approach with respect to Yiddish women writers, through dictating the themes deemed acceptable in writing by women and condemning works that dared to address subject matter beyond these confines.[52] Critic A. Glanz, for example, postulates that women should not seek to be "masculine," but rather, should produce "intuitive, feminine" work. As feminist writer, academic, and literary critic Joanna Russ demonstrates, these strategies limit women's ability to produce literature.[53]

Further, Yiddish journals tended to publish a very limited range of women writers, while overlooking all other Yiddish women writers. Within this limited range, it was also common to group divergent poets together solely on the basis of their gender. Yiddish poet Kadya Molodowsky mocks the inclination of Yiddish editors to pair two distinct women poets "as one kind, in one book, or on one page," even though often the only thing the writers have in common is that they are women and Yiddish poets.[54] Furthermore, editors of radical papers and journals included little critical discussion of women's role in Yiddish literature.[55] Yiddish writing by women was rarely reviewed in the literary journals of the time. The few reviews that were published tended to judge women's writing through a lens of stereotypical expectations and gendered assumptions. In fact, at times, women were not even seen as mature beings but as girls, as the title of Melech Ravitch's disdainful essay "Meydlekh, froyen, vayber—yidishe dikhterins" [Girls, women, wives—Yiddish poetesses] demonstrates.[56] The women were viewed not as writers, but as "women writers." As Hellerstein asserts, "Poems by women ... tend to be read primarily in reference to the writer's sex.... As of 1928, Yiddish did not possess a critical vocabulary for reading poems by women as poems."[57]

It was not uncommon for critics to place the responsibility for Yiddish literature on an individual woman writer, whose individual works were judged as representing the work of all women. Any perceived shortcomings by an individual woman writer were regarded as lowering the tone of Yiddish writing by women and of Yiddish literature in general. For example, in 1919, Glanz published a review in *Der tog*,⁵⁸ in which he harshly criticized the work of the previously lauded, admired, and widely-published Yiddish writer, Fradl Shtok.⁵⁹ In criticizing Shtok's writing, "Glanz expressed the deepest disappointment in his unfulfilled expectations of women writers."⁶⁰ Shtok thus became the token female who bore the burden for all Yiddish writing by women.

Feminist researcher Faith Jones demonstrates that a common tactic of reviewers was to contrast books by several Yiddish women writers in one review, with one of the books extoled at the expense of the others.⁶¹ This strategy of playing off one female writer against another reinforces the myth that only few, exceptional women are capable of producing quality work. Many reviewers have regarded gender as more relevant than the genre of writing. Jones cites an example of a review of "a non-fiction children's book about Israel" being appraised alongside "a book of adult poetry."⁶² These examples were not isolated incidents. As such, it is hardly surprising that there were complaints that "the doors of the Yiddish press are still strongly shut for us, women!"⁶³

Caustic critiques also maligned women writers and their work. The strategy of playing off one author against another further undermines women writers. Rather than valuing women's writing on its own merits, literary critics tended to see women's poetry as the inspiration for men's poetry. Glanz, for example, cast women poets as a collective Muse who would enrich the Yiddish poetic tradition, so that men could produce better works.⁶⁴ Additionally, editors such as Shmuel Rozhanski espoused the rhetoric of women's restrictions and exclusions, but did not follow through with greater inclusion and representation of Yiddish women writers in the publications they edited.⁶⁵ These attitudes and actions in the Yiddish literary community supported and maintained the underrepresentation of Yiddish women's writing in both publication and literary analysis.

The demeaning devices employed by male editors and critics were familiar to Lily Bes, who in her correspondence writes of her frustration with the light, frivolous treatment of Yiddish women writers.⁶⁶ Bes understood, as her poem's speaker suggests, that women's writing should not be treated dismissively, but rather, can and should be treated with dignity. The speaker concedes that her colleague can compete with dignity now, because her status is not yet equal to his—his life is not consumed by the oven, cradle, pot, and broom. However, Bes accentuates the temporality and temporariness of the colleague's elevated status through the use of *yetst* [now], echoing the *haynt* [today] of the preceding line. *Haynt* and *yetst* are juxtaposed against *morgn* [tomorrow] in the closing line. Thus, Bes does not regard her situation or the situation of women as permanent. She believes women will gain equality through imminent social change.

Bes draws on the trope of battle in the line "*Du vest ale shlakhtn gevinen tsum ambestn*" [You will win all the battles best][67] to emphasize the combative approach of her male colleague and the sense of embattlement of women writers like herself. This reflects the attacking tone of influential male literary critics who trivialized women's writing, confining it to stereotypical arenas and judgments, and who dismissed writing by women as having little or no merit.[68] Hence, as the speaker asserts, male poets can compete and win. Given the obstacles to publication, the ability of a significant number of Yiddish women poets, such as those noted in this essay, to continue publishing for three, four or more decades, is a testament to their talent and their tenacity.

Despite the gendered barriers that Bes confronts and articulates, the speaker in the poem believes in a better tomorrow. This conviction was empowered by the sweeping social changes in the status of women in Eastern Europe and in the New World. Women's struggle for equal rights was reflected in Yiddish poetry by women from the turn of the century.[69] The voice calling for justice, equality, and social change gained strength in the ensuing decades. Bes's voice, too, gains strength. "Tsu a kolege" concludes with a battle cry in response to the battle waged by the men, declaring that a new day is dawning, and, by implication, that women will gain the freedom, time, and social acceptability to pursue their writing.

This poem clearly articulates and exemplifies the barriers that some women confronted, including the tyranny of their domestic duties and the dismissive attitudes of male writers towards women writers and their work. It also depicts women's growing empowerment and hope for the future. The voice of the poet resonates for the reader, creating at first a feeling of defeat and despair at the difficulty and seeming-inescapability of her situation. The first stanza carries a sense of resignation, emphasized by the line "*Un mer hot far mir nit geklekt*" [Nothing else existed for me]. The second stanza invokes anger at her colleague's arrogance in comparing himself to her, when these limitations do not exist for him. Although she concedes that he is winning all the current battles, her tone grows more powerful. Her despondency is replaced with hope, concluding with a strong voice that imbues the reader with a sense of optimism for the forthcoming changes.

While the speaker in the poem appears self-assured and full of bravado, Bes's correspondence reveals a lack of self-confidence, shown in the begrudging way she discusses her work, and through her questioning, several times in the space of a short letter, whether others could create something better on this theme. This is of note, given that Bes was one of the most frequently published Yiddish women poets in *Di frayhayt* in 1928–1929. She seems highly conscious that she is not a sophisticated writer, as so urges talented women writers to take up this timely topic. Bes uses such strength in her poem, in contrast with her letter, because she aims to inspire her readers with a message of hope. In doing so, she draws on a model used by sweatshop poets such as Morris Rosenfeld and other *sotsyal-poetn*,[70] poets with a social conscience concerned with societal issues, including the lesser-known Anna Rapaport.[71]

Like other poems of the genre, the primary purpose of Bes's is to communicate a political message. Bes is able to do so effectively, because her poems are straightforward, forcefully spoken, and memorable. Bes seeks to motivate the reader with an idea that is expressed simply, then developed and repeated. This is a common trait of *sotsyal poezye*.[72] The poet uses everyday language, thereby ensuring that her poem is broadly accessible. Concise, monosyllabic words give strength and emphasis to the conviction of the speaker. The regulated prosody that Bes employs is an important trait of the social poem. Consistency of rhythm and simplicity of rhyme make the poem easy to remember.[73]

"Tsu a kolege" consists of two quatrains, with a simple metrics of alternating lines of six and four meters, creating a lyrical tone that is both unaffected and rousing. The traditional form of the poem—at a time when many Yiddish writers were experimenting with freer forms—gives the poem a *folkstimlekh*, or folksong-like quality, underlining its grassroots nature and connection with issues that concern common folk. In a sense, this traditional style emboldens Bes's expression of new political ideals and principles. The accessibility of the poet's style complements the everyday nature of the subject matter.

Bes's poem speaks of the future with optimism, yet, it is not prophetic. A better tomorrow did not come for her. It is not known whether Bes wrote or published further poems. It appears that no echo of Bes's writing remains, suggesting she did not manage to attain literary success. Bes's dreamed-of tomorrow did not come for Yiddish women poets *en masse* either. While Yiddish women poets gained greater prominence in the 1920s and 1930s, the Holocaust and its aftermath dealt decimating blows to Yiddish literature and culture. Women were doubly the victims, for much of their writing, printed primarily in journals and periodicals, did not survive. In addition, as Rosenfarb asserts, women's concerns were again pushed to the periphery in the face of pressing concerns over survival, immigration, and rebuilding community.[74] Thus, the silencing of women's voices intensified in the tomorrows that followed Bes's optimistic pronouncement.

## "Fun eynge vent"

Women's changing role is also a theme in "Fun eynge vent." Similar to "Tsu a kolege," this poem expounds new political ideas and ideals and heralds optimism at social and personal transition. "Fun eynge vent" articulates a rupture with the past, discarding the chaste and pious ways of the grandmother's generation of Jewish women and setting out on an adventurous new path in response to an inner revolt. The turbulence and transition in Jewish life at the time when the poem was published is reflected in the change in individual circumstances that the speaker seeks. The poem captures a woman's recognition that the old ways are cobwebbed and confining. The speaker affirms her intention to live a life of freedom. She refuses to be bound by societal conventions or communal expectations of how she should behave. In doing so, she defies the belief that women should adjust their actions in line with social norms.

Like "Tsu a kolege," the poem "Fun eynge vent" uses a first-person speaker, suggesting the poem is autobiographical. However, the poem could also represent another woman or even an image of the changing condition of Jewish womanhood. When read together with "Tsu a kolege," the two poems characterize either a woman at different stages in her life or perhaps two different women. "Fun eynge vent" represents a presumably younger woman who has greater freedom than the woman in "Tsu a kolege." In the absence of any accessible biographical information about Bes, it is not possible to speculate whether either of these poems depicts Bes's actual experiences. It is clear, however that both poems comment on the conditions that Jewish women of that time faced. The title "Fun eynge vent" immediately creates a sense of constriction and claustrophobia. Walls are a common trope in poetry, symbolizing the use and abuse of power and control through societal structures that seal people in or out. The description of the walls as *eng* [cramped, narrow, or tight] emphasizes the feeling of confinement from which the speaker seeks to escape. The use of the word *fun* [from] brings movement to the title, further underlining the speaker's need to break out of imposed boundaries and set herself free. The image of a woman confined behind the walls of her home is particularly potent when read in conjunction with "Tsu a kolege," emphasizing the power of the home to restrict women physically and creatively, thus fueling a desire to escape.

In the opening line of the poem, the speaker declares her indifference to the opinions of *"gute layt." Layt* literally means respectable, reputable, or proper people. The term implies genteelness. The addition of the adjective *gute* [good] reinforces the sense of respectability and adds a touch of irony.

Thus the speaker mocks the "good folk" who judge her because she chooses a different path in life. The opening line, later repeated, underlines the strength of the speaker's conviction and her sense of personal power in casting off social expectations.

The speaker states that, regardless of the opinions of others, she is repulsed by the cobwebs in the house. Her revulsion is powerful, representing complete rejection. Commencing the line with "For repugnant to me" creates enjambment from the previous line, linking the "good folk" with the repugnance. These threads are further interwoven with the image of the cobwebs. Cobwebs may be seen as "a symbol of human frailty and illusion."[75] Cobwebs appear where nothing is fresh or refreshed. Thus, the cobwebs may be regarded as representing the outmoded ways of the speaker's grandmother. The spun cobwebs are also reminiscent of the traditional female craft of spinning, a handicraft that had become superseded by the mechanization of the industrial period. This reinforces the speaker's desire to leave the traditions of the past behind and embrace modernity. Notably, both of Bes's poems contain an image of weaving.

Cobwebs may be considered beautiful, yet the speaker no longer sees any beauty in the pious ways that she rejects. While cobwebs appear fragile, they are in actuality strong. Similarly, while the role of religion was diminishing in Jewish communal life at this time,[76] religious mores retained a strong hold in many ways.[77] It appears that the speaker recognizes this strength, responding with repugnance and a powerful rejection. Yet, despite their strength, cobwebs may be easily destroyed and removed. This bodes well for the removal of religious restrictions.

Houses with cobwebs are associated with being untended or even unattended, playing on the untouched nature of those who are chaste. This connection is intensified when the speaker emphatically rejects pious chastity later in the poem. Cobwebbed houses also have a connotation of being dilapidated and frightening. This symbolizes the weakening of traditional religious structures of the past, even while a spider-web thread linking back to tradition remains. The cobwebs appear to be located in the speaker's house. However, this is not entirely clear, as in Yiddish, depending on the context, *der* may mean the, this, or my.[78] Possibly the speaker is expressing her repugnance for her grandmother's house, the house of pious tradition. In biblical literature, a woman is sometimes referred to as a *bayit*,[79] or house of her husband. As professor of religion Susan Niditch explains, the image in biblical literature of a woman as a vessel or house regards the woman solely in terms of her domestic, matrimonial, and maternal functions: "She is to be filled with her husband's seed.... As she contains and shelters the future child, so her realm is the home, the private realm of children and procreation."⁸⁰ This realm of religious expectation is rejected by the speaker in Bes's poem. The house may also be read as an allusion to domesticity or lack of domesticity as the speaker leaves tradition behind.

Symbols abound in the next two lines of the poem. The first is the speaker's description of being "drawn, just like a tramp to distant roads." The speaker flings off gendered expectations in applying an archetype associated with men to herself. Further, the tramp or vagabond is unencumbered, carrying little or no baggage. The tramp leaves the past behind physically and attitudinally and is self-reliant and independent, an explorer who roams freely. Yet this wanderer is not rich, having no assets and no material belongings.

The speaker's desire for freedom to follow her own choices is evident in her rejection of the expectations of others. Her longing to live like a tramp may also be read as symbolizing the desire to discard materialism and embrace the revolutionary politics of the time. This is reinforced with the later description of revolt brewing and resonates with the image of leaving behind the grandmother's pious ways. Further, Bes's poem was published in a revolutionary paper, at a time when many Jews were rejecting their religious heritage to embrace revolutionary politics.⁸¹ The speaker is drawn to distant roads, again stressing her desire to distance herself from closed-in religious ways.

There are two contrasting types of paths to which the speaker is attracted: unpaved paths of the open road and boisterous city streets. The dirt paths depict the speaker's desire to forge an unchartered path in life. This builds on the sense of freedom and adventure portrayed in the previous line of the poem. The explicit use of the word "open" accentuates her openness to new ways in life. It is questionable how much access Jewish women had to exploring the open road in the 1920s. Figuratively, however, women in this era were great explorers, developing alternative ways of existence as women and taking on new roles and pathways in life. Politically and culturally, they broke fresh ground, initiating significant social change.

At the same time as the speaker is drawn to dirt tracks, she is also attracted to the noisy city. In this respect, she typifies many young people of the era. Researcher Susan A. Glenn claims that many young Jews "were filled with a longing for change and excitement" that the city offered.⁸² This was true of many in Eastern Europe and the United States.⁸³ Within Eastern Europe, there was "substantial migration to urban centres,"⁸⁴ while most of the Jews who migrated to the United States "settled in cities where they clustered in districts close to downtowns."⁸⁵ Indeed, between 1880 and 1920, over a million Eastern

European Jews arrived in New York, where Bes's poem was published.[86] Thus, the longing for the noisy city may also be read as a metaphor for immigration.

The city symbolizes modernity. Cities presented fresh possibilities, particularly for women. As Hyman asserts, the urbanization that occurred at the end of the nineteenth century resulted in significant improvement in the status of women.[87] The city represented greater freedom for women, making movement to the city particularly attractive for those seeking to leave traditional religious mores behind. Cities also offered the opportunity to connect with like-minded people and become involved in a pulsing political and cultural life.

Noisy cities are the antithesis of open, dirt roads. Yet each brings the speaker into an extended environment that contrasts with the walls that currently confine her. The opposing attractions of rural areas and the city emphasize that the speaker is most strongly drawn to a process, not a particular place. She desires expansion and change. She seeks to escape the claustrophobia of her current life and is on the verge of a new beginning.

The expansion to which the speaker is drawn contrasts with the collapse of the past, as expressed in the line "*Es hot geplatst in mir di tsniyes fun mayn boben*" [My grandmother's piety has ruptured in me]. This is powerfully symbolic on a number of levels. *Tsniyes* has several different, though related, meanings: piety, modesty, and chastity. It is not clear which of these connotations Bes intended, and indeed, these three interpretations complement one another in characterizing a woman on the brink of modernity. The rupture with piety symbolizes the move away from religion and towards secularism, a journey often spearheaded by women, because women often gained access to secular education and ideas at an earlier time than their brothers did.[88] *Tsniyes* also depicts the traditional modesty and chastity that women had begun discarding at the turn of the century, as reflected in Yiddish poems by Paola R., Rosa Yakubovitch, Fradl Shtok, and others.[89] As Jewish women's sense of themselves as sexual beings ripened in the ensuing decades, expressions of sexuality became more apparent in Yiddish literature.[90]

*Geplatst* means burst, collapsed, cracked, or fizzled out. This may be read as an explosive rupture from the past or as a gradual breaking down. While the temperament in these approaches varies, both signify a crack that cannot be made whole. Thus, for the speaker, there is no turning back. The speaker uses *in mir* [in me] to describe the rupture. In articulating that the explosion has taken place inside of her, she accentuates the internal aspect of change. Further, this may imply an implosion rather than an explosion, as the speaker rejects the grandmother's ways.

The pious, chaste grandmother became a familiar image in Yiddish poetry as women cast off what they saw as repressive religious attitudes towards women.[91] It is noteworthy that women saw themselves as rejecting the ways of their grandmothers, as opposed to the ways of the rabbis. Traditionally, Jewish women's experience of religion was not centered within the synagogue, an institution that marginalized women. The Jewish religion has tended to treat females as observers of religious practice rather than as participants, shutting women out physically by segregating them behind the *mekhitse* [partition],[92] excluding them spiritually by not counting them in the *minyan*,[93] and not applying most of the commandments to them. As Hyman asserts: "The Jewish identity of Jewish women, then, was integrally connected with home and family life rather than with institutions."[94] Religious values and practices were passed matrilineally from the pious, modest grandmother to her granddaughters. Thus discarding the grandmother's ways became a trope for Jewish women of this time, who were actively embracing secularism.

The *tsniyesdike bobe* [the chaste, pious grandmother] from which young Jewish women wanted to escape was featured in other poems of this era, most notably, in Kadya Molodowsky's 1919 renowned cycle "Froyen lider" [Women's Songs].[95] Molodowsky's "Froyen lider" was widely acclaimed and would presumably have been known to Bes. While Bes's poem resonates and reflects "Froyen lider" in depicting the generational shift of young Jewish women rejecting the traditional ways of the grandmother, "Fun eynge vent" is far simpler in tone and content. Molodowsky presents vivid images of women whose lives have been constrained by traditional expectations and evokes the dilemmas challenging a young woman trying to escape. Both speakers give voice to their anger and rejection of confining ways. However, Bes's speaker merely declares so in a didactic manner. In contrast, Molodowsky's speaker confronts her grandmothers and casts off their piety, only to find herself in an impasse where tradition continues to shadow and limit her life. Bes's poem distils the message into a positive, one-dimensional punch. Molodowsky's poem is layered and multi-dimensional, presenting a deeper, more complex image than Bes's idealistic representation. Furthermore, Molodowsky's poem is aesthetically sophisticated, drawing on modern approaches to poetry, whereas Bes's poem utilizes simple rhythm and rhyme to convey her polemic. Bes's folksong-like approach makes her poem memorable. Molodowsky's evocative imagery and depth of exploration makes hers unforgettable. Molodowsky's sophisticated style and refined craft as a poet may have contributed to her ability to break through gender boundaries. In contrast, Bes, whose writing was impassioned but plain, seems to have been unable to endure as a poet. Nonetheless, both poets capture the zeitgeist of a generation of Jewish women in transition.

For Bes's speaker, this transition gained impetus through a sense of rebellion, as described in the line "*Es broyzt in mir revolt*" [Revolt is fermenting inside me]. *Broyz* may also mean seethe, reflecting the anger that gives impetus to revolt. The term revolt is powerful, given its association with the revolutionary movements that were gaining strength in Jewish communities at that time. Anarchist, communist, and socialist movements supported women's emancipation, at least in theory.[96] The publication of "Fun eynge vent" in a communist paper further underscores the sense of revolution.

In the poem, the speaker uses the simile of sparkling wine to describe her inner revolt. Wine is a symbol of celebration. Thus, the speaker may be seen as toasting her sense of resistance. At the same time, wine is connected with ritual blessing in spiritual Jewish life. The use of a symbol connected with religion to celebrate rejection of religious mores introduces a subversive note that further empowers the speaker's rebellion and flouting of conventions.

In the final quatrain, the speaker repeats her assertion "*Zoln gute layt mikh libn oder hasn*" [So let good folk either love me or hate me]. The repetition serves to accentuate her defiance and fortify her resolve. The poem concludes powerfully, with the speaker reiterating that it does not matter what others think, as she can no longer be any other way. Her need to be true to herself is stronger than her need to appease her community or live up to external expectations. The speaker's statement may be read as both her need to defend herself against judgment and her hope to inspire others.

In the closing line of the poem, the speaker asserts, "*Ikh kon shoyn mer...*" [I *can* no longer...]. Significantly, Bes did not use the phrase "*Ikh vil shoyn mer...*" [I no longer *want* to...]. This demonstrates the strength of the speaker's compulsion to live life differently. She feels she has no other option, regardless of the opinions of others and the impact that their judgment may have on her. Further, while "want" would signify a personal choice, the word "can" hints at social change as well as personal change. In making this statement, the poem concludes on a powerful note.

Stylistically, "Fun eynge vent" utilizes a very simple form of two quatrains of four lines each. The rhythm is regular; most lines are six meters. The closing line is five meters. Each line has a caesura, providing a natural pause halfway through the line. This creates a marching rhythm that reinforces the militant tone of the poem. It also gives the poem a song-like tone that enhances its popular appeal and makes it memorable. It is of note that only the second quatrain uses rhymes, and then only one rhyme (B, D). Thus, while the poem is rhythmically traditional, it does not use a traditional rhyme sequence.

The use of a traditional structure is diametrically opposed to the radical content and the rejection of tradition expressed by the speaker. Yet the folksong-like form gives the poem a down-to-earth tone that makes the political message accessible. "Fun eynge vent" is not high art; it is poetry for the masses. The simplicity of the poem gives the speaker natural appeal with the implicit message that if an ordinary woman can rebel, so too can the poem's readers.

The poem includes some notable word choices and interplays of sound. Bes uses alliteration throughout the poem, including in the repeated "d" and "v" sounds in the line "*Dervider mir di shpinvebs.*" The "v" sound is also used in "*vayte vegn.*" The combination of the releasing plosive "d" and the slightly restricted fricative "v" accentuates the tension between the sense of restriction and the desire for release. Sound and sense are also echoed in the line "*Geplatst in mir di tsniyes*," playing on the plosive "p" and the sibilant "ts" sound. This blending of plosives and sibilants enhances the sense of explosion. Thus the rupture is both heard and described. Similarly, the plosive "b" in *boben* and *broyzn* underpins the speaker's disdain for the past.

The speaker's voice is strong and defiant throughout. Her tone is self-assured. She is not portrayed as a victim; instead she is depicted as an agent of her own destiny. This is symbolic of the growing voice and power of Jewish women in the 1920s. The poet's rebellious voice and strong attitude remain constant throughout the poem. This is reflected in the constant rhythm of the poem and the repetition of the first line in the penultimate line. It is noted that the first published version of "Fun eynge vent" has a slight change in the penultimate line. In the earlier version, it reads, "*Zoln gute layt mikh shiltn oder hasn*" [I don't care if good folk curse me or hate me]. It is not known whether this is a typographical error, or whether the poet later changed the line. The use of the word "curse" signifies the strength and extent of disdain that the speaker encounters. The speaker's confidence, conviction, and ability to break away from the expectations of a controlling community are emblematic of the extraordinary strength of ordinary women in this period of powerful social change.

## *Conclusion*

Both of Bes's poems deliver strong, militant messages about women and change. Both describe the limitations of the female speaker's life and make a statement about who she is and who she believes she will become. "Fun eynge vent" is about breaking away from a tradition that has kept women bound, while "Tsu a kolege" heralds impending social change. Taken together, both poems speak of significant transformation—"Fun eynge vent" speaks of personal and situational change; "Tsu a kolege" relates to social change and its impact on the individual and on Yiddish literary culture. Both give the narrator agency in casting off the confines imposed on her and in being part of revolutionary change.

Bes's poems represent a powerful feminist voice in a time of turbulence and enhancement in the status of women in general and Jewish women in particular. The rebelliousness of Bes's poems captures a tone of her time. Bes boldly articulates some of the concerns and commitments of her generation. In both poems, Bes gives voice to anger and hope. These contrasting elements are essential in the struggle for equal rights. Moreover, in both poems, the speaker transforms her initial anger into impetus to seek change, with an optimism that is infectious. Her words are arrows in the fight for gendered justice.

Yet, as is the case with so many other Yiddish women poets of her time, Bes's writing is currently unknown. While we do not know the particulars of Bes's life, we feel, acknowledge, and share the power of her words—simple, heart-felt, ripe with rebellion, and with fervent belief in a brighter tomorrow. Perhaps that tomorrow never came for Bes and for many other women writers of her generation. But we should not leave her words buried in a forgotten past. Bes is one of many poets, whose work illuminates our knowledge and understanding of the Yiddish women writers who preceded us. In reclaiming the legacy of Yiddish women poets, it is incumbent on us to reclaim, as much as possible, the words of the forgotten women, little-known Yiddish women poets like Bes, who sought to inspire with courage, hope, and their belief in a world of equality.

## Notes

I am most grateful to Irena Klepfisz, Sue Kossew, Karen Auerbach, Melanie Landau, and Joan Nestle, who read and commented on various drafts of this essay. I am also very grateful to Sefra (Shifre) Burstin, Symcha Burstin, and Helen Burstin for their advice with the translations; to Amanda (Miryem-Khaye) Seigel for her assistance with accessing newspaper articles; and to Norma Fain Pratt, whose groundbreaking essay "Culture and Radical Politics," which included a brief extract of Bes's poem "Fun eynge vent," inspired me to seek out Lily Bes's writing. All translations are my own. Anyone with information on Lily Bes is requested to contact me.

1. Lexicons searched include Berl Kagan, ed., *Leksikon fun yidishe shraybers* (Nyu york: Rayah Ilman-Kagan, 1986), 99–100, and 618; Zalman Rejzn, ed., *Leksikon fun der yidisher literatur, prese un filologye, band 1* (Vilna: Kletskin farlag, 1928), 341; and Elias

Shulman, *Leksikon fun forverts shrayber: zint 1897* (New York: Forward Association, 1987), 11–12. Listing of 5,800 pseudonyms of Yiddish writers appears in Kagan, *Leksikon fun yidishe shraybers*, 561–812. Each page is divided into two columns, and each column is numbered as a separate page. Even so, it takes a lot space to list 5,800 pseudonyms!

2. Lily Bes, "Fun eynge vent" and "Tsu a kolege," *Di frayhayt*, January 20, 1929, 4.

3. While several of these previous poems also relate to pertinent themes of Jewish women's status, gender inequity and empowerment, and hence also warrant discussion, I have not been able to incorporate these into this essay, as I discovered these poems shortly before this book was going to press. I hope to prepare an article on these poems for publication in the future.

4. Tillie Olsen, *Silences* (New York: Delacourt Press, 1962), 39.

5. Norma Fain Pratt, "Culture and Radical Politics: Yiddish Women Writers in America, 1890–1940," in *Women of the Word: Jewish Women and Jewish Writing*, ed. Judith R. Baskin (Detroit: Wayne State University Press, 1994), 116.

6. Rokhl Holtman, "A gerekhte tayne," *Di frayhayt*, January 20, 1929, 4.

7. Lily Bes, "A land aza," *Di frayhayt*, December 23, 1928, 4.

8. Goldie Sigal, "The Flowering of Yiddish Literature," in *A Garment Worker's Legacy: The Joe Fishstein Collection of Yiddish Poetry, An Online Catalogue & Exhibit* [Montréal]: Digital Program, McGill University, 2001, accessed August 2, 2012, http://digital.library.mcgill.ca/fishstein/search.html.

9. Ezra Korman, *Yidishe dikhterins: antologye* (Shikago: L. M. Shtayn, 1928), xlvii; and Paula E. Hyman, "Introduction," in *My Life as a Radical Jewish Woman: Memoirs of a Zionist Feminist in Poland*, Puah Rakovsky, Paula E. Hyman, and Barbara S. Harshav (Bloomington: Indiana University Press, 2002), 3.

10. For further discussion of issues of gender in translation, see Uwe Kjær Nissen, "Gender in Translation," http://www.linguistik-online.de/11_02/nissen.html, translated by Jacek Krankowski, http://www.proz.com/forum/linguistics/7190-gender_in_translation.html, accessed November 16, 2011; and Hinde Ena Burstin, "Finding My *Vey*: Dilemmas of a Feminist Yiddishist Translator," *Bridges: A Jewish Feminist Journal* 14:2 (Autumn 2009): 44–55.

11. Chava Weissler, "Prayers in Yiddish and the Religious World of Ashkenazic Women," in *Jewish Women in Historical Perspective*, ed. Judith R. Baskin (Detroit: Wayne State University Press, 1991), 164.

12. See Gina Medem, *Di froy in der heym, in fabrik, in gezelshaftlekhn lebn* (Nyu york: Kooperativer folks-farlag fun Internatsyonaln arbeter ordn, 1937).

13. This letter accompanied Bes's submission of her two poems to *Di frayhayt*. The editor of the Sunday women's page reprinted the entire letter in Holtman, "A gerekhte tayne," 4.

14. See Ber Grin, "Yidishe dikhterins," *Yidishe kultur* (December 1973): 31.

15. Medem, *Di froy*, 9.

16. Olsen, *Silences*, 19–21.

17. See Adrienne Rich, *On Lies, Secrets and Silence: Selected Prose 1966–1978* (New York: Norton, 1979), 42–44; Joanna Russ, *How to Suppress Women's Writing* (London: The Women's Press, 1984), 6–12; and Lizbeth Goodman, ed., *Literature and Gender* (London: Routledge in Association with the Open University, 1996), viii.

18. Olsen, *Silences*, 167.

19. Chava Rosenfarb, "Feminism and Yiddish Literature: A Personal Approach," in *Gender and Text in Modern Hebrew and Yiddish Literature*, ed. Naomi B. Sokoloff, Anne

Lapidus Lerner, and Anita Norich (New York: Jewish Theological Seminary of America, 1992), 220–221.

20. Pratt, "Culture and Radical Politics," 125.

21. The prolific male poet A. Almi (Kh. Sheps) wrote the series of poems "Meydlshe gezangen" and upon the advice of I. L. Peretz submitted them for publication under a female pseudonym Esther Zaydler. One of these poems appears in Korman's anthology. Korman was seemingly unaware that the poem was written by a male. Notably, page 665 of Kagan's *Leksikon fun yidishe shraybers* lists Eliyohu Zaydler—but not Esther Zaydler—as a pseudonym for A. Almi. For further discussion of Almi and Peretz's collusion, see Rivke Kope, *Intim mitn bukh: mekhabrim, bikher, meynungen* (Paris: Drukeray Edison Poliglot, 1973), 60–62.

22. This is a list of the publications: Leah K. Hoffman, *In kinder-land*, 2d ed. (Nyu york: Kultur, 1921), 218 pages; Miriam Ulinover, *Der bobes oytser* (Varshe: Khayim Levin Epshteyn, 1921), 114 pages; Anna Bloch, *Poezye fun a litvisher meydl in afrike* (Johannesburg, 1921), 32 pages; Ida [Edith] Glasser-Andrews, *In halb-shotn* (Nyu york: Kultur, 1922), 68 pages; Yudika [Judith Tsik], *Naye yugnt* (Kovna: Likht, 1923), 40 pages; Sarah Reisen, *Lider* (Vilna: Farein fun yidishe shriftshteler un zhurnalistn, 1924), 96 pages; Rosa Yakubovitsh, *Mayne gezangen* (Varshe, 1924), 48 pages; Rosa Gutman, *Far gor dem noenstn: lider* (Berlin: Farlag Renesans, 1925), 16 pages; Rashel Veprinski, *Ruf fun fligl* (Nyu york, 1926), 60 pages; Pesi Hershfeld, *Koraln* (Shikago: Yidishn froyen kunstklub, 1926), 96 pages; Kadya Molodowsky, *Kheshvendike nekht* (Vilna: Kletskin farlag, 1927), 96 pages; Khane Vurtsel, *Hundert lider* (Nyu york, 1927), 128 pages; Rokhl H. Korn *Dorf* (Vilna: Kletskin farlag, 1928), 74 pages; and Esther Segal, *Lider* (Toronto: Zerubavel brentsh 219, I.N.A.P., 1928), 120 pages.

23. Korman, *Yidishe dikhterins*, vii.

24. Ibid., 359–370.

25. Kletsin publication data sourced from *Literarishe bleter* 1 (Friday, January 6, 1928): 21.

26. Rokhl Faygenberg, *A pinkes fun a toyter shtot: khurbn-dubova* (Varshe: Farlag gezelshaft, 1927), 148 pages.

27. Sh. L. Tsitron [S. L. Zitron], *Barimte yidishe froyen* (Varshe: Farlag gezelshaft, 1927). Farlag gezelshaft publication data sourced from *Literarishe bleter* 1 (Friday, January 6, 1928, 22).

28. Any attempt to compile such a listing would necessitate painstaking bibliographical research, for which accessible catalogues of Yiddish books would only be of limited use, according to Zachary M. Baker, Assistant University Librarian for Collection Development, Stanford University Libraries, email to author, July 28, 2012.

29. Also known as Klabund.

30. I. Rabinovitsh, comp., *Froyen literarishe zamlung* (Moskve: Tsentraln felker farlag fun F.S.S.R, 1928).

31. Ibid., 5.

32. Ibid., 5–6.

33. Morris Bassin, *500 yor yidishe poezye*, vol. 2 (Nyu york: Dos bukh, 1917). Volume 1 covers the period until 1910 and includes only one woman, the early eighteenth-century poet Geleh. A number of poems by unknown authors also appear in the volume. These may have been written by women.

34. Zishe Landau, ed., *Antologye: di yidishe dikhtung in amerike biz yor 1919* (Nyu york: Farlag yidish, 1919).

35. See Melech Ravitch, "Den mir hobn zuntshtn keyn andri (mekhaye) in der velt,"

## 48 Women Writers of Yiddish Literature

*Literarishe bleter* 5 (October 19, 1928): 830–831; Shmuel Niger, "Froyen-lirik," *Literarishe bleter* 5.46 (November 16, 1928): 909–910; and Z. Vaynper, "Undzere dikhterins," *Oyfkum* 3 (1928): 58–60.

36. Ravitch, "Den mir hobn zuntshtn keyn andri (mekhaye) in der velt," 830–831.
37. Niger, "Froyen-lirik," 909.
38. Holtman, "A gerekhte tayne," 4.
39. Kope, *Intim mitn bukh*, 39.
40. Holtman, "A gerekhte tayne," 4.
41. Irena Klepfisz, "Queens of Contradiction: A Feminist Introduction to Yiddish Women Writers," in *Found Treasures: Stories by Yiddish Women Writers*, ed. Frieda Forman, Ethel Raicus, Sarah Silberstein Swartz, and Margie Wolfe (Toronto: Second Story Press, 1994), 25.
42. Bes, "A land aza," *Di frayhayt*, December 23, 1928, 4.
43. Dovid Katz, "The Days of Proletpen in American Yiddish Poetry," in *Proletpen: America's Rebel Yiddish Poets*, ed. Amelia Glaser and David Weintraub (Madison: University of Wisconsin Press, 2005), 6.
44. Pratt, "Culture and Radical Politics," 129.
45. For further discussion, see Hinde Ena Burstin, "Finding My *Vey*: Dilemmas of a Feminist Yiddishist Translator," *Bridges: A Jewish Feminist Journal* 14:2 (Autumn 2009): 46.
46. Pratt, "Culture and Radical Politics," 132.
47. Holtman, "A gerekhte tayne," 4.
48. Klepfisz, "Queens of Contradiction," 25.
49. Pratt, "Culture and Radical Politics," 125.
50. Irena Klepfisz, "*Di mames, dos loshn*/The Mothers, the Language: Feminism, Yidishkayt, and the Politics of Memory," *Bridges* 4:1 (1994): 17; and Angus Calder with Lizbeth Goodman, "Gender and Poetry," in *Literature and Gender*, ed. Lizbeth Goodman (London: Routledge in Association with the Open University, 1996), 47.
51. Holtman, "A gerekhte tayne," 4.
52. See A. Glanz, "Kultur un di froy," *Fraye arbeter shtime* (October 30, 1915): 4–5; and Melech Ravitch, "Meydlekh, froyen, vayber—yidishe dikhterins," *Literarishe bleter* 4 (May 27, 1927): 395–396.
53. Russ, *How to Suppress*, 5.
54. Kadya Molodowsky, "Bagegenishn," *Literarishe bleter* (January 31, 1930): 95.
55. Pratt, "Culture and Radical Politics," 120.
56. Ravitch, "Meydlekh," 395–396. I have chosen to use the archaic term "poetess" in this translation in order to maintain the intent of the original Yiddish. While generally, I would use the term "women poets," this was inappropriate here, given that Ravitch described some female poets as girls, not women.
57. Kathryn Hellerstein, "A Question of Tradition: Women Poets in Yiddish," in *Handbook of American Jewish Literature: An Analytical Guide to Topics, Themes, and Sources*, ed. Lewis Fried, Gene Brown, Jules Chametzky, and Louis Harap (New York: Greenwood Press, 1988), 219.
58. A. Glanz, "Temperament," *Der tog* (December 7, 1919), 9. Glanz's criticism was so cutting that it is believed Fradl Shtok ceased writing in Yiddish after this review.
59. Shtok was the only female poet to be included in both Bassin's *500 yor yidishe poezye* and Landau's *Antologye: di yidishe dikhtung in amerike biz yor 1919*, published in the United States during this period. Further, just two years earlier, Shtok had been given

significantly more space in Bassin's anthology than any other female poet, with almost half the poems by women in the volume by Shtok.

60. Pratt, "Culture and Radical Politics," 122.
61. Faith Jones, "Criticizing Women," *Bridges* 13.1 (Spring 2008): 80.
62. Ibid.
63. "Tsu undzer lezer," *Froyen-shtim* 1 (May 1925): 4, cited in Joanna Lisek, "Feminist Discourse in Women's Yiddish Press in Poland," 104. Accessed October 7, 2009. URN: urn:nbn:de:kobv:517-opus-43494, URL: http://opus.kobv.de/ubp/volltexte/2010/4349/.
64. Glanz, "Kultur un di froy," 4–5.
65. See Shmuel Rozhanski, *Di froy in der yidisher poezye: antologye* (Buenos ayres: Yosef Lifshits-fond un der literaturgezelshaft baym yivo in argentine, 1966).
66. Holtman, "A gerekhte tayne," 4.
67. In order to maintain the original rhyme and rhythm in the literary translation, this line has been translated as "In every battle, you will win in the end."
68. See Niger, "Froyen lirik"; Glanz, "Kultur un di froy"; Ravitch, "Meydlekh"; and Ravitch, "Den mir hobn zuntshtn keyn andri (mekhaye) in der velt."
69. Kope, *Intim mitn bukh*, 55.
70. *Sotsyal poetn*, who first began publishing in the late eighteenth and early nineteenth century, wrote lyrical poetry that told of the hardships of life and the bitter struggle for justice.
71. Korman, *Yidishe dikhterins*, 47–50; and Pratt, "Culture and Radical Politics," 121.
72. For a discussion of exhortative poems, see Marc Miller, *Representing the Immigrant Experience: Morris Rosenfeld and the Emergence of Yiddish Literature in America* (Syracuse: Syracuse University Press, 2007), 64.
73. Ibid., 65.
74. Rosenfarb, "Feminism and Yiddish Literature," 217–218 and 226.
75. Jana Garai, *The Book of Symbols* (New York: Simon & Schuster, 1973), 98.
76. See Shmuel Rozhanski, "Di filzaytikayt fun der yidisher froyenvelt inem likht fun di yidishe poezye," in Shmuel Rozhanski, *Di froy*, 11–12; Korman, "Araynfir," in *Yidishe dikhterins*, xlvii; and Rivke Kope, "Naye tsaytn, naye tener," in Kope, *Intim mitn bukh*, 56. Also see Irving Howe, Ruth R. Wisse, and Khone Shmeruk, "Introduction," in *The Penguin Book of Modern Yiddish Verse*, ed. Irving Howe, Ruth R. Wisse, and Khone Shmeruk (New York: Viking, 1987), 11.
77. Howe, Wisse, and Shmeruk, *Modern Yiddish Verse*, 43.
78. For a discussion of issues in Yiddish-English translation of poetry, see Hinde Ena Burstin, "Culture, Meaning and Translation," in *Voices and Spaces: Indigenous and Multicultural Writers in Dialogue*, ed. Jennifer Martiniello (Canberra: Kenmarre Arts, 2006), 94–98.
79. *Bayit* is Hebrew for house.
80. Susan Niditch, "Portrayals of Women in the Hebrew Bible," in *Jewish Women in Historical Perspective*, ed. Judith R. Baskin (Detroit: Wayne State University Press, 1991), 29.
81. Rozhanski, "Di filzaytikayt," 11–12; and Norma Fain Pratt, "Transitions in Judaism: The Jewish American Woman Through the 1930s," *American Quarterly* 30: 5 (Winter 1978): 688–689.
82. Susan A. Glenn, *Daughters of the Shtetl: Life and Labor in the Immigrant Generation* (Ithaca: Cornell University Press, 1990), 46.
83. Howe, Wisse, and Shmeruk, *Modern Yiddish Verse*, 12.

84. Ruth Adler, *Women of the Shtetl—Through the Eyes of Y. L. Peretz* (Cranbury, NJ: Associated University Presses, 1980), 43.

85. "A Century of Immigration," Library of Congress, Home to Haven Exhibition, accessed July 9, 2012, http://www.loc.gov/exhibits/haventohome/haven-century.html.

86. "Jewish History Resources: New York Jewish History," New York State Archives, accessed July 9, 2012, http://www.archives.nysed.gov/a/research/res_topics_pgc_jewish_essay.shtml.

87. Paula E. Hyman, "Gender and the Immigrant Jewish Experience in the United States," in *Jewish Women in Historical Perspective*, ed. Judith R. Baskin (Detroit: Wayne State University Press, 1991), 224.

88. Iris Parush, "Women Readers as Agents of Social Change Among Eastern European Jews in the Late Nineteenth Century," *Gender and History* 9:1 (April 1997): 60–82; and Paula E. Hyman, "Discovering Puah Rakovsky," *Nashim: A Journal of Jewish Women's Studies and Gender Issues* 7 (2004): 101–102.

89. For examples of relevant poems, see Korman, *Yidishe dikhterins,* 59–61 and 75–100; and Kope, *Intim mitn bukh,* 56–57.

90. See Hinde Ena Burstin, "Female Fantasies from the Other Side of the Wall: Twentieth Century Lesbosensuous Yiddish Poetry," in *Jews and Sex,* ed. Nathan Abrams (Nottingham: Five Leaves, 2008), 38–51.

91. See "Froyen lider," in Kadya Molodowsky, *Kheshvendike nekht,* 11–19; and Miriam Ulinover, *Der bobes oyster.*

92. In synagogues at that time, and still in Orthodox synagogues today, a partition segregates the women from the men.

93. A *minyan* is the necessary quorum of ten men required for Orthodox communal worship.

94. Hyman, "Gender and the Immigrant," 233

95. Molodowsky, *Kheshvendike nekht,* 11–19. See especially page 11. Adrienne Rich's translation of Kadya Molodowsky's "Froyen lider I" is published in *A Treasury of Yiddish Poetry,* ed. Irving Howe and Eliezer Greenberg (New York: Holt, Rinehart and Winston, 1969), 284.

96. Klepfisz, "Queens of Contradiction," 33; and Pratt, "Culture and Radical Politics," 120.

# The Red Flower
*Rebellion and Guilt
in the Poetry of Celia Dropkin*

SHEVA ZUCKER

*In heysn vint* [In the Heat of the Wind], the only volume of poetry Celia Dropkin published during her lifetime, concludes with a poem called "Royte blum" [Red Flower] (p. 117, p. 58).[1] The very prominent placement of this poem at the end of the book suggests that Dropkin intended it as an explanation, a summation, and perhaps even a justification of both her preceding poetic oeuvre and of her life in general.

In a review of *In heysn vint* entitled "Di royte blum" [The Red Flower], which appeared in the newspaper *Der tog* shortly after the book's publication in 1935, Shmuel Niger, the foremost Yiddish literary critic of his day, says that the red flower is a metaphor for the poet herself.[2] I agree with Niger. Red, always the color of passion, suggests the poet's passionate untamable nature. Niger extends the flower metaphor to discuss Celia Dropkin's stance, not as an erotic poet but as a non-political poet in a highly charged left-wing literary scene. He writes:

> Why is the flower weeping? Because the field where the flower strolls, the field of poetry, is no longer in the flower field. Did not the poetry which is in style "plough up her maidenly garden?" Did it not bury deep in the earth [*glaykh gemakht mit der erd*][3] "the flowers everywhere?" Did she not sow both proletarian and anti-proletarian potatoes in her garden?

> Celia Dropkin is one of a very small number of poets who is happy and perhaps even proud that from amidst their potato-greens their red flower sprouts boldly-the red flower of purely personal lyric.... Poetry of the head is not for her. She is a heart poet.

Clearly, Niger is bothered, as were many other critics, by the highly personal and emotional nature of Dropkin's and women's poetry, in general.[4] He goes on to say, "It irks me that Celia Dropkin was personally compelling not only when writing her verse, it irks me that she included in her books things that were important only for her, and not the reader." Some of her poems remain, therefore, in Niger's eyes, "a purely personal memory, a private thing, stuff for an album, not lyric."

Although some readers may take exception to Niger's negative valuation of Dropkin's highly personal style, few can argue with his assertion that Dropkin's poetry is, for the most part, purely personal.[5] The poem "The Red Flower" is, I believe, even more personal than Niger realizes. Dropkin is not taking a stance as a non-political writer in a political literary milieu that produces only proletarian potatoes, for if she were, why would she have chosen to color herself red, of all colors? Rather, she is defining herself as a free spirit who, unable to repress her passionate and poetic nature, cannot conform to society's expectations for her as a respectable married woman. Indeed, illicit love and eroticism are the hallmarks of her love poetry.

The choice of the Yiddish word *"meydlshn"* [maidenly], which equates "girl" with "unmarried female" of whatever age,[6] suggests that the unrestrained freedom of maidenhood is now a thing of the past. The exigencies of married life demand that the narrator plough up her *meydlshn* flower garden, so that she may prepare the soil for more useful vegetables. Even so, here and there, a wild, red, purely decorative flower "weeping ... blossoms forth." In the first stanza, the use of the indefinite article "a" before "red flower" coupled with the participle "weeping" suggests that the poet, her girlhood barely behind her, does not yet have the courage to identify herself with the flower which, like her, struggles in painful isolation against all the forces that thwart its natural growth.

In the second stanza, despite the poet's increased efforts to conform by sowing good useful potatoes and weeding out the flowers everywhere, her "[my] beautiful red flower boldly blossoms forth." The poet's identification with the flower, indicated her by the possessive pronoun "my" and the adverb "boldly," expresses her now unambivalent triumph over repression and conformity. The placement of this poem, both at the very end of the book and also at the end of the section *"Hel bloye kareln-mayne kinder"* [light blue beads—(for) my children], a group of poems dealing mainly with children and motherhood, further accentuates this triumph. Indeed, in the innocence and beauty of her children and her uncomplicated relationship with them, she finds purity, comfort,[7] and renewed creativity.[8] Her garden becomes an image of both maternal and artistic fecundity, making the role of wife and mother that was to have constrained and shackled her, ultimately liberating.

Her poetry reflects these various tensions and passions that governed her life. Although she writes a good deal about and to her children, it is, not surprisingly, through her erotic poetry that she has left her mark on Yiddish literature. Celia Dropkin writes more explicitly and openly about love, sex, death, and the passions that build and destroy relationships than probably any other Yiddish poet—male or female. Her poetry invites us to explore dynamics of male-female relationships. I shall do so in this chapter.

Thus far, the most in-depth treatment of Dropkin's work is Janet Hadda's article "The Eyes Have It: Celia Dropkin's Love Poetry."[9] Using biographical material and the tools of psychological analysis on a dozen of Dropkin's love poems, it is Hadda's intent to explain how Dropkin's poetry reflects "the entangled mesh of feeling that forms its matrix: conflict, powerful, erotic longing, and forlorn loneliness."[10] While I find biographical information and psychological analysis highly illuminating in interpreting Dropkin's work, for me this is only one part of a more traditional close reading of texts. In my study, I include, therefore, not only love poetry, but also poems dealing with death and the family that shed light on Dropkin's sexual rebellion and guilt.

Because, as Hadda shows, the details of Dropkin's life do illuminate much of her poetry, I shall begin with these.[11] Born Celia Levine in Bobruisk, White Russia in 1888, she lost her father at an early age. According to Hadda, Dropkin engaged in a lifelong search for the nurture that was lost to her when her father died. In addition, the poet's mother, "whom she idealized ... was a rigid and unforgiving individual ... too absorbed in her own world to be truly available to her daughter,"[12] and certainly unequal to the task of compensating for the nurturing Celia never received from her deceased father. Dropkin's sexual encounters are, according to Hadda, an attempt to fill the resulting emotional void. Men became for her the source of mirroring and idealization, hence the affirmation, she never received from her parents. Love for Dropkin, says Hadda, "meant a combination of adult closeness and acceptance, combined with a freeing sexual contact. However, because of her early experiences, she also needed to be comforted and protected as if she were still a child."[13] This explains why being with her children often serves as an emotional haven and a balm to what she calls her "sick soul."

Dropkin began writing poetry in Russian while still a very young woman and was greatly encouraged by the Hebrew writer Uri Nisim Gnessin whom she appears to have idolized.[14] According to Hadda, her profound attraction to Gnessin may be explained by the fact that he was an idealizable man who also mirrored her longing to be seen and appreciated as an artist.[15]

When Dropkin was about twenty-one, she married Shmaye Dropkin, an active Bundist, and in 1912, she followed him to America, where he had fled for political reasons. Between 1910 and 1926, she bore six children, five of whom survived, and around 1917, she began writing poetry in Yiddish. The critic Norma Fain Pratt says that she lived "a conventional life"[16]—one that would seem to preclude the writing of poetry and the extra-marital sexual experiences she describes in her work. Yet both were central to her life. The red flower of creativity and passion would not be "weeded out."

Her children appear to have been an impediment to her time but not to her creative spirit. In fact, she wrote most of her poems during the 1920s and early 1930s, when her children were still at home.[17] She did not have appointed hours or even an hour set aside for writing, but rather, as her daughter Esther Unger recalls, "she worked on pieces of noodle paper, on scratch paper, on total chaos, on figuring out time."[18] This may explain why someone of her considerable talent managed to publish only one volume of poetry. She also wrote a number of short stories, which were included in the volume *In heysn vint* published posthumously by her children.[19] Later in life she took up painting. Photographs of some of these works also appear in that volume.

Dropkin is sometimes linked to the introspectivist group of Yiddish poets known as the *Inzikhistn*, but any real connection appears highly tenuous. This affiliation doubtless suggests itself because she wrote at the same time as they did. Indeed, she even published several poems in their journal and posed with them in a now famous literary photo. However, publication in a journal is, in and of itself, not sufficient proof of belonging to a group.[20]

Aaron Glanz-Leyeles, a founder, theoretician, and a leading *Inzikh* poet, also challenges this affiliation. In a note accompanying the publication of one of Dropkin's poems in "Dos lid fun khoydesh" [The Poem of the Month] in the *Inzikh* journal, he writes:

> Celia Dropkin once had a very close relationship to *inzikh*.... It bothers me that I don't see any clear signs of growth in her *Collected Poems*. The connection that she had to *inzikh* was, unfortunately, more superficial than internal.[21]

Leyeles's offensive tone notwithstanding, his conclusion is, I believe, correct. Other sources, such as B. and B. Harshav's *American Yiddish Poetry*, Reyzin's and Niger's entries under "Dropkin" in their respective lexicons of Yiddish literature,[22] and the 1971 edition of the *Encyclopedia Judaica*, corroborate this opinion. None of these works refers to Dropkin as an *inzikh* poet.

The more important proof is the textual evidence itself. In their literary manifesto, the *inzikh* poets advocated that a poem "express the organic relationship between outside phenomena and the self ... in an introspective and individual manner."[23] This "introspective manner" meant that the poet must "listen to his inner voice [and] observe his internal panorama-kaleidoscopic, contradictory, unclear or confused as it may be."[24] This constituted a rebellion against the well-rounded beautifully wrought "Impressionist poetry of mood and atmosphere ... written in a smooth poetic 'diction'"[25] characteristic of their literary forerunners *Di yunge* [Young Ones].

To express this frequently chaotic inner panorama, the *inzikhistn* applied the principles of stream of consciousness, representation through a splinter element rather than a full description, and simultaneity of experience.[26] Because they believed that each poem must have its own individual rhythm, they tended toward free verse (although not to the exclusion of regularly metered verse or rhyme), and they experimented with verse forms little used in Yiddish such as rondeaux, villanelles, and sonnet cycles.

Even though Dropkin's primary focus is on the self and her poetry is replete with conflicting emotions, she seldom presents the self as a kaleidoscopic personalized reflection of an internalized social world,[27] as the *inzikhistn* purport to do. Rather than a splintered representation of reality, expressed through stream of consciousness, she conveys the tension of two clearly articulated conflicting forces such as love and hate, the desire both to guilt. Nor is she concerned, as the *inzikhistn* are, with the historical and political world. Dropkin's poetic world encompasses only the self and nature and not the reflection of outer phenomena within her. Her nature poems such as "Zunfargang" [Sunset] (p. 13, p. 53), "Volkns" [Clouds] (p. 14, p. 36), and "Friling" [Springtime] (p. 15, p. 37) are finely wrought scene and mood poems in the manner of *di yunge* in which the poet, not personally intertwined with the subject, remains an admiring observer. Although she does at times employ free verse, and even more infrequently, blank verse, most of her poems are written in standard meters and traditional rhymes with great success. Her originality lies in her subject matter rather than in the linguistic or technical innovation stressed so often by the *inzikhistn*.

In defying most of the reader's traditional expectations about the treatment of themes such as love, sex, and death, Dropkin employs the technique of inversion. The feminist critic Annette Kolodny defines inversion of traditional images and associations so that they come to connote their opposites as one of the distinguishing features of much women's writing. She explains:

On the one hand, the stereotyped traditional literary images of women as, for example, the loving "Mom," the "bitch," the "Sex Goddess"—are being turned around in women's fiction.... On the other hand, there is a tendency to "invert" even more generalized traditional images and conventionalized iconographic associations so that they come to connote their opposites.... We seem to discover almost a conspiracy to overthrow all the nice comfortable patterns and associations of a previous (and, for the most part, male dominated) literary tradition.... Love is revealed as violence and romance as fraud; suicide and death are imaged as comforting and attractive while loneliness and isolation become, for their heroines, means to self-knowledge and contentment.[28]

As early as 1956, the Yiddish literary critic Sh. D. Zinger commented on this tendency towards inversion in Dropkin's poetry in pre-feminist *folkstimlekh* [folksy] style in an article in the magazine *Di tsukunft*:

> In the beginning, Celia Dropkin's poetry stunned those readers who expected pious *tkhinedike* (in the style of women's prayers) poems from female poets.... One had seldom before heard such honest open words from a Yiddish poetess as we find in Dropkin's volume of poetry, *In heysn vint*.[29]

Dropkin's poems are indeed, as Zinger says, very far from "*frumtkhinedike lider*" [pious poems in the style of women's prayers]. From the very first poem in both collections, "A zumer sonate" [A Summer Sonata] (p. 5, p. 3) in which she compares a lover's kiss to the sucking of snakes, Dropkin inverts most of the Yiddish reader's preconceived notions on almost every subject she explores. Supposedly loving hands are transformed into snakes ("Mayne hent" [My Hands]) (p. 50, p. 13); suicide seems sweet ("Baym fenster" [At the Window]) (p. 75, p. 8); and death appears like a beloved cavalier ("Dem meydl's toyt" [The Girl's Death]) (p. 84, p. 56). Sex does not bring closer spiritual union but rather, as she writes ("Es vilt zikh mir zen" [I'd Like to See You Sleeping]) (p. 55, p. 15), the desire to see her partner powerless and dead.

Yet, at the same time that Dropkin indulges in the most impious and hedonistic of sexual exploits, a part of her longs for a more traditional role, free from conflict, sin, and guilt.

The very structure of the first edition of Dropkin's poetry, arranged by the poet herself, we may presume, reflects this ambivalence. Divided into four parts, *In heysn vint* begins with a group of poems under the same heading that deals mainly with the erotic as well as the healing power of nature. Most of these poems have no first person poetic persona and when they do, as in "A zumer sonate" [A Summer Sonata] (p. 5, p. 3) or in "Nemt mikh tsu" [Take Me] (p. 22),[30] she is in relationship with no one except nature. The erotic thread is carried over into the second section "Tsirkus dame" [Circus Lady] and is there merged with the personal. These poems focus on the internal conflicts of the female persona trying to reach and sustain wild new heights of erotic experience while struggling against the forces of shame, guilt, and sin.

In the next section, "Baym fenster" [At the Window], these motifs are interwoven with the motif of death. While death is at times a healer and a haven from the soul's suffering, it is also a comfortless seducer and a termination that offers no resolution.

Only in the final section, "Hel bloye kareln—mayne kinder" [Pale Blue Beads—(for) My Children], does the poet find the peace and inner tranquility she craves. While being with her children cannot erase her guilt, it does, as she writes in the poem "Vi gut is mir" [How Good I Feel] (p. 106),[31] make her feel "far from longing and sin." Her children act as a balm to whatever dark and uncontrollable passions push her to these errant acts.

In addition to the shockingly open eroticism of Dropkin's poems, one is also struck by their almost total lack of Jewishness. In this, Dropkin is very much in the *inzikh* tradition. In rebellion against the social and national focus of the earlier generation of American Yiddish sweatshop poets and the more beautiful and "poetic" topics of *di yunge*, the *inzikhistn* stressed open thematic, insisting that a Yiddish poet need not write on specifically Jewish themes.[32] This credo, however, in no way, precluded the writing of poems on Jewish themes that poets like Glatshteyn and Leyeles certainly did even in their more militant, earliest years. Dropkin's poetry, however, if read in translation, divorced from the implicitly Jewish medium of the Yiddish language, would give the reader almost no clues regarding the Jewishness of its creator.[33] On the contrary, poems in which she takes on the personal of circus lady ("Di lid fun a getsn-dinern" [The Song of an Idol Worshiper]) (p. 28, p. 9) are flagrantly unJewish. The usual themes of Jewish poetry, in general, and, more specifically, Jewish women's poetry—pious ancestors, Sabbath candles, love of Israel and the Jewish people, God, and, after 1939, the Holocaust—are absent from Dropkin's poetry.[34] Was this a conscious rebellion against Jewish tradition or simply a reflection of the limited role religion and Jewishness in general played in her life? Her son, John Dropkin, suggests the latter. Neither Dropkin's upbringing nor her schooling had been religious. The extent of her Jewishness was, according to John, "just Yiddish."[35]

In contrast to writers like Anna Margolin or Kadya Molodowsky, hardly *frum-tkhinedik* themselves, she does not explicitly deal with her struggle with or rebellion against tradition.[36] Dropkin's poems do, however, tell of the tremendous emotional conflict wrought by exploiting her newly acquired freedoms to and beyond their limits and of the pain of being a slave to her passions. In so doing, she must surely have been aware of how radically she was inverting the reader's expectations of Yiddish women's writing.

"Mayn mame" [My Mother] (p. 48, p. 11) is probably Dropkin's most

"Jewish" poem. In it, Dropkin speaks of inheriting her passion from her widowed mother who had kept it submerged and hidden over years of self-imposed celibacy. Although Jewishness is never explicitly mentioned, the fact that the poem was written in Yiddish during the early decades of the twentieth century immediately conjures up specifically Jewish associations. Although by no means exclusive to Judaism, concern and compassion for the widow are significant Jewish principles. Dropkin's mother was, in fact, widowed young. According to John Dropkin, she was a very attractive woman; her relatives, the Golodietz family who took her and her two small children in after her husband's death, could well have afforded, and, indeed, benefitted from providing her with a dowry. Not remarrying seems, therefore, to have been a very conscious decision on her part. The poet describes her mother's decision not to marry again as *tsniesdik* [virtuous, modes, chaste]. Although the Jewish community generally encouraged widows to remarry, it also taught them that remaining alone was a higher ideal.[37] Because Dropkin's mother was not religious, her decision had more to do with her own psychological make-up, influenced perhaps subconsciously by attitudes and feelings inherited from the religious tradition than with belief itself.

The image of the wax candle in the poem begrudgingly lighting her days is an implicit allusion to the lighting of the Sabbath candles. The unspoken contrast between the begrudging wax candle and the hoped for spiritual satisfaction derived from blessing the Sabbath candles, one of a Jewish woman's most important *mitsves* [commandments], suggests that this tradition is not a source of joyous spirituality for the mother but rather of unnatural physical privation. As stated in the poem, the mother's decision, "never to be anyone's wife again," is not, however, motivated only by chastity. Her refusal to define herself ever again in terms of another person is both a declaration of independence and an act of rebellion against the prevailing mores. The repetition of the line emphasizes this stance.

Nevertheless, her independence is bought at a price. She must live with the loneliness and longing that she later bequeaths to her daughter. Language such as "absorbed deep within me," "hidden hot yearning," "underground stream," and "[deeply, (in Yiddish)] hidden desire" conveys the submerged unconscious nature of female sexual yearning. The very masculine and celebratory image of the mother's long hidden passion spurting openly from her daughter suggests the poet's rejection of her maternal legacy of chastity and sexual repression. In using the word "holy" to sanctify her mother's desire rather than her chaste resolve, Dropkin again inverts traditional expectations. She also, as Hadda points out,[38] links creativity to sexuality.

As if to explain what became of her liberated desire, Dropkin follows "My Mother" with "Di tsirkus dame" [The Circus Lady] (p. 49, p. 12), probably her best and best-known poem.[39] The circus dancer[40] is a metaphor for the woman as a daring sexual being, and the whole poem, an extended metaphor for the free woman in the sexual arena. The term "circus lady" conjures up the image of a dazzling exotic being of great physical prowess who, although in the limelight, exists somewhat on the periphery of respectable society. Her masterful balancing act puts her both supremely in control as well as detached and isolated from society seated in the arena and from the obviously phallic daggers beneath her. The seemingly contradictory descriptions of the daggers that appear to her to be shining in "a fiery circle" but are in actuality "cold" and "steel" suggest the warmth and ecstasy of physical union, of her "hot blood" heating up the cold dagger tips, can come only with the submission signified by falling. Then, and not before, can she move from being an object of desire to one who fulfills her own desires. But for the circus lady, falling, and hence sexual submission, also means death. She balances, therefore, between control and submission, for the moment, choosing the isolation of control.

While death is both alluring and frightening to the circus lady, it is purely a source of comfort and peace to the poet in "Baym fenster" [At the Window] (p. 75, p. 8.) Both the circus lady and the poet of "At the Window" are poised above the world, one in the arena and the other on the fifth floor. While the circus lady is the object of the crowd's envious but disapproving gaze, the poet in "At the Window" is unseen by the world below. Isolation brings the circus lady control, but for the woman in "At the Window," it yields only melancholy and the desire for death.

Death here, fused with the sidewalk, is personified lovingly with "mild grey eyes" and "kindly arms." Suicide, which offers the narrator the warmth and security of her childhood bed, appears to be an easy answer to her adult problems.[41] Here, as she contemplates flying to her end like a bird, she inverts the reader's notion of death as the demise of all hope and choice, envisioning it instead as the great liberator.

A similar inversion underlines the poem "Dem meydl's toyt" [The Girl's Death] (p. 84, p. 56),[42] in which Dropkin contrasts the constraints of living with the freedom of dying. The description of the dying girl lying "unashamed" with legs bared and shift lifted and smiling *tayvedik* [passionately, voluptuously] suggests that death transforms her, liberating her from the constraints that shame and modesty had imposed on her in life. While in other poems relationships with men are either deadly or dangerous, in the poem death itself is personified as male. It becomes the erotic partner, releasing in her a hitherto unexpressed passion and unabashed abandon.

And yet, while death at first appears to liberate the girl, it ultimately seduces and deceives. The word *maniet* [lures] and the lone caress, indicted by the use of the singulative verb construction "*tut a glet*" [does a caress], suggests that the girl does not choose death, but that death, playful and lascivious, like a rakish lover, seduces her. Death's pose as a "*liber kavalier*," which might be translated variously as a "dear or kind," "gentleman, partner, beau, suitor, or escort"[43] is only a disguise [*farkleydt*]. Although no longer modestly concealed, the girl's legs remain weary as the repetition of the phrase "*mate fis*" [weary legs] emphasizes. Death may literally uncover and reveal the body, but ultimately it can neither transform it nor enable the girl to transcend her weary corporeality. Even in Dropkin's love poems,[44] death often appears either in the literal or metaphoric sense. The poetic persona feels that to be in control, the submission or even death of her male partner is necessary.[45] Similarly, her need for love and cherishing is so overwhelming that she will seek these even if a part of her must die. In the poem "Zing ikh tsu dir" [So I Sing to You] (p. 54, p. 15), untitled in the first volume of *In heysn vint*, sexual union is depicted as annihilation through occupation rather than death through submission.[46] Images of the male sowing and growing bigger, culminating in the woman's gradual "dying," again bring out the tension between physical union and self-annihilation. The comparison between the sowing of a child and the sowing of "yourself" implies that the lover, like a child in embryo, becomes a parasite feeding off the woman and giving nothing in return. The normal planting of a child inside the female body leads to birth and to life. The lover's sowing leads instead to his growth and her spiritual diminution: "There's no room left inside me / for myself." Humiliated and degraded, the poetic persona's soul "lies like a dog at your [his] feet." Paradoxically, her ability to serenade him, even as she "*shtarbndik durkh*" [dies through / "dying into," in this translation] him, in both a sexual and spiritual sense, implies that she is willing and able to submit to him and even thrive creatively in this union. Perhaps she even celebrates the fact that in losing herself through him the boundaries between them are obliterated, albeit in a less than equal union.

The poem "Shpatsirndik iber vayse volkns" [Strolling Over White Clouds] (p. 53, p. 14) again expresses an unequal relationship between the poet and her lover. The poet's feeling of powerlessness under the actual physical weight of her lover's body bespeaks an emotional powerlessness as well.[47] On the most obvious level Dropkin is describing the post-orgasmic lull in which the lovers' souls leave their bodies to unite on a spiritual plane. Her sense of being physically entrapped reflects her feeling of emotional entrapment. While in reality, she is immobilized by the very "last," which means both "weight" and "burden" of his body on top of hers, in her fantasy they stroll together on an equal plane, over white fluffy clouds. His oppressively muscular body becomes a source of gentleness and love as it turns lighter and his face becomes transparent. This fantasy of lightness that culminates in them both dissolving like clouds suggests her desire for a more spiritual relationship and for escape.

As the lovers become more transparent and evanescent, their lips still remain. The poet describes her partner's lips three times: first blossoming gently, then blossoming somewhere far away as if through veils, and finally, swimming to her as if through a white cloud. On the literal level, the sustained presence of the ever-blossoming lips suggest that the lovers continue to kiss intermittently as their bodies disengage and the women's mind flies off into fancy. Because kissing is, in a way, the most gentle and intimate part of sex and is linked also to love in the greater sense, the constant presence of the lips accentuates her desire for more loving, gentler contact with him. It also suggests the possibility of verbal communication. In the poet's twice repeated description of his lips as "childlike-puffy," she strips him of all ability to dominate by bestowing on him the weakness, vulnerability, and awkwardness of a child. Only by this transformation can she have both union and freedom.

In contrast to the incorporeity the poet imagines in "Walking Over White Clouds," in the poem "Zoyg oys" [Suck Out] (p. 37, p. 24),[48] Dropkin explores the physical and emotional dynamics of what appears to be a sado-masochistic relationship. In both, however, she feels physically and emotionally overpowered by a dominant, more physically forceful male lover. In this poem, the lovers go beyond the bounds of an "acceptable" physical relationship. In so doing, they come to believe they embody a god who, in contrast to the stern, censorious Judeo-Christian God, "knows not that things are forbidden." Now godly vessels, they allow themselves to be ruled only by their passions and establish themselves as the measure of all things. The highly colloquial description of his god as one "*yos makht fun alts a tel*" [who makes a mess of everything] suggests that the arrogance of setting themselves up as divine must inevitably lead to human disaster.

The Christian and pagan imagery of hammering, burning, crucifixion, and sacrifice in the second stanza linking physical love to pain and also to proscribed forms of worship further accentuates the forbidden nature of the couple's unholy pleasures. Through crucifixion, the woman can, like Jesus, simultaneously suffer and be worshiped, becoming both the ultimate object of adoration and the ultimate victim.

If in stanza two, the poet is Christ, both tortured and idolized, and suffering for both their sins, in stanza three, she is merely the sinner. In inverting all standards of propriety and seeking the pain and humiliation of crucifixion, she must also endure the shame and guilt of her transgression. The illicit pleasures she and her partner enjoy can only lead to feelings of degradation and worthlessness. In entreating him to leave her "deeply ashamed, suck up and throw away," she, like the contrite sinner, requests the punishment she feels she deserves. Although he is her partner in sin, he is not her partner in both the pain and the punishment but shares none of the guilt. Knowing that a sexual act based on suffering, sin, and degradation can never lead to union but to the "mess" of a destroyed relationship, the poet exhorts her lover to "Be a stranger, and go on your way."

In other far less explicit poems to and about the significant men in her life, Dropkin develops the theme of guilt over her errant sexual behavior. In these, the man functions not as an accomplice but as a kind of conscience. In "Fun a lid" [From a Poem] (p. 85, p. 70), she imagines her father coming down to earth to comfort her. Because Dropkin's father died when she was very young, her image of him was most likely highly idealized, and she must have craved his approval, comfort, and guidance. Although in the poem, the poetic persona who is clearly here, as elsewhere, and extension of herself, imagines that her father had come down to earth to comfort her, the shift in tense from past in the first four lines to present thereafter suggests the discrepancy between the supposed purpose of his imaginary visit and the actual outcome. We cannot comfort her. Nor does he react to her "*mayism*" [deeds] with tenderness, pride, or even anger, but rather, like herself, with helpless despair. Dropkin here is indicting herself for not being the kind of daughter that would make her father proud. While she in no way blames him for his reaction, she makes him join in her suffering over the shame and guilt of her wayward life.

Similarly, in the poem "Tayerer" [Dear One] (p. 66, p. 62), dedicated to "Shin," who is almost certainly her husband Shmaye, she senses the disapproval of a central male figure. Hadda correctly observes that "the poem's fourteen lines are technically a sonnet, but the distribution of lines is not standard. The form thus provides a backdrop for a discussion of life that will not proceed along predictable lines" (p. 109). In this work, the poet asks her husband to understand that it is not her intent to deceive or to hurt him.[49] The vagueness of the lines, "To flee... Whither and to whom? I know and I don't" suggest that her lovers are interchangeable and indistinguishable while his acceptance and love are critical.

Although his goodness and honesty stand in contrast to her errant behavior, he like she, suffers for her sinfulness. Her apparent disregard for marital fidelity may seem to put her in a position of power, but her supposed freedom makes her instead a slave to her passion, and as she sees it, a helpless victim of inability to control her actions. In her mind, his virtue and his right to punish her make him more powerful. She, like guilty straying child, must plead for his love and forgiveness. The hauntingly simple line "*Vi ikh layd, vi ikh layd*" [How I suffer, how I suffer] conveys the anguish of a guilty soul driven by forces beyond her control to commit sinful acts.

Perhaps it would be naïve to suppose that any Jewish woman writer, born at a time when most of the women around her were still "*frum-tkhinedik*" [pious in the style of women's prayers], could celebrate the pleasures of the body with such seemingly reckless abandon and suffer no devastating emotional consequences. If this poem is any indication, this writer could not. Although Dropkin and so many other women poets of her day lived free and even bohemian lives, eons away both in deed and spirit from the lives of their pious mothers or, at least, grandmothers, we must not forget that these changes came about in no more than a generation or two. Perhaps the break was not as complete as it appears at first. Although it is true that Celia Dropkin inverted our traditional expectations of the Jewish woman writer, making her name synonymous with sexual rebellion and female eroticism in Yiddish poetry, there is another side to her writing, a side that simultaneously reveals intense inner struggle and conflict.

To surrender to one's passions as Dropkin did, means, ultimately, to be ruled by them and not to rule over them. The attitude she frequently displays, an attitude certainly not incompatible with her religious tradition, shows a soul wracked by guilt, shame, and fear of being punished for her sins. She frequently describes herself as weakened by that very passion which, at first, seems to have liberated her from the constraints of convention. In "Vi zaftik royte epl" [Like Juicy Red Apples] (p. 69),[50] for example, she expresses the fear that "the worm of passion ... will devour me to death."

Death, simultaneously frightening and fascinating, is a frequently recurring theme in Dropkin's poetry. In allowing her passion to rule her, she paradoxically links herself more to death than in life. The haunting lines in "Ikh bin dayn feyike shilerin" [I Am Your Faithful Pupil] (p. 36)[51] "*Vos tifer ikh kuk in di soydes fun libe, / vert der toyt mir alts liber, alts liber*" [The deeper I look in the secrets of love, / death becomes dearer and dearer] speak powerfully to this point, as do, of course, several of the poems discussed earlier in this chapter.

For Dropkin, as for her most celebrated poetic persona, the circus dancer, life is a balancing act in which she walks a thin line between being a daring adventuress above the arena and wanting to fall, a kind of death in which she would relinquish some of that mystique and power for a more traditional submissive role within life's arena.

Significantly, in ending the book with "The Red Flower," Dropkin points to a reconciliation of the constant inner and external conflict between erotic adventurer and the more conventional wife and mother. Despite the poet's attempts to grow only useful potatoes, i.e., to conform to convention, the flower of passion and creativity will not be weeded out. Only here at the very end does the poet relinquish her feelings of guilt and shame and accept herself as the wild, unrestrained red flower. Ultimately, by subverting our traditional expectations as she struggles within and against them herself, Dropkin allows passion and freedom to triumph. Partly against society's, and indeed, her own, wishes but partly in keeping with her own deepest desires, her red flower boldly blossoms forth.

## Notes

This essay was originally published as Sheva Zucker, "The Red Flower—Rebellion and Guilt in the Poetry of Celia Dropkin," *Studies in American Jewish Literature* 15 (1996): 99–117. Purdue University Press kindly gave permission to reprint the essay. Fair use and other considerations made some editing necessary.

1. I shall give the page number of each poem, first, as it appears in Celia Dropkin, *In heysn vint: Lider fun Tsilie Drapkin* [In the Hot Wind: Poems of Celia Dropkin] (Nyu york, 1935), and then, as it appears in the edition published by her children, entitled Celia Dropkin, *In heysn vint* (Nyu york, 1959). All translations, unless otherwise indicated, are my own.

2. Shmuel Niger, "Di royte blum" [The Red Flower], review of *In heysn vint* by Celia Dropkin, *Der tog* (New York) 1 March 1936.

3. I offer the Yiddish in brackets when I feel that the English cannot fully capture the meaning and feeling of the Yiddish. In the translation of the poetry, I have aimed more for accuracy than poetic quality, though I hope that the latter is not totally absent.

4. The poet and critic Yankev Glatshteyn responded similarly. In the magazine *Yidishe kemfer* (December 14, 1956), he wrote that, in 1928, he had judged Dropkin's poems to be too personal. At that time, he had said that "she enjoyed pouring out her feelings more than the pleasure of writing." By the time he wrote this later article, he had revised his thinking so that he saw the extreme emotionality of her work as one of its chief virtues. "Her poems," he writes, "have in them a power that does not allow them to be limited or restrained."

5. The critic Janet Hadda comments on the close, and frequently identical, relationship between the poet and the "I" of her lyric in her article "The Eyes Have It: Celia Dropkin's Love Poetry," in *Gender and Text in Modern Hebrew and Yiddish Literature,*

ed. Naomi B. Sokoloff, Anne Lapidus Lerner, and Anita Norich (New York: Jewish Theological Seminary of America, 1992), 96. Indeed, Hadda suggests that this connection is more pronounced in Dropkin's poetry than in the work of many other poets. She writes, "To suggest that the 'I' in her writing is somehow unrelated to the woman and her feelings denies the essential lyric quality of Dropkin's work in the service of a literary myth." Similarly, Kathryn Hellerstein, in an article in the same volume entitled "From 'Ikh' to 'Zikh': A Journey from 'I' to 'Self' in Yiddish Poems by Women," writes, "Dropkin writes love poems in which it is natural to assume that the poetic 'I' corresponds transparently to the woman writing the poem." (She then goes on to analyze the poem "Odem" [Adam] in which this transparency is deceptive.) Given the highly personal nature of Dropkin's lyric, it is not surprising that none of her poetry deals with political themes. Her only somewhat "political" poem is "Tsu a tokhter" [To a Daughter], dated 1940 and published therefore only in the second edition of *In heysn vint*, page 83. Here she writes of giving her daughter Esther a wool scarf so that she will not get cold at the numerous political demonstrations she attends. Esther, according to her brother John, was an active communist in those days. The wool scarf is also, of course, a metaphor for the mother's loving and protective response to her daughter's vulnerability; the political here is clearly secondary to the personal. Had Dropkin's oldest son John not made me aware of it in an interview with him and his wife Ruth in Brooklyn, New York, in July 1990, the political element would not have been obvious from the poem itself.

6. It is not surprising that the word "girl" would also imply "unmarried female" for in a culture that saw marriage as the only legitimate option for adults, unmarried women were almost always girls or very young women.

7. Dropkin expresses the idea that her children provide a sort of emotional haven for her and an escape from her "sin" in the following poems: "Vi gut iz mir" [How Good I Feel] (p. 106) and entitled "Mit penimlekh ful freyd" [With Faces Full of Joy], (p. 91 in the 1959 edition); "Ikh vel antloyfn" [I Will Run Away] (p. 102, p. 93); and "Ikh tulie tsu" [I Cuddle] (p. 97) and entitled "S'faln shtile trern" [Quiet Tears Are Falling] (p. 85) in the 1959 edition. In the previously mentioned article, Janet Hadda also discusses this aspect of Dropkin's work, pp. 108–109. She says, "The children anchor her, remind her that she has a life apart from her world of love and longing outside the home. Moreover, their purity allows her to tap into something within herself, a feeling from her past, when she was not yet prey to the complications and miseries of her current existence, and when she was free from the self-censure that she expected, as well, from her social milieu."

8. The poem "In mai" [In May] (p. 104, p. 91) conveys the mother's sense of renewed wonder and vigor as she participates in her child's fantasy life.

9. Janet Hadda, "The Eyes Have It: Celia Dropkin's Love Poetry," in *Gender and Text in Modern Hebrew and Yiddish Literature*, ed. Naomi B. Sokoloff, Anne Lapidus Lerner, and Anita Norich (New York: Jewish Theological Seminary of America, 1992). The critic Dan Miron also concentrated heavily on Dropkin in his article "Why There Was No Women's Poetry in Hebrew," in the same journal. However, he is concerned only with the poem "*A kush*" [A Kiss], which the Hebrew poet Uri Nisim Gnessin "translated" from the original Russian into Hebrew.

10. Ibid., 93.

11. For biographical information on Dropkin, see Zalmen Reyzin, ed., *Leksikon fun der yidisher literatur, prese un filologie* [Lexicon of Yiddish Literature, Press and Philology], (Vilnius: B. Kletzkin), 1928 ed., s.v. "Drapkin Tsilie" and *Leksikon fun der nayer yidisher literatur* [Lexicon of New Yiddish Literature], 1959 ed., s.v. "Drapkin Tsilie."

12. Hadda, "Eyes," 97.

13. Ibid.

14. For a lengthy discussion of Dropkin and Gnessin and an analysis of how Gnessin "translated" Dropkin's poem "*A kush*" from the original Russian version, (of which the Yiddish, dedicated to him, is a translation) into Hebrew and what this suggests about the differences between male and female writers in Hebrew literature, see Dan Miron's article "Why Was There No Women's Poetry in Hebrew," *Gender and Text in Modern Hebrew and Yiddish Literature*. Janet Hadda also discusses Dropkin's relationship with Gnessin on page 99 of her article. For another discussion of Dropkin and Gnessin, and particularly the poem "*A kush*" and the similarity between Dropkin's story "Bela iz farlibt" [Bella is in Love] and Gnessin's story "Etsel" [Alongside] see H. Binyamin, "Tsili shel Gnesin" [Gnessin's Tsili], *Siman kria* 12–13 (February 1981): 240–241. See also the poem "A kush," *In heysn vint*, 1935, titled "Un durshtik trink ikh" [And Thirstily I Drink], *In heysn vint*, 1959, dedicated to Gnessin. John Dropkin says that his younger brother Henry was named "Uriel" in Hebrew after Gnessin.

15. Hadda, "Eyes," 99.

16. Norma Fain Pratt, "Culture and Radical Politics: Yiddish Women Writers, 1890–1940," *American Jewish History* 70.1 (1980): 84.

17. One wonders how a mother of five in those days even managed to find a moment to herself, let alone the leisure to write poetry and have the sort of romantic adventures described in her work, yet Dropkin did both. It was not easy, but according to son John, her husband Shmaye Dropkin helped with the housework much more that did most husbands in those days. He was also proud of her accomplishments and actively supported her writing. The children seem to have been little affected or impressed by the fact that their mother was a writer. John, the oldest, says that as a child he knew his mother wrote but he did not know she was a "writer." As to the extra-marital affairs, according to John, his mother and father loved each other and certainly did not have an "agreement" or what would be considered an "open marriage" today. Although Shmaye Dropkin was surely cognizant of the fact that his wife had extra-marital affairs, he did not approve, but obviously tolerated it. He, as far as his son knows, did not have sexual relationships outside the marriage. Despite Celia's dalliances, their son remembers his parents' marriage as being a happy one. The couple was very active socially, and Shmaye was very proud of his talented wife.

18. Pratt, "Culture and Radical Politics, 84.

19. John Dropkin says that most of Dropkin's short stories and her serialized novel were written from 1928 to 1934 in Bluefield, West Virginia, and in Virginia, the two southern towns in which the family lived because their father Shmaye got a job managing a factory. The alien environment in which Celia Dropkin found herself proved favorable for writing. She had no friends to take up her time. All but the youngest child were in school, and she finally had the time to concentrate more on her work. In order to make money, she wrote short stories for the *Forverts* and a serialized novel, *Di tsvey geflin: roman fun yidishn lebn in amerike* [The Two Feelings: Novel of Jewish Life in America], which ran from March 31, 1934 to June 6, 1934. Although John Dropkin never read the novel himself, he described it as "strictly potboiler stuff, *shund*" [literary trash]. He remembers her writing it and discussions about it at home as well as the editor Abe Cahan's exhortations to "put in a little human interest," that is to say "sex."

20. A reprint of this photo appears in Benjamin and Barbara Harshav, eds., *American Yiddish Poetry: A Bilingual Anthology* (Berkeley: University of California Press, 1986), 36. The Harshavs also pointed out that publication in a journal is, in and of itself, not sufficient proof of belonging to a group. On page 37, they write, "Over one hundred

poets and writers participated in *Inzikh,* and surely not all of these were members of the group."

21. Aaron Glanz-Leyeles, *Dos lid fun khoydesh* [The Poem of the Month], *In zikh* 21 (February, 1936): 103.

22. Zalmen Reyzin, ed., *Leksikon fun der yidisher literatur, prese un filologie,* 1928 ed., s.v. "Drapkin Tsilie" and *Leksikon fun der nayer yidisher literatur,* 1958 ed., s.v. "Drapkin Tsilie." The 1971 edition of the *Encyclopaedia Judaica* lists the following poets as members of *Inzikh*: Aaron Glanz-Leyeles, Yankev Glatshteyn, Nokhn-Borukh Minkoff, Yankev Stodolsky, B. Alquit, Mikhl Likht, Bernard Lewis, Alef Katz, Kalmen Heisler, and Reuven Ludwig. Celia Dropkin is not among them, and I don't believe we should attribute this either to oversight or sexism.

23. Harshav, *American Yiddish Poetry,* 38.

24. Yankev Glatshteyn, A. Leyeles, and N. Minkov, "Introspectivism" [Manifesto of 1919], *In zikh: A Collection of Introspective Poems* (New York: Max N. Maisel, 1920), reprinted in Harshav, *American Yiddish Poetry,* 774.

25. Harshav, *American Yiddish Poetry,* 33.

26. Ibid., 41.

27. Ibid., 38.

28. Annette Kolodny, "Some Notes on Defining a 'Feminist Literary Criticism,'" *Critical Inquiry* (Autumn 1975): 75–92.

29. Sh. D. Zinger, "Ven du vest dem toyt in libe derkenen" [When You Recognize Death in Love], *Tsukunft* (October 1956): 374–75.

30. The poem "Take Me" is called "Eint bin ikh" [I Am Lonely] in the 1959 edition and is on page 41.

31. The poem "How Good I Feel" is called "Mit penimlekh ful freyd" [With Little Faces of Joy] in the 1959 edition and is on page 91. The line quoted in English is "*Vayt bin ikh fun benkenish fun zind*" in the original Yiddish.

32. Harshav, *American Yiddish Poetry,* 780.

33. Janet Hadda also comments on the lack of Jewish themes in Dropkin's poetry on page 95 saying that "she rarely uses the imagery of Jewish life—neither religion nor Eastern European folk tradition." Hadda also conjectures that Dropkin's disinterest in grappling with the issues of specifically Jewish female expression may account for some of the critical silence surrounding her work. She suggests, however, that the nature of her subject matter may have more to do with this relative silence.

34. Dropkin has only one poem, unpublished, which is clearly a reaction to World War II. I am grateful to John Dropkin for sending me a tape of his mother reading this and other poems. The poem is called "Shevere gedanken" [Heavy Thoughts]. Despite the inherently political nature of the topic, the poem deals with the Holocaust in a purely personal manner.

35. According to John Dropkin, unlike his father Shmaye who ran away from home to escape his stringently orthodox father, his mother had not been raised at all religiously, and so felt no need to rebel against religion. Indeed, if she had, this would most likely have been reflected on her poetry. Dropkin was not militant in any way. The family never had a *seyder* or a Chanukah celebration. The only deference they paid to the Jewish calendar was in buying the children new clothes around *Rosh Hashanah* [the Jewish New Year] and Passover. The only concession made to *kashrut* was not eating shrimp or pork. They even ate bread on Passover, and John Dropkin remembers, with some amusement, walking to an Italian neighborhood to get it. The children were all sent to Yiddish afternoon schools and were all allowed to drop out!

36. Interestingly, although the writing of such poets as Anna Margolin, Fradl Shtok, and Kadya Molodowsky was hardly *"frum-tkhinedik"* [in the pious style of women's prayers], the public still seemed to expect that from women. There is a certain logic to it since each of these writers did have first-hand knowledge of the religious world, either in her own upbringing or through her mother or grandmothers. See particularly Kadya Molodowsky, "Froyen lider" [Women's Songs], *Khesvendike nekht* (Vilna: Kletzkin Publishers, 1927), 11–19 and Anna Margolin, "Mayn shtam redt" [My Ancestors Speak] (Nyu York, 1929), 10–12. These poems are also available in translation. Poems I and VII of "Froyen lider" translated by Adrienne Rich appear in Eliezer Greenberg and Irving Howe, eds., A *Treasury of Yiddish Poetry* (New York: Schocken Books, 1974), 284–285. Poems II and VI translated by Irving Feldman appear in Irving Howe, Ruth R. Wisse, and Khone Shmeruk, eds., *The Penguin Book of Yiddish Verse* (New York: Penguin, 1988), 320–323. Two complete translations of the poem, one by F. Peczenik and one by Kathryn Hellerstein, appear in the journal *Yiddish* 7, nos. 2–3 (1988): 174–186. "Mayn shtam redt" is translated by Adrienne Cooper in Melanie Kaye/Kantrowitz and Irena Klepfisz, eds., *The Tribe of Dina: A Jewish Women's Anthology* (Montpelier, VT: Sinister Wisdom, 1986), 148–149.

37. It is true that Judaism, unlike Christianity, never posited celibacy as a higher ideal than marriage or than remarriage. Certainly, widowers and widows were encouraged to remarry. Men, particularly, were encouraged to remarry when their children needed a mother. It was also believed that male sexual desire had to be satisfied and marriage provided a legitimate avenue for that need. While women were certainly also encouraged to remarry, some literature offers the conflicting view that, although not possible or practical for most women, not remarrying was on a higher moral level. For example, eighteenth-century memoirist Gluckel of Hameln attributes her decision to remarry to her weakness and sinfulness. In *The Memoirs of Gluckel of Hamel*, trans. Marvin Lowenthal (New York: Schocken Books, 1977), 223–224, she writes, "Aye, sinner that I am, I should have married off my (daughter) Mariam and giving no thought to a second marriage done what beseems a good, pious Jewish woman; leaving behind the nothingness of this world, I should have taken myself, with the handful that remained me, to the Land of Our Fathers.... But my sins brought it to pass that God led me to other thoughts, and held me unworthy of it." Similarly, "A Widow's Prayer" found on page 88 of *Hours of Devotion*, a collection of prayers for women, may also be expressing the hope that worthy and pious women need turn to no man for help in their bereavement. Here the widow asks God to be her support and her mainstay: "Let me not fall into the hands of men, to stand in need of their gifts and presents, but do Thou feed and sustain me, for Thy mercy is exceedingly great.... Be Thou our Support and Helper in time of need."

38. Hadda, "Eyes," 97.

39. There are two different ending to the poem. In both editions of *In heysn vint* the last line is *"Oyf avere antbloyzte shpitsn/vil ikh fain"* [On Your Bare Points/I Want to Fall]. Levitan translates it simply as "I want to fall." In E. Korman, ed., *Yidishe dikhterins: antologye* (Shikago: L. M. Shtayn, 1928), 163–64, this is followed by the line *"Nor ikh hob kin mut"* [But I Have No Courage]. I don't believe that this difference significantly changes the reading of the poem. In either case, even though the narrator wants to fall, she does not. Falling is both attractive and frightening to her for it implies a kind of death.

40. The literal translation of *"tsirkus dame"* is "circus lady," but Levitan translates it appropriately here as "circus dancer."

41. "At the Window" is another example of a poem in which an imaginary retreat

into childhood, this time the speaker's own, provides an escape from the complexities and pain of adult life. At the same time that the retreat seems sweet, as does the suicide that would allow it, one must also see that the image of childhood presented here is ultimately a sad one. As Hadda points out, "Only a child whose comforts had been meager indeed would be likely to find a source of gratification and mirroring in as cold as potentially harmful a resting place as a concrete sidewalk" (107).

42. It is quite possible that Dropkin's poem was inspired by the painting "Death and the Maiden" (1915) by the Viennese Expressionist artist Egon Schiele. In the painting, both the maiden and death lie on a sheet as death caresses the maiden, paralleling Dropkin's motif of death uncovering the maiden and caressing her now bared legs. Her legs appear quite muscular and heavy, reminiscent of the "*mate*" [weary] legs in the poem. The mood of the two pieces is, however, somewhat different. While in Dropkin's poem, the maiden seems happy to be lured by the rakish seducer death, in Schiele's painting, death and the maiden cling to each other in seeming desperation. According to the art critic Alessandra Comini in *The Fantastic Art of Vienna* (New York: Knopf, 1978), "Death and sexuality played prominent roles in Schiele's tragically short life" (22). Although Dropkin did not actually begin painting until 1953, she was always interested in modern art. Given this interest and her propensity to these themes, it is not unreasonable to assume that she was familiar with and influenced by Schiele's work, and particularly this piece. It is also possible that both works are responding independently to a well-known motif.

43. Uriel Weinreich, *Modern English-Yiddish Yiddish-English Dictionary*, s.v. "Kavalir."

44. Hadda characterizes the love poems this way: "...what emerges most clearly is a predominant mood of unhappiness and longing; a forlorn quality dominates, although, to be sure, there are also poems in which the poet's words are strong and confident" (97).

45. See, for example, the poems "Ikh hob dikh nokh nit gezen" [I Haven't Yet Seen You] page 55 and with the slightly different title "Es vilt zikh mir zen" [I'd Like to See You] page 15 in the 1959 edition, and "Es iz in dem aza tsoyber" [There Is Such Magic in It], page 59 and with the slightly shortened title "Aza tsoyber" [Such Magic] page 60 in the 1959 edition.

46. Also translated by Adrienne Rich in Irving Howe and Eliezer Greenberg, eds., *A Treasury of Yiddish Stories* (New York: Holt, Rinehart & Winston, 1969), 168.

47. The last two lines of the poem are different in the two volumes of *In heysn vint*. In the 1934 edition, they are "*shvimen tsu mayne brenedike lipn / dayne royte, kindish-pukhke*" [swimming to my burning lips, / yours red and childlike-puffy lips]. The 1959 edition reads "*shvimen tsu mir / dayne royte, kindish-pukhke lipn*" [swimming towards me / your red, childlike-puffy lips]. On the assumption that Dropkin herself had something to do with the change, I have translated the second version.

48. This poem is untitled in the 1935 edition but is referred to in the table of contents as "Du kvelst" [You Are Overjoyed], the beginning of the first line. Seymour Levitan translated the poem.

49. See note 17 for a discussion of the Dropkin marriage.

50. The poem "Like Juicy Red Apples" is called "Fal ikh tsu der erd" [I Fall to the Earth] in the 1959 edition and is on page 17.

51. The poem "I Am Your Faithful Pupil" is called "In di soydes fun libe" [In the Secrets of Love] in the 1959 edition and is on page 72.

# Borrowed Shoes
## *Shira Gorshman's Politics of Literature*
### Faith Jones

Shira Gorshman's remarkable life led her back and forth between towns, cities, and countryside in Eastern Europe and both pre-statehood Palestine and post-statehood Israel, where she took part in a variety of Zionist and Soviet experiments in economic and social organization.[1] She did not begin writing for publication until her thirties, by which time she had a wealth of life experience and a sharpness of observation that became the foundation on which she built her creative life. Although her first book did not appear until she was in her mid-forties, she succeeded in publishing ten books of stories, memoirs, novellas, travelogues, and character sketches. Her writing remains less well known than that of some other Yiddish writers, with little recent critical notice taken of her work, and her life story is incompletely documented.

Gorshman was born in 1906 in Krakes (Krok in Yiddish), Lithuania. Her father divorced her mother when Gorshman was only a month old.[2] Her father became a *poresh*, a Talmudic recluse who frees himself from earthly relations in order to completely immerse himself in study. Her mother later remarried, but Gorshman's stepfather was violently abusive to her. When she was still a young child, her maternal grandfather intervened and took Gorshman away:

> One time [when her stepfather was beating her] my grandfather came in and tore me from his hands. He faced him and said, "Hershel, hit me! Why are you hitting someone smaller than you? What a hideous display."[3]

From then on she lived with her grandparents, and became particularly close to her grandfather, whom she continued to adore until her final days, notwithstanding the distance between her life choices and her grandfather's expectations of her. Gorshman's grandmother was harder to love, a tough, combative character, but Gorshman later credited her with teaching her skills in the garden, in tending animals, and around the house. Gorshman's grandfather gave her a traditional education, with more emphasis on religious learning than was usual for girls. She studied Bible and even some Talmud, although she was not particularly interested in religion and did not pursue this area of study.

At the age of fourteen, Gorshman left her grandparents' home and moved to the nearby city of Kaunas (Kovno in Yiddish), where she became active in Zionist organizations.[4] In the Zionist circles, she met and fell in love with the man she was to marry. Within four years, Gorshman had married and decamped for Palestine with her husband and baby. They joined an unusual commune, *G'dud ha-Avodah Trumpeldor* [Joseph Trumpeldor Labour Battalion]. This group settled *kibbutzim*, but also served as mobile labor for building infrastructure that was needed in the emerging *yishuv*. Like most early kibbutzim, the members lived together on their pooled income, with little personal property. Founded in 1920, *G'dud ha-Avodah* ultimately involved 650 people. The group had several splits, the largest of which, in 1927, essentially changed the group. A small, further-left faction of 115 people, according to Gorshman, left Palestine to found a commune in Crimea, where the Soviet authorities were eager to establish Jewish farming.[5] Gorshman threw her lot in with this group. She was by then divorced from her first husband and had three daughters.

The commune that the former pioneers founded was called *Voya Nova* [New Way]. Unlike *G'dud ha-Avodah*, it was agricultural in focus. Gorshman and her daughters arrived in 1928. Gorshman took on the running of the dairy operations. She was at this time ideologically committed to the idea that Jews should be regular workers, not intellectuals and professionals. She believed if Jews lived this way, "then people would see there is no difference" between Jews and Gentiles.[6] She became skilled at animal husbandry and was proud of her ability to oversee five hundred head of cattle. But Gorshman was not entirely suited to life on a collective farm. She had a pugnacious character and was often in trouble with the governing council of the collective. For example, one day in 1929, she discovered that two members of the collective, who worked under her in the dairy operations, had turned the young calves out to pasture without first giving them water. This was dangerous for the calves as they had no water supply all day. She got so infuriated that she hit and injured the two thoughtless young men.[7] For this, she had to come before a tribunal of the farm's governing council. Visiting the commune at this time was a group of artists from Moscow. They had come to paint the commune and its way of life, perhaps sent on an official delegation to create Soviet art.[8] And "they wanted to have a look at the idiots who came from Palestine," as Gorshman said later. The artists attended the tribunal, among them Mendel Gorshman, who quickly became enamored of her:

> He saw the work, and he said he would help me work in the stables. I didn't want that. He didn't understand it wasn't simple. In a little while, he talked to me about love. I told him I didn't need it. You have talents, you have easy work, and I don't understand what it is. Because in the shtetl my grandfather taught me Bible, but not art. You are still young, and I don't know how you live. I suspect that your children will have to sell newspapers on the street, and I don't know about that. This isn't my thing. But don't talk to me about love, because I'm not ready for that now. He went away with the brigade of artists, and in the middle of 1930, June, when one of the people from the commune was arrested, he came back to the commune. He said all the right things: he'd never met anybody like me. And I said my own things. And I wish now I hadn't done some things [...].[9] I stuck to my guns. I told him no, and he left. In February in 1931 he came back to the commune. I lived with three other commune members in one room. [...] This was the third time he'd come back, but not in vain. [...] He knew that if I left I wouldn't be milking cows, and I liked the cows. [After he left] I was sitting there and one of the girls I lived with came and was waved a book and said, I found this in your bed. When I looked at it I didn't understand what it was. It was a note of credit. It was a way I could go with the book [to a bank] and I could get money.[10]

Gorshman needed to decide what to do. She was by now in love with Mendel Gorshman, but was concerned that their lives were too different. She also did not want her children to have a stepfather, because of her own experience as a stepchild. The six hundred rubles Gorshman had left her was a considerable sum of money, and she worried about being indebted to him. In addition, there was another man interested in marrying her, a non–Jewish professional she met in town when selling milk. She sent the money back to Mendel Gorshman in Moscow. She had to borrow postage money from her other admirer, since as a commune member she had no personal property. About those years, she remembers:

> In a month or a month and a half, Mendel Gorshman came back, in 1931, and he said to me, Everything else I can stand, but that you should throw such a stone at my head, that I can't stand. I sent you the money to do with what you wanted. If you didn't want anything for yourself, you could give it to the children. But why did you send it to me? And how could you behave so badly just out of pride. And so I told him, I love you no less than you love me. If you tell me that my children will never feel that you are their step-father, then I will leave the commune and go with you to Moscow. And that's what happened.[11]

Gorshman and her three children moved to Moscow and began a new kind of life there. As Gorshman indicates, she knew very little about art, which was not only her husband's profession but his mode of living. Her upbringing in a traditional *shtetl* family, and especially because she was raised by old-fashioned grandparents, had not prepared her for modernity. In Kovno she had thrown herself into left–Zionist politics, and within a few years was working as a laborer in rural Palestine and then Crimea. Except for perhaps those few years in Kovno, she had no exposure to manifestations of modern culture. But with her immersion in Mendel Gorshman's circle of artists and writers, she began to see that cultural work could be as satisfying as physical labor and that the meaning of art could be as meaningful as other forms of knowledge. Of that, she writes:

> And so gradually, listening to reputable, honorable people [Mendel Gorshman's artist friends], I began to understand that as well as Bible, Holy Books and Prayers, there were also other things in this world, such as: exhibitions of art and sculpture. And this is what actually led me to literature. It was Nikolai Nikolaievitsh Kupriyanov who said casually to me that if my Yiddish is better than my Russian, I should start writing in Yiddish. And that's what happened.[12]

As Gorshman herself pointed out, in some ways she had always been a writer. Her mother kept her childhood writings until they were destroyed in the war,[13] and she wrote letters to her grandfather after she moved to Kovno and Palestine, letting him know about her marriage and children, even though he did not approve of her Zionist activity or her lack of religiosity.[14] However, she began writing for publication after receiving encouragement from her husband's circle of friends in Moscow, and her first publication came about with the advice of Leyb Kvitko, one of the leading Soviet Yiddish writers. She recounts that time in these words:

> I had a written a story "The Fellow-eater" and I left it on the desk and I was washing the floor in the kitchen because it was my turn to clean the shared kitchen. Kvitko came to me with the papers, and said, did you write this? And I said yes. "Good lord," he said, "why have you kept silent? Good God. I knew that all mothers give their children the breast so they can eat. But this is the first time I've read a story about a mother who locks her son in the drawer of a dresser because he always wants to eat." The story is published, it's called "The Fellow-eater": this is a parasite that lives inside you and keeps eating, because the child is never sated and is growing up in a very poor family. This story I keep including in my books. That was my first, serious story that I wrote and it was judged to be the kind of story Sholem Aleichem couldn't write. Not that it's better than Sholem Aleichem! But that's what the critics said. [...] Leyb Kvitko, who was a wonderful writer, well-known over the world, he said "even if you write nothing else, with just this story you'll be recognized in our literature."[15]

Kvitko appears to have immediately grasped Gorshman's unique place in Yiddish literature and the themes and vision that would serve her throughout her career. With the story "Der mit-eser" [The Fellow-eater], Gorshman shows her penetration of the dilemmas faced by women. Extreme poverty in the prewar *shtetl* is a common theme in Yiddish literature. That this poverty strains family relations and makes parents despair of caring for their children is also well explored territory. Gorshman's contribution is to show women's ambivalence towards their children and the way that poverty turns the normally joyous activities of women's lives, such as breastfeeding, into corrosive duties that warp the family structure. Gorshman's early publications included stories in the journals *Heymland* [Homeland], *Der shtern* [The Star], *Der emes* [Truth], and *Eynikayt* [Unity], as well as in anthologies.

Gorshman's living situation during the war and Holocaust is not clear. She was probably still in Moscow with her husband and children, by then teens and young adults. One daughter died of starvation. Gorshman attributed this to her and her husband's inability to wheel and deal as necessary in the wartime economy: "We couldn't do anything for her, couldn't buy and sell, or whatever."[16] Later stories indicate she may have spent some time in Central Asia at this time or just following the war, but this is not certain. She visited her mother in Lithuania just before the outbreak of the war (her grandparents were already dead), and this was apparently the last time she saw any of her family of origin. Her many stories about the Holocaust and the few memoir sketches of her grandparents show how deeply affected she was by her own personal losses and the end of the *shtetl*. Late in her life, she exhibited some symptoms of survivor's guilt when asked directly about Krok:

> It's hard, almost impossible, to talk about it. I don't feel I have the right to mourn it, or to remind anyone of it. They left the train thinking they were going to bathe. But it wasn't a bath. Everyone knows what it really was. They went in the front, and dead bodies were thrown out the back. To speak about it is nearly impossible.[17]

Gorshman re-visited Krok in the 1970s and 1980s as a guest of the Lithuania Writer's Union. These visits re-traumatized her, for example when she saw farming occurring on the site of a mass grave and when she went to the house of a former neighbor and saw Jewish ornaments they had clearly pilfered from the house of a deported family or perhaps from a family they had helped massacre in the Lithuanian pogroms of 1941.[18]

The Holocaust featured in some of the stories in her first book, *Der koyekh fun lebn* [The Power of Life], published in 1948, with illustrations by her husband. There were also stories based on her time in Palestine, though these stories avoided political messages about Zionism and focused on collective labor and other stories based on *shtetl* life. Not all these subjects were equally welcome in the Soviet literary landscape of the era. A review by the well-known writer, translator, and pedagogue Noyekh Lurye in the journal *Heymland* embodies the difficulties she faces. On the one hand, Lurye perceptively notes that a certain kind of female character shows up repeatedly in these stories: "[A] woman with a good, motherly heart and an eccentric, almost angry manner of speaking, which makes her good-heartedness richer and gives her flavor."[19] This character's resemblance to Gorshman's grandmother is probably not a coincidence. He goes on to praise some of the folkloric aspects of the stories, such as a story in which a woman goes to her husband's grave to request intervention with God—a practice not found in normative, rabbinic Judaism. He is also positive about stories set in the commune, which show peasant laborers and their dedication to work, and the Soviet systems of social organization. They also show a strong connection of Jews to the land and to their non–Jewish neighbors. These characters, Lurye says, behave as members of a socialist collective and take their strength from this collective:

> This Soviet atmosphere, which fills the works so naturally, as air fills space, is an indicator that Shira Gorshman is absolutely not condemned to nourish herself cooking and devouring the old, gathered leftovers of her memory. She is situated in close contact with flow of Soviet life and can serve up very worthy contemporary work.[20]

However, Lurye dismisses the stories of Palestine excepting one story that speaks of disillusionment: it "shows the bitter fate of the rebellious pioneers."[21] And, although he had praised some folkloric aspects of the *shtetl* stories, he also judges them to be the least interesting:

> The writer doesn't show us any processes, any characters, that haven't been written of a great deal in our literature. We also do not find any fresh views of well-known phenomena, a viewpoint which can mirror the present-day condition of our consciousness.[22]

He describes a few of these stories thus:

> An empty, humorous piece about a slow-witted, small-town, old Jewish lady ("Chaya-Rokhe the Lost"); a story which is more suited to "Kav ha-Yoshor" [Righteous Measure, an 18th century book of moral instruction] than to a book by a Soviet writer ("The wise geese"). A picture of bitter poverty and helplessness, truly choking backwardness ("The fellow-eater"), richly and skillfully written and all the same stuck in the scope of ethnographic exoticism.[23]

One can't help but feel the confusion of these messages for the writer. Folkloric details are good; ethnographic exoticism is bad. Stories of the old days are boring, but the character they contain of the harsh, older Jewish woman is interesting. One can sense Lurye, as well as Gorshman, walking a line whose exact demarcation is changing under their feet. And indeed, they were right to be cautious. The issue of *Heymland* in which her book was reviewed was the last issue of that journal; the review was the last Yiddish work Lurye published in his lifetime.[24] The newspaper *Eynikayt* covered a reading Gorshman gave at the state library of Belarus in its October 2, 1948 issue.[25] Within a few weeks, the magazine had folded. By mid–December 1948, Stalin's "anti-cosmopolitan campaign," in which up to seventy percent of the named individuals among the censured were Jewish,[26] and a simultaneous campaign of repression against Jewish institutions and cultural figures, transformed Yiddish culture in the Soviet Union. Publishing came to a halt and was slow to pick up even following Stalin's death and Khrushchev's 1956 speech acknowledging Stalin's crimes.

By 1961, Khrushchev's "thaw" reached a stage where Yiddish publishing could again take place.[27] However, the twelve-year gap proved extremely damaging. Gorshman's friend Leyb Kvitko was among the writers killed in the so-called "Night of the Murdered Poets" in 1952.[28] Other writers and cultural figures who were central to Soviet Yiddish cultural life—the great Dovid Bergelson among them—died with him. Many more stopped writing. More importantly, Yiddish literacy and interest in Jewish culture had been seriously undermined; the audience for Yiddish was diminished and unsure of its relative worth in the new political situation. Gorshman herself came through the anti-cosmopolitan campaign without attracting official notice. This was probably a reflection of her lower profile than most of the victims, who were better-known and influential. She later said that she herself did not suffer. However, she cannot have avoided being affected by the murder of her friends and the general dissolution of the Yiddish cultural infrastructure that sustained her intellectually.

Although Mendel Gorshman was able to make a living as an illustrator, it is not known what Gorshman did for a living in Moscow. At the time of the reemergence of Yiddish publishing, Gorshman was clearly ready with material. In 1961, a slim volume of her stories was brought out by *Yidish bukh* in Warsaw, where Yiddish publishing remained strong relative to the Soviet Union. Publication in Poland was a frequent strategy by Soviet Yiddish writers, who had uncensored mail access to Poland and did not consider publishing there to be an act of dissidence or one that might bring them to official notice.[29] The stories in *Dray un draysik noveln* [Thirty-Three Stories] were generally very short, but must have been written during the years of repression, when

Gorshman could not know if there would ever be a market for them. Like many of Gorshman's books, the stories are divided into sections by theme. Two brief memoirs are followed by sections called "Women," "Communards," "From Hell," and "Pity for Living Things." Gorshman was not averse to reusing stories from her previous book, a habit she continued throughout her creative life. The section "Women" includes two stories about abortion, "A rakhmones af di mantsbiln" [Pity the Menfolk] and "A vayberisher shmues" [A Women's Conversation]; a story about domestic assault, "Tsvishn berg" [Between Mountains]; a reprint of "The Fellow-eater"; and a story about an unwed mother and her accepting, joyful grandparents "Der driter dor" [The Third Generation]. Although not all the stories focus on women's issues, even those in other sections of the book are often told from a female character's point of view, and include many strong-willed, tough heroines who take risks, are competent in non-traditional roles, and survive against the odds. The story "Lebn un likht" [Life and Light], from the Holocaust series, describes the terrible choices women living in the ghettos had to make once pregnancy was made illegal. Another Holocaust story "Bobe Malke" [Grandma Malka], a reprint from *Der koyekh fun lebn*, tells the story of a midwife who avoids deportation by pretending to be a Gentile, but who takes her revenge on collaborators, though it may endanger her own survival.

The major player in the new Yiddish publishing of the 1960s was the journal *Sovetish heymland* [Soviet Homeland]. *Sovetish heymland* was largely a literary journal, but also published folklore, political commentary, and other non-fiction essays. As a state-supported publication, it enjoyed both a significant print run and a huge page count. It was edited by Arn Vergelis, a poet turned pundit, and published by *Sovetskii Pisatel*, which also published books. Publication in *Sovetish heymland* or a *Sovetskii Pisatel* book was the main route for Soviet Yiddish writers to gain an audience. *Sovetish heymland* also played a propaganda role, which may have been its actual *raison d'etre*, in the Soviet effort to appease American Jews and to counter accusations of anti–Semitism.[30] Gorshman was one of only a handful of women who published frequently in this journal. *Sovetskii Pisatel* also brought out a translation of *33 noveln* in 1963. In 1974, a collection of the great majority of her works to that date,[31] *Lebn un likht* [Life and Light], was published by *Sovetskii Pisatel*, which also brought out a Russian translation in 1979. Gorshman may have intended this four-hundred page work to stand as her lifetime collected works, presumably feeling she was getting on in years. Nonetheless, she did not at this point rest on her laurels. Her fourth book, *Ikh hob lib arumforn* [I Love to Wander], was published as a supplement to *Sovetish heymland* in 1981. In 1984, another large compilation of her stories, *Yontef in mitn vokh* [Mid-week Holiday], was released.

In spite of these successes, Gorshman remained bitter about her writing life in the Soviet Union. Late in her life, she told an interviewer:

> Because I didn't write about the great, shining party that would bring freedom to all people, and about the dear leader of all peoples. Therefore very little of my work was published there.[32]

She also claimed that Vergelis asked her to write positively about Stalin, but this makes no sense. Before and after the 1948–1961 repression of Yiddish publishing, she was published and reviewed in the main Soviet Yiddish organs. By 1961, when Vergelis was the editor she most needed to please, nobody was expected to write paeans to Stalin. Gorshman was even allowed to publish a story about false accusations during the Stalin era.[33] Her post–1961 works include a number of stories that are somewhat rebellious. The long story "A basherte zakh" [Something Predestined] includes a character who, although a specialized engineer with important work to do building society, suddenly finds himself demoted, then fired, for reasons that are never explained but hint at a sudden change in official policy, corruption, nepotism, or who knows what. The abortion story "Pity the Menfolk" hints at class disdain between the female abortionist and her less-educated patients. In a variety of small ways, Gorshman shows the failure of the Soviet Union to bring about a unified, classless society with neutral relations between ethnic groups. This is not to say she did not pander at times. Perhaps inevitably, she made sure to include pro–Soviet messages, particularly if telling a specifically Jewish story. This was perhaps meant to counteract accusations of clannishness. The stunning story "Life and Light" ends with the character who has survived the Holocaust expressing her pride that her son, born after her husband's death in the ghetto, has taken after his father and become a Young Communist. Her many stories of Crimean commune life might similarly be said to counter Jewish specificity with a Soviet vision of collectivization and productivization of Jewish labor. She did not, however, see these things as a sell-out or see herself as a "true believer." Later in life Gorshman told an interviewer that she was never able to bring herself to attend the memorial services for the August 12, 1952 murdered writers.[34] Although she loved Kvitko, she could not stand his and others' complete accommodation to the Soviet system. In a fond, sad essay about Kvitko, she says:

> It would have been better if the murdered writers hadn't believed so fully, it would have been better if Kvitko hadn't dedicated himself totally to everything Soviet, and to the great cutthroat. Better if he were guilty, Reb Leyb Kvitko. The

pain would be as great as ever, but the guilt and the knowledge of it would alleviate the enormous suffering.[35]

Overall, Gorshman's regular publications in *Sovetish heymland* and her books that appeared in Yiddish and Russian do not speak of a system that singled her out for neglect. What is certainly true is that Vergelis kept strong control over publication in his journal and that he considered himself the only possible curator of Yiddish literature in the Soviet system. His personal posturing was a huge irritation to writers, which may form the basis of Gorshman's later claim that he attempted to force her to write more programmatically. There were also structural impediments to what could and could not be written. Gorshman was not able to return to the topic of Palestine and its pioneer era until her move to Israel in 1990. Gorshman may also have retrospectively misremembered how much she was published because so little notice was taken of her work when it was published. While occasionally the subject of serious literary criticism,[36] she did not garner the amount of attention that many of her male counterparts did. This may be a reflection of the place of women both in Yiddish literary culture and in Soviet ideology. While in theory both systems embraced women as equal participants, the places opened up for them, while greater than in earlier eras, never came close to the space afforded men. Gorshman is not considered or is barely mentioned in numerous books and essays about Soviet Yiddish writers, both those published in the Soviet Union and those published outside of it.[37] She also lacks the intrinsic interest of those who were politically victimized. Among North American Yiddish readers and scholars, the execution of Kvitko, Bergelson, and others in 1952, has become the central issue surrounding Soviet Yiddish for Western literati; those writers garner most of the scant attention the Yiddish world turns on Soviet writers.[38] However understandable this is, it leaves us with a situation that perpetuates Gorshman's marginality. Another way in which she was marginal was in her choice of genres. Although she wrote a few novels and novellas, she primarily wrote stories, while Yiddish and Soviet critics were more focused on novelists.[39]

Mendel Gorshman died in 1972.[40] In 1990, Shira took advantage of Gorbachav's opening up of emigration to Israel. One of her daughters had either moved there previously or immigrated at the same time. She lived in Ashkelon and became active in Yiddish cultural life in Israel. Although already in her mid-eighties, she energetically re-published many of her stories from her earlier books since the Soviet imprints were basically unavailable in Israel. She also wrote new works and re-wrote works that she had self-censored under the Soviet regime. Her new work was strong on memoir sketches—very short pieces that described a single incident or person—but also included some short fiction. Her only novel, *Khanes shof un rinder* [Chana's Sheep and Cattle] was one of five Yiddish books Gorshman published in Israel.[41] Her book of brief, impressionistic sketches, *On a gal* [Without Malice], was translated into Hebrew. She won two literary awards in Israel: the Dovid Hofshteyn Prize, awarded by the Yiddish Writers Union of Israel, in 1991 and the Hamlin House Prize awarded by the Histadrut, in 1994. Yiddish in Israel was severely attenuated, and she was hardly a household name, but she expressed satisfaction with her life and with the small apartment she shared with one of her daughters, because it afforded her space to write.[42]

Gorshman was also critical of Israel and modern Israeli society and was characteristically caustic on the subject. When she won the Hofshteyn prize, she apparently gave an acceptance speech that articulated her main complaints, namely that Israel was too dependent on American money, did not support Yiddish, did not ensure economic justice even within its own borders, and did not care about anyone outside its borders at all. She paraphrased her speech this way to an interviewer:

> I'm applauding, I'm happy, you're happy, but I have to tell you that I am walking in borrowed shoes.[43] That's not comfortable. The dress is comfortable, but the shoes aren't. You are ready to take from America, but never will you reach into your pocket to give five shekels for Yiddish literature. And Yiddish literature is a holy thing. It is the real holy language. Those that went to Auschwitz, many of them didn't read or scream in Hebrew, they screamed "God, you're blind and deaf, look what is happening to your children." There's a verse by King Solomon in Ecclesiastes: "it wasn't, it isn't, it won't be"—referring to justice. The Americans build houses and sell them for millions of dollars but those who live there won't open the door to a mother and child. It's very good that you have asphalt roads, cars, and the successful people can sit in them and drive fast, this is all well. But what's bad is that they forget the majority, which has no cars. And outside Israel there are children dying of hunger. Let Israel be eternal. This is good. Because without Israel we're nothing. We'll be murdered the way the 6 million were. But it should be better than it is.[44]

Possibly her adjustment to modern Israeli society was made more difficult by her memories of the idealistic pioneer movement and the hard labor she and her comrades had performed in the service of nation-building:

> I live now in an apartment building among people who only eat, sleep, and worry about themselves. They don't begin to know how much blood and toil was expended so that they should be able to come to Israel.[45]

And although she found a receptive home in Israel for her writing, she apparently missed the natural conviviality of the Moscow cultural scene she and

Mendel Gorshman had so easily moved in. This short anecdote from one of her last books sums up the situation:

> They told me that writers get together in the evenings at Agnon's house. Naturally, I went there as soon as possible. There were already a lot of writers gathered when I got there. Some sat, some walked around. I went over to a seated writer and said:
> [in Hebrew] "Do you speak Yiddish?"
> [in Hebrew] "No, no, no, what do you think?"
> "There's no need to shout."
> I went over to another one and asked again, as I asked everyone. He said in a beautiful Yiddish:
> "I can't. But there's a woman sitting over there, she's a Yiddish writer."
> My soul brightened. In two steps I was beside her. It's true, she was a Yiddish writer. She even showed me her book, taking it out of her bag. She asked:
> "Do you have a book out?"
> I showed her "Chane's Sheep and Cattle."
> She looked and it and wanted to know:
> "How much does it cost?"
> "15 shekels."
> "That's all? Mine costs 25. So I can't exchange books with you."
> I didn't want to trade with her anyway. I found myself thinking:
> "It's a shame you don't sell burekas."[46]

Gorshman's last book was *In di shpurn fun G'dud ha-Avodah* [In the Footsteps of the Labor Battalion], published in 1998, in which she finally returned to the story of her early experiences in pre-statehood Palestine. She died in 2001 in Ashkelon, a few days before her ninety-fifth birthday.

As a whole, Gorshman's work shows some stable features beginning with some of her earliest work. "Bobe Malke" published in her first book, portrays the kind of folk heroine who reappears throughout her work. Malka the midwife is devout but not tied to norms of religious piety; she uses the mushrooms growing in the cemetery to make liniments for her patients. This angers the town rabbi. Malka is thus suspended between life and death, even before the war comes. When the war does come, she first disguises herself, then carefully plans and carries out revenge on a collaborator who is enriching himself from the houses of his former Jewish neighbors. Like many later Gorshman characters, she is shown as independent of mind, able to act in her own best interests, able to be violent, and both a unique individual and tied to the Jewish people and Jewish fate. As one critic put it:

> A master of the novella, Gorshman described deep psychological experiences and created unusual portraits of people. The central hero in her work is the woman as a folk-figure in the uneasy historical epoch [...]. This very figure, through whom the writer embodied the important problems of reality, always appears in

a time when the foundations of old forms of social organization are broken, and new relationships and alliances in social life and in the life of a new kind of family are being constructed.[47]

These same themes reappear in her stories of Palestine, the Crimea, and the *shtetl*, as well as her other Holocaust stories, and illuminate some of her most fascinating work. But not all her stories follow this pattern. In her stories of modern Soviet life in particular, her characters and situations stray quite far from these motifs. Not all her women characters are heroic, able to fend for themselves, or in control of any part of their fate. Her story "A Yapanisher shirem" [A Japanese Parasol] takes place entirely among middle-class Muscovites. The main character is a woman who has allowed her life to be completely bound up in her husband. She takes pleasure from helping with his work and has allowed herself to become isolated from her one remaining family member (others perished in the war). When her happy existence is undermined, this character struggles to remember her own identity and to create the life she needs. The story "Shkheynim" [Neighbors] takes place among Jewish evacuees to Central Asia during World War II. This story asks questions about the gendered nature and experience of famine and starvation. The main character and her son are housed with a couple, who are musicians. The musicians are worldly and cosmopolitan, but the main character begins to see that their relationship is by no means a modern marriage. As food becomes scarcer, relations between the neighbors become strained, the husband becomes more autocratic, and the wife more cowed. When the main character is allowed to return to Russia, she does so with her pride intact. But her female neighbor is not able to escape her situation and remains as trapped as ever. The story "Tsvisn berg" [Between Mountains] is also set in Central Asia. The narrator, who is apparently from Russia, is befriended by a local woman. Although she speaks limited Russian, this new friend gradually makes the narrator understand that she is regularly beaten by her husband. Neither the narrator nor the abused woman is able to change this situation.

The story "A basherte zakh" is unusual among Gorshman's oeuvre. While most of her stories are under ten pages long, "A basherte zakh" is about forty pages. It centers on a Jewish couple whose daughter becomes a seamstress for a local theater troupe. She falls in love with and marries a non–Jewish actor, who moves into the family home. The parents are at first unsure, but soon begin to adore their new son-in-law. Their lives are punctuated by the difficulties of navigating through bureaucracy. The father is an engineer who loses his job, and the son-in-law has trouble securing roles from a dictatorial director. The family is visited by their small-town Gentile in-laws, who sprinkle the daughter with hempseed to promote fertility. The daughter does indeed become joyously pregnant. This story has no particular suspense, but it is an engrossing portrait of family life in what must have been fairly common set of circumstances—a mixed marriage, not enough housing, the petty malice of apparatchiks—and its image of the ability to find joy in these surroundings feels authentic.

Gorshman witnessed at close hand numerous distinct manifestations of Jewish existence in the twentieth century: the *shtetl*, settlement in Palestine, Soviet collectivization, and Moscow intellectual life under a variety of ideological regimes. She was also highly influenced by the destruction of the traditional communities of Eastern Europe, a fate she personally avoided but strongly identified with. In her fiction, survival always exacts a spiritual price. Her life story is marked by a purposeful quest for integrity. In making *aliyah* to Palestine and working hard labor, and again in leaving Palestine for a Crimean commune, and finally in leaving Moscow for Israel, she attempted to find a situation that allowed her to live her ideals. Her work celebrates women who are as uncompromising as she was and mourns women who lack the means to live uncorrupted lives. She, like many of her characters, insisted on the need to live a life consonant with their professed beliefs about right and wrong. When she arrived in Moscow, she came late to Jewish modernity. She arrived fully formed, with an already established identity and a sense of her own competence. Nurtured by Moscow intellectual circles, she was able to live her ideals partly through writing them, although not perfectly while she was constrained by Soviet policy. But she was never totally comfortable with her new situations, any more than she had been in the religious atmosphere of the *shtetl*, because she was uncompromising in what she demanded for herself and others.

Gorshman has failed to gain a wide audience as evidenced by the lack of translations and critical attention partly because the mantle of Yiddish literary life has fallen squarely on the United States, which Gorshman neither visited nor wrote about. She is not made fascinating by being a symbolic martyr of Stalinist crimes, and she is further unappealing to American tastes because of her dedication to leftist politics, a dedication that survived her disillusionment with Stalinism and the Soviet experiment. Critics prefer writers of longer works than her typical miniatures, and we must also consider the fact that Soviet, Israeli, and American critics are all less eager to write about women writers, particularly those who, like Gorshman, fixed their artistic gaze on women's lives. But Gorshman deserves to be better known and more widely read. Her work is both penetrating and subtle, and it rewards re-reading and analysis.

## Notes

Where the stories discussed in this essay may be found in Yiddish, Russian, Hebrew, and English.

"Der miteser" [The Fellow-eater]
  YIDDISH: *Der koyekh fun lebn, 33 noveln, Lebn un likht, Yontef in mitn vokh*
  RUSSIAN: *Tret'e pokolenie, Zhizn' i svet*
"A rakhmones af di mantsbiln" [Pity the Menfolk]
  YIDDISH: *33 noveln, Lebn un likht, Yontef in mitn vokh, Vi tsum ershtn mo.*
  RUSSIAN: *Tret'e pokolenie, Zhizn' i svet*
  ENGLISH: http://debbienathan.com/i-feel-sorry-for-these-men-a-yiddish-story-about-abortion/
"A vayberisher shumes" [A Women's Conversation]
  YIDDISH: *33 noveln, Yontef in mitn vokh*
  RUSSIAN: *Tret'e pokolenie*
"Tsvishn berg" [Between Mountains]
  YIDDISH: *33 noveln*
  RUSSIAN: *Tret'e pokolenie*
  ENGLISH: *Bridges* 14 no. 2 (Fall 2009)
"Der driter dor" [The Third Generation]
  YIDDISH: *33 noveln, Lebn un likh.*
  RUSSIAN: *Tret'e pokolenie, Zhizn' i svet*
"Lebn un likht" [Life and Light]
  YIDDISH: *33 noveln, Lebn un likht*
  RUSSIAN: *Tret'e pokolenie, Zhizn' i svet*
  ENGLISH: http://jewishfiction.net/index.php/publisher/articleview/frmArticleID/124
"Bobe Malke" [Grandma Malka]
  YIDDISH: *Der koyekh fun lebn, 33 noveln, Lebn un likht, Yontef in mitn vokh*; also in the anthology *Dertseylungen fun yidishe sovetishe shrayber*
  RUSSIAN: *Tret'e pokolenie, Zhizn' i svet.*
  ENGLISH: *Beautiful as the Moon, Radiant as the Stars*
"A basherte zakh" [Something Predestined]
  YIDDISH: *Lebn un likht, On a gal*
  RUSSIAN: *Zhizn'i svet*
  HEBREW: *Bli marah*
"Khanes shof un rinder" [Chana's Sheep and Cattle]
  YIDDISH: earlier versions of the story appeared in *Lebn un likht* and *Yontef in mitn vokh.*
  RUSSIAN: *Zhizn' i svet*
"A Yapanisher shirem" [A Japanese Parasol]
  YIDDISH: *Lebn un likht, Vi tsum ershtn mol*
  RUSSIAN: *Zhizn' i svet*
"Shkheynim" [Neighbors]
  YIDDISH: *Lebn un likht*
  RUSSIAN: *Zhizn' i svet*

An additional story, which is not discussed in this article, is available in English:

"Nit oysgeredt di hertser" [Unspoken Hearts]
  YIDDISH: *Lebn un likht*

Russian: *Zhizn' i svet*
English: *Found Treasures*

1. Other spellings of her name include Shirke Goman, Shire Gorman and Szyrke Gorszman. She was previously known as Shira Kushnir (either her maiden name or that of her first husband).
2. Interview with Frieda Forman and Sue Fishkoff, Ashkelon, Israel, January, 2 1995. Interview audiotape courtesy of Frieda Forman. Many of the details in my essay are taken from this interview. All translations are mine unless otherwise identified.
3. *Shire Gorshman: Lite, Palestine, Krim*. Film interview by Boris Sandler; produced by Sandler and *Forverts*, 2009.
4. Chaim Beyder, "Shire Gorshman, zikhroyne levrokhe" (obituary), *Forverts*, April 13, 2001; "Gorshman, Shira," *Leksikon fun yidishe shrayber in ratn-farband* (Nyu York: Alveltlekhn yidishn kultur-kongres, 2011).
5. The rest of the group remained in Palestine, but by 1928, the G'dud ha-Avodah banner was dissolved and its construction focus was lost. Members dispersed to their kibbutzim and pursued other ways of earning a living. See Ben Halpern and Jehuda Reinharz, *Zionism and the Creation of a New Society* (New York: Oxford University Press, 1998).
6. Forman and Fishkoff, interview, 1995.
7. This incident forms the basis of an episode in her novel *Khanes shof un rinder* [Chana's Sheep and Cattle].
8. A few years later Mendel Gorshman went to Birobidzhan to paint Jewish life there as well. See "Boyung in birebidzhan," *Forpost* 2 (1936): 128–129; and Israel Rabinovitsh, "Naye geshtaltn: di yidishe oytonome gegnt in kunst," *Forpost* 2 (1936): 218–224.
9. As Gorshman indicates very delicately here, sexual mores were loosened in the commune, perhaps because most members were young and had no parental influences nearby. Both in stories and in interviews, she described the tension between sexual liberation and pressure to be sexually available. See, for example, her story "Hoykhe shveln," about an attempted rape, which appears in *33 noveln* and *Lebn un likht*; and her interview with Boris Sandler in the film *Shira Gorshman: Lite, Palestine, Krim*.
10. The story of Gorshman's romance with her second husband is told in different versions, with slightly differing details in the film *Shira Gorshman: Lite, Palestine, Krim* and in Gorshman's interview with Frieda Forman and Sue Fishkoff. Direct quotes are from the Forman and Fishkoff's interview, 1995.
11. Ibid.
12. Shira Gorshman, "Vi bin ikh gekumen tsum shraybn," *On a gal* (Tel Aviv: Yisroel-bukh, 1996), 14. Kupriyanov was an artist and illustrator.
13. Forman and Fishkoff, interview, 1995.
14. Shira Gorshman, "Vi bin ikh gekumen tsum shraybn," *On a gal* (Tel Aviv: Yisroel-bukh, 1996), 11–13.
15. Forman and Fishkoff, interview, 1995.
16. Ibid.
17. Sandler, "*Shire Gorshman: Lite, Palestine, Krim*."
18. Ibid.
19. Noyekh Lurye, "Der koyekh fun lebn," *Heymland* 6 (1948): 137.
20. Ibid., 139.
21. Ibid., 140.

22. Ibid., 138.
23. Ibid.
24. According to the *Leksikon fun der nayer yidisher literatur*, he did publish a book in Russian in 1957. His death in 1960 meant that he did not live long enough to publish again in Yiddish. See *Lekiskon fun der nayer yidisher literatur* (New York: Congress for Jewish Culture, 1963), vol. 5, col. 35.
25. Y. Volfson, "Literarishe ovnt in mozir," *Eynikayt* 119 (Oktober 2, 1948): 3.
26. Yaacov Ro'i, "Anticosmopolitan Campaign," *YIVO Encyclopedia of Jews in Eastern Europe*, 8 July 2010, 8 July 2012, http://www.yivoencyclopedia.org/article.aspx/Anticosmopolitan_Campaign.
27. This summary cannot begin to explore the many ways Yiddish was viewed and officially dealt with in the Soviet Union. Repression did not begin in 1948 and did not end in 1961. However, for Yiddish writers, these were the most difficult years. Schools were closed as early as the 1930s, and even after the "thaw," limits remained on what could and could not be discussed in print. Yet official support of some publishing organs before and after the anti-cosmopolitan campaign allowed Yiddish writers to reach an audience much larger than that of most American or Israeli Yiddish writers, and Yiddish culture remained highly developed much later than in other places. For full discussion of these issues, see Gennady Estraikh, *In Harness: Yiddish Writers' Romance with Communism* (Syracuse: Syracuse University Press, 2005) and *Yiddish in the Cold War* (London: Legenda, 2008).
28. Although this term is the most common one used in English, it is a misnomer and may obscure the real nature of the event. The majority of those killed that day were not writers but members of the Jewish Anti-Fascist Committee. My thanks to Gennady Estraikh for this observation, as well as for many other useful comments on this essay.
29. Gennady Estraikh, *Yiddish in the Cold War* (London: Legenda, 2008), 72.
30. Gennady Estraikh, "*Sovetish Heymland*," *YIVO Encyclopedia of Jews in Eastern Europe*, 20 October 2010, July 8, 2012, http://www.yivoencyclopedia.org/article.aspx/Sovetish_Heymland.
31. The Palestine stories and a number of other early works from *Der koyekh fun lebn* were not included.
32. Forman and Fishkoff, interview, 1995.
33. I have not seen this story, but it is described in Elias Schulman, "*Sovietish Heimland*: Lone Voices, Stifled Creators," *Judaism* 14, no. 1 (1965): 63. Schulman cites this story as appearing in *Sovetish heymland*, issue 1 of 1963.
34. Forman and Fishkoff, interview, 1995.
35. Shira Gorshman, "Kvitko," *On a gal* (Tel Aviv: Yisroel-bukh, 1996), 134. For a nuanced treatment of Yiddish writers' embrace of Soviet ideology, see Gennady Estraikh, *In Harness: Yiddish Writers' Romance with Communism* (Syracuse: Syracuse University Press, 2005).
36. See Hersh Remenik, "Shira Gorshman," in *Shtaplen* (Moscow: Sovetskii Pisatel, 1982), 340–349. One oddity of Remenik's essay is that he is apparently unable to refer to the Jewish-specific "*khurbn*" (Holocaust) in discussion of Gorshman's Holocaust stories, and so refers throughout his essay to "*der groyser foterlendisher milkhome*," the Great Patriotic War, the Russian name for World War II.
37 She does not appear in Joshua Rothenberg, *Fun amol un fun haynt* (Tel Aviv: Farlag Perets, 1990); Yeḥezḳel Lifschits and Mordechai Altshuler, eds., *Briv fun Yidishe Sovetishe shraybers* (Jerusalem: Hebrew University, 1979); Irving Howe and Eliezer Greenberg, eds., *Ashes Out of Hope: Fiction by Soviet-Yiddish Writers* (New York: Schocken

Books, 1977); Shmuel Niger, *Yidishe shrayber in sovet-rusland* (Nyu York: Aroysgegebn fun Sh. Niger bukh-ḳomiṭeṭ baym alyelṭlekhn yidisher ḳulṭur-ḳongres,1958); Khone Shmeruk, Benjamin Harshav, Abraham Sutzkever, and Mendel Piekarz, eds., *A shpigl af a shteyn* (Tel Aviv: Goldene keyt, 1964); and many other volumes. Nakhman Mayzel's *Dos Yidishe shafn un der yidisher shrayber in sovetnfarband* (Nyu York: Ikuf farlag, 1959) makes two very brief mentions of Gorshman, but it is difficult to find them because she's listed in the index as Shire Gornshteyn—a sign that the indexer had never heard of her.

38. The neglect of Soviet-Yiddish writers is quite overwhelming and can hardly be overstated. While I am here discussing the particulars of Gorshman's trajectory, it should be noted that even the most important of the Soviet Yiddish writers are not well served by current scholarship or translations, even Bergelson remains greatly under-researched.

39. An interesting point of comparison with Gorshman's situation is that of Minsk poet Rokhl Boymvol. Like Gorshman, there was no particular reason Boymvol escaped notice in the Stalin era; and like Gorshman, Boymvol eventually went to Israel and carried on publishing there in Yiddish. However Boymvol was not as prolific as Gorshman, which may have affected the critical interest in her. In addition, Boymvol wrote largely about motherhood, a topic unlikely to interest mostly male critics. See Rina Lapidus, "Rakhil Baumvol (1914–2000): The Joy and Creativity of Motherhood," in *Jewish Women Writers in the Soviet Union* (New York: Routledge, 2011), 106–118.

40. Artists Trade Union of Russia, *The Register of Professional Artists of Russian Empire, USSR, Russian Emigration, Russian Federation and the Republics of Former Soviet Union (XVIII–XXI Centuries)*, http://painters.artunion.ru/e2-07-1.htm (February 2, 2013). Mendel Gorshman's Russian name was Mikhail Efimovich Gorshman.

41. Two earlier versions had been published in the Soviet Union. Neither of those is included the sections set in Palestine.

42. Forman and Fishkoff, interview, 1995.

43. Gorshman apparently meant this literally. She did not have enough money for elegant shoes to wear to her own prize ceremony.

44. Forman and Fishkoff, interview, 1995.

45. Shira Gorshman, "Vi bin ikh gekumen tsu shraybn," *On a gal* (Tel Aviv: Yisroel-bukh, 1996), 13.

46. Shira Gorshman, "Ba agnonen in shtub," *On a gal* (Tel Aviv: Yisroel-bukh, 1996), 36.

47. Chaim Beyder and Refoel Blumenfeld, "Shire Gorshman, zikhroyne levrokhe" (obituary), *Forverts*, April 13, 2001, 24.

# From Diamond Cutters to Dog Races
## *Antwerp and London in the Work of Esther Kreitman*

DAFNA CLIFFORD

Reading through the three volumes that constitute the collected works of Esther Kreitman, one is continually confronted by two questions: how is it that such a talented storyteller wrote so little? And then, after deeper reflection on the circumstances of her life, how did she manage to write anything at all?

Esther Kreitman, or more accurately, Hinde Esther Singer Kreitman, was born in Bilgoraj, a Polish *shtetl* near Lublin, in 1891, and died in London in 1954. Toward the end of her life, she wrote a story called "Di naye velt" [The New World, 1949] narrated in the voice of a newborn infant.[1] The child describes being rejected at birth by her mother and ignored by her father, and even by her grandmother, because she was a girl. Despite the author's attempt to maintain a light narrative tone, the bare facts of the matter still elicit a series of pained exclamations from the narrator at this mistreatment of the helpless little girl. Given into the care of a wet nurse with six children of her own, the new baby is taken away to live in a tumbledown shack crammed with a horde of small children and a husband who makes his poor living repairing bits and pieces in the same small room. As there is no floor space for another cot, the little guest is placed under the table, where she remains with the filth and cobwebs of the underside of the table in her eyes. The story finishes with the tiny heroine overcome with despair at the realization that there is no place for her in the "new world" into which she has been born.

The details in this story, with which Kreitman's son, Maurice Carr, was evidently familiar from his childhood, reappear more than forty years later in an article he wrote for *Commentary* magazine, entitled "My Uncle Yitzhak."[2] The irony of this title in a piece that is almost as much about his mother as his uncle, Isaac Bashevis Singer, would not have been lost on Kreitman. To this day, there appears to be only one article about her in which any mention of her more famous brothers is deliberately eschewed.[3] She would have seen in this further relegation of herself merely one more example of the unequal treatment she believed she had always received from her parents and society, compared with her brothers. "*Di naye velt*," on the surface an unassuming little tale, contains the foundation myth for Kreitman's art in its most basic and explicit form. It is about her sense of rejection by her mother, discrimination against her by her parents because she is a female, and her consequent relegation to the arid role of household drudge. Her creative strategy is to transform the suffering and bitterness of her own destiny into works of art, and in doing so, as Norich observes bracingly, "to distance herself from the limitations imposed on her own life."[4]

It was, indeed, a bitterness over which she came to exercise considerable artistic control, even if she never fully overcame it. Whatever the truth about the precise conditions in which she actually spent her early years, the legacy of that time was a nervous disposition and chronic eye trouble that culminated in the loss of one eye. She also suffered from an unusual form of epilepsy known as "partial complex seizures." These differ from the better-known grand mal and petit mal in that "they erupt out of normal behavior and are therefore not recognized by observers as attacks."[5] Janet Hadda's graphic description of the nature of these attacks in her biography of Isaac Bashevis Singer concludes with the information that the patient may have a number of seizures one after the other over several hours or even days. Moreover, it would seem that Kreitman occasionally also had other seizures, at least according to her brother's descriptions of them, which were closer to those of grand mal epilepsy. It goes without saying that in the Warsaw of the 1890s and prewar 1900s, no adequate medical care was available for her illness. Not surprisingly, perhaps, her family considered her behavior aberrant, hyperemotional, and hysterical. Maurice Carr describes how, during a visit to his relatives in New York after Kreitman's death, he fell out with Bashevis and never spoke to him again after his uncle observed offhandedly, "Your mother was crazy."[6]

Although humiliated and insulted by her family's unconcealed opinion of her mental health, she made good use of this motif in her writing. Dovid Berman, one of the protagonists of the novel *Brilyantn* [Diamonds] (1944),[7] published during the Second World War in London, says to his sister, Jeannette, "*nisht bekhinem bistu take meshuge*" (61) [It's not surprising that people think you're mad]. Later in the narrative, Jeanette's mother, Rokhl, thinks of her daughter as *aza shtik meshugas* (247), and muses to herself, *ver veyst, tsi zi iz nisht, kholile, arop fun zinen* (248). The pious interjection *kholile* "God forbid," which the religious woman would not omit, even in her most explicitly wounding thoughts, shows what Kreitman felt she was up against. The choice of name for this character, a hysterical young woman who dances wildly about the house in a mad ecstasy and confused reality with the romantic novels she absorbs in great numbers, is a sly reference both to herself and to her brother Israel Joshua, the object of her greatest envy and admiration. In his last novel, *Di mishpokhe karnovski*,[8] there is a pathetic spinster named Jeanette, a character who is hopelessly out of touch with reality and compensates for her loneliness by identifying with the heroes of the romantic novels she reads all day while tending to her scholarly, cantankerous father in his bookshop.

The subject of reading, specifically in relation to the question of who is allowed to read and who is not, is the focal point of her first book, the autobiographical novel *Der sheydim-tants* [*Danse macabre*], 1936, translated with the title *Deborah*, 1946).[9] If the extraordinary household in which Kreitman grew up is known at all to the non–Yiddish-reading public, it is usually through the translations of her brother Isaac's stories and especially of his memoir, *In My Father's Court*.[10] Enthusiasts of Yiddish letters may also be familiar with Israel Joshua's memoir, *Fun a velt vos iz nito mer* [Of a World Which Exists No More],[11] published posthumously in New York in 1946. *Deborah*, however, presents the remarkable Singer parents, Pinkhos Mendl and Basheve, perhaps more authentically. The nostalgia, pain, guilt, and idealization that characterize her brothers' reminiscences are absent from Kreitman's narrative, written as it was before the Holocaust. On the other hand, her version of Singer family life lacks the technical control of Israel Joshua's and the thematic focus of Bashevis's. Her own childhood and youth still lingered as raw experience in her mind, with the residue of the anger at her mother and jealousy of Israel Joshua still too suffocating.

According to her portrayal of her parents, Kreitman's grievance against them stems from her father's refusal to let her study and her mother's lack of support and encouragement for her daughter's ambitions to make something of herself. Paradoxically, Basheve Singer's impressive intellectual gifts had been nurtured by her own father, a rabbi renowned in his day for his intellectual acuity and spiritual stature, who had nonetheless allowed his daughter access to virtually the same education that was reserved in those days for sons.

Pinkhos Mendl, a rabbi, zealous Hasid and incorrigible mystic, blamed his wife's education for her self-possession and rationalist approach to religious as well as practical matters. Determined to avoid the mistake made by his father-in-law, Pinkhos Mendl was careful not to allow his daughter to become intellectually independent. Although Kreitman describes in *Deborah* how her heroine/counterpoint hides books on top of the oven in order to read them secretly when she has a moment to spare, she also emphasizes how very little time or strength she has to devote to the learning and self-improvement she dreams of, as she is the family drudge. Because of the contradictory association of reading with guilt and resentment as well as with the love and happiness forbidden to her, Deborah's bouts of madness are preceded by a sudden physical inability to read:

> If only she could read! But no sooner did she set eyes on a book, than a cloud of specks, like a swarm of troublesome insects, began to dart about all over the printed page, and these hovering specks would make her quite dizzy. The empty room around her would sway drunkenly, and she would have to put the book aside. And then a host of strange fancies would take possession of her mind. She could not shake them off, no matter how hard she tried.... The next day a different canker would prey on her mind. The more it festered the more she would struggle to remove it; but soon she would have to acknowledge defeat [*Deborah*, 339].

In the Singer household of Kreitman's youth, someone had to see to the running of the household while her mother lay on the sofa reading, and this task fell to Deborah/Hinde, as the only other resident female. This picture of Basheve Singer as basically indifferent to the housewife's obligation to perform certain domestic chores and, indeed, as too weak even to think seriously about taking them on, is vividly corroborated by I. J. Singer in his memoirs. In his version, too, his sister sees to the housework while his mother lies eternally on the sofa with a book in her hand, rising only to prepare the occasional inedible meal. In his account, however, the tone is neither resentful nor accusatory. He merely notes dryly that his parents would have been a perfectly suited couple if his father had been his mother, and his mother had been his father. Referring to Bashevis's comments about Kreitman's writing, Clive Sinclair locates the structural weakness in *Deborah* in the lack of any attempt "to fuse autobiographical and fictional elements; what was not autobiography was simply wish fulfillment."[12]

In an extravagant gesture of reproach to her mother when their quarrels become unendurable, Deborah agrees to an arranged marriage with a man she has never met. This event is the turning point in the novel, as it was in the author's own life. Deborah marries a Hasid who left Poland to escape conscription into the Russian army and leaves Warsaw to live with him in Antwerp. Of his mother's first novel, Carr later remarked that "The matchmaking episode was true to life."[13] That Kreitman hardly bothers to disguise the story of her own marriage in her novel is, no doubt, a sign of the recklessness that so disturbed her parents and brothers, but it is also a measure of how disastrous the marriage was. Maurice Carr writes discreetly of his father that he was a *schlemihl*.[14] Of Deborah's husband Berish, Kreitman writes that "she remained as much a stranger to her husband as when she had first set eyes upon him (although she was more and more conscious of his love for her)" (*Deborah*, 338). But although Esther left Avrom Kreitman many times, she always returned to him.

Neither the sense of indebtedness to Pinkhos Mendl, as the incarnation of the virtuous Jew that permeates the writings of Isaac Bashevis Singer, nor the obsession with Jewish history, the great tragic theme of Israel Joshua Singer, is the focal point of Kreitman's work. Curiously, her treatment of the same material is more timeless and less dated than that of her brothers, possibly because of the slightly detached tone of her writing. What is fascinating about Kreitman's take on the same historical period and personal origins is that she included all the standard elements of Yiddish fiction of the time, but the truthfulness of her portraits of female and non-Jewish characters makes her work seem both more modern and more European. Most obviously, she deals more powerfully and convincingly with intergenerational conflict between mothers and daughters, as well as with the usual tension between fathers and sons. The lure of Zionism, communism, and political activism for the disaffected youth brought up on an exclusive diet of Jewish religious texts and practice are all duly chronicled, as in the movement from the *shtetl* to the city within Poland followed by emigration to the West, although here it is Belgium and England, rather than America. The transition from scrupulous religious observance is accomplished in a sentence, as if the whole process of removing the heavy yoke of the tradition that regulates every aspect of life in a hasidic home had occurred almost inadvertently: "She had discarded her wig, her husband had removed his beard" (*Deborah*, 332). With this extraordinarily casual remark, Deborah summarizes the state of piety in her marital household. Above all, of course, the subject of madness is treated with a sensitivity, precision, and black humor that are virtually exclusive to her in Yiddish fiction, unlike, for example, the famous portrait of Mirl Hurvits in *Nokh alemen* [When All Is Said and Done],[15] where, for all Dovid Bergelson's sympathy, the heroine's self-destructive behavior is condemned as the result of weak self-discipline and moral confusion.

Kreitman's ability, in the words of S. S. Prawer, "to reproduce the texture of experience, the physical and mental together,[16] comes especially to the fore when she is demonstrating the mechanism by which protracted periods of humiliation push an eager, willing, and impressionable young person into a cycle of depression and rebellion. Having thrown herself away on a loveless marriage in order to spite her mother, Deborah then takes almost immediate exception to Antwerp. Too late, she realizes the enormity of the mistake she has made: "She had abandoned herself, gloatingly, to an *idée fixe*, that everyone, including her own mother, hated her and was anxious to get rid of her; a prey to this delusion, she had deliberately brought disaster upon herself, hoping thus to inflict pain upon others—a fantastic imaginary act of revenge on imaginary persecutors ... with what terrible results!" (*Deborah*, 332). Nevertheless, Kreitman repeats this pattern eight years later in her next novel, *Brilyantn*. In this narrative, during one particularly hefty argument between the adolescent Gitele Kornhendler and her hated stepmother, Gitele's father intervenes and says that if she doesn't like the situation at home, she is welcome to leave "*az es gefelt dir nisht, kenstu dir geyn gezunterheyt*" (*Brilyantn*, 23). This is the relevant emotional situation for Kreitman, an essential unhappiness that reappears in careful patterning throughout her work. Her maturation as an artist may be measured by the way she learned to expose the pain of rejection and incompatibility within the family with increasing humor.

In *Brilyantn*, Kreitman looks at the unraveling of the Jewish family against the backdrop of life in a modern city. Much more a proper family saga than *Deborah*, *Brilyantn* is an investigation that expands to include three generations of the Berman family as well as friends and associates. Whereas in *Deborah*, the blame for family disruption was attributed to the intractable personality of the mad daughter, here it is the eldest son, Dovid, who leaves home because of constant rows with his father. While the plot of *Brilyantn* might superficially appear to be yet another version of the trials and tribulations of *shtetl* Jews undergoing the transformations brought about by emigration and Westernization, the novel exudes a sense of easy familiarity and confidence in its portrayal of the Yiddish-speaking communities of Antwerp and London virtually unique in the literature. Antwerp is undoubtedly ideal for this purpose because of its special social structure. The area where the Jews engaged in the diamond business live and work may still be referred to as the ghetto, but anti–Semitism is not at all an issue here. On the contrary, the Jews are unstintingly voluble in their gratitude at being allowed to enjoy the peace and plenty of life in Belgium. In the single incident of overt prejudice in the text, when a trade union leader tells the militant communist Laybish that Jews are, unfortunately, not accepted as union members, the interview is conducted with impeccable courtesy, even friendliness.

With the depiction of Antwerp in *Brilyantn*, Kreitman moves far beyond the vestiges of the *émigré* novel to be found in *Deborah*. She had, of course, left Warsaw before the First World War, and had been living in London for thirty years by the time for second novel was published.[17] There is no longer any trace of homesickness for Warsaw in the part of the novel set in Antwerp, and the chapters dealing with the Bermans after their flight to London are frankly a love letter to England. Carr writes that his mother never stopped talking about her parents, Warsaw, and *di alte heym* generally.[18] Be that as it may, her literary depiction of Antwerp evolved radically over the years since her unhappiness there during the early months of her marriage and subsequent brusque departure. Dovid Berman, the scion of hasidic forebears, ever on the lookout for what he calls a *"pshore tsvishn got un eyrope"* [a compromise between God and Europe], walks around with copies of Spinoza and Darwin in his pocket. Moreover, he regularly buys two season tickets to the opera, one for the Flemish, and one for the French. Despite the apparently limited social contact they have with non–Jews, the characters easily navigate the internal complexities of Belgian society and celebrate its popular culture exuberantly.

Kreitman is able to evoke the atmosphere of Antwerp and to show how a "diamond Jew" like Gedalia Berman has the strength and endurance of the stones he works with. He is not destroyed by emigration and the inevitable decline in his fortunes. All in all, he is probably the most intriguing of Kreitman's fictional creations, and certainly the most contradictory. Having married his Rokhl for love, he proceeds to treat her with nothing but disdain, addressing her as "ox" and "cow" [*oks* and *beheyme*]. Yet when his elderly father appears unexpectedly on the doorstep of the splendid Berman London residence, Gedalia showers every attention on his parent and spares no trouble in trying to reproduce the religious environment his father was used to in his Polish *shtetl*. Far from having succumbed to the vulgar materialism of which he stands accused by his father, Gedalia reveals an artistic soul and a completely unself-conscious readiness to do whatever is required to keep the family going, including household shopping and cooking. When Rokhl becomes too ill and absorbed in her own thoughts to prepare the Passover meal, Berman turns his hand to all the necessary activities, most of which he would not previously even have been able to name. In one striking image, for instance, he is said to "examine an egg for blemishes with exactly the same attention that he devotes to studying a diamond" (*Brilyantn*, 294).

Indeed, the text abounds in beautifully arranged *tableaux vivants* of

Antwerp street life. Before dawn, the milkman sets off on his delivery rounds, and the housewives in the poorer streets sweep the pavement in front of their houses and polish brass door knockers, all the while exchanging friendly greetings in Flemish with Dovid Berman. Even from the perspective of the older generation, Antwerp is described with affection, but when the narrative turns to the younger age groups, their joyous acculturation is unequivocal. In particular, the chapters describing the Kermesse, the annual fair, succeed in recreating the smell of the streets (*khazer-shmalts*, in fact) and "all kinds of mussels and worms" (*Brilyantn*, 42), the casual drunkenness, and sexual encounters, including those of Dovid Berman and Jules Zweigenbaum, with a degree of plasticity, detail, and vividness that makes them a kind of Yiddish paraphrase of a Breughel painting.

Kreitman's great strength in this second novel is her ability to conjure up the milieu of the *brilyantn yidn*, with its intricate social psychology and technical terminology. She was, in fact, much praised for this in Yiddish literary circles from the first appearance of *Der sheydim-tants*. In a letter dated 1 January 1937, sent from Tel Aviv, the Yiddish writer Y. Papiernikov compliments her on her recent book, declaring that he agrees with the well-known contemporary Yiddish writer Yoysef Opatoshu, "*ikh halt mit Opatoshun, az ir kent shraybn.*" Opatoshu himself had written to her on 30 January 1936 to congratulate her on her achievement in *Der sheydim-tants*. Writing with uncharacteristic laconicism, Opatoshu scribbles briefly "*mayn libe Ester Kraytman, ayer bukh 'Der sheydim-tants' iz mir gefeln.*" Doubtless intending to encourage her, he says that it has some good chapters and that she is a great scholar, "*zeyer a groyse melumedes,*" but somewhat spoils the good impression by not trusting her to decipher the Hebrew word *melumedes* without putting in the vowels for her. On the other hand, it is also possible that Opatoshu, like many Jews, include the vowels to demonstrate his own competence in matters *loshn-koydeshdik*. In any case, his letter concludes with the exhortation to her to persevere with her writing—"*shraybt*!"

Who are these *brilyantn yidn* she described so successfully? Largely first and second generation *shtetl* Jews, they lived for the most part crowded together in poverty. The technical side of the business was divided among *shnayders, shlayfers,* and *klivers,* specialist cutters and polishers. Great fortunes were not the province of the technicians, but of the important merchants, and to a lesser extent, if they were lucky, of the *meklers,* the middlemen. Already a long-term London resident herself, Kreitman gives the protagonist, Gedalia Berman, important business dealings with Hatton Garden even before he moves there at the outbreak of the First World War. Kreitman has a fresh approach to her subject matter, and in a witty reversal of the usual stereotype, the pawnbroker in London is one of the few non–Jewish characters with a speaking role in the narrative. With the scene shift to London, the linguistic style changes abruptly to include many more foreign words than the odd phrase thrown in to establish setting and character in the Belgian part of the novel. She does, however, maintain a fondness for certain idiomatic expressions that she uses frequently in all her writing, such as *mentshn, vos kenen a kats dem ek nisht farbindn* [people who can't tie a bow on a cat's tail], which is also one of Bashevis's favorite terms of disparagement.

Nevertheless, as soon as the Bermans arrive in London, the text undergoes distinct stylistic changes in both dialogue and descriptive passages. First and foremost, whole sentences in English suddenly appear in the narrative. Kreitman evidently expected that her readers would either be interested in screaming newspaper headlines about current murder trials and horse-racing results, or else that they would appreciate the local color. The difficulties experienced by the refugees are enumerated with relatively sober dispassion compared with the intense personal suffering of the heroine in *Deborah*. In general, the fictional element in *Brilyantn* quickly becomes subordinate to the author's interest in describing the world she sees around her, rather than in plot and character development. Dialogue is subsumed to a passion for reportage, and the emotional states of her protagonists and the interactions among them are mostly conveyed in the voice of the omniscient narrator. On the other hand, the peculiar facial expression, dress, and demeanor of the wealthy Jews who come to meet the Belgian refugees at a London railway station in 1914 are caught with malicious accuracy, as are the indignities imposed on the refugees by the unfamiliarity of their new surroundings. With undisguised glee, Kreitman catches the particularly English mixture of amateurism and goodwill that sometimes cancel each other out, but reserves her most acid comments for the refugees themselves:

> The little tables, as if by their own accord, filled up with people from the same social background. At one small table sat several young people, talking non-stop about the loftiest matters for days at a time before, during, and after meals. Shakespeare never left that table for a minute, Bernard Shaw, Ibsen, Heine, Goethe, Homer, Rembrandt, Michelangelo, the intellectuals discussed every conceivable subject; and loudly too. They were experts in everything—fine art, music, literature... [*Brilyantn*, 218].

What Kreitman especially deserves to be better known for are her piquant Yiddish vignettes of London life. For example, Gedalia Berman's first visit to Hatton Garden takes place in a classic urban landscape of horse-drawn carriage, pea-soup fog, and the ubiquitous black soot of the years before the Clean Air Act. One landlady, a former immigrant herself, is now so well acculturated in Britain that she fries kippers for her lodger's breakfast. In addition, despite frequent interjections about the injustices of the reigning social system, the text includes passages expressing genuine surprise at the British worker and his serene lack of interest in work. In one lovely scene, a group of navvies gather round an improvised coal fire, preferring a desultory chat about the weather to repairing the road. The foreman—and this is obviously what really impresses the narrator—remarks to the only eager worker *"vilst arbetn, arbet"* [if you want to work, work] (*Brilyantn*, 211). Themes relating to English social history are woven into the account of Jewish refugees who, along with women, are entering the mainstream national economy because of wartime manpower shortages. Women bus conductors, who appeared in London during the First World War for the first time, make their debut here in Yiddish narrative prose. For the same reason, the recently arrived refugees are in demand for employment in their areas of professional competence, especially tailoring, sewing uniforms, and boot making for the army. *Der khoyv legabe king un kantry* [one's duty to king and country] (236), inspires an atmosphere of liberation in the capital:

> Everywhere in the munitions factories, on the trams, omnibuses, and even the trains, women were working.... Even the "Soho-types," pick-pockets, and "Aldgate boys" had to take women's power into account, and had stopped laughing at the policewomen.... Jewish girls too had found out that there was demand for secretaries, and that one could learn shorthand and typing on a six-month course.... Their mamas wanted to make brains out of them, not factory hands [236].

The beau monde of 1914–1915, the officers and other ranks with their girls, throng the side streets of Soho, and London literary society has its headquarters in a favorite café. "This café was in a little street where were sold glazed clay pots from which thousands of years ago, all sorts of pharaohs and other Caesars drank spiced wine; where in nearly every other shop window all kinds of Egyptian, Roman, and Greek gods were displayed for sale, and where Chinese gods with fat paunches smiled down at the passers-by" (248). Such old curiosity shops, despite their distinctively London flavor, strongly recall the amazing junk shop in I. J. Singer's early story *"Altshtot."*[19]

English coloring, place names, cultural institutions, and language are a richly integral part of Kreitman's work. Rokhl Berman and her daughter, Jeannette, go to Bournemouth for Rokhl's health. Whitechapel Road, with its shops, houses, and poor inhabitants, is described at length. Soldiers on leave sing "It's a Long, Long Way to Tipperary" in Hyde Park. At Speaker's Corner, a nationalist exhorts his listeners to "Remember Nelson!" while a pacifist cries, "Down with the warmongers!" and the suffragettes chorus, "Mrs. Pankhurst here too! Hear! Hear! Good old Mrs. Pankhurst!" (283–84), in English in the text. Significantly, the disintegration of the Berman family is attributed to the character flaws of its individual members, among which obstinacy and intolerance are paramount, rather than to the malign influence of English example. After years of bitter family quarrels over his failure to earn a living, in a last, desperate bid for self-respect and economic independence, Dovid Berman takes the king's shilling and volunteers to serve the war effort as a frontline soldier. The narrative ends with Jeannette more manic, pretentious, and unstable than ever. In 1918, Gedalia Berman, now a widower, returns to Antwerp, in order to realize his plan to marry Gitele, his son's discarded mistress and mother of his grandchild, in a quasi-incestuous union that echoes that of Jacob and Dinah Ashkenazi in I. J. Singer's novel *The Brothers Ashkenazi*.[20]

The long road to assimilation that winds unsteadily through *Brilyantn* cuts a straighter swathe through the fourteen stories in the collection published as *Yikhes* (1949). Many of the pieces in this volume are slight, but Kreitman's treatment of theme remains strong. What lends an air of subtlety to the transition from tradition to modernity, from Warsaw to London is the emphasis on individual psychology in Kreitman's depiction of a wide range of characters. In the story "Dogs," she shows an impressive grasp of betting procedures and jargon, rattling off dialogue including such expressions as *di eynshilingdike* and *di bookies* mixed with imagery chosen from more traditional sources, *me khapt di tsaytungen vi matse-vaser* [the newspapers went like hotcakes]. The story is a study of a compulsive gambler called Tom whose inability to control his obsession with dog races humiliates his wife and forces the family into permanent poverty. Themes taken from her own life recur in various guises in Kreitman's work. Among these, the most prevalent are women who suffer from their husband's inability to support their families, women who attract general opprobrium at their own weddings because of their inappropriate behavior, and deeply fraught mother-daughter relations. In addition, the stories are strikingly full of injustice and inequality between siblings. "Yikhes," the centerpiece of the collection, is about the bitterness of a young woman who resents the imbalance in love, support, and approval between herself and her sister. The discrepancy in parental love is highlighted in the contrast between their weddings. One is celebrated in grand style, because the parents are pleased with the match with a distinguished scholar. The other daughter, who makes a poor choice of husband, marries without the attendance of any of her close relatives.

Variations on the theme of emotional rejection of females in Kreitman's work include mothers who rebuff their daughters but who are themselves ignored and demeaned by their husbands. Reb Meirl, in the short story of that name, forgets that his wife is in the room even when she is standing there next to him.[21] Strong women do exist in her narratives, but their presence is used to underline another form of injustice, namely that, like Toybe in the story "Yikhes," they are not paid for their household work. In "Zeygers" [Clocks], a charming tale set in London during the Blitz, a mother murmurs a prayer to God to protect her *shlekht kind* [bad child] (*Yikhes*, 68). English is used extensively in this text not only to show the encroachment of the language into Yiddish-speaking homes but presumably because no Yiddish equivalent could convey the exact nuance Kreitman wanted. The "bad daughter," who prefers to remain in her "room," translated parenthetically as *shtub*, wishes "good night and good luck" before her mother descends for another night into the bomb shelter in the basement of a church, where local women knit away the hours waiting for the all-clear siren. This intimate family portrait includes domestic details relating to the process of acculturation of the immigrant community. Bella, the daughter of *di mises djaykobs*, is an assiduous follower of the BBC broadcasts guiding and encouraging the nation through the war, especially favoring morale-building programs, such as the one instructing listeners on how to do their morning exercises.

In her description of the undramatic events of ordinary life, in which she shows characters who are not obviously exceptional, Kreitman alters our way of appraising the so-called commonplace. Turning her own melodramatic tendencies to good effect is only one of her techniques. In fact, she excels generally in revealing feeling and states of mind in people who would otherwise be almost invisible. The essence of her writing is that it attempts, as Jeremy Ahearne writes in another context, "to affirm the resilience and inventiveness of 'ordinary men and women' against the analyses which present them as entirely informed or crushed by the economic and cultural apparatuses which set the terms of social life."[22] Moreover, Kreitman's contribution to Yiddish literature and culture is more varied than her relatively small output might suggest. From a series of letters in the YIVO archives,[23] it is evident that she was, perhaps somewhat surprisingly, considered the only one in London who could be expected to provide material about the English Jews fighting in the Spanish Civil War for the Museum of the Jewish Fighter in Spain, set up in Paris in 1937. Unfortunately, there are no letters from her, but the letter-writing conventions[24] of the time indicate the range of subjects covered and the degree of closeness of individual correspondents. There are virtually no letters in the collection that do not touch upon the *modus operandi* of the small Yiddish journals around the world in which Kreitman's novels were serialized or where her stories were printed, though not always for immediate payment.

Although she continued to work for most of the war, by 1945 she could no longer concentrate on her writing. As she confesses to Moyshe Schulstein, with whom she conducted a warm and candid correspondence, she is too *zatshmelyet* [stunned] by what has happened to the Jews in Poland. Schulstein answers her on 24 October 1945 from Paris:

> *Du darfst shraybn un shraybn mayn tayere. Ver den volstu gevolt zol shraybn? Efsher vilstu dos iberlozn far di, vos kumen nisht? Mir zenen azoy veynik gebibn in Eyrope az mir zoln zikh kenen farginen dos fargenign fun shvagn.*
>
> [You must write and write, my dear. Who, do you think should write then? Perhaps you want to leave it for those who will not come after us? Too few of us remain in Europe for us to allow ourselves to keep silent.]

Conventional wisdom about Kreitman, inasmuch as such a thing can be said to exist at all, has tended to concur with Clive Sinclair that "the same tradition that nurtured her brothers, that gave them the intellectual and moral fortitude to reject it, simply smothered Esther."[25] In a slightly more giving vein, Bashevis said of her, "She did not write as well as I. J. Singer, but I do not know of a single woman in Yiddish literature who wrote better than she did."[26] Both of these views are doubtless correct as far as they go, but do not take into account the inherent obstacle to wider diffusion of her work presented by the very nature of her subjects. Antwerp and London were not part of mainstream Yiddish literary or scholarly interest during her lifetime, and that situation has not altered appreciably since her death. Recognition is long overdue of her contribution to the dissection of community dynamics in the closed hasidic world she understood so well.[27] She wrote about power, its abuse, and those systematically excluded from taking an active part in the narrative of their own lives. She gave moving and powerful expression to the need for the recognition of the dignity of women, while maintaining a strong emotional attachment to the society she criticized so feelingly.

## Notes

This essay was originally published as Dafna Clifford, "From Diamond Cutters to Dog Races: Antwerp and London in the Work of Esther Kreitman," *Prooftexts* 23:3 (2003): 320–337. Indiana University Press kindly gave permission to reprint the essay.

1. Esther Kreitman, "Di naye velt," in *Yikhes* (London: Narod Press, 1949).
2. See Maurice Carr, "My Uncle Yitzhak," *Commentary* 94: 6 (December 1992): 25–32.
3. Faith Jones, "Esther Kreitman: Renewed Recognition of Her Writing," *Canadian Jewish Outlook* 38: 2 (March/April 2000): 17–18.

4. Anita Norich, "The Family Singer and Autobiographical Imagination," *Prooftexts* 10:1 (January 1990): 93.

5. Janet Hadda, *Isaac Bashevis Singer: A Life* (Oxford: Oxford University Press, 1997), 43. Hadda's study combines the freshness and excitement of her personal contact with Singer himself and members of his close entourage, with the perspectives of a practicing psychoanalyst and literary critic. She considers in depth the personalities and destinies of generations of his forbears as well as those of his two siblings, who were also Yiddish writers. The material that Hadda presents is one of the most valuable resources currently available in the study of Kreitman's life and works.

6. Carr, "My Uncle Yitzhak," 26.

7. Esther Kreitman, *Brilyantn* (London: W. & G. Foyle, 1944). All translations from this novel are my own.

8. I. J. Singer, *Di mishpokhe karnovski* (Nyu york: Matones, 1943).

9. Esther Kreitman, *Der sheydim-tants [Danse macabre]*, first published in Warsaw (1936) and in London (1946) by Virago Press in the English translation by Maurice Carr, under the name of its eponymous heroine, *Deborah*.

10. I. B. Singer, *In My Father's Court* (New York: Farrar, Straus and Giroux, 1962).

11. I. J. Singer, *Fun a velt vos iz nito mer* (Nyu york: Matones, 1946).

12. Clive Sinclair, *The Brothers Singer* (London: Allison and Busby, 1983), 51.

13. Ibid., quoting Maurice Carr, 39.

14. Carr, "My Uncle Yitzhak," 30.

15. Dovid Bergelson, *Nokh alemen* (Vilna: Kletzkin, 1913).

16. S. S. Prawer, "The First Family of Yiddish," *Times Literary Supplement* 29 April 1983, 420.

17. From 1936, Kreitman was closely involved in the marketing of her books. In his compendious volume *Yiddish Culture in Britain* (Frankfurt am Main: Peter Lang, 1990), 383, Leonard Prager notes that "in the early days she sold her novels from her home address, 56 Lordship Park, N 16." Many of the letters therefore have to do with the practical difficulties involved in posting copies of her books abroad, given that neither she nor the potential bookseller could usually afford the postage. She also persisted in trying to communicate with writers who interested her, even when they had no demonstrable connection with her own world of Yiddish letters. Having published George Bernard Shaw's *Intelligent Woman's Guide to Socialism and Capitalism* in Yiddish in Warsaw in 1930, she sent him a copy of her translation and was rewarded with a letter in which he says that he is returning the book to her as he can't read a word of it, and, in any case, he never accepts unsolicited manuscripts. Nonetheless, he does suggest helpfully that she get in touch with Victor Gollancz, the most important Jewish publisher in London, "especially if your manuscript has a left-wing tendency." Stefan Sweig, also true to form, writes on 30 June 1939, from a London address, urging her not to lose heart in the face of the prevailing indifference among English publishers to books describing a Jewish milieu, "*weil gerade in den letzten Jahren zuviel davon erschienen ist und merkwuerdigerweise gerade die Juden unter den Lesern und Kaeufern von Buecher* [sic] *mit juedischen Problemen nichts mehr hoeren wollen nachdem sie den ganzen Tag genoetigt sind, daran zu denken.*" What, one wonders, did she make of that?

18. Carr, "My Uncle Yitzhak," 26.

19. I. J. Singer, "Altshtot," in *Antologye fun der yidisher proze in poyln tvishn beyde velt-milkhomes*, ed. A. Zeitlin and J. J. Trunk (Nyu york: CYCO, 1946).

20. I. J. Singer, *Di brider ashkenazi* (Warsaw: Brzoza, 1936; New York: Maks N. Mayzil, 1937).

21. Kreitman, "Reb Meirl," in *Yikhes*.

22. Jeremy Ahearne, *Michel de Certeau: Interpretation and Its Other* (Cambridge: Polity Press, 1995), quoted in Andrew Klevan, *Disclosure of the Everyday: Undramatic Achievement in Narrative Film* (Trowbridge, Wiltshire, 2000), 6.

23. Kreitman archive, YIVO, New York, I am grateful to Yeshaya Metal, who, as public service librarian at YIVO, photocopied the Kreitman archive for me.

24. No letters from before 1934 appear to have been included in the archival collection. The first, dating from February of that year, is a typed communication from *Dos fraye vort*, a Yiddish weekly edited by Dr. I. Steinberg from 151 Whitechapel Road, notifying Mrs. Kreitman that her story "Dzhek" was printed that day and that it was very good. Steinberg asks her to write something for the paper, specifying that he would like *bilder fun yidishn London* [pictures of Jewish London] and that it should be something more than just a single, isolated episode or random event. On March 12, 1934, he invites her to a meeting to discuss ways of increasing the circulation of *Dos fraye vort*. On November 5, 1935, Hayyim Brzoza of the Brzoza Publishing House writes her from Warsaw that he has placed notices about her book in *Haynt*, *Moment*, and *Literarishe bleter*. Furthermore, he is about to set sail for America, and assures her that he will give her warmest greetings to her brother, in the singular, therefore meaning Israel Joshua, who is mentioned again in a letter written two days later, when Brzoza promises to print her book on the same quality paper as her brother's book. Moreover, he is going to print her novel under the name *Dvoyrele* at the same time as her brother's latest work. There is also a copy of the publishing agreement, dated June 3, 1935, in which Hayyim Brzoza undertakes to print eight hundred copies of *Dvoyele* and to send five hundred of them to Kreitman. By April 17, 1937, in the last letter of the series, the novel is referred to as *Sheydim-tants*.

25. Sinclair, *The Brothers Singer*, 40.

26. I. B. Singer, quoted in Hadda, *Isaac Bashevis Singer: A Life*, 136.

27. In the section on Esther Kreitman in her recent book (Ruth R. Wisse, *The Modern Jewish Canon: A Journey Through Language and Culture* [New York: The Free Press, 2000], Wisse notes that Kreitman's early emigration removed her from the environment in which other women were writing and publishing in Yiddish. She speculates about "what kind of writer Kreitman might have become had she spent the formative 1920s in Warsaw, as did her brothers, instead of in London, where the Yiddish writers formed only a tiny enclave within Anglo-Jewish literature." This perspective suggests a wholly dampening effect on Kreitman's art, but it has to be balanced against the stimulation afforded by her experiences in London and Antwerp. Between 1936, the year in which her first novel was published and her death in 1954, Kreitman was in continuous correspondence with Yiddish writers in Europe, Israel, and North and South America. However, the cumulative effects of the physical and mental illness from which she suffered, intensified by poverty and an unhappy marriage, made her a difficult person to deal with. Some of the letters to her in YIVO archive involve heated exchanges about imagined slights and insults, about which her correspondents try and sooth her injured feelings. Even had she remained in Warsaw, she might therefore have been unable to sustain supportive friendships with fellow writers.

# To Dive into the Self
## *The* Svive *of Blume Lempel*

ELLEN CASSEDY *and*
YERMIYAHU AHRON TAUB

> One dives into the self—
> and behold—a svive.
> Malka Heifetz Tussman
> in a letter to Blume Lempel[1]

The word *svive* means environment or atmosphere and connotes fellowship and connection, suggesting a place where one belongs, a home. Over the course of her life, Blume Lempel (1907–1999) experienced multiple dislocations and upheavals.[2] As her friend and colleague, the Yiddish poet Malka Heifetz Tussman (1893–1987), eloquently expresses, the home or *svive* that Lempel came to inhabit was a portable one of her own making. The unconventional personal milieu that she created for herself was grounded in a fierce sense of self and included a distinctive and multi-faceted role within the world of postwar Yiddish letters. Out of this self-made *svive* came a profoundly original oeuvre, distinct in its unusually bold and diverse set of subjects centered on women's experiences, its radically experimental narrative strategy, and its dazzlingly poetic prose style.

Born in Galicia, Lempel spent her early adulthood in Paris and fled to safety in New York just before the outbreak of World War II. Once settled in the United States, she was one of a very few writers who continued writing in Yiddish into the 1990s. Although the small and shrinking Yiddish literary world had its limitations and frustrations, in many ways it served her well. Her short stories, which are the focus of this essay, were published in Yiddish periodicals on several continents. Many of them were collected in two volumes: *A rege fun emes* [A Moment of Truth], published by I.L. Peretz Publishing House (Tel Aviv) in 1981; and *Balade fun a kholem* [Ballad of a Dream], published by Israel Book Publishing House (Tel Aviv) in 1986. She received numerous prizes, and despite the shattering of Yiddish culture during her lifetime, she maintained long-lasting and mutually sustaining literary friendships with other Yiddish writers around the world.

Women's lives and women's points of view are central to the great majority of Lempel's short stories. Her work not only plumbs her own life, which spans a wide range of places, eras, and cultures, but it also imagines a remarkably wide range of characters and occurrences far outside her own experience. Although the subject of the Holocaust is deeply embedded in her work, she does not confine herself to this theme. Some stories explore the consciousness of characters with seemingly ordinary lives. Others describe characters living on society's margins, including troubled refugees and survivors. A number of stories deal with subjects that many other writers of her time considered taboo, such as abortion, incest, and rape. Lempel's fiction not only opens a window into past eras of twentieth-century Jewish life, especially women's lives, but also provides acute and enduring insights into the human condition.

Lempel's work is characterized by lyrical powers of empathy, sharp and often satirical observations, and an unorthodox approach to narrative that she perfected in defiance of literary convention. Mirroring the uprooted situations of her protagonists, many of Lempel's stories lack orderly plot progression, transitions, conventional pacing, and clearly delineated endings. Full of restless flashbacks and unsettling imagery, they roam from place to place and from era to era, moving between present and past, Old World and New, and dream and reality. The fractured, disrupted, and unresolved narratives convey with stark clarity the enduring effects of the forces of historical upheaval on the individual.

## *From Galicia to New York*

Lempel experienced those forces first-hand. Born Blume Leye Pfeffer during the first decade of the twentieth century, she was raised in what she described as "a white-washed room by the banks of a river that had no name."[3] Her birthplace was Khorostkiv, known as Chorostków in Polish and Khorostkiv in Yiddish, in Galicia; it was a region of shifting nationality. The town belonged to the Austro-Hungarian Empire before World War I, to Poland between the two wars, and to Soviet Ukraine after World War II.

Blume's father, Abramshe, was a butcher, "a simple person" with a black beard—so strong, she recalled, that "he could carry a calf on his shoulders from the slaughterhouse to the butcher shop," a distance of nearly a mile. Her mother, Pesye, was blond and blue-eyed, with translucent pale skin. She read novels, subscribed to a newspaper from the nearby city of Lviv, and was considered cultured by the townspeople.[4] Although Blume's older brother, Yisroel (1899–1944),[5] received a formal education, her own schooling was sporadic. For a few years she attended a religious school for girls and a Hebrew folk school, and at times a tutor came to the house, but as she later recalled in an interview with the Yiddish scholar and journalist Itzik Gottesman, "my father believed that all a girl needed to know was how to cook a pot of food, sew a patch, and milk a cow."[6]

"In Poland I didn't write at all," she remembered. "I only dreamed of writing."[7] As she dreamed, she stored up observations that would later appear in her work. Her childhood self remained accessible to her all her life as "the girl who was, the girl whose tides ebb and flow on my sandy shores to this day."[8] Characters based on girlhood memories appear in vivid relief. Aunt Rokhl sits at her machine "sewing bridal garments for other women's weddings. She sews and sews, until white begins to show in her jet-black braids."[9] Zosye, "the bookkeeper's pampered daughter, is riding her bicycle, her windblown hair as blond as the furniture in her father's parlor."[10] A blind beggar sits in the market square "on a low stool with her petticoat touching the ground, a brass cross dangling on her bosom, and a string of beads in her hand."[11] Here is "Reyzye Paltiels with her gold tooth, the tooth through which she filtered her rippling octaves. Reyzye was the only girl in town who could sing 'Aida' with all the frills and trills, like a real diva."[12] And here is Grandma, "a little woman of few words. She scurried about the house as quiet as a hen, even pecking like a chicken at her meager crusts of bread, which she hid in the pocket of her velvet underskirt."[13]

For a time, the world of Blume's childhood seemed safe and secure. As the first-person narrator in "Even the Heavens Tell Lies" puts it:

> Enclosed within my father's words and my mother's tears, the world came to me as a completed picture, and I accepted its preordained colors and nuances as part of the natural order. Just as the sun rose every morning behind our barn and set every evening behind the tree that my father pointed out with his finger, so I stayed within the picture frame, walking in the light, avoiding the shadows, never straying beyond the borders. The house where I was born and grew up was my personal fortress.... When my father shut the gate every evening, I was certain that nothing bad would befall me.[14]

When Blume was twelve years old, however, the comforting sense of order began to crumble. Her mother died of a heart ailment, and her father quickly remarried. Blume was pressed into service as a housekeeper and nursemaid for the new couple and their young child. Her brother Yisroel, eight years her senior, who had become involved in militant communist activity,[15] was caught and imprisoned, and then escaped and went into hiding. Lempel remembered the police arriving at the house in the middle of the night to search for him, ordering everyone out of bed and stabbing into the mattresses while cursing the "filthy Jews."[16]

Yisroel fled to France, and in 1929, at twenty-two years old, Blume, too, left Khorostkiv, intending to become a pioneer in Palestine. On the way, she stopped off in Paris to visit her brother, who had settled in the Jewish immigrant neighborhood of Belleville. Captivated by the city, Blume abandoned her pioneer plans. She attended night school and read books in French and Yiddish. Here, against all odds, her dream of becoming a writer began to take shape. Her brother urged her to abandon her literary ambitions—only an educated person could write, he maintained. And her living situation made writing difficult. As she recalled:

> We all lived in one room—my brother, his wife, their two children and I. My bed was shoved under their bed. The children slept together in another bed. A table, a few chairs—it was horrible. Not a place where you wanted to write or where you could write. There was nowhere to put down a piece of paper.[17]

Nonetheless, she did write, mostly love poems and short stories, in Yiddish, and she began to show her work to others. On one occasion, a Yiddish journalist

> invited me to his home so that I could read him my stories—he couldn't decipher my handwriting. After I read a page or two, he proposed to me. He was on his way to Argentina, and if I agreed to marry him, he said, we could help each other. This incident set back my belief in a writing career.[18]

To make a living, she first found employment sewing handbags and then took a job in the fur industry, where she met Lemel (Leon) Lempel (1911–1986). The couple married and two children, Paul (1935– ) and Yolande (1937– ), were born. The Paris years were exceptionally happy ones for Lempel. Once again she took mental notes that later found a place in her fiction. "When one is young in Paris," she wrote years later in her story "The Victim,"

> the city seethes and storms every month of the year. Storms rage on the street, in the house, on the boulevards and in the alleys, and especially in Montmartre—storms of artists, athletes, and professional idlers, revolutionaries, fascists, and partisans for every imaginable cause.[19]

In 1939, as Hitler's power grew, Leon became convinced that the family needed to escape from Europe. He managed to secure immigration papers from the American consulate, and the Lempels sailed for New York. Before they left, Blume burned all of her writings.[20]

## New York Debut

Blume loved her adopted city and intended to return there.[21] In the end, however, the Lempels settled permanently in New York, first in an apartment in Brooklyn and later, in 1950, in a house in Long Beach, on Long Island, not far from the sea. Here, once again Lempel began to write, and, for the first time, to publish. Her first published story, "Muter un tokhter" [Mother and Daughter], appeared in *Der tog*, a Yiddish daily newspaper, in 1943 under the pseudonym Rokhl Halperin, her aunt's name.[22] A few years later, Lempel forged a connection with the *Morgn frayhayt*, a Communist Yiddish daily. The editor, Paul (Peysekh) Novick (1891–1989), presented her with the Yiddish typewriter that she used for the rest of her life.[23] In 1947, the paper serialized *Tsvishn tsvey veltn* [Between Two Worlds], her sweeping, panoramic novel of Paris between the world wars. In this early work, many of Lempel's powers of characterization and description are on display, along with her interest in taboo themes. Amid a vast cast of characters and multiple plot lines, a romance between a Jewish woman and a Nazi takes center stage. Flashbacks into the *shtetl* past punctuate an evocation of the increasingly anti–Semitic terrain of the 1930s, along with finely tuned observations of Parisian high society and compassionate portraits of the marginal and downtrodden. Some of this material Lempel later reworked in short stories. In 1954, the Philosophical Library, a small New York press, published the novel in English translation as *Storm Over Paris,* under the name Blanche Lempel.

After this promising literary debut, however, Lempel's writing career went dormant. Her responsibilities increased at home when her aunt Rokhl moved in with the family, a third child, Steven (1945– ), was born, and Leon's young nephew, Michael Klahr (1937–1998), who had been orphaned during the Holocaust, joined the family in 1946. As before, although she did not write during this period, Lempel gathered impressions for later use. In "The Death of My Aunt," she draws upon Rokhl's life story, illuminating her psyche from one angle after another in a typically disjointed narrative that jumps from modern-day New York City to prewar Poland, from bedtime story to passionate romance, from old age confusion to girlhood dreams. Although the narrator's failure to reach the old woman's bedside in time to ease her passing causes her great anguish, Lempel grants her aunt a kind of immortality by bringing her to life on the page. The story ends on a transcendent note:

> I freed the imprisoned soul, which then rose, fluttering softly, and wafted away to the exalted place for which it was destined, leaving behind the body as a gift for Mother Earth.[24]

"Cousin Claude" tells the story of the adopted orphan nephew from the point of view of the family's young daughter, who watches from the pier as

> at the end of the gangplank, a little boy appeared with a black beret pulled over his ears. He wore short pants and no socks. Instead of a shirt, a torn sweater covered his narrow shoulders, from which a brown backpack hung open and empty.[25]

Claude's adjustment to his new country, with its new language, a new family, and a new school proves difficult. He and the narrator grow increasingly awkward with each other as they reach adolescence. After leaving home, he becomes an accomplished artist. Years later, the narrator is moved to learn that just as his arrival is forever sealed into her consciousness, so, too, he has never forgotten his first glimpse of her from the deck of the ship. The bond between the two is fragile but unbroken:

> Her two thin braids tied with red ribbons and her two frightened eyes took up more than half of her face. She was looking at a ship in the port, and her ribbons were reaching out toward it. They came close, very close, but they never quite touched the ship.[26]

Even more than her family responsibilities, however, it was the devastating news from across the Atlantic that brought Lempel's literary output to a standstill. Back in Khorostkiv, she learned that her father's wife and their young son had been seized and killed by the Nazis, after which her father had set fire to the family home and hanged himself. On the day before liberation, her beloved brother Yisroel, who had joined the French Resistance, was arrested and shot in Lyon, leaving a wife and two sons.[27] Describing her state of mind during this period, Lempel later said, "When our great Holocaust with its vast cruelty was revealed ... I was catapulted into a deep despair. The past was a graveyard; the future without meaning."[28] Increasingly despondent, she again began to burn her work. "I needed to write," she recalled, "but I couldn't. I didn't have time to write. It was a strain to write. And for whom should I write? Tomorrow another Hitler would come, or another Stalin, and burn everything, lay everything to waste."[29]

Finally she stopped writing altogether. "I sat paralyzed within a self-imposed prison," she said later. "The years went by, many desolate, fruitless years."[30]

## Rebirth from the Ashes

Then came a turning point. A friend who wrote Yiddish fiction, Reyzl Glass Fenster (1909–?), suggested that she dedicate herself to writing about the cataclysmic destruction that was consuming her. The unexpected proposal "opened a psychological door," Lempel said later:

> Before my eyes stood my annihilated people, encircled by flames, without an exit. I accompanied them in the sealed train cars, trudged with them on the death marches. Their ashes were reborn before me. I saw them in their humiliation, in their dejection, and I felt I must speak for those who could no longer speak, feel for those who could no longer feel, immerse myself in their unlived lives, their sorrows, their joys, their struggle and their death.[31]

Lempel had found her calling. Just as she spoke of the dead rising up from the ashes within her imagination, so her own work—burned more than once by her own hand—experienced a rebirth. In the wake of catastrophe, she had come to understand, "we, the survivors, must write the reality, paint it, immortalize it in stone, engrave it in people's minds—so that such a disaster will never again be possible."[32]

Having left Europe on the eve of World War II, Lempel had not personally experienced the terror of the roundups, mass executions, and concentration camps. Accordingly, while her work was to provide glimpses of these horrors, they would not be her central subject. Alexander Spiegelblatt, a writer and editor associated with *Di goldene keyt* [The Golden Chain], the preeminent Yiddish literary journal published in Tel Aviv, wrote:

> She does not attempt to record the horrors of the Holocaust years in the manner of those Jewish writers who witnessed those events firsthand. Blume Lempel needed to find other dimensions for her encounter with the Holocaust.... In her stories, the gruesome deeds of the murderers are almost always mentioned only incidentally. It is not about them that she wants to tell.[33]

As Spiegelblatt understood, Lempel's subject was not primarily the annihilation but its aftermath, not the annihilated themselves but "the survivors, the broken people who attempt after the war to establish a new link to life, and who through it all remain broken."[34] Lempel shared in the bereavement, loss, and profound trauma that afflicted these "broken people" and devoted herself to expressing the experience of displacement, flight, and adaptation, and the special burden of remembrance and retribution, grief and guilt, carried by the living.

Lempel started writing once again. As she embraced her new literary mission and undertook to reinvent herself as a writer, her creativity began to flow.

It was a while before she began to seek publication, however. "My writing seemed to me a personal matter," she said later, "a mute exchange of feelings, from them to me and from me to them, the slaughtered, the burned, those suffocated in mass graves, the sacred martyrs of human evil." It was another friend from the world of Yiddish letters who persuaded her to share her new work. 'One fine day I happened to run into the poet Chaim Plotkin [1910–1996]," she later recalled. "It was he who took me by the hand and led me back onto the literary path."[35] In the late 1960s, her poems in English and Yiddish began appearing regularly in small English-language literary publications and in Yiddish journals. Over the next two-and-a-half decades, her short stories were published in Yiddish publications around the world, including *Di zikh, Naye tsaytung,* and *Yisroel shtime* in Tel Aviv, as well as the New York publications *Zayn, Tsukunft, Undzer eygn vort, Yidishe kultur, Forverts, Yidisher kemfer,* and *Algemayner dzhurnal,* and *Khezhbn* (Los Angeles), *Letste nayes* (Australia), *Undzer veg* (Paris), and *Dorem afrike* (Johannesburg, South Africa).

## *"I like to start at the end..."*

The short stories that constitute the core of Lempel's oeuvre are characterized by boldly unconventional narrative techniques, a daring range of subject matter, and a highly original style. Lempel's narratives do not follow traditional formulae; instead, they seem raw and fractured. Some resemble collages, whose carefully arranged fragments reverberate against one another. Many make use of modernist or surreal techniques such as jarring juxtapositions, dream symbolism, flashbacks, free association, and frequent crossings of the border between fantasy and reality. "I like to start at the end and work backward," Lempel said. "Or start in the middle. Or begin with some strange subject and then change the character entirely and start all over again."[36] Adding to the turmoil, she sometimes switches tenses or even changes from third-person to first-person narration in the middle of a passage.

Lempel's narrative strategy was ideally suited to the task she set for herself. The drama in her stories consists not in how the plot moves from point A to point B, but rather in how she forces the reader to experience jaggedness and disjunction. "The narrative element is not central in Blume Lempel's stories," Spiegelblatt wrote. "For her, what is essential is the pondering, the seeking, the getting to the bottom of things, the constant drive to attain 'the moment of truth.'"[37]

Thus, the boundaries between the real and the unreal can be fragile and permeable. Vast cosmic landscapes rub up against domestic scenes. Deep abysses, birds of prey, bags of bones, and acts of suicide keep company with cups of coffee at the kitchen table and cozy Sabbath meals. Multiple time periods co-exist on a single page. As Yonia Fain (1914– ), an artist and Yiddish writer in New York, comments in a 1986 letter to Lempel:

> Throughout the stories, time undulates, not measured or divided into past, present, and future. As long as we are alive, we carry all times within ourselves simultaneously. And who knows for sure what is fact and what is dream? And who can say with certainty how much arrival there is in going away, and how much going away in arriving? ... These and many other questions are woven in a natural way into your work.[38]

In the story "Yosemite Park," for example, as the narrator steps off a tour bus in front of the awe-inspiring Bridal Veil waterfall with her camera and binoculars, she is overtaken by a memory from the Old World: "From underneath the ruins of time a bride stepped forth, a refined young woman with flaming red hair." As the narrator explains, "Sometimes a present-day experience becomes entangled with a long-forgotten event that once affected me. When past and present meet, the flash of their collision lights up the vanished time in full color." In the folkloric tale that unwinds, complete with its own bridal veil, the sound of a shofar resounding in the hills of the Old World mingles with the honking of the bus driver's horn.[39]

Abrupt, dizzying shifts from the everyday to the celestial characterize "My Friend Ben," a story of a flirtation between two middle-aged protagonists. One morning, Ben drops in on the narrator and sits down at the piano and

> sound merges with sound, spiraling into a storm of emotions. The music ferments and overflows into my bloodstream and I absorb it into my being.
> Inside her solitary cell, the Persona forgets about her chains and rises on fantasy-wings. Clad in a tunic threaded with gold, she dances wantonly before an ethereal vision who swells, takes form, and becomes flesh and blood, his narrow hips swaying before her in velvet and silk. Limbs outstretched, he dances with menacing drama. The music froths and foams. Snorting bulls thunder into the arena.[40]

A moment later, the two friends are seated at the kitchen table with coffee and strawberries, and the narrator is attempting, not entirely successfully, to tamp down Ben's smoldering passion by asking after his pets.

Not only Lempel's narrative strategies but her range of subjects, settings, and characters is extraordinary for Yiddish fiction. Many of her stories open a window on the Old World, yet for Lempel, her Eastern European roots are not the primary focus but rather one landscape among others. Along with deeply felt accounts drawing upon her Galician childhood, she vividly evokes a wide array of other times and places and the life experiences of people—

especially women—with very different life experiences, offering insight into aspects of Jewish experience and women's experience close to our time.

In several stories set in prewar or wartime Paris, for example, we meet women who are depicted with unfailing empathy even as they stray outside the norms of their Jewish community. In "Her Last Dance," Simone Bonmarchais, the Jewish mistress of the chief of police, navigates the glittering, perilous world of Nazi-occupied Paris with a primal insistence on survival—until the moment when she drops her carefully constructed mask.[41] In "A Moment of Truth," Lily Brown marries a sadistic Nazi doctor, then denounces him.[42] And in "The Rendezvous," the protagonist stands trial for murdering her Nazi lover.[43] All of these stories display Lempel's gift for portraying women armed with few resources who are forced to make life-altering decisions.

Contemporary American settings characterize many of Lempel's stories, though here, too, she often reaches far beyond her own experience to explore the lives and psyches of women very different from herself. "The Bag Lady of Seventh Avenue" takes us to the ladies' room in New York City's Penn Station, where the narrator, a suburban train commuter, forms a bond with a homeless woman. Characteristically for Lempel, it is an empathic but unusual bond: "I found myself thinking of bizarre gifts for her," the narrator says: "feathers from the bird that hides its head in the sand, bouquets of desert flowers, miniature seashells, each shell a tower reaching for the heavens."[44] "Pachysandra" introduces us to the anguish of a deeply religious African American woman who tells a lie to save a life and then waits for God to punish her for her sin.[45] "A Little Song for a Jewish Soul" takes us to a Long Island synagogue, where the narrator is surprised when a young gentile folksinger shows up to say *kaddish* for his deceased girlfriend. Typical of Lempel, the narrator is haunted by the suffering of the unknown young woman who has died. "As night fell, her sad Jewish eyes looked out at me from the dark windowpanes."[46] She cannot rest until she has imagined the young woman's life and death and paid her own tribute to her memory.

Sometimes faced with impossible choices, Lempel's women largely resist grand, heroic action. Yet neither are they defined by passivity. Rather, they engage in a restless struggle with memory, shifts in consciousness, and thorny choices. They struggle to confront the madness of history and sometimes to fend off the oncoming madness of the self. In "Even the Heavens Tell Lies," a woman who has been deeply scarred by the Holocaust tells us:

> When I crossed the ocean, I carried with me the habit of speaking to the shadows, and it became my way of life.... I live on the sidelines, like a stranger in my own world. I live with the snakes and scorpions, with the black leeches in my brain, in my blood.[47]

This protagonist finds consolation in naming the flowers in her garden after friends and family members lost in the Holocaust. The protagonist in "Waiting for the Ragman," too, wrestles with the burden of a lost world:

> After all these years, I'm still lugging the past behind me—the house, the street, the village, the town.... I take up my load of memories and begin to cast off the yesterdays that weigh so heavily on the present.... I'm still waiting for the ragman to come, to take the heavy pack from my bowed shoulders and toss it into his wagon."[48]

Often, Lempel's women are propelled by their encounter with powerful natural forces, which can be feverish and erotically tinged or full of horror. A common image is of a horrifying void. "The Power of a Melody," for example, opens with a wasteland:

> Far, far away, in the regions of the world where all is encased in ice, there is no marking of time. No seasons, no renewal and no withering away—only a vast, enshrouded world where frost and snow and primeval winds go unrecorded in any chronology. There, where all paths come to an end, the footsteps of eternity make no imprint in the void.[49]

In "En Route to Divorce," Phyllis Shtromvaser leaves her husband. Of Phyllis, Lempel writes, "she went into his arms as if into a castle, and she went out as if from a prison." Phyllis is on her way to Reno when she looks out the window of the plane "into a world of sheer oblivion, a world untouched by human hands, unchanged since the six days of creation.... All around stretched a blue transparent void." Phyllis has been looking forward to the freedom promised by the women's liberation movement. Yet now the emptiness outside the window seems like a mirror of her own unraveling life. The "world without doors, without locks, fences, or borders" seems less like a welcome opportunity to express herself than a terrifying void.[50]

As this passage and other occasional references make clear, Lempel was aware of the women's movement of the 1970s and sympathized with women, like Phyllis, whose lives were transformed by it. Because women's lives, women's consciousness, and women's strong sense of self were so central to Lempel's work, one could characterize her as a feminist writer. Yet most likely the label would have made her uncomfortable. There is no evidence that she associated herself with the feminist movement, and it appears that she arrived at her woman-centered literary perspective on her own.

Although the natural world is a source of terror to Phyllis, other protagonists find there a welcome dwelling-place, often in unusual ways. They form profound bonds with cats, with a monkey in the zoo, even, on more than one occasion, with an insect. In "Neighbors Over the Fence," for example, a cautious cross-cultural friendship between a Jewish woman and her widowed Italian neighbor blossoms when Mrs. Zagretti knocks on Betty's door to discuss the death of a housefly she has come to treasure as a soulmate. She feels for the fly, the last of its kind, and senses—correctly—that Betty will understand.[51]

In "Even the Heavens Tell Lies," the protagonist hides in the forest to escape persecution during the Holocaust, becoming one with her environment:

> The darkness that had once frightened me became my protector, sheltering and hiding me and revealing my secret to no one. The wind mingled my scent with the smells of the forest. The rain washed away my footprints. I followed the animals and kept away from people. The wind brought me the smell of berries, a dead bird, the rotten carcass of a half-devoured creature. Under cover of night, propelled by hunger, I pursued these scents. The forest took me in without tears, without words, receiving me with an impersonal indifference, a naked, frank, and savage truth. For the worm in the grass, the rabbit in the thicket, the tree, the star, the nuts, and for me: one and the same truth.[52]

The theme of hiding, particularly in the natural world, recurs frequently in Lempel's work. Perhaps it sprang in part from her sense of having a hidden identity as a Yiddish writer disguised as a suburban housewife, a woman apart with an inner life all her own. Central to that inner life, and that of many of her protagonists, is the enduring trauma of the Holocaust. Sudden glimpses of the *khurbn* are an important element of many stories. "Yosemite Park," for example, unexpectedly ends with the tears of the Old World bride ascending

> into the clouds, where they mingled with the tears of all the incinerated brides that rose with the smoke from the chimneys of Auschwitz. Thus joined together, they drifted over sea and shore, suspended in the veil of eternity.[53]

"A Snowstorm in Summerland," which describes a married couple's road trip to Florida, also ends with Holocaust imagery—the onus of history carried by the survivors—as the two settle into their room at the Holiday Inn:

> The bed is made up with white pillows and woolen blankets. Under the pink lampshade on the night table, two candies are waiting to gladden the heart. Reluctant to enjoy all these good things, I stand at the window. I see the distant forest from which there was no escape. I see the faces of loved ones and the faces of strangers. I want to bow my head to the ground and beg forgiveness from the bones that were denied a proper burial.[54]

For Lempel, the Holocaust was sometimes obscured, as if behind a cloud, but never distant, a primal event whose devastating impact could never be escaped.

Like several other stories, "A Snowstorm in Summerland" offers a wry portrait of married life, with the grumpy, practical-minded husband serving as the foil for the wife, who is absorbed in her dreams, memories, and imagination. Many other stories, however, explore far more daring terrain.

"The Debt," for example, opens with an image of a young woman lying "face up on the operating table. Her upper body was firmly secured with plastic straps, her knees up, her bare legs spread."[55] Lempel's unflinching description of the abortion blends straightforward description with poetic and deeply personal imagery to powerful effect. In the words of the Yiddish scholar Sheva Zucker, Lempel "is always ... pulling back the veil that covers hidden sexual desires, unsaid words, and unrealized dreams...."[56]

"The Little Red Umbrella," for example, introduces us to the erotic imaginings of a middle-aged woman as she anticipates a blind date:

> The rendezvous with the poet came like a jolt from the very heart of life, awakening the butterflies from their lethargic dozing. White silk wings hovered in the air. The studio apartment, which a moment before had been cold and dark, brightened with an ethereal light. The walls began to sing again.[57]

In "Even the Heavens Tell Lies," we share the erotic sensations of a breast-feeding mother:

> When the sky is blue, the gladiolus laughs with my cousin Gitl's sensuous mirth. Her pink goblet with its red rim reminds me of Gitl's half-parted lips, always eager to be fruitful and multiply. At twenty she was already the mother of two sets of twins. Whenever she was nursing a child, her mind would flood with intoxicating notions. She kept her grey eyes lowered, ashamed to raise them lest her thoughts be revealed. Perhaps she asked God to forgive her for feeling such hot lust for her husband.[58]

And in "The Death of My Aunt," an elderly woman calls upon her religious faith as a shield to protect her from her erotic fantasies:

> "Rokhele, darling, open the window, I'm dying for you!" His red-hot eyes burn holes in the windowpane. I cover my face. I don't want to look at him. I don't want to see the net he's spreading for me. I grab the holy book lying on the table. All the virtues of my mother and father come to my aid. And even though I don't turn around, I feel that he's still there—so sad, so forlorn.[59]

In its cool precision and its audacious subject matter, "Oedipus in Brooklyn" surpasses all of these stories. Having been turned down by Avrom Sutzkever, the editor of *Di goldene keyt*, who considered it too shocking to publish,[60] the story appeared for the first and only time in the collection *A rege fun emes*. Lempel retells the ancient legend from the point of view of a contemporary Jewish mother who becomes involved in a sexual relationship with her blind son. Her matter-of-fact narration vibrates against an eroticized natural landscape as the two move inexorably toward their doom. In Lempel's hands, the plot is thoroughly believable. As one critic put it, "the quiet, understated tone she employs even in describing shocking scenes"[61] binds our sympathies to the characters even as they step into forbidden territory:

> Danny opened the door of his mother's room, felt his way to her side, and patted the blanket. He had dreamed that a man was in bed with her....
> Frightened, Sylvia encircled him with her bare arms and tried to soothe him.[62]

Along with her experimentation with time and tense and her unconventional subject matter, Lempel's poetic use of language, too, was distinctive. For all of her rule-breaking as a writer, her words, in her stories no less than in her poems, were chosen with painstaking precision. Many readers commented on the poetic power of her prose. Her fellow Yiddish writer Malka Heifetz Tussman wrote, "I don't see the word 'poem' on top of ["My Friend Ben"]. Nonetheless, I see your story as a poem—maybe four or five poems.... Yes, you are a poet."[63] Another colleague, Chava Rosenfarb (1923–2011), agreed. "I admire the beauty and austerity of your language," she wrote. "You are so economical, careful not to waste a single word."[64]

Examples of Lempel's poetic prose abound. In "Waiting for the Ragman," for example, a characteristic passage is packed with dense, idiosyncratic imagery, as the narrator engages playfully and emotionally with an animated natural world:

> The young Passover sun liked to play with the colored glasses that stood on the sideboard in honor of the holiday.... As I lifted my hands in the air, the beams rained down over my head like a golden raisin wine that began to ferment inside me. Unheard tones resounded from the deep. The sun recorded these unwritten notes, and I myself composed the lyrics: promise-words for tomorrow, for later, for next Passover when I would be a child again.[65]

In "The Debt," the young woman lying in bed in the abortion clinic refuses a pill for her pain and instead escapes into "the green meadow of her youth," where Lempel creates a dazzling blend of splendor and menace, as well as beauty and violence:

> [T]he girl playing with pieces of broken glass ... finds a miraculous splinter that reveals a wondrous world of red and green and blue. Strings of beads, green pearls. The nettles sparkle like seven suns and the stones in the road are golden coins.
> The blond peasant boy from across the river sticks out his foot to trip her and snatches away the magic shard.... The boy has smashed the magic glass, stomped it to pieces.[66]

With their exceptionally wide range of subject matter, locales, characters, and eras, Lempel's stories never feel repetitive; the specific drama of each protagonist is always compelling. Yet with their recurring narrative elements, themes, and style, they cohere into a unified whole. Chava Rosenfarb wrote that she experienced *Balade fun a kholem*, Lempel's second collection, not as a series of separate stories but as "a kind of original, sweeping novel that encompasses the life of our generation."⁶⁷

## The Svive of Yiddish Letters

For Lempel, writing in Yiddish was a carefully considered choice that brought both costs and benefits. Although spoken in Jewish communities around the world, Yiddish was never the dominant language of any country. After World War II, the Yiddish literary world lost its European core and was dispersed on several continents. Over the course of Lempel's career, it grew increasingly marginal, with a smaller and smaller readership. Yet the Yiddish literary world also worked to Lempel's advantage and helped her talent to flower.

Although she spoke English at home with her husband and children and published some of her poems in that language, Lempel felt the Yiddish language to be an essential part of her literary vocation. "Yiddish is in my bones," she wrote. And furthermore, as she notes:

> when I hear my mother's "Oy!" I lift my eyes to heaven and hear God answering me in Yiddish. The birds, real and imagined, speak Yiddish, and the wind at my window speaks Yiddish—because I speak Yiddish, think Yiddish. My father and mother, my sisters and brothers, my murdered people seek revenge in Yiddish.⁶⁸

Writing in Yiddish enabled Lempel to preserve her connection to her perished people as a whole. It was also a means of sustaining her particular tie to her adored brother. In Paris before the war, Yisroel had discouraged her from writing. Now, from beyond the grave, he functioned as her muse:

> My older brother, who watches over me, tells me what to write in Yiddish. I can't very well tell him not to speak in the language of exile.... Now he watches over me, directing my stories from beyond the grave with a sure touch. This is how it was. This is what happened. So must it be recorded.... You survived to bring back those who were annihilated. You must speak in their tongue, point with their fingers....⁶⁹

Like others who wrote in *mame-loshn*, the Jewish "mother tongue," after World War II, Lempel often felt isolated. "I have no one," she told Gottesman in 1985.⁷⁰ She asserted that she rarely participated in Yiddish cultural activities in New York, citing the difficulty of traveling to the city from her home in suburban Long Island. It seems likely, however, that the distance was more than a matter of geography and that her isolation was, at least in part, her own choice. "She isolated herself," her granddaughter recalled. "When you're that deep into your internal world—she could have been in Times Square and she would have been isolated."[71] Thus, although her work itself was characterized by unusually intimate portraits of human consciousness, as a person Lempel remained private, even somewhat reclusive. As she put it:

> To this day, I hide my literary existence under my apron. If you asked my neighbors about my writing, they'd look at you and think you were crazy. Even people who have lived here for 25 years don't know.
> Writing for me is a private matter, separate even from my own family. I don't like to write when my husband is in the house. It presses on me—I'm not free. Free is only when I know I'm alone. Then I'm free to write what I want.[72]

In her personal life, Lempel kept her literary identity separate from those around her. Writing in Yiddish meant that her children, her neighbors, mainstream writers, and the public at large were unable to read her work. As a writer, she frequently concealed the details of her personal life. For instance, her correspondence includes letters from several editors pressing for information about who she was and where she had come from. To reviewers, too, her identity was often a mystery. Some speculated incorrectly that she had survived a concentration camp or that she was a young woman.

Lempel's carefully guarded persona, it appears, freed her to "dive into the self." Isolation, in part a matter of circumstance and in part deliberately sought, afforded her the liberty to pursue her own idiosyncratic vision, her *dybbuk*.[73] Deeply faithful to her own path, she did not feel part of a literary "school" or trend in any language. Asked about writers who had shaped her, Lempel could not cite any. "I feel I don't borrow from anyone," she said.[74] In response to a query from Spiegelblatt, who wondered about her artistic, philosophical, or psychological influences, she mentioned Sigmund Freud and the philosophers Spinoza and Bergson, but only in passing. "I've taken a look here and there," she said, "but not more than that."[75] Critics sometimes drew parallels between Lempel and other writers, such as Dovid Bergelson and Lamed Shapiro,[76] but all agreed that she was difficult to categorize and that reading her work was an experience like none other.

Yet, although Lempel profited from isolation when it suited her, in many ways the Yiddish literary world was a true *svive* that offered her support, fame, and companionship. In 1970, as her mature creative period began to develop, she was fortunate to win the support of Abraham Sutzkever, who was renowned in the world of Yiddish letters as a poet, as a cultural hero for rescuing treasured Jewish texts in the Vilna Ghetto during World War II, and as the founder and editor of the leading Yiddish literary journal, *Di goldene keyt*, which was published in Tel Aviv. Sutzkever's encouragement and guidance were profoundly important to many postwar Yiddish writers. He and Lempel corresponded for many years. After receiving her first letter of acceptance from *Di goldene keyt*, Lempel recalled:

> I still remember how surprised I was at the warm answer. I remember even that it was a cold, cloudy winter day, but for me spring gardens burst into the most beautiful bloom.... The energy that I had conserved in my youth came out from under my apron.[77]

While another editor might have tried to rein Lempel in, smooth out her rough edges, or tame her bold choices, Sutzkever never did. Instead, he was deeply affirming of her individuality:

> You have your own words, your own observations, your own madness, which you scoop out from within yourself like shovelfuls of hot coals.... Your talent is not an ordinary one—of that I am sure.[78]

"I write not for my readers but for myself," Lempel responded. "I write for the dybbuk that is seeking a transformation through me."[79] Sutzkever wrote back without delay. "For that dybbuk must you write!" he urged. "You must write for yourself and for me and for that chosen reader whom every true talent brings into being through the magnetic power of the work itself. Sincerely and with much belief in you...."[80]

From the very beginning, Sutzkever held Lempel to the highest standards:

> I detect in your creativity a burning impatience. And because your very real talent interests me, allow me to say this: you must be more patient, must deliberate over every line.
> Your prose is in essence poetic, and therefore it must be pure and careful, like pure poetry.... There are writers—and perhaps great ones at that—for whom the power of the writing is in the prose itself. For you, the power of the prose is in the poetry. Every drop is as important as the rushing current.
> I write this to you because I believe strongly in your talent. But to talent must be added another talent—the talent to steer the talent.[81]

He also urged her to "keep writing in Yiddish. You have a Yiddish heart, not an English one."[82]

Sutzkever's encouragement played a central role in sustaining Lempel's commitment to her writing. As her career progressed, she found other literary figures who also provided significant support. In 1979, she hired Binem Heller (1908–1998), a distinguished Yiddish poet in Tel Aviv, to shepherd *A rege fun emes* to publication. Over a period of two years, Heller in Tel Aviv and Lempel in Long Beach, New York collaborated. Heller negotiated terms with Peretz Publishing House in Tel Aviv and suggested the stories that should and should not be included in the collection. He urged Lempel to include even her most daring stories, ones that had been rejected, including "Oedipus in Brooklyn," which Sutzkever himself had turned down. He suggested new titles for several stories, proofread the manuscript, and oversaw the cover design, printing, and binding. His regular expressions of admiration no doubt provided important sustenance to Lempel. "You are one of the best and most original storytellers in Yiddish," he wrote in a letter.[83]

Lempel's *Balade fun a kholem* entailed a similar collaboration, this time with the Tel Aviv poet, I.Z. Shargel (1905–?), who served as a volunteer adviser and editor to Israel Book Publishing House. Once again, a warm correspondence developed, as Shargel read every story, suggested word changes, and sent Lempel his own books for her comments.

Both volumes received glowing reviews in Yiddish newspapers and magazines in New York, Israel, and Australia. "The sound and the style were new and surprising for Yiddish literature," wrote Alexander Spiegelblatt. "One immediately recognized an expert literary talent ... that conveyed Jewish fate in the years after the Holocaust ... in a unique and deeply personal manner...."[84] "A consummate master of poetic narrative," wrote Yonah Berkman in Melbourne, Australia.[85] "An original and remarkable writer ... a great achievement," wrote Eliahu Shulman in New York's *Forverts*.[86]

An impressive string of literary prizes followed. Lempel received the YKUF Prize for Literature awarded by the *Yiddisher kultur farband* (Jewish Culture Association, New York, 1981); the I. J. Segal Prize awarded by the Jewish Public Library in Montreal (1983); the Osher Schuchinski Prize awarded by the Atran Center of the Congress for Jewish Culture (New York, 1985); and the Chaim Zhitlowsky Prize for Literature (New York, 1989).

From the 1960s through the early 1990s, when she was in her late eighties, tirelessly and successfully Lempel submitted her work to publications all over the world. Often a single story was published more than once. In addition, Lempel's arrangement with the publishers of her two books required her to handle the distribution and the orders herself.[87] Although she claimed to despise this aspect of the writing life,[88] she devoted herself to the task with great seriousness. Within her personal papers, lists of addresses, orders, and correspondence with critics and fans throughout the world are carefully filed. Some were renowned Yiddish literary figures; others were simply individual readers.

As a result of these efforts, her work became known throughout the Yiddish literary network, and other writers began to seek her out. Much like the regulars at the cafés of Vilna or Warsaw in earlier eras, the diminishing ranks of Yiddish writers in the second half of the twentieth century sustained one another. On occasion, Lempel attended meetings of Yiddish writers in New York. For some years, she met regularly with the New York writer Nosn Brusilov (1892–1977). She vacationed in Florida with members of the Montreal Yiddish community. On occasion, she met face-to-face with individual Yiddish writers in New York, Montreal, Paris, and Israel. And she conducted a voluminous correspondence. The warmth and liveliness of the letters she received, preserved within her papers, make clear that she invested considerable energy in her epistolary friendships. A particularly intimate friend and frequent correspondent was Chava Rosenfarb, of Montreal, who introduced herself to Lempel through a letter in 1982. "I've been reading your work in *Di Goldene keyt*," she wrote. "I feel very close to your way of writing, to your style. Who are you?"[89] The two women exchanged regular letters until 1990, critiquing each other's work, revealing their struggles with writing and publishing, sharing their views of other writers, and offering news about their families. Malka Heifetz Tussman, who lived in Berkeley, California, also forged a warm and supportive friendship with Lempel despite the many miles separating the pair.

Old age did not slow Lempel's creative output. When her husband Leon died in 1986, she wrote in a poem that she felt "like a mummy/ wrapped in tears/ silent" with "nothing more to tell/ nothing more to say."[90] In fact, however, she had not finished telling. "Pastorale," a story published in 1988, is a poignant depiction of an elderly woman with an ailing husband, a precise evocation of the grumpy exchanges at the breakfast table, the husband's methodical raking of autumn leaves, the understated but dreaded approach of mortality:

> Now I'm knitting a sweater for my husband. I'm in no hurry. An unbidden voice whispers that I should take my time. As long as I knit, I hold the Angel of Death at bay.[91]

Lempel's stories and poems continued to be published in the 1990s. On October 20, 1999, she died of cardiac arrest in her Long Beach home at the age of 93. An article in the *Forverts* stated:

> With the passing of Blume Lempel, Yiddish literature has lost one of its most remarkable women writers, whose number today is already terribly meager.... An empty spot has opened in the galaxy of talented women Yiddish writers. Alas, it is not clear who can take her place.[92]

In a 1931 letter, the celebrated Yiddish writer Chaim Grade (1910–1982) noted how sad it was that Lempel's talent had flowered so late, at a moment in history when few could read her words in the original. But perhaps, he said, this was inevitable. Lempel belonged to her time and no other:

> It is enough to make one weep, that you appeared in our literature at a time when so few good readers remained. But perhaps it could not have been otherwise. Perhaps your magical, sweet, lyrical tone could not have come into being any earlier than our autumn years.... You are a modern writer in the most beautiful sense....[93]

Although she sometimes claimed to write only for herself, and although she was committed to the language of her murdered people, Lempel sometimes expressed frustration with her situation as a Yiddish writer. She yearned for a larger readership. World languages like English, she wrote in a letter to the Yiddish poet Osher Jaime Schuchinski, "have readers young and old. Everything gets reviewed. Among us, on the other hand, there is talk only of Sholem Aleichem, Mendele [Moykher Sforim], and [I.L.] Peretz. No one knows about the living writers."[94]

Lempel made repeated attempts to reach out to English-language readers, with mixed success. Having seen her novel published by a small publisher in 1954, Lempel unsuccessfully submitted the manuscript to a major literary agency in the 1970s, hoping for republication. Some of her poetry was published in English. She hired translators to translate some of her short stories, a few of which were published in the Jewish magazines *Bridges* and *Midstream*. She tried, without success, to find a publisher for an English-language collection of her stories. Late in her life, her story "Correspondents" appeared in English in *Found Treasures*, the groundbreaking English-language anthology of Yiddish women writers published in 1994. No doubt she would have been gratified to know of other English-language anthologies published in the years since her death, including *Beautiful as the Moon, Radiant as the Stars: Jewish Women in Yiddish Stories* (2003); *Arguing with the Storm: Stories by Yiddish Women Writers* (2008); and *The Exile Book of Yiddish Women Writers* (2013).[95] In years to come, as new generations of readers encounter Lempel's work, whether in the original Yiddish or in translation, they will have the opportunity to step into her *svive*. As they do, they will be richly rewarded.

## Notes

1. Letter to Blume Lempel from Malka Heifetz Tussman (1893–1987), January 23, 1975, BL's papers, courtesy of Paul Lempel.

2. Lempel sometimes stated her date of birth as 1910. Her obituary in the *Forverts* and her son Paul assert it was 1907. "Blume Lempl [sic], a modernistishe yidishe shray-

berin," by Sore-Rokhl Schaechter, *Forverts* November 5, 1999. Interview with Paul Lempel, Eastchester, New York, July 26, 2008.

3. One-page autobiography written for acceptance of the Chaim Zhitlowsky Foundation award, dated December 17, 1989, BL's personal papers.

4. From "*En Commemoration*, for the children and children's children of Israel and Chaye Pfefer," BL's personal papers.

5. Dates provided by Robert Pfeffer, Yisroel Pfeffer's son, email communication to the authors, January 20, 2012.

6. Videotaped interview with Blume Lempel conducted by Dr. Itzik Gottesman, Long Beach, NY, 1985. Courtesy of Itzik Gottesman.

7. Ibid.

8. Blume Lempel, "Dos vartn afn shmatilnik" [Waiting for the Ragman], in *Balade fun a kholem* (Tel Aviv: Farlag I. L. Peretz, 1981), 153. All translations are by Ellen Cassedy and Yermiyahu Ahron Taub and will appear in their forthcoming collection.

9. Blume Lempel, "Der toyt fun mayn mume" [The Death of My Aunt], in Blume Lempel, *A rege fun emes* (Tel Aviv: Farlag yisroel bukh, 1986), 48. All translations are by Ellen Cassedy and Yermiyahu Ahron Taub and will appear in their forthcoming collection.

10. Lempel, "Images on a Blank Canvas," in *Rege*, 70.

11. Lempel, "Waiting for the Ragman," in *Balade*, 151.

12. Lempel, "Even the Heavens Tell Lies," in *Rege*, 23.

13. Lempel, "Waiting for the Ragman," in *Balade*, 157.

14. Lempel, "Even the Heavens Tell Lies," in *Rege*, 20.

15. Pfeffer, e-mail, 2012.

16. Troim Katz Handler, interview, Long Beach, New York, June 7, 1992. Courtesy of Troim Katz Handler. Also see Troim Katz Handler, "Blume Lempel," in *Jewish Women's Archive: A Comprehensive Historical Encyclopedia*, Jewish Women's Archive, March 1, 2009, http://jwa.org/encyclopedia/article/lempel-blume.

17. Gottesman, interview, 1985.

18. Ibid.

19. Lempel, "The Victim," in *Balade*, 63.

20. Gottesman, interview, 1985.

21. Ibid.

22. *Der tog*, 12/2–3/43. Cited in Berl Kagan, *Leksikon fun yidishe shraybers* (Nyu york: Ra'aya Elman-Cohen, 1986). Also cited in notes, March 9, 1982, BL's personal papers.

23. Gottesman, interview, 1985.

24. Lempel, "The Death of My Aunt," in *Rege*, 55.

25. Lempel, "Cousin Claude," *Rege*, in 194.

26. Ibid., 201.

27. Gottesman, interview, 1985.

28. Acceptance speech, YKUF Prize, May 31, 1981, BL's personal papers. YKUF, the *Yidisher kultur farband* [Jewish Culture Association] was founded in Paris in 1937, then later moved to New York and operated until 2006.

29. Gottesman, interview, 1985.

30. Acceptance speech, YKUF Prize, May 31, 1981.

31. Ibid.

32. Ibid.

33. Alexander Spiegelblatt, "Durkh a shparune," review, *Di goldene keyt* 106 (1981): 196.

34. Ibid., 198.
35. Acceptance speech, YKUF Prize, May 31, 1981. Plotkin was a New York poet born in Poland.
36. Gottesman, interview, 1985.
37. Spiegelblatt, "Durkh a shparune," 196.
38. Letter from Yoni Fain to BL, July 27, 1986, BL's personal papers.
39. Lempel, "Yosemite Park," in *Balade*, 249 and 248.
40. Lempel, "My Friend Ben," in *Rege*, 150.
41. Lempel, "Her Last Dance," in *Balade*, 135–147.
42. Lempel, "A Moment of Truth," in *Rege*, 115–130.
43. Lempel, "The Rendezvous," in *Balade*, 11–22.
44. Lempel, "The Bag Lady of Seventh Avenue," in *Balade*, 91.
45. Lempel, "Pachysandra," in *Rege*, 29–36.
46. Lempel, "A Little Song for a Jewish Soul," in *Balade*, 172.
47. Lempel, "Even the Heavens Tell Lies," in *Rege*, 26.
48. Lempel, "Waiting for the Ragman," in *Balade*, 148.
49. Lempel, "The Power of a Melody," in *Rege*, 242.
50. Lempel, "En Route to Divorce," in *Balade*, 102, 94, and 96.
51. Lempel, "Neighbors Over the Fence," in *Rege*, 101–108.
52. Lempel, "Even the Heavens Tell Lies," in *Rege*, 22.
53. Lempel, "Yosemite Park," in *Balade*, 254.
54. Lempel, "A Snowstorm in Summerland," in *Balade*, 212.
55. Lempel, "The Debt," in *Rege*, 109.
56. Sore-Rokhl Schaechter, obituary, *Forverts*, November 5, 1999.
57. Lempel, "The Little Red Umbrella," in *Balade*, 125.
58. Lempel, "Even the Heavens Tell Lies," in *Rege*, 27.
59. Lempel, "The Death of My Aunt," in *Rege*, 53.
60. Sutzkever's letter to BL, August 22, 1971, stated: "It is a very strong story—perhaps too sensational, too shocking in its theme," BL's personal papers.
61. Hertz Kalles (1905–1988), remarks at I.J. Segal Prize ceremony, October 1983, in Montreal, BL's personal papers.
62. Lempel, "Oedipus in Brooklyn," in *Rege*, 174.
63. Letter from Malka Heifetz Tussman, May 26, 1973, BL's personal papers.
64. Letter from Chava Rosenfarb, May 16, 1986, BL's personal papers.
65. Lempel, "Waiting for the Ragman," in *Balade*, 160.
66. Lempel, "The Debt," in *Rege*, 114.
67. Letter from Chava Rosenfarb, 1986.
68. Blume Lempel, "The Fate of the Yiddish Writer," *Yidishe kultur* 48 (November-December 1986): 20.
69. Ibid.
70. Gottesman, interview, 1985.
71. Interview with Vivien Krieger, New York, NY, July, 25, 2008.
72. Gottesman, interview, 1985.
73. In the Jewish tradition, a *dybbuk* is the wandering soul of a dead person residing within the body of a living individual.
74. Handler, *Jewish Women's Archive*, 1992.
75. Letter to Spiegelblatt, October 27, 1982, BL's personal papers.
76. Kalles, remarks, 1983.
77. Letter to Spiegelblatt, BL's personal papers.

78. Sutzkever to BL May 4, 1974, BL's personal papers.
79. BL to Sutzkever, May 29, 1974, BL's personal papers.
80. Sutzkever to BL, June 7, 1974, BL's personal papers.
81. Sutzkever to BL, June 16, 1971, BL's personal papers.
82. Sutzkever to BL, June 24, 1977, BL's personal papers.
83. Heller to BL, November 1, 1979, BL's personal papers.
84. Letter to Spiegelblatt, BL's personal papers.
85. Yonah Berkman, "*A Rege fun emes*," review, *Letste nayes* (July 5, 1981): 8.
86. Eliahu Shulman, "A merkvirdike zamlung dertseylungen," review, *Forverts*, March 22, 1981, 11.
87. Lempel, "The Fate of the Yiddish Writer," 22.
88. Gottesman, interview, 1985.
89. Rosenfarb to BL, September 22, 1982, BL's personal papers.
90. Blume Lempel, "Widowhood," *Di tsukunft* 93: 1–2 (Jan/Feb 1987): 22.
91. Blume Lempel, "Pastorale," *Di tsukunft* 95: 4 (Nov/Dec 1990): 36.
92. Mordkhe Bauman, "Blume Lempel, di shrayberin un der mentsh," *Forverts*, December 3, 1999.
93. Letter from Chaim Grade, August 3, 1981, BL's personal papers.
94. Letter from Osher Schuchinsky, April 12, 1987, quoting BL's letter to him, February 16–17, 1987, BL's personal papers.
95. Frieda Forman, Ethel Raicus, Sarah Silberstein Swartz, and Margie Wolf, *Found Treasures: Stories by Yiddish Women Writers* (Toronto: Second Story Press, 1994); Sandra Bark, *Beautiful as the Moon, Radiant as the Stars: Jewish Women in Yiddish Stories* (New York: Warner Books, 2003); Rhea Tregebov, *Arguing with the Storm: Stories by Yiddish Women Writers* (New York: Feminist Press, 2008); and Frieda Johles Forman and Sam Blatt, *The Exile Book of Yiddish Women Writers* (Holstein, Ontario: Exile Editions, 2013).

# "Of all the men I am the most manly"
## Aspects of Gender in the Poetry of Khane Levin

JOANNA LISEK

Of all the men I am the most manly.—Khane Levin—*Tsushteyer*[1]

Yiddish literature, by its very egalitarian nature, was quicker than Hebrew literature to accept women's voices. This was due in part to women's weaker facility with Hebrew and to the fact that, at the beginning of the twentieth century, Yiddish poetry departed from collective subjectivity in favor of individualism, psychologism, and lyricism.[2] In addition, Yiddish poetry was more predisposed to expressions of intimate experiences than Hebrew literature, which was dominated by national-historical bombasticism. Also, Yiddish literature more readily accepted the expression of female eroticism and sexuality to the extent that it was liberated from the traditional model of femininity forged by religion and folklore. For example, in New York, the center of modern Yiddish literature, poets such as Celia Dropkin and Anna Margolin were redefining the concepts of love, death, and gender.[3] Yet the courageous, innovative female voice did not only come from poetry written in the United States. As a result of the Russian Revolution, subversive women's poetry, including works that tackled gender issues, existed for a while in Europe too.

The most eminent proponent of the blossoming creativity of female Jews affected by the Russian revolution was the Kharkov-based writer, communist, and feminist Khane Levin.[4] She was the first woman in Soviet Russia to broach the problems of modern women's identity in her work. Unfortunately, even today, her artistic accomplishments are only known within a small circle of scholars.[5] Furthermore, not only was she on the margins of the androcentric canon of Yiddish literature, she has also been excluded from the current reclaimed canon of Yiddish women writers.[6] In this chapter, I would like to correct that situation. Since Levin's life constitutes an important context for reading her texts, I start with a brief biography.[7]

Khane Levin was born in Ekaterinoslav (currently Dnipropetrovsk, Ukraine) on May 3, 1900, the third of seven children. Before the revolution, around 48,000 Jews lived in Ekaterinoslav, which was at the time an important center of Jewish culture. Khane's father, Shaya Levin, who died in 1941, was a gravedigger. He is remembered by his family as a very devout Jew. Scant information is available on Khane's mother, Sofia, née Grynberg, who died either in 1954 or 1953. Khane attended Russian and Jewish schools, and before the revolution, she worked as a dressmaker, as well as in a shop. She began writing poems at an early age. First, she wrote in Russian, and then, persuaded by Leyb Naydus, she started to write in Yiddish. The timing suggests that she must already have been writing in 1915 when Naydus was in Ekaterinoslav. This pattern was a regular occurrence. Female poets would often begin by writing in languages other than Yiddish, and only following the intervention of a Yiddishist, a writer occupying a place in their lives, such as a brother, husband, or lover, did they decide to develop their talent in Yiddish.

The opportunity to be printed, meanwhile, often came from their connections with editors and publishers.[8] Reading the short autobiographies contained in Ezra Korman's *Yidishe dikhterins*, one is struck by the role the women ascribe to their "patrons" who introduced them to Yiddish poetry.[9] If one studies their private lives, it becomes clear how much relations with men influenced the chance of being published. Female writers, not treated as equal partners in the male-run presses, were usually pushed into the *froyen-vinkl* [women's corner]; they could expect protectionism more than actual recognition of the merits and significance of their work. Levin's own début came in 1918 on the pages of the St. Petersburg publication *Folks blat*. Her poems were also included by Peretz Markish in his anthology *Trep*, published in Ekaterinoslav in 1921. During the civil war in Russia, she joined the Red Army, where, according to her family, she was the partner of the commissar, who died in 1922. This relationship produced a child who may have died very early or who may have been still-born. After the revolution, she studied at the Teaching Seminary and briefly worked in Jewish schools. Between the wars, Levin lived in Kharkov, which at the time was an important site of Yiddish culture.

She was given an apartment at *Slovo* [Word], a house for writers where Leib Kvitko and Perets Markish also lodged. Levin became friendly with Kvitko and Markish, as well as with Itzik Feffer. They were all regular guests at her home. Her life partner was the famous actor Adolf Vinogradsky, who went by the stage name Dolya Vinogradsky. Following the common trend in revolutionary circles, the couple did not formalize their relationship.

Levin's most important volume of poetry, *Tsushteyer* [Contribution], was published in 1929 in Kharkov. The volume features a series of pieces entitled "Froy" [Woman], as well as "Eyne vi asakh andere" [One Like Many Others], a series about the experiences of a female soldier. Before the outbreak of the Soviet-German war, she published four more poetry collections: *Oyg oyf oyg* [Eye to Eye], 1933; *Kleynikaytn* [Trifles], 1933; *Di yingere fun mir* [Younger Than I], 1934; and *Eygns* [Own], 1941. Like Kadya Molodowsky, Levin was an accomplished Yiddish poet in terms of the number of her publications. Additionally, Levin issued six books for children and numerous short stories. In 1939–1940, she studied at the Foreign Languages Institute in Moscow. She survived the war in Buzuluk, which is within the Orenburg region. In 1945, she lived in Moscow, but afterwards she moved to Kharkov permanently. Following the war, like many others, she sought refuge from the rigid norms imposed on art and literature by the political system by writing children's literature. She published poetry for children in Ukrainian and Russian. Her closest writer friends were arrested in connection with the campaign against Jewish intellectuals and activists of the Jewish Anti-Fascist Committee and murdered on Stalin's orders in 1952. Levin was afraid that she would share the same fate. Although she continued to publish in the Moscow-based *Sovetish heymland*, she remained outside mainstream Yiddish literary life. She died on January 19, 1969.

In this chapter, I use a gender perspective to explore those motifs in Levin's work in which she redefines the Jewish female identity in the context of social and customary changes brought by the October Revolution. I examine those aspects of Levin's oeuvre that make her an original and innovative poet and distinguish her work from Soviet Yiddish literature. This is not, therefore, a presentation of her whole corpus. I omit her children literature, short stories, and folk poems. Instead, I select works that contain universal elements, are relevant for today, and illustrate her greatest artistic achievements.

## *Mother*

The issue of the trauma of wartime experiences from 1917 to 1921 is central to "Froy," Levin's feminist manifesto. That work concentrates on the problem of being a woman who is unable to carry a baby to term and give birth to it.[10] This extremely powerful work, which opens her début poetry collection, is a cry for the rights of women, whose bodies always become spoils in times of historical uncertainties. Levin writes of the rapes carried out by men and of the massacres of pregnant women. Not satisfied with a description of events from the observer's point of view, such accounts from pogroms have a long tradition in Jewish poetry, Levin, in striving for subjectivity, makes one of the victims of the male barbarism the subject of the poem:

> Before whom,
> before whom am I to bare my pain?
> No longer can I silently suck on my wound!—
> Each night I dream of women,
> and each bewails a child.
>
> Who will share with me my cares?
> Who will relieve me in this hard world?
> Each night I dream of women,
> Pulled by their hair to the door...
> Women thrown on tables.
> Their knees pulled apart by strange hands.—
>
> Every moment thrown on the rubbish pile
> are bits of children's and women's bodies—terror and shame...
>
> It is hard,
> but I am ashamed to disappoint,
> because my country is beautiful
> and the joy of a festive morning
> awakes in my country—
> ears full of grain,
> but for me
> and for my fate
> empty...
>
> I too ploughed and sowed,
> for myself
> the ear
> I toiled hard.
> It should not be so,
> It should not happen so,
> that the mother's body becomes a coffin for the child![11]

This poem reaches a shocking strength of expression by introducing an almost naturalistic description of the terrorizing of women by tearing babies from their wombs. Their tragedy is described in two respects: first, the loss of a child, and second, taking away that element of humanity that is shame and the opportunity to have a say in the fate of one's own body. Levin evokes the world of nature, the grain, full of ears, which brings to mind a woman's pregnancy. The child growing in the women is affectionately described as an ear. The motif of ploughing and sowing are metaphors often used for fertilization. Here, the woman herself is ploughed and sowed, becoming "soil" for the new life. The man does not appear as the one making the decision about conception. The woman has "toiled" to grow a person inside herself. Yet this hardship turns out to be in vain; her body has become a coffin for the baby. The women in this tragedy have become entirely alone. Their husbands are blind to the rapes carried out on their own wives, finding an effective anaesthetic in alcohol. They do not preserve the memory of the babies killed in the womb. Women, on the contrary, have their bodies marked by the stamp of tragedy, retaining a memory of the death caused in them. Levin speaks brutally of the tragedy that may be understood only by women who have experienced the death of another person in their own live bodies:

> Our husbands have grown used to seeing us with our lords,
> they drink all night with a tab till morning,—blind.
> But the naive female body cannot forget
> the simple joy of the growing baby.
>
> Every particle of my body is full of wild despair and lament,
> the pain chokes me—I have no strength left.
> I was called upon to be the mother of the enlightened generation,
> and I am given—its autopsy in my belly.[12]

A woman emerges from such a traumatic experience mutilated, no longer able to treat relations with a man as before, anxious about and fearing sex: "A pair of joined lips causes me pain, / unease strikes, like night sweats thick as honey."[13] At the end of the poem, Levin changes her strategy, moving from an individual subject to a collective one. She speaks in the name of women who are given the chance to demand their own rights. As a result of the revolution that shook the former social order, a crack appeared in the patriarchal history of humanity. The foundations of the system of subordination of one sex to the other seemed for a moment to be shaken. Of course, one must stand up to men for the rights of women and mothers. It is necessary to make the most of the moment and "cast off the burden of our sex":

> We all have a pass,
> For a moment we are
> outlaws from obedience to our sex.
> The lioness comes to the lion at the time of love,
> the vixen comes to the fox for rights-of-women and mothers
> and we—
> chosen from generations—calling ourselves "man and woman,"

> at the body's cage
> cast off the burden
> of our sex.¹⁴

Levin's poem breaks all the taboos associated with maternity. Moreover, the figure of the woman-mother serving in the 1920s as a target in anti-feminist discourse becomes an active participant in feminist rebellion and the main subject of its efforts.

The issue of single motherhood is an important theme in Levin's poetry. One poem, "Kinder zaynen kleyn, vos konen kinder visn" [Children Are Small, What Could They Know], is a record of a man splitting with and abandoning a woman and their young daughter after finding a new partner. The child is familiar with this situation from the lives of her friends, but now has to face up to the fact that this has happened to her. She realizes this when the father only comes in the evening to visit his old home and abandoned family. The drama of the situation is heightened by the child's naive statements and questions:

> Vita's daddy bought a new mummy.
> A whole new mummy on a new street.
> And now he just visits Vita's mummy. [...]
> Does daddy live at work now? Does he sleep in the factory? [...]
> How can daddy live on a different street?
> He's daddy, how can he be a guest?¹⁵

From the child's perspective, the change in her parents' relationship is an incomprehensible part of the games grown-ups play, an absurdity at odds with reason that shatters the order in the world. The tragedy of the child, and at the same time of the mother, unable to do anything to change the course of events and protect her child from unhappiness, is emphasized by the ironic verse recurring in the poem like a refrain: "The years of childhood bliss, what could children understand." The stereotype of carefree childhood is unmasked as false, as the child, as yet not protected by the armour of experience, is all the more defenseless in becoming the victim of the affairs of the father, who has "bought a whole new mummy." The childish language exposes the brutal truth about the "modern" relations between men and women based on free love. The poem finishes with the moving image of the daughter and mother, all the closer to one another as they are united by shared unhappiness:

> She nestles her warm body to her mother,
> To mother's cheeks, to mother's mouth.
> I will always, always love you more and more!
> What twaddle, silly, go to sleep sooner,

> because father will be angry,
> But the fond words have lost their power,
> And the child weeps ever louder, despairing in the night [...]
> Blonde and grey hairs are plaited.
> They weep, like two women, left just the same.
> And at the foot of the bed quietly looks on
> a little rabbit with stitched-on eyes,
> with its sewn mouth it sucks on a carrot
> and is not moved by any little, trembling tear.[16]

Other poems by Levin, for example, "Shuld" [Guilt], describe the struggle of the woman and mother in the reality of daily life after breaking up, when she has to meet the challenge of fulfilling both roles, mother and father, which turns out not to be entirely possible:

> Nobody should think,
> that time heals wounds,
> women once left still weep,
> and I too weep every night
> Not because sometimes
> I cannot sleep at your cradle,
> but I always want to lull you,
> comfort my lonely fortune.
> Meanwhile you need my love,
> you bear my name,
> Upon myself I take it
> to be mother and father.
> Only your childish voice torments me,
> when I hear and see—
> to every strange man you say Daddy,
> you cuddle up to others' knees.
> Do I caress you little,
> in tenderness I do not cease,
> I can do everything,
> but one thing—not,
> I cannot bring back your father.
> This is why I feel guilt
> under your pure gaze,
> to every strange man you say Daddy,
> you cuddle up to others' knees.
> Nobody should think,
> that time heals wounds,
> when children miss their fathers,
> mothers weep at night.[17]

The presence of the child makes it impossible to submit to the passage of time and forget about the man with whom there was once a connection. Since the child is a continual manifestation of its father, for the woman, the relationship with him cannot become just part of the past. The child's longing for her father still keeps the wound of the breakup fresh, and even worse, it awakes a feeling of guilt in the woman, regret that she cannot give the child its father. The woman's loneliness is heightened by the feeling of the child's being alone.

Levin's motherhood poems offer insights into the huge gulf dividing the male and female experience of parenting, specifically, men's lack of access to the bodily dimension of pregnancy, when one's body becomes a cradle for another, and woman's inability to reconcile the tragedy of the loss of a child to the consequences of broken relationships and the woman's lot, raising the "fruit" of the meeting of woman and man.

## Clothes

Another important subject in Levin's poetry is the generational conflict between the traditional, small-town Jewish women's identity and the modern identification of the woman living in the rhythm of the big city, the combatant with political and feminist ideas. One manifestation of this conflict, depicting women's changing relationship with their own corporality, is the motif of differences in the way mothers and their daughters dress.

Clothes are a significant social and cultural code.[18] Changes in clothing are an important vector in revolutions in standards and social changes. Traditional historical narratives treated fashion, the world of silks and fineries, in a marginal manner, yet in *belles lettres*, the status of the choice of clothing is preserved as a system of identifying signs. The type and change in clothing played a particular role in Jewish culture. During the Diaspora, Jews were on the one hand dressed by non–Jews with signs of their identity, for example, pointed hats, intended to counteract contacts between Jews and Christians, and on the other hand, Jews kept themselves distinct by maintaining their own unique style of attire. Furthermore, clothing is regulated by Jewish religious law and by tradition. Jewish religious law forbids imitation of *chukas hagoyim* [non–Jewish clothes]. Today, generally recognizable are, above all, male Jewish wear, such as *tallitot* [ritual prayer shawls]; *tallit katan* [under-waistcoats with tassels]; *yarmulkes* [headcoverings that form a whole system of distinguishing marks for the various branches of Judaism]; and Hassidic coats, white stockings, and *shtreimlech* [fur caps]. Yiddish prose is dominated by descriptions of men symbolically changing from Jewish clothes to the so-called European style, with the protagonists cutting their sidelocks, shaving their beards, and shedding their coats as manifestations of their social aspirations and changes in worldview.

*Sheytlekh* [women's wigs] and bonnets concealing, depending on their degree of orthodoxy, either the shaven heads of married women or their cut hair, are now less commonly associated as an element of traditional Jewish dress. This no doubt results from the marginalized role of women in Judaism and androcentric description of men's clothing as a synecdoche of the entire Jewish community. An excellent portrayal of the simplified approach in which universal equals male may be found in an excerpt concerning Jewish clothing in the memorial book dedicated to Pińczów, Poland:

> Jews in Poland dressed like the Polish nobility, but by the 15th century like burghers. At the time when Poles were changing their dress (robes) to European clothes, Jews were forbidden to dress in the same way, and they remained with the old style of bourgeois clothing. With time, such clothes became a tradition among Jews, and the long gabardine began to function as a normal Jewish outfit. The Jews from Pińczów, who had come from Bohemia and Moravia, in the 16th and 17th centuries, wore bekishe[19] and sheepskin jackets, and at the front taleskotn[20] and arbekanfes.[21] On the head, a hat.[22]

There is not a single word in this passage on the traditional clothing of Jewish women. This leads to a linguistic exclusion by which the expression "Jews in Poland" refers only to the male half of Jewish inhabitants. Notably, the description of clothes distinguishing a Jewish woman refers especially to her marital status. For example, her traditional attire makes it clear if she is single, married, widow, or *agunah*.[23] This was related to the social role, particularly of wife and mother, designated to her.

The motif of dress, closely related to the issues of corporality, held an important place in the work of female Yiddish poets, often appearing in the moment of confrontation of the traditional lifestyle of mothers and modernity of their daughters. The ideal of *tsnue*, the virtuous woman, the model of womanhood ordained by traditional Judaism, provides the context for this intergenerational dialogue. Anka Grupińska describes "the ideal Jewish woman" as "modest, silent and hard-working, patient, obedient to God and subordinate to her husband, unaware of her needs, not remembering herself."[24] Furthermore, the contemporary *tsnue* from the ultra–Orthodox quarter of Jerusalem dresses "in a black scarf fitting tightly to her smooth (shaven) head, black stockings, a dark blouse carefully buttoned up to her neck and at the wrists."[25] Shedding the headscarf or wig, taking off the thick stockings, or pulling up the sleeves has the same status as cutting sidelocks or exchanging the long coat for a tailcoat and the fur cap for a bowler.

The young woman in Levin's poetry looks at the elements of her mother's dress as attributes of virtuousness, respected but rejected. Levin's poem "Kleyder" [Dresses] is a clear rebellion against covering up, swathing, or hiding the female Jewish body with the intention of preventing its beauty from attracting male gaze and tempting males to touch. The young woman's dresses alienate her from her mother's world; they do not carry information about belonging to the Jewish world, and furthermore their rather unfeminine cut erases the divide between the sexes, which is also forbidden by religious law[26]:

> In my short dresses,
> with no collar and no sleeves,
> as smooth, simple, as men's shirts,
> in my mother's eyes I look
> wild and strange,
> embarrassed, she looks away from me,
> and stares at the floor.[27]

Both women watch each other. The mother is embarrassed by her daughter's body. The roles are somehow reversed; the mother is less experienced in terms of corporality and less accustomed to female sexuality than her daughter. She is uneasy and shocked to look at a body that she gave birth to:

> Mother glances at my young slender body,
> Embarrassed she looks with aversion and pain.[28]

The daughter analyzes her mother's dress, which becomes the carrier of signs of the sexual potential of the Jewish woman, reduced to a procreative function. The thick creases hide the contours of the body bring to mind babies' cradles, and at the same time, they are filled with snow, symbolizing the embers of the body, cooled and frozen by virtuousness:

> they are wide, long,
> arranged into thick creases—
> each crease—a cradle filled with snow.[29]

The tips of the shoes that appear from under the edge of the mother's dress contain encrypted information about the borders of the world they traverse, namely "from the market to the porch in counted steps." The horizon of the mother's world is marked out by the home and the marketplace. These feet, dressed in plimsolls, are the busiest part of her figure. They are compared with "heads of mice," which have to work quickly but "unhurriedly." What does an "unhurried run" mean? The mother's hurry is different from that of her daughter. It is not chaotic, but ordered; the mother's plimsolls are bustling, but they walk circles like "the hands of an old clock." In the mother's world, time runs in circles; everything has its time. The old clock marking the run of mummy's plimsolls is the rhythm of life ordered according to Jewish tradition; it ticks off the "home hours," because home is the mother's universe.

Entirely different is the hurry of the daughter; she must be "nimble" to manage to jump into a rushing tram or car. The daughter explains the customs of her modern world, unknown to her mother, as if to a child:

> Dear mum!
> Every morning
> there's this custom here—a certain time
> when I have to free my step and speed up,
> for me alone it will not wait
> the tram, or car.
> The car is strict—
> I must be agile
> so that sometimes I can run
> and jump into it.[30]

The daughter cannot restrain her body with dresses in the style of her mother; they do not suit the pace of the city.

Yet it is not only external reality that forces one to throw off the long, respectable dresses, there is pressure from the inside too. The young woman does not want to put out the fire of her desires. She rejects modesty and shame, wanting to burn in the flame of desire without restrictions and the boundaries of moderation and caution, even if this brings with it the risk of loss, of burning out:

> My dear mum,
> my old mum!
> What shall we do with your dresses,
> you tell me.
>
> With your long dresses
> and with my lustful hands
> which I stretch towards the sun—
> without the manacles of sleeves.
> I'll leave them
> naked,
> brown,
> black,—[...][31]

This does not mean, however, that she eliminates the aspect of her body's fertility. As she says, "Nobody ever caught the sun. / And the sun will not catch me!" She counts on the fact that she too might become a mother, but the child she bears will be the fruit of her passion, burnt by the sun of the lust of its mother's body:

> If I have a child—
> If I should have one child—
> a daughter, or son—
> let it be black
> with lips full of red.
> still in its mother's body
> soaked with the sun![32]

In this poem, the freeing of the arms from the manacles of the sleeves appears; the bare arms become a symbol of sexual freedom in women's Yiddish poetry. We may ask why the poet's attention is concentrated on the arms. We may seek the reasons in the role of female arms, emphasized in Judaism and deriving from its patriarchal order. The Talmud, giving the reasons for removing from women the privilege and obligation to study the Torah, explains that the wisdom of a woman lies in her hands,[33] not her head. This is another incarnation of the archetype of the woman as spinner; her vocation is weaving.[34] The roots of this are biblical. In the extract from the Book of Proverbs describing *eshet khayil*, a woman of valour, crucial for the model of Jewish womanhood, the activity of her hands is stressed:

> A woman of valour, who can find?
> far beyond pearls is her value [...]
> She seeks out wool and linen
> and her **hands** work willingly [...]
> She considers a field and buys it,
> from the fruit of her **handiwork** she plants a vineyard.
> She girds her loins with might
> and strengthens her **arms** [...]
> She puts her **hand** to the distaff,
> and her **palms** support the spindle.
> She spreads out her **palm** to the poor
> and extends her **hands** to the destitute.[35]

In Levin's poetry, clothes are not used only as a pretext for presenting intergenerational dialogue and showing the distancing from the traditional world of the mother. They also remain an expression of the quest for a definition of the woman's own sexuality. The protagonist of Levin's poems balances between elements of male and female identity, and the expression of this becomes her clothes and shoes—for example, her heels. High heels have become a symbol of a woman's sex appeal. The protagonist rejects feminine shoes with heels in favor of a wide shoe with a flat heel, allowing her to move in an "anti-feminine" way. While the rhythm in which she lives makes her dispense with graceful movement, her walk becomes the expression of the new roles that the modern woman wants to fulfil. "Eylndik un menerish" explores that sentiment:

> Hasty and manly is my walk,
> the flat heel of a wide shoe.
> My walk is brisk,
> my pace quick,
> in the day of all the men I am the manliest:
> Deftly I bear the load of the city,
> Stiffly it sounds—my hasty walk.[36]

However, being "the manliest of all the man" is scrupulously staged, to an extent constituting a performance constructed for daily use, a battle with "natural" womanhood, with the still present legacy of the mother forming the female identity:

> Ever better I recognise myself
> and every time
> I paint myself
> a new print.
> Even the cigar, which so harms
> the corners of my mouth,
> is there because
> I am ashamed to look like myself
> and like my mother's wedding veil.[37]

The masculine cigar, a Freudian phallic symbol, also a marker of strength and power, becomes the antithesis of the mother's wedding veil. The mother's veil, with all the weight of its gender background, is the quintessence of Jewish womanhood. Jewish girls were traditionally raised with marriage in mind. While still in the cradle, the baby would be sung lullabies by her mother about her ideal future. Whereas a boy was wished that he would grow up to be a *talmud khokhem*, the epitome of good wishes for a daughter were the images of her future fiancé. For an adult woman in the patriarchal system of traditional Judaism there was no other social role, guaranteeing acceptance and respect, than the function of wife and mother. The young woman from Levin's poem feels in herself the presence of the instilled model of womanhood, but learns to recognise herself. However, this self-awareness leads her to a capable, deliberate creation of herself, despite the gender circumstances. In this poem, the veil forms a kind of mirror. The woman feels that under the masculine "print," which she lends herself, her face still shows through. The wedding veil is also a symbol of modesty and innocence, which is developed in the next part of the poem:

> I cover my face to no one,
> my arms are bare
> along the street they glide.
> By day anybody can take me by the naked arm,—
> I am ashamed to show them my anger.³⁸

Referring to the veil that closes the previous stanza, the woman declares, "I cover my face to no one," which, in the context of the next verses, is a confession of rejection of the *tsnue* model and, like in "Kleyder," the naked arms become a manifestation of this. The bare arms are again a symbol of freedom, and their "gliding," lifted like wings, is also emphasized. But while social custom, manifested in ways including physical proximity, removal of barriers and bodily distance, and ease of touch, arouses in the woman aversion and anger, she is unable to show this. That would be at odds with the modernity for which she stands. The day is the time of masculinity, yet by night Levin's protagonist wants to set free her femininity muffled in the hard, manly self-image created in the day:

> But at night,
> when there is no one to please,
> I so desire for you to tell me:
> —Yours
> And let it seem wild to you
> let it seem strange to you,
> notice how womanly-delicate
> are the tips of my shirt.³⁹

At night, she wants her partner to perceive in her delicateness, femininity, not to be entirely deceived by her man's shirt, but to see under it her woman's body. The "tips of my shirt" may be interpreted as the tips of the collar, but also as the nipples pointing through the shirt. She knows that, in the new form of relations shaped in revolutionary circles, this may seem strange and too primitive, but in the night sexual freedom, understood also as a lack of steady relationships burdened by the duty of fidelity and exclusivity, ceases to be the longed-for victory of the social revolution. In the woman, there awakes then a desire for the feeling of mutual belonging. She wants to shed the cocoon of masculinity:

> I am so tired
> with the hard, manly day.
> The night is heated
> the night is dark
> and I am still a woman.⁴⁰

Privacy, intimacy, and sexual desires, shown as attributes of the night, arouse the feminine aspects of identity.

In the four-part poem "Nekht" [Nights], Levin further deepens the contrast between the masculine day and the night, as under its cover the woman wants to again become a little girl in her relationship with her lover, exude an atmosphere of subtlety, tenderness spiced up with infantilizing. She writes:

> My dear,
> do you want to listen to me?
> Is it true that the night entreats you with caresses?
> The silence keeps you sweet, like a lamb....
>
> Today I want to be a little girl again,
> a grain of joy,
> on your frowning lips
> a sunny-rabbits smile
> I will let out without a mirror.
>
> Did you think that with my plaits
> I'd cut off my girlish subtlety?
> Oh, you....[41]

Here the symbol of the change in the use of the "masculine" day—that is, the world of the struggle for universal ideas—is cutting off the plaits. Incidentally, in the earliest photographs that have survived of her, Levin has her hair cut very short.

## Soldier Woman

The clearest transgression of gender roles in Levin's poetry is the motif of the Jewish woman soldier. When reading her series of soldier poems, we need to remember that Yiddish literature did not have a tradition of battle poetry and did not develop protagonists who were heroic in the European conception.[42] Alien to it was the ideal of gallant patriotism, the expression of which was death on the battlefield. This was of course connected to the existence of the Jewish nation in the Diaspora, which lacked its own army. Although so-called historical songs were written describing the havoc of war and the pogroms, the songs were from the perspective of the victims, emphasizing their martyrdom.[43] In the nineteenth century, when Jews were conscripted by force into the tsarist army, the songs of recruits became popular. These songs, written in a lamenting tone, portrayed going to the army as the loss of one's own identity.[44] The protagonist of Khane Levin's poetry, a volunteer female soldier, breaks taboos in two ways: as a Jew and as a woman.[45] The essential prop in Levin's war poetry is a rifle, which functions in various contexts of meaning. It becomes the main symbol of departure from the Jewish world. The poem "Tsushteyer" describes a meeting with the mother on their ancestors' burial mound, where the mother bewails not the dead, but her living daughter, screaming at her in despair, "Who do you take after? Not after me, not after Dad. After a goy, after a *shikse*!⁴⁶ Our daughter is playing with a rifle!"⁴⁷ Here, the rifle is an object from outside of Jewish reality. To the mother, firing the rifle is like cutting oneself off from the heritage of the ancestors, alienation. The daughter does not try to soothe her mother's despair. On the contrary, she makes the iconoclastic declaration on the family grave:

> Mother, long live the earth!
> I can also saddle a horse
> with a goy. Like a *shikse*
> I kissed in the bushes.
> The world is burning and the girl is glowing
> They give me a cold rifle.
> They envelop me—two hot arms.
> Like a vagrant, like a goy
> on a horse...
> at the front ... in the fire.⁴⁸

The soldier's experience is interwoven in Levin's poetry with entry into the world of sexuality. In the army, the old prohibitions and norms cease to apply as rituals and conventions are put aside, and one goes with the voice of impulse, longing. The war strips the body of all secrets. On the one hand, through the death and massacre visible everywhere, and on the other, through the physical proximity of men's and women's bodies. In "Eyne vi asakh andere" [One Like Many Others], Levin presents the resting army by writing "they are not heroes, not knights,"⁴⁹ and after the battle they begin to tell obscenities about women, such as "brothers, I have a wife—oh ho ho! What a rascal, how she sings! And her breasts...—oh! like this, like this they are!," "Everyone panting ... hungry for women,"⁵⁰ the poet summarizes. In these conditions, death and eroticism form an inseparable whole, and the lover of the protagonist of the war series, who may be treated as the poet's alter ego, when he wants to make love, leads her among the graves amid the moss, and nearby:

> A harmonica screeches in the field.
> Some soldier-boy dances happy and well,
> The slaughtered calves smell alarmingly,
> Of phlegm, wormwood, and blood.⁵¹

In the next part of this poem, the rifle, itself, is an undoubtedly masculine attribute of power, possessing the characteristics of a phallic symbol. When the couple are lying next to one another, the declaration occurs:

> Empty in the body and the hearts,
> She is disgusted by her own breasts.
> She is disgusted by the rifle, black,—
> Damp from the grass and the kisses...[52]

In the game of love, the young girl is rather passive. It is she who is led and kissed; she looks at the sky and the moon and recalls the story of Rachel, daughter of Laban, who when leaving her father's home with Jacob, secretly stole her father's idols and hid them under her saddle. When Laban caught up with the escapees and demanded the return of the idols, Jacob, not knowing about Rachel's deed, warned that if his father-in-law should find the stolen idols on somebody's person, the perpetrator would die.[53] However, Rachel did not allow her camel to be searched, citing menstrual indisposition, though according to the rabbinical interpretation she died when giving birth to her next child, Benjamin, as a result of Jacob's words, and was buried by the road.[54] Levin refers to this story in her poem describing the evening embraces on the front line:

> Rachel shamed her male saddle,
> And under it hid the house idols
> This is why she died on the road,
> Her trail—split in two...[55]

In Levin's poetry, Rachel's conduct takes on a doubly symbolic meaning. First, it is an expression of the impossibility of completing cutting oneself off from the world in which one grew up, with the desire to keep something of value from the family home. Second, in refusing to come down from the camel because of menstruation, Rachel becomes a symbol of the model of womanhood defined in categories of weakness, powerlessness, and delicateness, but also impurity. Often these two motifs are developed in Levin's poetry: the problem, in the face of the revolution, of breaking off from the values instilled in the Jewish home, and issues of the dilemma between femininity and masculinity understood from the point of view of gender.[56] She is well aware that the social revolution has permitted women to enter male roles and to sit on the male saddle, as the verses on Laban's daughter describe. And that is why in "Di vig" [The Cradle], Levin writes, "You have made me the same as a man in the yoke of the sword and the rifle."[57] In spite of this, though, she remains in the yoke of womanhood. After the war, she faces the challenge of being a mother, and several verses later in the same poem declares, "I love my child, yet heavy for me is the cradle."[58] It is hard for her to meet the challenges of normal motherhood when she has the feeling that she has given birth to the country in which she lives:

> The girl made her contribution
> to the world borne of her blood and flesh.⁵⁹

She is torn between her home, symbolizing the woman's space, and the male reconstruction of the country, between her love for her child and that for the homeland, and between being a mother and being a citizen. "Di vig" continues:

> My country,
> my Soviet country!
> You stand above me,
> so huge,
> so bright,
> still I break away from my doorstep
> and my mother's heart
> I leave
> on the handle of my door.⁶⁰

This leads to a gender aspiration. She wraps her masculine relationship with her country in her feminine corporality:

> My country,
> my Soviet country!
> You swelled high like a man
> in the delicate mother's body,
> in the mother's tissue!...
> Like a man I break
> Amid your brightness
> And remain on the doorstep...—
> Still I must be a mother,
> Must be a woman.⁶¹

The transgression turns out to be not quite possible, and Levin's protagonist is in spite of everything the heir of Rachel, who under her men's saddle, kept the idols of femininity.

## Lover

Levin's poetry is also courageous and bold in erotic themes. She portrays the sexual revolution that took place during the wave of socio-political changes. Her poems are expressions of the quest for redefinition of one's own sexuality. She describes the longing for "ordinariness," which is the desire to find a partner before whom a woman will not be ashamed to show her feelings and who will father the child for whom she yearns. However, in this ordinariness from which the "mother's wedding veil" shows through is to be based on the principles of equality and freedom. From "Prost" [Simply]:

> I am like my mother—
> It hurts me—I weep.
> I love—I want a child from you.
> But in the fortune of the four walls of your world I will not be imprisoned,—
> I too have a separate
> key to the door.
>
> For me awaits the street.
> for me awaits work.
> And equally with you I pay
> the world a debt.
> And if needs be—
> You know—
> I can die
> far from those I love.
> far from my quiet yard!
>
> And if needs be—
> You know—
> my teeth and lips
> the reeking dressing
> will take.[62]

This expected partnership in the relationship with the man is not meant to be a gift or a favor, but thoroughly "developed." The modern woman has already left the space of the home that belonged to her for centuries, and now she works just the same and may fall in battle just the same. As a result, there is no argument for denying her right to a "separate key to the door" or for subordinating her life to the man's priorities. Yet what is terrifying in the new reality freed from conventions, is the woman's possible treatment as a sexual object for a night. The sexual revolution has brought with it the model of casual relationships, associating it with prostitution. Understood here, it would seem, as sexual contacts are deprived of feelings and bonds:

> Why does it happen so,
> as it happens,
> that the woman's flesh becomes a shelter
> for making it through the night?
> The bodies of women, like apples
> munched lecherously,
> lie like rubbish
> on every road and path…
>
> It hurts me and I weep
> who should I be ashamed to?
> Who will tell me, that a rest
> I have not honestly earned?
> Now,

> at rest,
> I demand the debt of my womanhood—
> the debt of a mother's rights
> and of the father of my child.[63]

In the new, post-revolutionary reality, however, thinking about a steady relationship might be treated as a lack of progressiveness, a legacy of the bourgeois mentality against whose conventions the social revolution and the changes in social mores it brought were rebelling. The woman from Levin's poem confesses that the trappings of romantic love have become outdated, passé, but she has within herself the desire for a steady relationship, although she knows that this exposes her to ridicule and incomprehension. From "Zay dokh nit keyn kind" [Don't Be a Child]:

> Don't be a child,
> Who will laugh at you?
> Is it truly a disgrace for a man—
> to enter the house
> and do nothing bad to her?
>
> Explain to me,
> whom can it harm
> that some night
> is not used in a night-time way?
> Don't be angry,
> don't call me "bourgeois"—
> I just want to grasp,
> what I so far don't understand.
>
> Perhaps someone will be bored by the song
> of the moon and the roses,
> but is it truly a disgrace—
> to search for this one in hundreds, a thousand,
> search for this one
> and for this one to be a woman?[64]

This does not mean, however, that we do not find the record of many sexual experiences and a variety of partners in Levin's poetry. In one of her poems, "Trink ikh vayn" [I Drink Wine], there is even an indication of looking for affection in the arms of both men and women:

> And that my heart is a pitcher of joy
> I knelt down,—
> whether it be men, or women—
> I love all, all are close.[65]

In "Nekht," she attempts to convey the dynamic of a woman and man coming together by building a quivering, panting atmosphere, in which the nature of the experience is the blending of activeness and passivity, distancing and nearing, fullness and longing, and lack and fulfilment:

> I stroke your hair,
> I envelop you,—
> fullness in my heart,
> on my lips silence.
> I explain nothing,—
> I ponder.
> It is night.
>
> Quietly I laugh,
> quietly I call.
> I do not see you,
> I look for you—
> I find your neck
> and throat.
> I am hot—
> I worry,
> I leave,
> I come back,
> I lie still without strength. Surrendered.
> It is night...[66]

Sometimes these are sexual encounters for just one night, leaving behind shame and hurt, like in verse IV of the Nekht poems. In this description of a nocturnal encounter with a man another strategy has been chosen, concentrating on a detail, the pillowcases:

> There's a kind of hot night,
> and at night—heated pleasures,
> why did we break out in joy?—
> For heady wine and honey!
> You said:
> in the courtyard the dog will bark,
> but the dog—you remember—did not bark.
> It put its head in my lap,
> quite normal, rustic, calm.
> You remember how happy you were?—
> Without yapping the dog greeted me...
> You led me by the hand
> like a big—small child.
> You said:
> —The pillowcase is clean,
> lie down,
> rest,
> rest...
> You put the pillow down for me

and arranged it under my head.
There's a kind of hot night,
and at night—heated pleasures.
And we broke out in the joy
of heady wine and honey!

On the pillow remained a stain,
a stain, of blood, or wine.
I left your room
and never returned.
You will not call me to you again,
and I will not come alone.
I am ashamed now to meet
a simple rustic dog.[67]

This poem is based on an ambiguity of the dog and the stain. On a clean pillowcase put on for the lover, a red stain remains. The stain could be wine, the symbol of amorous pleasures, or blood, the symbol of the suffering and pain left in the woman by the chance nature of this meeting, the pain that her body will also be "munched lecherously,"[68] and will become just "a way of making it through the night"[69] as Levin writes elsewhere. A similar ambiguity is represented by the dog. In one way, the dog is a normal, friendly guardian of the house, but in another, at the end of the poem, the words about the dog, "I am ashamed now to meet / a simple rustic dog,"[70] may refer contemptuously to the man who for only one night put a clean pillow under her head and who never again came calling.

The repeated verses on breaking into "joy of heady wine and honey" evoke the metaphor of love from the *Song of Songs*, in which the combination of honey and wine has an unequivocally erotic meaning, with the image of the intercourse of the bride and groom described as an entry to the garden, associated with consumption of honey and wine:

> I went into my garden, my sister, the bride,
> I found my myrrh with my balsam,
> I ate my slice with my honey,
> I drank my wine with my milk.
> Eat, my friends,
> drink and get drunk on my love![71]

In his superb analysis of *Song of Songs*, Othmar Keel shows the deeply culturally rooted meaning of shared consumption of honey and wine by a man and woman as a metaphor of the bliss of physical love; honey is the sweet aspect of love, and wine is the daze caused by it. Keel cites other ancient texts that introduce honey and wine into their description of the closeness of lovers.

For example, in the Sumerian song of love, the delights of the honey-scented bed are described like this:

> My brother led me to his house,
> he laid me on the honey-scented bed,
> my beloved, sweet, clutched to my heart
> after many, one after the next touches with the tongue,
> one after another, my brother,
> he with the most beautiful face, did this fifty times.[72]

And on the Old Babylonian plate depicting the sexual act, during which the woman drinks wine, we see the following inscription, which in a frank way shows the connotations of wine and love:

> My God! Sweet is the drink of the landlady,
> Like her heady drink sweet is the vulva,
> sweet is the drink
> like her labia, so sweet is her vulva,
> sweet is her drink.[73]

Levin therefore combines in her description of the intercourse of the woman and the man archetypal images with contemporary details such as the white pillowcase, obtaining a dichotomous situation of an object in which the area of enjoying pleasures is a temporary break from the real order of reality, after which the person is again condemned to solitude. For a brief moment, the desired model of mythical unity and closeness to another person is realized, but afterwards, there is a return to strangeness and distance and from the honey and wine remains only a stain on the pillowcase, a sign of suffering, disgrace, or tainting. For centuries, the connotation of a red stain on the sheets was as a symbol of loss of virginity, a sign of the wedding night.

The steady relationship, the longing for which appears as a motif in Levin's poetry, ultimately also brings disappointment in the form of the inevitable alienation and distancing oneself from partners, which results in aversion to bodily contacts:

> I drink wine,
> but no longer that one.
> Again joy,
> yet much smaller.
> I sing songs, like before,
> but my dear is far away.
> No,
> not far,
> quite close to me,—
> he drinks wine and sings,

on my table he lies,
but his gaze is far and distant.
I cease to worry about it—
I have new,
fresh,
arms.
Late at night from the street
another visits me.
My heart is a pitcher of joy.
I am ready to embrace anyone.
I sing loud, even louder,
Let him see and long again.
And that my heart is a pitcher of joy
I knelt down,—
whether it be men, or women—
I love all, all are close.
Only to that one,
the most strange—
I fear
to fix my gaze.
I hug
the wall,
let it not touch my hand.
I turn up my collar around my neck,
for he once embraced it.

First-born, first-born, I am your wife.
Your pain rests in my flesh...[74]

This poem exudes the whole scale of often contradictory feelings that the woman harbors in relation to her partner, of whom she calls herself his wife. The poem ranges from longing and the desire to arouse jealousy, to anger, searching for joy in infidelity, to fear, aversion, which do not, though, exclude the feeling of a profound connection and corporeal belonging. This poem too refers to the symbolism of wine, playing with the meanings of wine as a drink and wine as a metaphor for amorous pleasures. The statement at the beginning, "I drink wine, but no longer that one," turns out to be a confession on the new "other" partner who gives the freshness of his arms and allows her to sing the songs of love. The joy of the relationship "on the side" is partial, though: to an extent it only serves to arouse longing in the regular partner. The alienation of the one who ought to be closest to her pushes the woman into the arms of men and women, because her heart is—and here again the metaphor referring to wine—a pitcher of joy, which must have an outlet. This brings with it the growth of barriers, distance in relations with her husband, who, however, in the culmination of the piece is ultimately called "first-born," someone who still continues to have priority. Just as the mother cannot renounce the bodily bonds with the child in her womb, a bodily symbiosis exists with the man; his frustrations pass through her body, maturing like the fetus inside her.

## Conclusion

In her poetic credo "Di shure, vos mir libn" [The Verse That We Like], Khane Levin expressed the hope that her poems might find an audience to whom some aspect of her oeuvre would speak and who might open her books:

> I know you are not thunderous
> and you are not resounding, my words,
> but maybe you will reach someone—
> in joy or in sorrow.
> The beating of the heart
> too is only heard,
> when to someone's breast
> you press your ear.
> The mute bird's cry
> of the amazing falling bird
> arouses in us fear
> and does not allow the eyes to know sleep.
> Childishly tangled words,
> tiny tears falling from the lashes,
> how often do they chain us to the spot
> and throw us on our knees.
> Behind the mute bird's cry,
> behind the childish joy, the mother's tears—
> behind all of this I have directed
> every drop of blood in my veins.
> Honest joy and unfeigned suffering
> from myself and from you I always demanded.
> Be not like cold mirrors,
> my verses!...
> Everything I say,
> I say from the depths of my heart,
> These are my only treasures,
> my own.
> I wish for this one happiness,
> I wish for this one joy,
> that for some man, child, woman old or young
> one of my poems,
> just one verse,
> one word
> shall become so near and dear,

> that this book will open itself
> with the verse that is sought.
> Not dead,
> not blind,
> not praising is this book.
> It feels, it knows....[75]

Unfortunately, Levin's books have stayed closed. Her poetry is marginalized within women's Yiddish literature, as well as within Yiddish literature, which itself occupies a peripheral place in the world literary canon. She therefore suffers a triple marginalization. To date, her writings have not enjoyed the same attention, for example as those of Celia Dropkin, Anna Margolin, or Kadya Molodowsky, whose works have been translated into English and have thus acquired a wider readership. This may be the result of the political and territorial circumstances that placed her works outside of the main current of research on Yiddish literature. The lack of attention, however, is not due to the artistic value of her writing, the excellence of which was perceived immediately upon publication of her début volume. In the magazine *Di royte velt* [The Red World] in 1929, Yekhezkl Dobrushin wrote that the standard of the collection *Tsushteyer* placed it among the most outstanding achievements of Soviet Jewish poetry.[76] He stressed that what distinguished Levin's poetry from other contemporary Yiddish poetry was the very clearly marked—in an innovative, original way—female subjectivity that bonded all Levin's works together. As he writes, "Khane Levin's book *Tsushteyer* is a monolith devoted to one and the same *froyen-frage* [women's issue], or rather *mame-frage* [mother's issue], the subject of the woman in contemporary Soviet reality."[77] The entirely new element introduced by Levin's poetry to Jewish Soviet poetry is, according to Dobrushin, the attitude to corporality, which he terms "love for the body."[78] Summarizing, he describes Levin's works as poetry of protest and suffering, but he quickly adds that it is also full of faith and optimism. This assurance of the optimistic meaning of Levin's work is of course made in respect to the particular conditions the poet was writing under—in a system in which every poem was judged according to the categories of the political ideology, and where an accusation of creating works lacking the required trends could lead to denial of an artist's living, arrest, or even execution. Critical texts written by the authorities of the time, Dobrushin's among them, did not just, as is usually the case, influence the development and reception of an author's work, but also its very existence. An accusation of pessimism was a serious charge since faith in the glorious socialist future was compulsory. That is why Dobrushin, clearly positive in his attitude to Khane Levin and her poems attempted to extract the elements that matched the optimism that the system dictated. He did, though, accuse her of excessive saturation of certain poetic extracts with personal sorrow, yet ultimately his verdict brings salvation. He writes that "Khane Levin portrays the set of experiences and women's issues in an optimistic light, which comes from the processes of reconstruction thanks to which we have now achieved the transformation of the woman into a creative person of work with equal rights."[79] I think that this part of the review shows clearly the restrictions that she had to face to keep the female aspect of her work from dominating the asexual "person of work," how much care she had to take to prevent the difficult challenges of modern womanhood, the painful experiences from drowning out the youthful optimism which, though without doubt present in her work, is not obvious, but tangled in the baggage of suffering and doubts. Reading Levin's poems and collections that were published after 1929, we see that the passion, rebellion, and pugnacity that were fully revealed in the first collection are somewhat muted. This was no doubt influenced by the intensifying repressiveness of the system, as well as the efficient method of Soviet nationalization of creative output through guaranteeing of a job and a set of privileges for subordinated artists and writers. Remember that in the 1930s Khane lived in an artists' house, collecting a regular fee, which made both her and her family's existence dependent on her published works being ideologically acceptable.

This review by Dobrushin also reveals a certain specter that hangs over the reception of Khane Levin, namely that the Jewish Soviet literary elite soon became androcentric,[80] with Itzik Feffer, Perets Markish, and Leib Kvitko[81] as the canonical artists; their work was treated as a kind of template. Despite his praise for her invention and innovativeness, Dobrushin had to discern in it influences of the poetic style of Feffer, the rhythm of Markish, and the worldview of Kvitko. Ultimately they were seen as those who defined Soviet Yiddish poetry, and even today there is a cult around them, overshadowing such creative personalities as Khane Levin. A distinct and sad confirmation, but also a depiction of certain mechanisms of this dominance of the classics is given by the recollections of Levin's daughter, Eda Vinogradsky. When I discovered that Levin's daughter had published a commemorative text, I approached it with high hopes, counting on an interesting contribution to the poet's biography, but above all a source on the poet deriving from the closest person to her, who could remember her from before the war, the daughter's account of her mother. How great was my disappointment, though, when in the article entitled "Поэты моего детства" [Poets of My Childhood], I found recollections of Kvitko, Markish, and Feffer. As Vinogradsky notes, they were "friends of my mother, the poet Khane Levin, beginning her creative journey together with them."[82] Despite the existence of so many analyzes and memorial papers on these three, Levin's daughter devotes her whole essay to them. Only by reading between the lines may a few biographical facts be teased out. Why does Vinogradsky not write about her mother? She wanted to write about what she thought was important and of significance for everyone, specifically, the canonical authors. Having lived day to day with her mother, Eda does not perceive the need to share her recollections of her. She only relays what she remembers from the visits to their home of the "great poets," for, as she writes in her last sentences, "They were the giants of Jewish poetry of the 20th century. They were known not only in our country, but around the world. Our nation can be proud that it gave us poets of this magnitude."[83] Yet sometimes giants block the view of the horizon. My overarching goal in this chapter is to remove from the shadow of the giants Levin's legacy to Yiddish poetry.

## Notes

Vadim Levin and William Vinogradsky, the living descendants of Khane Levin, kindly gave permission to publish her poems.

1. Khane Levin, *Tsushteyer* (Ukraine: Melukhe-farlag fun Ukraine, 1929), 14.
2. See Dan Miron, "Why Was There No Women's Poetry in Hebrew Before 1920," in *Gender and Text in Modern Hebrew and Yiddish Literature*, ed. Naomi B. Sokoloff, Anne Lapidus Lerner, and Anita Norich (New York: Jewish Theological Seminary of America, 1992), 65–91. There were of course female Hebrew poets, such as Rachel Morpurgo (1790–1871) and Rachel Bluwstein (1890–1931), but here I am interested in modern women's poetry, which in 1928 was extensive enough for Ezra Korman to publish *Yidishe dikhterins: antologye* (Shikago: L. M. Shtayn, 1928).
3. On Celia Dropkin, see Janet Hadda, "The Eyes Have It: Celia Dropkin's Love Poetry," in *Gender and Text in Modern Hebrew and Yiddish Literature*, ed. Naomi B. Sokoloff, Anne Lapidus Lerner, and Anita Norich (New York: Jewish Theological Seminary of America, 1992), 93–112 and Agnieszka Legutko, "Cyrkowa dama—poezja Celii Dropkin czytana z perspektywy genderowej," in *Nieme dusze? Kobiety w kulturze* jidysz, ed. Joanna Lisek (Wrocław: Wudawnictwo Uniwersytetu Wrocławskiego, 2010), 207–242. On Anna Margolin, see Abraham Novershtern, "'Who Would Have Believed That a Bronze Statue Can Weep': The Poetry of Anna Margolin," *Prooftexts* 10: 3 (1990): 435–468.
4. On Jewish literary life in Kharkov, see Gennady Estraikh, "The Kharkiv Yiddish Literary World, 1920s–mid-1930s," *East European Jewish Affairs* 32, no. 2 (2002): 70–88. Estraikh mentions Levin in his volume.
5. A short biographical note on Khane Levin may be found in Chaim Beyder, *Этюды о еврейских писателях* (Kiev: Izdat of "Spirit i litera," 2003), 170; she is also mentioned in Nachman Mayzel, *Dos yidishe shafn un der yidisher shrayber in Sovetnfarband* (Nyu york: Ikuf, 1959).
6. Evidence of this is the omission of Levin's poems from Barnett Zumoff's bilingual English-Yiddish anthology of women's poetry *Songs to a Moonstruck Lady: Women in*

*Yiddish Poetry* (Toronto: TSAR Publication in association with the Dora Teitelboim Center for Yiddish Culture, 2005).

7. My thanks go to Vadim Levin and William Vinogradsky for helping to establish the details of Levin's life for me.

8. Norma Fain Pratt, "Culture and Radical Politics: Yiddish Women Writers, 1890–1940," *American Jewish History* 70 (1980): 81–82.

9. See Ezra Korman, *Yidishe dikhterins: antologye* (Shikago: L. M. Shtayn, 1928).

10. On matriarchs in Yiddish poetry, see Kathryn Hellerstein, "The Metamorphosis of the Matriarchs in Modern Yiddish Poetry," in *Yiddish Language and Culture Then and Now*, ed. Leonard Jay Greenspoon (Omaha: Creighton University Press, 1998), 201–231. Also see Joanna Lisek, "Jidisze mame—ciało i mit" [Yidishe Mame—The Body and the Myth], *Tsvishn* 3 (2010): 4–11.

11. Levin, *Tsushteyer*, 7–8. Unless noted otherwise, all works were translated by Joanna Lisek.

12. Ibid., 8.
13. Ibid.
14. Ibid., 8–9.
15. Khane Levin, *Eygns* (Kiev: Melukhe-farlag, 1941), 58–59.
16. Ibid., 60–61.
17. Ibid., 64–65.

18. For more on the motif of dress in Yiddish women's poetry, see Joanna Lisek, "Peruka, chodaki i jedwab. Poetyckie sukienki w jidyszowej szafie," *RitaBaum* 17 (2011): 18–23.

19. *Bekishe* is a type of men's coat lined with fur, cut at the waist and decorated on the chest, reaching down below the knees. It served as clothing for traveling and hunting.

20. *Tales kotn* is a type of waistcoat sewn from two straight pieces of white linen or woollen cloth put on over the head and tied at the sides, on the four edges of which tzitzit are attached.

21. *Arbekanfes* is an undergarment covering the chest and upper part of the back. The name is used interchangeably with *tales kotn*, but here it is a separate item of dress.

22. Mordechai Shinar, *Sefer-Zikaron le-ḳehilat Pints'ev: in Pinṭshev ṭogṭ shoyn nishṭ* (Tel Aviv: Irgun Yots'e Pinṭshev be-Yiśra'el uba-tefutsot, 1970), 42.

23. *Agunah* refers to a woman whose husband has left without a divorce or a woman whose husband is missing.

24. Anka Grupińska, *Najtrudniej jest spotkać Lilit* (Kraków: Wydawn Austeria, 2008), 124; on traditional dress among ultra–Orthodox women see Sima Zalcberg, "'Grace Is Deceitful and Beauty Is Vain': How Hassidic Women Cope with the Requirement of Shaving One's Head and Wearing a Black Kerchief," *Gender Issues* 24:4 (September 2007): 13–34.

25. Grupińska, *Najtrudniej jest spotkać Lilit*, 188.
26. Deut. 22: 5.
27. Levin, *Tsushteyer*, 16.
28. Ibid.
29. Ibid., 17.
30. Ibid., 17–18.
31. Ibid., 18.
32. Ibid.
33. Jerusalem Talmud, Sotah 3: 16 a; see Rachel Biale, *Women and Jewish Law: The*

*Essential Texts, Their History, & Their Relevance for Today* (New York: Schocken Books, 1984), here: *Study of Torah*, 29–41.

34. This does not mean that there were no female Jewish scholars of the Holy Scriptures. For their names, see Emily Taitz, Sondra Henry, and Cheryl Tallan, *The JPS Guide to Jewish Women: 600 B.C.E–1900 C.E.* (Philadelphia: Jewish Publication Society, 2003). The issue of the ban on women studying the Torah was itself discussed. Eminent rabbis often had well-educated daughters. It is not the exceptional person who may be remembered and discovered that is the issue here, but rather certain general cultural mechanisms. On woman's weaving, see also Exodus 35:25.

35. Proverbs 31, 10–31.
36. Levin, *Tsushteyer*, 14.
37. Ibid.
38. Ibid., 14–15.
39. Ibid., 15.
40. Ibid.
41. Ibid., 35.
42. See Ken Frieden, *Classic Yiddish Fiction: Abramovitsh, Sholem Aleichem, and Peretz* (Albany: State University of New York Press, 1995).
43. See Jean Baumgarten and Jerold C. Frakes, *Introduction to Old Yiddish Literature* (Oxford: Oxford University Press, 2005), 328–341.
44. See Shaul M. Ginzburg and Pesach S. Marek, *Еврейскія народыя пъсни въ Рассіи* (Saint Petersburg: Voskhod, 1901), 283–302.
45. Interestingly, Yiddish dictionaries do not give the feminine form of the word for soldier, *zelner*.
46. A *shikse* is a non-Jewish girl.
47. Levin, *Tsushteyer*, 123.
48. Ibid.
49. Ibid., 74.
50. Ibid.
51. Ibid.,75.
52. Ibid., 75–76.
53. Moses 31: 30–35.
54. Louis Ginzberg, *The Legends of the Jews*, Vol. 1, Project Gutenberg, http://www.gutenberg.org/dirs/etext98/1lotj10.txt.
55. Levin, *Tsushteyer*, 76.
56. On intergenerational dialogue in women's poetry in Yiddish, see Kathryn Hellerstein, "The Metamorphosis of the Matriarchs in Modern Yiddish Poetry," in *Yiddish Language and Culture Then & Now*, ed. Leonard Jay Greenspoon (Omaha: Creighton University Press, 1998), 201–231.
57. Levin, *Tsushteyer*, 19.
58. Ibid.
59. Ibid., 124.
60. Ibid., 19–20.
61. Ibid., 20.
62. Ibid., 11.
63. Ibid., 12.
64. Ibid., 13.
65. Ibid., 30.
66. Ibid., 34.

67. Ibid., 37–38.
68. Ibid., 11.
69. Ibid.
70. Ibid., 38.
71. Song of Songs 5: 1.
72. Quoted in Othmar Keel and Bolesław Mrozewicz, *Pieśń nad Pieśniami: biblijna pieśń o miłości* (Poznań: Zysk i S-ka, 1997), 176.
73. Ibid., 195.
74. Levin, *Tsushteyer*, 29–30.
75. Levin, *Eygns*, 3–4.
76. See Yekhezkl Dobrushin, "Undz Tsushteyer [vegn Khane Levins lider-buch]," *Di royte velt* 11–12 (1929): 181–189.
77. Ibid., 182.
78. Ibid., 186.
79. Ibid., 189.
80. A clear example is the chapter "Soviet Yiddish Literature," in Sol Liptzin, *A History of Yiddish Literature* (New York: Jonathan David Publishers, 1972). In that chapter, of the almost 30 writers described, there is not a single woman.
81. This of course did not save them from execution if they were seen as enemies of the system.
82. Eda Vinogradskaya, "Поэты моего детства" [Poets of My Childhood], *Вестник народного университета еврейской культуры* No. 6 (2000): 181.
83. Ibid., 189.

# The Iron Rod of Desire
## Imagism and Modernism in Anna Margolin's Drunk from the Bitter Truth

PAULA HAYES

As a reader and a critic, one of my more pressing questions about Anna Margolin's writing is how the aesthetics of her poetry is to be positioned within the broader category of modernism. Placing Margolin's poetry within the matrix of turn-of-the-century modernism is challenging, if not wholly problematic, insofar as her work does not fully reflect the core tenets of any single aesthetic theory. Does Margolin's poetic modernism correspond to the popular literary movements of her day, specifically the Yiddish movements of *Di yunge* [The Young Ones] and *Inzikhistn* [Introspectivists]? Is Margolin best classified as a feminist modernist whose poetics lends itself to comparisons within the Yiddish modernist canon, as well as outside of it? There are multiple ways of reading Margolin. We may read her as a Yiddish counterpart to the Anglo-modern Imagists Amy Lowell, T.E. Hulme,[1] and Hilda Doolittle (H.D.). If we read Margolin's work as a counterpart to Anglo-modernist Imagism, we must recognize that her images are more impressionistic than they are concise, and therefore in some ways, they break from Imagism's focus on creating physical, concrete images. In other ways, Margolin may be read as a precursor to a second wave of Jewish-American poets, which includes Muriel Rukeseyer and Adrienne Rich. In fact, Adrienne Rich's interest in translating Margolin's may indicate a degree of continuity and heritage shared between Margolin as an early modernist poet and later modernist, feminist poets.

Comparing T. E. Hulme's "Autumn" to three poems with the same title by Margolin sheds light on the relationship between Anglo-modernism's version of Imagism and Margolin's Yiddish Imagism. T. E. Hulme's "Autumn" (1909) is often praised as the first Imagist poem. The poem is short, consisting of only seven lines. The poem demonstrates a form that values the restraint of passion and strong emotion, hence alluding to a return to the classical poetic devices found not only in classical European poetry but also in classical Chinese and Japanese poetry. In the opening of Hulme's poem, we encounter a speaking voice, as well as an image of the speaker as he walks in a city at night during the autumn months. The speaker is an active observer of the scenes around him, including both city life and nature. The poem is sharp and uses concise language that makes distinct comparisons between images throughout—comparing the color of the moon to the face of a farmer and the stars in the night sky's horizon to the faces of children. In Hulme's version of modernism, both objects and colors find their corollaries. One image invokes the next image so that the poem's images are framed, and the speaking voice in the poem is framed by the perspective of what is seen and observed. By contrast, in Margolin's three poems entitled "Autumn,"[2] the images cannot be contained by the speaker's mere observation. With Margolin, there is an abundance and an overflow of emotion that spills out, over, and onto the image. In Margolin's modernism, the images are not used to convey simple scenes but are used to imprecisely convey emotions and moods. Margolin's imagery is disruptive while Hulme's imagery is an imagery of containment. One of Margolin's "Autumn" poems opens with the line "In the hot sharp glare of that dense wild garden."[3] Each successive line is a continuation of the pile of images preceding it so that each line builds image upon image until at last there is a climax created out of the images. Using nature as a voice for the feminine, Margolin writes in her own version of "Autumn" how nature "shrieks."[4] The civility and the classical restraint so characteristic of Hulme's "Autumn" is absent in Margolin's several "Autumn" poems, as Margolin uses imagery to open up the otherwise closed subject of female expressiveness.

In spite of the fact that Margolin never participated *exclusively* in any one literary or aesthetic movement of Yiddish modernism, she was well acquainted with the artistic creeds, tenets, and manifestos of several literary groups, including *Di yunge* and *Inzikhistn*. The renowned Margolin scholar Abraham Novershtern argues that if we go by Margolin's chronological age we should naturally count her as a contemporary of *Di yunge*; however, as Novershtern points out, given the fact that Margolin does not appear as a poet on the Yiddish literary scene until around 1920, this would place her as coming of age much later and as a contemporary of *Inzikhistn*.[5] This is not to say that a chronological placement is the only consideration when positioning a poet within modernism; there is also the consideration of whether a poet's work aesthetically fits within a literary movement's objectives. Arguably with the rise of Yiddish modernism at the turn of the century, Yiddish poets were quite aware of the broader Anglo-modernist movements. As many American Yiddish writers were immigrants or from immigrant families, they often drew ideas from non–American forms of modernism, such as Russian Introspectivism, Russian Acmeism, German Expressionism, and nineteenth-century French Symbolism.[6] For instance, *Inzikhistn*, represented by Aaron Glantz-Leyeles's collection of poems, *Labirint*, and by Jacob Glatstein, held the view that modernist poetry should become a form of existentialist poetry centered upon the expression of the inner self. As Benjamin and Barbara Harshav observe in Glatstein's poetry, "the Introspectivist poet wears the armor of silence toward politicized society, and tries to liberate words from the burden of sense."[7] Both *Di yunge* and *Inzihkistn* had to decide how to interpret the influence of French Symbolism on the creation of modernist verse. French Symbolism, as exemplified by Charles Baudelaire's poetry, placed a great emphasis on conveying a world of the senses. By moving away from the political and ideological, movements such as *Di yunge* and *Inzikhistn* collectively helped to invent a Yiddish modernism that would deal with matters of the self as opposed to political and ideological matters. In the history of Yiddish modernism, we see the artistic, aesthetic debates that took place between *Di yunge* and *Inzikhistn*; perhaps because of the debates that took place within these two art circles, both movements helped create a change in the intellectual atmosphere for writing Yiddish poetry. Unlike the proletarian or "Sweatshop Poets," *Di yunge* and *Inzikhistn* placed an emphasis on using poetics to capture self-expression, putting new importance on the construction and revelation of self-identity. *Di yunge* relied heavily on using a lyrical voice, as well as on the construction of symbols, moods, and images. *Di yunge* placed a greater importance on using moods to capture the poetic self; whereas *Inzikhistn* focused more on the emergence of a philosophical, existential view of the self.

Ruth Wisse says of *Di yunge* that "probably in no artistic group did aestheticism seem as anomalous as among the Yiddish poets in New York during the first decades of this century"[8] because of the socio-economic composition of the movement. Since the participants of *Di yunge* were ordinary workers, craftsmen who worked at common trades, we might expect to see *Di yunge* representing the proletarian or offer aspirations toward the bourgeoisie. Yet, as Wisse attests the general disposition of the participants in *Di yunge* was one where there was "the expression of feelings through the evocative symbols rather than by ideational statement; emphasis on musical rather than pictorial correspondences between the arts with a resulting stress of sound patterns and oral effects."[9] Wisse also points out that *Di yunge* "reacting against the bourgeoisation of culture" was able to move Yiddish modernism in the direction of internal feelings; for as Wisse writes, "[t]he movement inward dictated an immediate shift from the realm of ideas to that of moods."[10] There is a retreat from proletarian ideological concerns that we discover in *Di yunge*, as the search within for emotions and moods and the representation of these moods through prosody, rhyme, and lyric shift the emphasis away from social concerns. The result is *Di yunge* produced a move in Yiddish poetics toward more individualistic concerns. Artistically, the poetry of *Di yunge* appropriated the legacy of French Symbolism in new ways by muting the symbol or image. *Di yunge* wrote poems intending to incite a set of emotions in the reader's mind through the use of a symbol or image, but without overly emphasizing the symbol or image itself, so that the end result was *the experience of a feeling or mood*, such as the exuberance of youth or nostalgia for the past. In the poetry of Mani Leyb and Moyshe-Leyb Halperin, we find that the means by which a symbol or image is muted is through the use of a lyric form; there, in the modernism of *Di yunge* poets, we discover a focus on the *lyrical nature of the speaker* that conveys to the reader the poem's dominant mood. When reading a *Di yunge* poem, in order to trust the mood of a poem, we must trust the speaker and what the speaker is telling us.

A good example of Margolin's taking a similar approach in her poetry is "The Song of a Girl." While I am not suggesting that we read "The Song of a Girl" as an example of a *Di yunge* poem, I am suggesting that Margolin's exploration of what it means to navigate between the construction of a lyrical "I" and that of self-expression places her firmly within the middle of the two major Yiddish poetry movements of the early modernist era. Additionally, we see where Margolin is exploring the modernist problem of how to interpret the influence and legacy of French Symbolism. The first two stanzas of "The Song of a Girl" demonstrate Margolin's construction of a lyrical voice and potentially an autobiographical one.[11] In the first stanza, we encounter the speaker's excitement, as a rush of emotion causes the speaker to remember "a song without words."[12] The lyrical voice embodies sound, musicality, but the indication in the line is that the lyrical voice may be devoid of language or may move to a space outside or beyond language. The lyrical voice becomes a negation of the power of language to render artistic productions of representation, including the speaker's memories. Yet, there is also present in "The

Song of a Girl" the Imagist impulse to create images that produce comparisons between experiences and an external reality that extends past the feeling of the experience itself; we see this in the two opening lines of the second stanza. Margolin writes, "Faces fluttered like blossoms in the wind,"[13] making a comparison of Imagist style between the faces she encountered in an unnamed past experience that is now recalled in the poem and that of the blossoms of flowers. In the second line of the second stanza, the images take a decisively different turn as there is a comparison between "quivering lips" and "flaming wounds."[14] The imagery is darker and more romanticized. Who is the speaker positioned behind the lyrical "I" in "The Song of a Girl," and how do we separate the speaker from her lyrical voice? How do we separate the lyrical voice from the poem's images?

By combining the lyrical voice with image, Margolin is forging her own path between the two dominant Yiddish modernist poetic movements of her day; she is moving in and out, as well as between the spaces of the self and self-discovery that *Di yunge* and *Inzikhistn* encouraged. We may see glimpses of the influence of *Inzikhistn*'s vision for the modern poem to occur as an expression of existential reality, while also traces of *Di yunge*'s preference for the lyric mode, the evocation of moods, and the muting of images and symbols. As Wisse writes of the *Di yunge* poets, "The Yunge concentrated on precisely the most personal of their moods and feelings: loneliness, estrangement, guilt, boredom, unrequited passion."[15] In truth, we find each of these moods present in Margolin's poetry. Yet, because Margolin did not belong entirely to any of the literary movements of her day it seems the case that she felt relatively free as a poet to pull principles from often competing strands of modernism, combining aesthetic theories at will.[16]

The experiential in Margolin's poetry often takes a dark, brooding turn, where the reality of the artist's world is mysteriously transformed into discordant, monstrous images. This transformation of reality into its opposite, into nightmarish scenes, seem strikingly familiar to the poetic methods of Baudelaire and Edgar Allan Poe, the American inheritor of French Symbolism. Margolin's poem "Dear Monsters" allows for the speaking subject to enter into a maze of wandering "among people, along friendly roads."[17] Soon, the images turn to distortion, become "quiet, dreamy"[18] as the speaking subject is forced to encounter her own thoughts of loneliness and alienation. The memory of a lost love is too much for the speaker to bear so she turns inward, where she is met with unspeakable depths of despair, as the image of her absent beloved becomes negatively misshapen into "the tramp of armies in the streets" and "silhouettes."[19] There is a kaleidoscopic effect, as emotional truth, veiled and hidden through the construction of poetic masks, is overlaid with the fusion of nature and cityscapes. The speaker's voice is lost, almost drowned, amidst the grotesqueness of her landscape, as city scenes and the natural terrain of mountains become like monsters. The speaker struggles against the monsters and the grotesque landscape to save her voice: there is the "howl" and "roar,"[20] guttural utterances that sing beyond the imagination and negatively transcend language. As the speaker moves through her heart-rending cries, finally the lyrical voice progresses to weeping: "the heart weeps like a stray sheep,"[21] so that even the sound of the weeping is more animalistic than human, a bleating that once again pushes against the boundaries of what can be articulated through language. In Margolin's poetry, emotions represent a greater force to be reckoned with than that of language; for, emotions are associated with the primal essence of existence. This is not to say that language is not of vital importance to Margolin; her experimentation with rhyme and half-rhyme is certainly an indicator of her awareness of the pliability of Yiddish. But, for Margolin it seems language, through its pliability, is at times to be made subservient to emotion.

In Margolin's "Over Brown Roofs," the speaker describes both a powerful emotional state derived from the fading of love and the feelings of obscurity and isolation of walking a city street[22]; however, in this instance, Margolin does not turn to the grotesque to explain her feelings. She instead uses impressionistic images such as a sun casting a light just above the rooftops. And in place of the anxiety and fear the speaking subject expresses elsewhere in poems such as "Dear Monsters," here that sense of anxiety becomes hushed. Language is not spoken word but song, allowing the poetic voice and the speaking subject to embody lyric, as the speaker's desire and her state of missing her beloved becomes a song producing cadences. The poem evokes the sensation characteristic of T. S. Eliot and Baudelaire of describing in sensual terms the sheer emptiness of the metropolis and the unrequited love that is the outgrowth of the modern mind's inability to attach itself to any one thing, to the objective world, or any condition of permanent existence.[23] The melancholia experienced as the result of being separated from one's beloved along with the anonymity and depersonalization of a metropolis conjoin. A simple image of the light cast by the sun onto the city streets creates a mood in the poem of emotional and psychological detachment, as well as discontentment. There is the feeling of a distant autobiographical presence in the poem, as the lyric submerges the reality of the speaker. The reader's consciousness, by *feeling* the images more than *seeing* the images, is raised to the level of the poem's mood. Taken together, Margolin's poems strongly exhibit the modernist themes of discontentment, emotional detachment, and psychological isolation.

In addition to looking at the relationship between Margolin's poetry and the Yiddish movements of *Di yunge* and *Inzikhistn,* Margolin's personal relations shed a great deal of light on her intellectual and emotional development as a young, Yiddish female poet. To fully value and appreciate her poetry, we must search for ways to reconcile the contradictory and sometimes peculiar elements of her life. Anna Margolin, the literary pseudonym of Rosa Lebensboym (1887–1952), was born in Brest-Litovsk, Belorussia. Throughout her years as a poet, she struggled to find recognition among her male Yiddish contemporaries in the Lower East Side of New York. Margolin's early introduction to modernism correlates with her first visit to New York in 1906. It was in New York that Margolin struck up an acquaintance with Chaim Zhitlowsky, author, socialist, and major champion of Yiddish. Caught somewhere in the emotional space between girlhood and womanhood, she gravitated toward Zhitlowsky, and in time, became romantically involved with him. The relationship with Zhitlowsky was not permanent, but it did establish a semi-lasting pattern in Margolin's life: becoming intimately connected with men she deemed as intellectual partners. While it would be tempting to suggest that Margolin saw in Zhitlowsky an artistic mentor, I think perhaps more to the point is that Margolin through each of her relationships with prominent intellectuals may have been seeking out a relationship of gender and social equality, even if the attempts at finding this level of equality in some regard may have failed. Regardless of the motivations that lead Margolin into her relationship with Zhitlowsky, she became disillusioned and disenchanted by it. Margolin returned to Europe, where she traveled through London and Paris, two of the major centers of modernism. In Warsaw, she found a new love in the modernist writer, Moshe Stavsky. She lived with Stavsky in Warsaw, but the marriage proved by all accounts to be as unsatisfying as her earlier love affairs. With Stavsky, Margolin had a son, Naaman. Making what was a relatively unusual decision for a young woman of the era, Margolin chose to leave both husband and son.

Fleeing the domestic roles of wife and mother, Margolin returned to New York in 1913, this time making America her permanent home. Exactly what the concept of home meant to Margolin, who was at the time still very much alive in the revelries of her youth, it is quite impossible to say.[24] But it is clear that Margolin's new life in New York allowed her to evolve into her self-chosen roles of writer and poet. By twenty-six, she had travelled the world, become a divorcee, mother, intellectual, laborer, and a burgeoning writer. By 1913, she had seen some of the most prominent sites for Jewish, Yiddish, Russian, and Anglo-American and Anglo-European forms of modernism—Palestine,

Paris, Warsaw, London, Odessa, and Konigsberg. She had associated with anarchists, proletarians, socialists, political leftists, and Jewish nationalists[25]; she had attended socialist lectures and was versed in the secular Jewish Enlightenment, the *haskalah*. During Margolin's childhood, her father had encouraged her education, which was an unusual circumstance for a Jewish girl; she learned and spoke multiple languages. Her mind was primed for a spiritual and a secular perspective toward the arts when, in 1917, Margolin fell in love with Hirsh Leyb Gordon and married for the second time. Two years later, her relationship with Gordon proved, like her first marriage, to be unrewarding. During a period of estrangement from Gordon, she moved into a relationship with Reuven Azyland, the Yiddish poet and one of the founding members of *Di yunge* movement.[26] In time, Azyland's acceptance of Margolin's temperament, and perhaps his genuine admiration for her brilliance and mystical charm, flowered into the stability of a lifelong partner. Literary history tells us that Margolin had hoped to showcase Yiddish poetry for the world and bring Yiddish poetry into the forefront of the modernist scene. Much of Margolin's literary career was punctuated by a series of minor triumphs; her audience was mainly put together of Yiddish speaking Eastern European intellectuals, often first generation immigrants to America. At one point, Margolin wrote a short column for the New York Yiddish newspaper *Der tog*; the column was rather aptly titled "A Woman's World." Margolin sporadically published in journals associated with Yiddish modernism, such as *Di naye velt* and *Tsukunft*.[27] It was through these early attempts, her exploration of different literary avenues and genres, even her failures in love that led Margolin to become the poet she did.

In 1923, one year after the publication of T. S. Eliot's definitive modernist text and *tour de force The Waste Land*, Margolin edited a less than successful anthology of Yiddish poetry.[28] Though Margolin's anthology did not achieve the acceptance she had planned, still the effort testifies to her optimistic pursuit of Yiddish poetry's entrance into the broader spectrum of modernist literature. Not only did Margolin struggle to bring Yiddish modernist poetry into the larger canon of modernism, she also faced a second battle, as a female poet, of gaining the recognition she deserved in Yiddish literary circles. Her one significant triumph came in 1929, in mid-life and already past the trials of youth, while in her forties, with the publication of *Lider* [Songs or Poems].[29] Margolin's *Lider*, like T. S. Eliot's *The Waste Land*, gives truth to Arthur Symons's claim that the modernist poet should express a "disembodied voice" as the ideal form of poetry. *Lider* testified to the modernist assertion that myth, symbol, and image could be fused with the lyric mode. Like her

Anglo-modernist contemporaries, Margolin's Yiddish-modernism explored how the use of myth, symbol, and imagery could be used to convey modernity's fragmented world of "broken images."[30] Symons's claim that Symbolism is "a form of expression, at best but approximate, essentially but arbitrary, until it has obtained the force of a convention, for an unseen reality apprehended by the consciousness"[31] is an example of how modernism sought to use myth, symbol, and image as a way of describing the indescribable, the unspeakable, and the unutterable. Margolin's *Lider* was republished posthumously in 2007 under the title *Drunk from the Bitter Truth*; this bi-lingual Yiddish-English volume is a testament to the ineffable beauty of her aesthetic style. Three main techniques emerge in Margolin's *Drunk from the Bitter Truth* that when taken together come to characterize her own version of modernism: the poet's reliance upon the lyric mode or lyric form, a keen attention to the use of symbols and imagery, and a preoccupation with constructing autobiographical masks or poetic personae.[32]

The Yiddish scholar Barbara Mann refers to Margolin's poetic style as "an example of what might be called in retrospect 'Jewish imagism.'"[33] Mann's argument is that Jewish Imagism encountered a different set of restrictions placed upon it when it came to considerations of how art and poetry should be created; and, in part, many of these restrictions came from within Judaism. Largely, Judaism's prescription coded into the commandment of "thou shalt have no graven images" and "no other gods before me" translated, historically, as an anxiety and nervousness toward creating certain forms of representational art. What was to count as a "graven image?" As Mann states, "An awareness of the Second Commandment prohibition was also implicit in the rejection of forms of cultural expression that were not explicitly didactic or ideological."[34] Margolin's poetry runs against this grain of using art for "didactic or ideological" purposes, deliberately using images that may be deemed as idolatrous. Margolin's Imagism does not produce a poetics that moralizes or that embraces social or proletarian concerns. Mann also notes that as a result of the second commandment in Judaism it produced among some Yiddish modernist poets "an anxiety regarding image making" and this anxiety "undergirded pantheistic treatments of the natural world and descriptions of a new, more embodied sense of self."[35] Here, too, Margolin breaks away from Jewish cultural expectations as her poetry is full of natural images, many of which could be deemed as a "pantheism" or as representative of a plurality of views on the relationship of self, particularly the feminine self, to nature and to God.

As part of Margolin's Imagism, we find certain motifs in her poetry: gods, priests, dusk, darkness, night, the beloved and the lover of the beloved, guards and guardians, dreams, smoke and fog, gardens, trees, beggars, terror, silence, muteness, voice and speaking, shadows, the deep and the void, swords, sorrow, monsters and the monstrous, gold, sky, air, gentleness, the hues of purple and blue, sculpture, masks, veils, hardness, death, love, letters, dust, flowers, woods, piety and the pious, drunkenness, light, secrets, forgiveness, sin, the sun, and falling stars. These motifs place Margolin in the company of the Symbolists and demonstrate her indebtedness to Baudelaire and Verlaine, but the motifs also hark back to an earlier form of Romanticism. Additionally, the images evoke the German *Götterdämmerung*, even Wagner's cycle of operas, *Der Ring des Nibelungen*, with its excessive mythologizing and romanticizing. In "A City by the Sea," a prime example of Margolin's ability to bring together Symbolism with Romanticism, we find that the speaker's mind is lost amidst memories of a time she cannot clearly recall. In the poet's hazy daydream, the city is enclosed by a sea, a place where the speaker once heard Chopin's nocturnes and where she watched couples dance a waltz. The speaker's youth has elapsed and "the dancers waft by and vanish like phantoms."[36] In her modernism, Margolin's use of images are imprecise, yet are connected to both an existential, thinking consciousness that possesses memories. While Margolin's use of images lack the concreteness that a reader might anticipate coming from an Imagist writer; nonetheless, her images trigger an emergence of a feminine self that remembers, dreams, even yearns.

In poems such as "We Went Through the Days," Margolin's use of images is less than material, breaking with the prescriptions typically associated with Imagism. In "We Went Through the Days," Margolin writes in the opening of the poem, "We went through the days as through storm-tossed gardens" while the activity of the lovers uplift their spirits to become "like happy creatures and clever, playful gods."[37] The transgressive and idolatrous imagery is deliberate and self-consciously formed. Margolin's Imagism is not the "*direct treatment of a thing*" that defines Ezra Pound's Anglo-modernist Imagism, but is instead a form of Imagism that breaks the "thing" being described into an impressionist scene, where the senses and the self begins to unite and where autobiographical revelation is couched behind the haze of images. The images in Margolin's poetry cause the reader to "see" the scene as though looking through a screen, a film, or a veil. Often, the speaker's identity in Margolin's poems is split: this fractured representation of self at times embraces the role of the beloved, the recipient of love, and at other times plays the role of the pursuer of the beloved. What we find in Margolin's poetry is her unusual ability to break the speaker's self-identity into two parts: into an autobiographical

"I," who remembers, possesses memories, and holds desires for past and future and into a self that moves further from the autobiographical "I" into selfhood. If we examine the whole of Margolin's poetry, there we will discover a dualism between the lyrical "I" and the existential self. This may be Margolin's ability to bring together and merge *Di yunge*'s focus on a lyrical "I" with that of *Inzikhistn*'s focus on the existential self. In Margolin, the merging of these two Yiddish aesthetic movements produces the poetical convention of a dualism of self-expression, where self-expression is caught, almost trapped, between a lyrical "I" and the existential self of being. Yet, both parts of this dualism, the lyrical "I" plus the existential self, when put together move us in the direction of a Yiddish poetics that is deeply concerned with the formation of selfhood. Yiddish poetry concerned with selfhood is one step in the longer history of the evolution of a poetic modernism concerned with the self-identify of identity politics.

In an exchange of personal letters with Reuven Ayzland, Margolin compares the creative process of the poet to that of a sculptor.[38] Margolin's fascination with sculpture as an analogy or metaphor for the poet's creative process helps to locate Margolin's aesthetic interests along the broader spectrum of Anglo-modernism's desire to transform the poem into an art object of objective contemplation. In Anglo-modernism, the poem could undergo this transformation into object through the consideration of other art mediums, namely by looking to the visual arts and plastic arts for models. Ezra Pound's early modernist poem "To Whistler, American" is one such example. In that poem, the speaker is feeling his way through the timeline of history seeking out the shadowy formations of a national identity that may also double as a cultural identity for the creation of poetry and art.[39] The speaker finds his way to poetic inspiration by first looking to painters from Albrecht Durer to James Abbott Whistler. The speaker's search takes him through "sketches" that are done "in the mood of Greece" and that pass through "that mass of dolts."[40] Pound's insistence that the poet is not after ideas, but is instead after a "vortex" of inspiration is comparable to the Yiddish *Di yunge*'s insistence that a poem should express the mood and not a world of ideas. We may consider Pound's interest in the English painter Wyndam Lewis, Pound's later participation in Vorticism, as well as Amy Lowell's and H. D.'s incorporation of geometrical lines, painting, and sculpture into their poetics, each as instances where the modernist Imagist poet perceived his or her task as analogous to that of a painter or sculpture.[41] Pound, for example, once noted how in his composition of his quintessential Imagist poem, "In a Station of the Metro," that instead of writing a poem describing his emotional experience of the metro station, he could have just as easily chosen another medium, such as paint or sculpture to offer the representation of feeling.[42] Modernism's hope of reconstituting the elemental nature of the poem as an art object required that there be a model to follow: the rigidity, toughness, plasticity, and permanency of the visual arts provided this model. Margolin's posturing in *Lider* is in keeping with Anglo-modernism's dalliance with the visual arts. As Novershtern remarks, for Margolin, "Sculptural concision is never the real essence of the personae presented in her poetry; it is only a pose."[43]

Not only is Reuven Azyland's relationship with Margolin a good source for understanding Margolin's theories on modernist poetics, we also learn from her relationship with Azyland something of the emotional anguish Margolin may have felt at her choice to desert her infant son, leaving him in Palestine in the company of her ex-husband, Moshe. While it is impossible to understand with certainty Margolin's decision to abandon her son, it is plausible to assert that the emotional impact of her choice may be traceable in a number of her poems, such as "What Do You Want, Mary?" Although the poem may be read and interpreted as symbolizing the Christian figure of the Virgin Mary, the selection of a Christian theme for a Yiddish poet is strikingly out of place. Margolin's selection of Mary (or Mari in some translations) makes the speaker's persona less accessible to the Yiddish or Jewish reader. Margolin writes her own mythos of Mary, transforming her into a modern and a pagan. Additionally, "What Do You Want, Mary?" may serve as the means for Margolin's rather personal exploration of motherhood; it is possible that Margolin's feelings of lost love for her son, and even feelings of guilt for leaving her son, are transferred within the poem onto the figure of Mary. "What Do You Want, Mary" refashions the image of the Christian Virgin Mary into a woman who faces the inner struggles of her own incapacity to embrace the trials of motherhood.[44] The poem gives the vague impression of a domestic scene, one filled with misery, loneliness, and seclusion. A poetic technique that Margolin relies on in the poem is repetition. However, in the instance of this poem, Margolin's repetition of the question "What do you want, Mary?" takes on a feeling of *universalism*, as the speaker probes deeper into what it is that *any* woman truly wants. The poem questions whether the domestic role of mother is what a woman wants or what *all* women even want; as the poem builds in its momentum, the role of motherhood is overshadowed by the speaker's longings. In place of motherhood, Mary speaking in the voice of the lyrical "I" in the poem answers the rhetorical question, posing "I want my feet rooted in the earth."[45] The warmth of the earth and its fresh fields stands in sharp contrast, as well as in tension to her "stern"[46] domestic abode.

We find Mary is placed into a perpetual state of waiting, spending her nights alone. "What Do You Want, Mary?" is an enactment of the feminine voice wrestling to come to terms with a woman's assigned social place as mother, while hoping to transcend the social restrictions of gender.

In Margolin's "What Do You Want, Mary?" we find where Mary is faced with the choice of living a life enclosed within the domestic sphere, with its daily responsibilities and illusions of love, or with the decision to escape the boundaries of the domestic, abandoning motherhood and freeing herself to discover an existence apart from domestic obligation. Faced with these two choices, Mary chooses her existential freedom, or at least the longing for this existential freedom is made clear and overpowers the other considerations of social roles in the poem. In the second half of "What Do You Want, Mary?" the language of the poem shifts from focusing on Mary toward a much more subjective use of the lyrical "I." This shift to the lyrical "I" signifies the poet's self-identification with the poem's own constructed myth of Mary. In the second half of the poem, Mary, by burying herself within her own subjectivity, becomes metaphorically delivered into a state of nature. And though there is seemingly a greater sense of danger for Mary waiting for her outside the domestic sphere, or so the mood of the poem seems to convey, there is also the reward of discovering how the feminine is connected to areas beyond the social. The poem's tempo picks up speed as Mary slips further and further into an overwhelmingly impressionistic world of nature. Similar to what we would expect to find in a poem by H.D. where nature becomes a transcendent force, amoral and sensual, here too in Margolin's "What Do You Want, Mary?" we find nature as a primal source for the emergence of feminine self-expression. The sun penetrates; the rain is "savage" but dowses Mary in its kisses, as a storm overtakes her by "bending" Mary to its own will.[47] In H. D.'s early modernist text *Sea Garden* (1916), we come across images of nature as aggressive, vigorous, and lusty. Margolin's images of nature, too, are lusty, and mostly tinged with the melancholic. The melancholia in Margolin's poetics may have been an indicator of her own mental struggles, the possible phases of depression she faced, even a foreshadowing of the reclusiveness that would overtake Margolin in the last part of her life. In general, we may surmise that Margolin's "Mary Poems" use untamed nature as a symbol for the liberty of the female spirit.[48] In other Margolin poems, the wildness of gardens and the harshness of the seasons become symbols for describing the feminine as a borderless essence. In "Mother Earth, Well-Worn, Sun-Washed," there is a close association of femininity with uninhabited nature.[49] The lyric voice takes on the persona of the earth, a goddess form, yet also, paradoxically enslaved to the sun.

The earth is bound in "long blind silence," strong and active but assigned to a subjected condition that stands in stark contrast to the freedom of the sun's hot, burning rays.[50] The speaker calls herself "beloved," but describes herself as a "dusky slave" and a "mistress"[51] to the sun. To be the beloved, to be a woman, is to be a pagan, a goddess, and to worship the sun.

Many of Margolin's poems express a private spirituality, while simultaneously exploring the secular and the pagan. Several of her poems tend to confront and challenge God, as though written from the perspective of a female Job. There is, in fact, such a deeply entrenched sense of suffering in Margolin's poetry that it is difficult to assign all of the suffering to secular themes. To be sure, there is a component of suffering in Margolin's poems that is nothing short of a Job-like experience as the poet wrestles with the meaning of God and God's existence. The poem "Mary's Prayer" is another example of the way in which Margolin takes up the symbol or mask of the Virgin Mary, and here too much like the Anglo-modernist Imagist, H. D., Margolin is concerned with mytho-poetic constructions that create autobiographical masks. Though the poem expresses many feminist concerns, it also conveys a heightened sense of spiritual desolation.[52] "Mary's Prayer" depicts Mary as suffering as a result of her own silence, or perhaps suffering from God's silence *toward* her. Instead of portraying Mary as consoled, Margolin renders an image of Mary as desperate, fearful. As readers, we do not necessarily emerge from either "What Do You Want, Mary?" or "Mary's Prayer" with a sense that Mary's selection by God as the vessel of holy life is something that Mary herself wanted; the chosen stature of Mary is not the prominent element of Margolin's poems on Mary. In "Mary's Prayer," Margolin's allusions to the immaculate conception is told in frightening terms, revealing Mary's fear. The result is that a quite human image of Mary emerges. We see Mary's flaws, how she struggles and wrestles with the responsibility that has been handed to her; we even see Mary's desire to deny her chosen status and escape from it. Here, we may find a comparison between Margolin and the Russian poet Anna Akhmatova's poem "Lot's Wife"[53] and its exhibition of Russian Acmeism. In Akhmatova's "Lot's Wife," we find the Jewish story of Lot's wife being turned into a pillar of salt as reconceptualized from the perspective of the wife. Traditionally, in the account from the *Tanakh*, we are not given the name of Lot's wife. Yet, Akhmatova takes the image of this unnamed woman and returns to her a sense of dignity and humanity, as we come to understand the desire of Lot's wife to see the place she loved, her home and homeland, one last time. In Akhmatova's rendering of Lot's wife, we feel the wife's pain; yet, in the same instant that Akhmatova is humanizing Lot's wife, she is also using the image of Lot's wife as a mask to cover the self-expression of the poet. In a similar manner, Margolin uses the image of the Christian Mary to mask and conceal self-expression. We may look to other examples of female modernist poets using historical figures to construct masks; take for instance H. D.'s poem "Helen." The poem published in 1928 stands as an example of Anglo-modernism's ability within the movement of Imagism to confront socially taboo subjects, such as female sexuality, gender, and female expressiveness by constructing masks: either autobiographical masks or as a masking of self-expression.

"Mary's Prayer" wrestles rather genuinely with questions of sin and repentance, while exploring Mary as God's guardian and servant. Unable to ascertain where God is, Mary takes an unconventional path to finding God, by using her sin as a path. Should we interpret Margolin's line that the "flames of sin and tears"[54] is a path to God as being a theological statement on Margolin's part? Is it a literary statement signifying the influence of Baudelaire? In Baudelaire, sin is an ontological category, but also a form of personal, individualistic rebellion, as iniquity becomes the language of the poet.[55] God's silence toward Mary stands as a paradox in the poem when placed beside Mary's activity of building God a "nest" of adoration."[56] The "nest" is the product of Mary's "love"; yet, the "temple" is the product of Mary's meekness.[57] We may ask whether Margolin's image of Mary's "temple" is fashioned after a Jewish temple, or if this is a pagan temple fashioned after the modernists. The "nest" is a symbol of the domestic, the comfort of that space, but that is in tension with God's own silence. Love is active, but worship and servitude is submissive. Here, too we must inquire about Margolin's intentions in selecting her imagery. We see once more the dualism present in Margolin—a passive self, but also an active one. There is an active vision of God, but also the silence of God as a passive form of the divine. The last three lines of the poem reveal a dark night of the soul, as Mary is shown to be completely still, waiting, as God moves *through* her.[58] Margolin's image of God's passage over and through Mary gives an echo of the Twenty-Third Psalm, yet other images depict spiritual struggle in the mythical and pagan language of war. Yet ultimately, in "Mary's Prayer," the image of God depicted more nearly approaches Zeus than the Jewish God.

The poem "Portrait" makes reference to God's secret election of a "scorned woman" and her "elevation" above those who mock her.[59] In "Portrait," Margolin is demonstrating her acknowledgment to *Di yunge* while also breaking with *Di yunge*'s belief that poetry reveals authentic self-expression, and perhaps her dedication of the poem to the founder of *Inzikhistn*, Glantz-

Leyeles, indicates a preference for *Inzikhistn*. While the reader might expect from the title of the poem for the content to offer a genuine representation of the poet, there is no exact rendering in "Portrait." Instead of offering a precise self-portrait as might be anticipated, Margolin describes herself through the gendered lens of an objectified woman, as one caught up in the unpleasing gaze of others, an imagined other. In this way, Margolin is more like the *Inzikhistn*; for, Margolin shuns the task of self-portraiture in favor of creating a mask that holds her own sense of subjectivity at bay while paradoxically using the mask to explore an existential nature of the self.[60] Reading the first stanza, the reader may question who exactly is being rebuked in the poem. Is the speaker rebuffing God for filling the woman's life with a grief so profound that it "inflamed her," or perhaps society for its "mockery" of the woman's condition?[61] Margolin's "Portrait" plays upon the poet's realization that art fabricates a version of truth, comparing the truth of selfhood to an "empty house."[62] The image of the mirror in the second stanza recalls Yiddish modernists such as Mani Leyb's construction of self-portraiture, only to turn and reject the image of the mirror; thereby, signaling a refusal to surrender to a complete acceptance of *Di yunge*'s aesthetic ideals. "Portrait" tends to proclaim the voice of the poet's subjectivity as *damned* to a state of *otherness*. Thus, the unidentified woman in the poem is symbolically shown to suffer from the poem's inability to perform its single and primary function: namely to speak for the subjectivity of the poet and artist. Given that the poem cannot perform what it is designed or defined to do, to speak or reveal authentic subjectivity, the poet herself feels the weight of what it means to lack voice. Margolin's admission of poetry's failure to present authentic forms of self-representation is evident in the last stanza of "Portrait." The speaker, after admitting that her "mask" is a form of "silence" or of silencing the truth of the self, the speaker is symbolically smothered or suffocated by the inability to achieve a unification between subjectivity (the poet's revelation of an authentic self) and the construction of the poetic mask. The poem ends with a "burning madness" that is connected to "her throat" that stifles creativity and creative freedom.[63] We may question whether Margolin's intention was to create a parody, almost, of *Di yunge*'s attempts to capture accurate self-description only to show that such attempts become too restrictive; the poem appears to favor the existential approach to the formation of self, a theme more appropriate for an *Inzikhistn* poet.

The past, for the modernists, represented a way of escaping the angst and uncertainties of modernity by reclaiming an imagined, long-lost ancestral past. In many ways, Margolin's emblematic poem "Once I Was a Youth" serves as an intra-textual response to Anglo-modernism's obsession with locating a primal, unclaimed golden era in the past of western civilization. Yet, the effect of the poem in its ironic temperament is to question modernism's great appeal toward the classical past as a moral source of authority. The poem may also play upon the novelty of *Di yunge*'s belief in *l'art pour l'art*. Relying on the modernist technique of bringing together incongruent images, often from multiple time periods, as a way of showing the need to bridge the present moment with the past, "Once I was a Youth" brings together classical images— the philosopher Socrates, the Roman ruler Caesar, and Jesus, the Jew, the Nazarene. Novershtern, refers to "Once I Was a Youth" as a poem "marked by an explicitly negative identification of the lyrical persona."[64] Novershtern defines the speaker's persona as "negative" because each persona seems to defy attempts to claim a complete, whole identity, crashing against the boundaries of definition—"neither feminist, Jewish, nor modern."[65] Novershtern reasons that Margolin's placement of "Once I Was a Youth" at the opening of her book *Lider* counters the aesthetic principles of *Di yunge*. Mani Leyb's *Lider* opens with a poem of self-portraiture—"Mani Leyb's aim was to draw an accurate self-portrait in the spirit of the Romantic tradition, which highly valued sincerity. In contrast, in 'Once I Was a Youth,' Anna Margolin declared her contrary aim to *escape* self-portraiture."[66] Novershtern goes on to note, "Once I Was a Youth," represents a form of "cultural hybridism—the formation of a persona which both comprises femininity and masculinity, both Jewish and secular qualities ... the secular element in her poetry takes on a sort of pagan hedonism."[67] While Margolin was using the modality of the lyric and the lyrical voice in the construction of a personal poetics, her purpose was likely to achieve self-concealment, self-effacement, and the alienation of the speaker's intentions. The fact that the speaker's persona resists complete identification with any one form of social, cultural, historical, or even gender categorizations is precisely what makes the poem function as a work of modernism. The *negative lyrical moments* of the poem are created as the speaker of the poem adopts a series of imprudent, masculine facades that hide the poet's true feminine identity as a Yiddish woman living in the modern age. The lyrical voice of the speaker is a transcendent element in the poem and repositions itself as part of, in the words of Novershtern, an "amoral world of philosophy, beauty, art and sculpture."[68] In a somewhat unsettling way, yet in an attempt to reclaim a historical possession of Jewish history as a marginalized source of western civilization, the lyrical construction of the speaker's voice in "Once I Was a Youth" works to declare the Greco-Roman world as effeminate and ineffectual. In what is almost a Nietzschean condemnation, "Once I Was a Youth" reproaches western civilization for its historical parade of immoral conduct and chides Christianity for its feebleness, all the while assigning strength to the Jews. There is a dim tone the poem communicates, as if to inquire what will be the fate of the Jewish people at the hands of western civilization?

The advent of Christianity, too, holds a paradoxical position in the poem, as Jesus, a Jew, is considered "the weakling from Nazareth" contrasted against the "wild stories about the Jews."[69] The poem is deliberately and self-consciously ambiguous in its representation of Christianity, and in particular in its representation of the relationship of Judaism to Christianity. The pagan roots of Christianity are present in the poem, as the image of Jesus is depicted on par with the Greek Socrates and the Roman Caesar; yet, the coupling of Jesus with the "wild stories of the Jews" also places Jesus in the company of the Jews, and in a sense, reconstructs an atmosphere of historical and social confusion over what to do with the figure of Jesus. Does Jesus belong to the culture of Hellenism and Greco-Romanism? Is Jesus a figure belonging to classical antiquity? Is Margolin going so far as to reclaim Jesus, perhaps as she does with the figure of Mary, as belonging to Jewish culture? Is there a reconstitution of the Jewishness of Jesus in the poem? These questions are complicated by the fact that Margolin assigns the word "weakling" to the image of Jesus, and this seems to force a historical and cultural alignment of Jesus with classical antiquity. Furthermore, the images in "Once I Was a Youth" hold violent connotations. Socrates as an ancient father of secular rationalism, a keeper of wisdom, and a typological figure of a prophet is condemned to death for his treason against the youth of Athens and his alleged irreligious claims against the gods of Greece. While the history of Socrates is neither directly told nor narrated in Margolin's poem, Socrates does function in the poem as an example of a condensed symbol. It is what the reader may likely associate with Socrates, as with Caesar and Jesus, that are important in the poem, not only what Margolin chooses to directly state or to conspicuously omit. Condensed into the symbol of Socrates is the likely association of his death by hemlock and his inability to successfully defend himself against the tyranny of the Athenian courts; thus, as a symbol in the containment of the poem, Socrates stands as the first tragic, violent moment in the evolution of western culture's historical consciousness. On the other end of the scale stands Jesus, likewise a condensed symbol in the poem, as the persecution and crucifixion of Jesus becomes the last tragic, violent moment in the ancient history of the Greco-Roman world out of which is birthed a new consciousness in western civilization. Underlying these definitive, yet tragic-violent moments, that alter the collective consciousness of western civilization, is the marginalization of the Jewish people. And so, too, the "wild stories of the Jews" stands as a condensed symbol in the poem for those who stand at the fringes of western culture.

The feminization of Socrates, Caesar, and Jesus may also be connected to the way that the language of Yiddish was thought of as a feminized language, the language of women's prayers or grandmother's stories.[70] As Allison Schachter has noted, "Secular writers who wrote in Hebrew and Yiddish could not totally divorce these languages from their gendered associations as they competed, with each other and with writers in other European languages, for newly sex-integrated Jewish audiences."[71] Part of the Jewish project of modernism in literature was to create a new Jewish culture that would exist "along new national and ethnic lines, aiming to create a national (not territorial) literature that represented a Jewish culture unmarred by racialized and gendered stereotypes."[72] Contained within the project of modernism is how to construct an image or images of home, homeland, and national culture. In Margolin's poetics, the reader is left wondering and asking, where is home for Margolin? As poems like "Once I Was a Youth" indicate, home is always displaced, marginalized, put off, and caught in the act of perpetual invention and re-invention, ensnared as it is between the cultural spaces of other nations, other cultures' narratives of identity.

In Margolin's modernism, in place of a search for home, there is the personal and the emotional; yet, the personal and the emotional are equally displaced. A good example is "Just One Poem," in which Margolin intimates that behind all of her poetry is the autobiographical impulse to repeat the story of her own personal sense of "despair and pride," until finally language itself becomes exhausted.[73] The fact that personal truth can never fully be revealed causes language to falter. Sensuality is conveyed in many of Margolin's poems, especially in the poems that are overtly melancholic. Margolin's work reveals a great sense of drifting, as though labyrinths fill the heart, mind, and soul of the poet. Consider "I Have Wandered So Much," which rather oddly uses highly masculinized images to convey a woman's insatiable thirst for love. In that poem, Margolin describes her drifting as "through hearts like wastelands."[74] None of the images in "I Have Wandered So Much" express female passivity or even modesty. Instead, the poet overturns these stereotypes about a woman's accepted role as pristine, pure, and demur. Margolin describes, what are perhaps her own many love affairs, as the effect of "bad blood" and "the iron rod of desire."[75] By removing Victorian sensibility and using the imagery of war, combining Symbolism and returning to the traces of Romanticism, Margolin places the woman as the victor, the valorized, and the *conqueror* (and not the conquered). Yet, for all its hardness, Margolin's poetry makes a plea to the listener, to the absent lover, and to the beloved—"Be kind."[76] Margolin's poetry is a beautiful expression of the hard and soft impulses of the female spirit. Her artistic life was spent in the search of the darker beauty of hiding self from self, shadow from shadow. But always the shadows are lightened just a little by the light of Margolin's longing, a particular longing that culminates in the descent of day as it shades itself into night to find, embrace, and belong eternally to that intangible world of love, spirit, even God.

## Notes

All the poems discussed in this essay are published in Anna Margolin and Shirley Kumove, *Drunk from the Bitter Truth: The Poems of Anna Margolin* (Albany: State University of New York Press, 2005).

1. For an understanding of Hulme's contribution to Anglo-modernism, see T. E. Hulme, "Romanticism and Classicism," in *Speculations: Essays on Humanism and the Philosophy of Art*, ed. Herbert Read (New York: Routledge, 2014), 111–140. In the essay, Hulme argues that poetics should steer away from the excesses of Romanticism and return to the restraints offered by Classicism.

2. The three poems are published in Anna Margolin and Shirley Kumove, *Drunk from the Bitter Truth: The Poems of Anna Margolin* (Albany: State University of New York Press, 2005): 117, 125, and 131.

3. Ibid., 117.

4. Ibid.

5. Abraham Novershtern, "'Who Would Have Believed That a Bronze Statue Can Weep': The Poetry of Anna Margolin," *Prooftexts* 10: 3 (1990): 437.

6. For an understanding of the relationship between French Symbolism, Anglo-modernism (Anglo-American modernism), and Russian Acmeism, see Elaine Ruskino, "Russian Acmeism and Anglo-American Imagism," *Ulbandus Review* 1:2 (Spring 1978): 37–49.

7. Benjamin and Barbara Harshav, *American Yiddish Poetry: A Bilingual Anthology* (Stanford: Stanford University Press, 2007), 50.

8. Ruth R. Wisse, "*Di Yunge* and the Problem of Jewish Aestheticism," *Jewish Social Studies* 38 (1976): 266.

9. Ibid.

10. Ibid., 266–267.

11. Naomi Brenner, "Slippery Selves: Rachel Bluvstein and Anna Margolin in Poetry and in Public," *Nashim: A Journal of Jewish Women's Studies & Gender Studies* 19 (2010): 105–106. Additionally, for a discussion of how Margolin's lyrical "I" may be musically translated into lyricism for performance arts, see Adrienne Cooper, "Making Music with Anna Margolin: Creating 'Shake My Heart Like a Copper Bell': A Poet, a Composer, an Interpreter—Three Lives in Yiddish Art," *Bridges: A Jewish Feminist Journal* 15: 2 (Autumn 2010): 39–49.

12. Kumove, *Drunk from the Bitter Truth*, 227.

13. Ibid.

14. Ibid.

15. Wisse, "*Di Yunge*," 267.

16. Novershtern, "Who Would Have Believed," 437–441. Novershtern argues that many of *Di yunge* poets, such as Mani Leyb, valued sincerity and accurate self-portraiture. By comparison, Margolin sought to hide the self behind persona and masks.
17. Kumove, *Drunk from the Bitter Truth*, 101.
18. Ibid.
19. Ibid.
20. Ibid., 103.
21. Ibid.
22. Ibid., 119.
23. For a historical context of T. S. Eliot's encounter with the material of the French Symbolist Charles Baudelaire, see John Morgenstern, "The 'Center of Intensity': T. S. Eliot's Reassessment of Baudelaire in 1910–1911 Paris," *Religion and Literature* 44:1 (Spring 2012): 159–167.
24. Cooper, "Making Music with Anna Margolin," 43.
25. Ibid., 45.
26. Faith Jones, "Criticizing Women," *Bridges: A Jewish Feminist Journal* 13: 1 (2008): 78. Jones details the significance of Margolin's relationship with Ayzland as it relates to Margolin's development as a poet. Jones quotes from letters exchanged between Ayzland and Margolin wherein Margolin discusses her poetic style, including her breaking of tradition with Yiddish poetry of using precise rhyming schemes. Margolin describes in her letters with Ayzland her choice to use rhyming patterns that are near-rhymes as an artistic device.
27. For historical background on the emergence of female Jewish writers in the 1920s and 1930s as it parallels new social roles for women within the practice of Judaism, see Norma Fain Pratt, "Transitions in Judaism: The Jewish American Woman Through the 1930s," *American Quarterly* 30: 5 (1978): 681–702. Pratt makes the argument that during the 1920s and 1930s Jewish women began to recreate the social expectations of women and work to form more progressive norms for women, including the ability to be involved in the arts. Pratt's argument is that the changing structure of social roles for women between the late nineteenth century and early twentieth century paved the way for female Jewish poetry. Pratt also discusses the sexism and discrimination that female Jewish writers faced during the era. Pratt links her argument of changing social roles for women with the alterations in Jewish religion, particularly Reform Judaism.
28. In 1923, Anna Margolin edited and self-published *Dos yidishe lid in amerike—1923*, an anthology of contemporary Yiddish poetry in which she excluded her own work. See Kumove, *Drunk from the Bitter Truth*, xx. Her single volume of eighty poems, *Lider*, was issued in 1929 by Orion Press in New York. Abraham Novershtern edited a Yiddish edition of the volume, which was published in Jerusalem by The Magnes Press in 1991.
29. For a brief discussion of the publishing success of Anna Margolin's *Lider*, see Jones, "Criticizing Women," 77. For a discussion of how Anna Margolin's publication of *Lider* was part of a proliferation of Yiddish poetry during the 1920s, see Novershtern, "Who Would Have Believed," 434–436. Additionally, see Brenner, "Slippery Selves," 108–110.
30. T. S. Eliot's version of modernism argued that tradition, ancestry, and religion had become broken sources for the modern poet. The fragmentation produced by modernity's mechanizations, technological changes, the rise of the metropolis, and the loss of confidence in organized religions inform the major themes in Eliot's writing and of High Modernism in general. Modernism's concentration on disillusionment, disembodiment,

### 178   Women Writers of Yiddish Literature

and ironic distance between the subjective nature of art and the poem and the objective nature of art and the poem define much of Anglo-American poetry written during the 1920s and 1930s. A strong correlation may be drawn between Margolin's Yiddish-American modernism, as it also contained themes of confronting modernity's fragmentation of society, the loss of faith in tradition, and the modern experience of being uprooted from one's historical ancestry. Like Eliot, Margolin's poetry offers an ironic voice and an ironic distance between subject (speaker) and object (images described).

 31. Arthur Symons, *The Symbolist Movement in Literature* (New York: E. P. Dutton, 1919), 1.

 32. Novershtern, "Who Would Have Believed," 448–453. Additionally, for a discussion of Margolin's use of the autobiographical and the construction of the "autobiographical self," see Brenner, "Slippery Selves," 105–106.

 33. For an overview of Yiddish modernism and imagism, see Barbara Mann, "Picturing the Poetry of Anna Margolin," *Modern Language Quarterly* 63:4 (2002): 501–536.

 34. Ibid., 502.

 35. Ibid., 502–3.

 36. Kumove, *Drunk from the Bitter Truth*, 17.

 37. Ibid., 23.

 38. Novershtern, "Who Would Have Believed," 441–444.

 39. See Ezra Pound, "To Whistler, American," *Poetry* 1 (October 1912): 7.

 40. Ibid. For a discussion on Pound's use of the poem "To Whistler, American" and how the poem represents an early invention in the theory of Imagism, see the insightful article by Bartholomew Brinkman, "Making Modern Poetry: Format, Genre and the Invention of Imagism(e)," *Journal of Modern Language* 32:2 (2009): 26.

 41. To read more about Pound's theory of the vortex in Imagism, see Eliot Wineberger, "The Vortex," *Chicago Review* 51, no. 4, 52, no.1 (Spring 2006): 186–202.

 42. For further discussion of how Pound conceptualized the poem "In a Station of the Metro," see Brinkman, "Making Modern Poetry," 28.

 43. Novershtern, "Who Would Have Believed," 441.

 44. For a discussion of another one of Margolin's "Mary Poems," specifically "Mary's Prayer," see Kathryn Hellerstein, "Translating as a Feminist: Reconceiving Anna Margolin," *Prooftexts* 20: 1 & 2 (Winter/Spring 2000): 191–208. Hellerstein argues that the way in which a translator chooses to translate the language and images in Margolin's poems may be influenced by the translator's own feminist views or concerns with Margolin's themes. Hellerstein also holds the view that Margolin's poems are more directly modernist in their aesthetic constructions, often in contrast to many of her Yiddish female poet counterparts of the era. Hellerstein indicates that in addition to Margolin's more obvious modernism, it is possible to interpret feminist themes in her poetry.

 45. Kumove, *Drunk from the Bitter Truth*, 185.

 46. Ibid.

 47. Ibid.

 48. Furthermore, I am using the term "the Mary Poems" as a way of grouping, classifying, and characterizing Margolin's poems that refer to the Virgin Mary. Margolin wrote seven poems using the Virgin Mary as the central symbol of the poem. The poems that I am arguing comprise Margolin's "Mary Poems" are the following: "What Do You Want, Mary?" "Mary's Prayer," "Mary and the Priest," "Lonely Mary," "Mary and the Guests," "Mary Wants to be Beggar Woman," and "Mary and Death." See Kumove, *Drunk from the Bitter Truth*, 183–205 for these poems.

49. Kumove, *Drunk from the Bitter Truth*, 5.
50. Ibid.
51. Ibid.
52. As part of my critical reading of Margolin's poems, I hold that spiritual desolation as a tenet of modernism is a thematic concern that Margolin has in common with poets such as T. S. Eliot, Ezra Pound, and Muriel Rukeyser.
53. The translation of the poem "Lot's Wife" that I am using appears in Anna Akhmatova and D. M. Thomas, *Anna Akhmatova: Selected Poems* (New York: Penguin Classics, 1995), 55.
54. Kumove, *Drunk from the Bitter Truth*, 189.
55. For a good discussion of the use of sin and vice as aesthetic categories in Baudelaire's poetry, see Tony W. Garland, "Brothers in Paradox: Swinburne, Baudelaire, and the Paradox of Sin," *Victorian Poetry* 47:4 (Winter 2009): 633–645.
56. Kumove, *Drunk from the Bitter Truth*, 189.
57. Ibid.
58. Ibid.
59. Kumove, *Drunk from the Bitter Truth*, 7.
60. Novershtern, "Who Would Have Believed," 457.
61. Kumove, *Drunk from the Bitter Truth*, 7.
62. Ibid.
63. Ibid.
64. Novershtern, "Who Would Have Believed," 440.
65. Ibid.
66. Ibid., 441.
67. Ibid., 453.
68. Ibid., 440.
69. Kumove, *Drunk from the Bitter Truth*, 3.
70. Allison Schachter, "Modernist Indexicality: The Language of Gender, Race, and Domesticity in Hebrew and Yiddish Modernism," *Modern Language Quarterly* 72:4 (December 2011): 493–520.
71. Ibid., 499.
72. Ibid.
73. Kumove, *Drunk from the Bitter Truth*, 175.
74. Ibid., 29.
75. Ibid.
76. Ibid.

# Forgotten Playwright
## *Kadya Molodowsky and the Yiddish Theater*

### Debra Caplan

In 1934, Kadya Molodowsky (1894–1975), author of three highly regarded books of poetry and the most prominent female writer in interwar Poland, published a series of sharply critical theater reviews in the Warsaw Yiddish paper *Fraynd*. In spite of having no professional experience with the theater prior to writing these reviews, Molodowsky indicted the offerings of the Warsaw Yiddish stage in the confident, if exasperated, didactic voice of an experienced and established theater critic. "To produce a play—new or old—means to interpret the play, so that one will get something out of it," she wrote in her first review. "In the Skala Theater's interpretation of *The Inspector General* there is not a single central moment. Nothing is emphasized at all."[1] Even more egregious to Molodowsky, the director seemed unaware of moments where the playwright had explicitly highlighted various themes or elements. "What is left? Everything is washed-out, lackluster. There is no concept."[2] In subsequent reviews, Molodowsky continued to accuse aspiring high-art directors of transforming literary dramas into trashy, melodramatic *shund*. A few years later, Molodowsky would turn to writing her own plays in an attempt to add a new dramatic voice to the Yiddish stage that had so profoundly disappointed her.

This essay is the first to assess Molodowsky's multifaceted contributions to the Yiddish theater during the interwar period. Molodowsky is best known for her accomplishments as a prolific Yiddish poet and children's author. Yet her oeuvre also included theater criticism along with three inspired and innovative dramas: *Ale fentser tsu der zun* [All Windows Face the Sun, 1938]; *Nokhn got fun midber* [After the Desert God, 1949]; and *A hoyz af grand strit* [A House on Grand Street, 1953]. All have yet to be critically assessed. Indeed, Molodowsky's multifaceted contributions to the professional Yiddish theater have been consistently overlooked by scholars and critics. Molodowsky's colleagues tended to ignore her dramas even as they lauded her poetry in prominent journals; her plays were thus likewise rarely produced by the directors of the interwar Yiddish stage, who were nearly all men.[3] Even Zalmen Zylbercweig's encyclopedic six-volume *Lexicon of the Yiddish Theater* omits Molodowsky from its otherwise comprehensive survey of Yiddish playwrights, actors, directors, and theater critics.[4] Similarly, the scant existing scholarship on women's involvement in the Yiddish theater focuses exclusively on female stage performers, disregarding the careers of the few women who, like Molodowsky, sought to enter the almost exclusively male-dominated backstage spheres of playwriting, directing, managing, and dramatic criticism.

Yet in spite of this lack of recognition, Molodowsky's theater writing represents a significant contribution to the Yiddish stage and marks the first emergence of a prominent female voice in modern Yiddish drama. Molodowsky was the first woman to write Yiddish theater criticism under her own name. She may have even been the first woman to write Yiddish theater criticism at all, though the proliferation of pseudonyms among Yiddish theater critics makes the claim impossible to fully determine. Moreover, Molodowsky was not only the first and only published Yiddish female playwright in interwar Eastern Europe, but she was also an innovative modernist playwright in a dramatic tradition in which theatrical modernism more often than not was the brainchild of visionary directors rather than writers. Like Itzik Manger and other better-known dramatists, Molodowsky turned to children's theater as the inspiration for her modernist dramatic experimentation.[5] Unlike her male counterparts, Molodowsky had already established her reputation as a talented children's writer long before she began writing plays for children in 1938 with *Ale fenster tsu der zun*. This play, though never staged and largely ignored by the literary establishment, was far more stylized and innovative than the children's theater productions of her more famous colleagues, and represents a near-complete fusion of Molodowsky's two literary genres of modernist poetry and children's literature. Though nearly forgotten in the annals of Yiddish theater history, Molodowsky was, in fact, a talented theatrical modernist, whose contributions have been too long overlooked: an extraordinary outlier in an interwar Yiddish culture in which dramatic writing and theater criticism were seen as exclusively male realms.

Molodowsky was indeed rare among women writers in aspiring to be a Yiddish dramatist and a theater critic. Prior to Molodowsky, few women had ever tried their hands at Yiddish playwriting. Those who did write plays received scant recognition from their male peers, let alone publication or stage productions. For an aspiring female Yiddish playwright, director, or critic, there were virtually no role models or success stories of women who had succeeded as professional writers in the Yiddish theater. Although there were only a few areas of modern Yiddish culture in which women did not fully participate, playwriting was a consistent exception throughout the history of modern Yiddish theater. Even as women became increasingly well represented among prominent Yiddish writers of poetry and prose in the first decades of the twentieth century, playwriting remained an all-male enclave, as did stage direction, production, theater design, and dramatic criticism. Yet while they were almost completely absent from the literary and production-oriented professions of the Yiddish theater, women were remarkably present on the Yiddish stage as actresses.

Actresses dominated the professional Yiddish theater from its very inception, when sixteen-year-old Sega Segal married actor Sakhar Goldstein in order to secure her mother's permission to join the Goldfaden Troupe.[6] Many of the most popular and enduring plays in the Yiddish theater, for instance Abraham Goldfaden's *Shulamis*, Jacob Gordin's *Mirele Efros*, and Sh. Ansky's *The Dybbuk*, prominently featured powerful and unforgettable heroines. These leading roles required extremely talented and versatile actresses who could carry the entire show. Actresses such as Bertha Kalish, Keni Liptzin, Bertha Gersten, Esther Rokhl Kaminska, Bessie Thomashefsky, and Molly Picon had enormous followings of dedicated fans, and their names were prominently featured on billboards and newspaper advertisements for their productions, often placed above the playwright or the director.[7]

Still, in a period in which it was common for male actors to run their own theater companies, it was extremely unusual for women to do the same. Some women, for example, Bessie Thomashefsky, Jennie Goldstein, Sara Adler, Paula Dreiblatt, and Ida Kaminska, were occasionally intermittent company heads. These arrangements rarely lasted since the actresses tended to quickly cede control to their husbands or sons.[8] Keni Liptzin was the sole exception, but her company was entirely subsidized by her husband, a successful and wealthy publisher. It was likewise rare for star actresses to write their own material, though those with a literary flair frequently wrote best-selling memoirs.[9] Female stage directors were also somewhat unusual in the Yiddish theater. Two major exceptions were Ida Kaminska and Klara Segalovitch; female stage designers, critics, and producers were virtually unknown.[10] Molodowsky's entrance into theater criticism and playwriting in the mid- to late 1930s was a contentious and unprecedented move for a female writer. A survey of Molodowsky's background provides some insights into her professional activities.

Molodowsky was born in 1894, the daughter of a forward-thinking *maskilic* Talmud scholar and community teacher who took it upon himself to provide her with a thorough education in Bible, Talmud, and Hebrew. As a young woman, she moved to Warsaw and became a teacher. By day, she worked as a kindergarten teacher in the Yiddishist schools of the Central Yiddish Schools Organization (TSHISHO), and by night, she taught Hebrew and Yiddish literature to working adults at a community school. In 1920, her literary career was launched when prominent fellow writers Dovid Bergelson, Yehezkel Dobrushin, and Pinchas Kahanowich [Der Nister] published her poetry in *Eygns* [Ours], their anthology of young local talent.[11] Encouraged by the support of the literary establishment, Molodowsky began to publish her poems widely in newspapers and journals. Her first book of poetry, *Kheshvendike nekht* [Nights of Heshvan], appeared with a leading press in 1927.[12] The book was well-received and earned laudatory reviews in the most important Yiddish newspapers in interwar Poland from prominent literary critics and fellow writers.[13] Over the next four decades, Molodowsky would continue to publish her poetry to great acclaim and develop her reputation as a talented and prolific Yiddish poet and prose writer.

The poems published during Molodowsky's first decade as a professional writer exhibit a strong feminist voice. In sequences like "Froyen lider" [Women's Poems], Molodowsky struggles to find common ground between her identity as a modern Yiddish writer and her subjugated role as a woman within traditional Jewish religious culture.[14] In the 1930s, Molodowsky found a new interest in writing for children, drawing upon a decade of experience as a kindergarten teacher to craft the children's stories and poems in a second collection, entitled *Mayselekh* [Stories], published in 1931. This book was extraordinarily well-received and was widely reviewed by all of the major Yiddish papers in Warsaw and abroad. Selling even more copies than *Khesvendike nekht*, *Mayselekh* secured Molodowsky's international reputation as a rising star on the Yiddish literary scene. Along with a steady stream of stories for children published in the Yiddish press, Molodowsky published *Dzshike gas* [Dzshike Street] in 1933. That work focused on larger political and social concerns and had a much more mixed reception among her colleagues. Some derided her poems, in the words of one critic, as "daintily feminine love-songs" rather than serious poetry.[15] For a poet like Molodowsky, who had fought vociferously against being categorized as a "women poet" writing "women's poetry," these reviews were particularly distressing. It was within this context, in the immediate aftermath of the tepid reception of *Dzshike gas* and the implied accusations that her poetry was not "serious" enough for her overwhelmingly male colleagues, that Molodowsky began to publish her theater reviews in Warsaw's Yiddish newspapers and journals, the only female voice in an entirely male-dominated sphere.

Molodowsky's first theater review, published in May 1934, was of a new Yiddish production of Gogol's famous comedy *The Inspector General*. In an innovative twist, the director cast actress Rokhl Holtzer as Khlestakov, the play's male protagonist who wreaks havoc on a small town by falsely claiming to be a government official. One might imagine the feminist Molodowsky of *Khesvendike nekht* and "Froyen lider" championing this unconventional casting of Khlestakov. But instead, Molodowsky accused the director of corrupting Gogol's masterpiece. Holtzer was indeed a talented actress, she conceded, but there were too many challenges for her to overcome. Of the actress Molodowsky writes, "She needed to portray Khlestakov, a civil servant from a hundred years ago, a Russian, and a man. Rokhl Holtzer is a good actress, but she took on an insurmountable burden."[16] Was this a response to the critics of *Dzshike gas* who charged Molodowsky with writing frivolous "women's poetry" or an effort to distance herself from the perception that her work was all about defending women? We might imagine so, though Molodowsky never quite makes her motives as a theater critic clear. Indeed, this review marked the only time that Molodowsky ever explicitly wrote about the role of women on the Yiddish stage. Given Molodowsky's frequent poetic commentary about the role of Jewish women in modern society, the lack of attention paid to the position of Yiddish theater women in these reviews is noteworthy and may best be understood within the context of the critical response to *Dzshike gas* in the Yiddish press.

Over the next few months, Molodowsky continued to publish her theater reviews in the Yiddish communist paper *Fraynd*, where she served as literary editor. Some of the performances she reviewed were, like the Skala's production of *The Inspector General*, aspiring high-art productions intended for an intellectual audience of Yiddish writers, artists, and cultural activists. Molodowsky, however, was rarely impressed. Typical was her review of a new translation of an Alexei Tolstoy play at Warsaw's Kaminski Theater, in which she charged the production team with transforming a decent literary play into its complete opposite, namely a trashy American-style melodrama. Calling the production a "corruption of a literary classic," Molodowsky wrote of a flawed translation that "left no trace of humor" and sharply criticized the weak artistic vision of the director who "did not know where [the stage direction] was coming from."[17] In her review of Sholem Aleichem's *Napoleon's oytser* [Napoleon's Treasure], originally published as *Di goldgreber* [The Gold Diggers] staged by the renowned avant-garde Yiddish director Michał Weichert (1890–1967), Molodowsky was more forgiving of the director's failure to transform a literary masterpiece into a fully realized stage production. In order to properly stage a Sholem Aleichem text, Molodowsky declared, the director would need to find the visual equivalent of the great writer's famously sophisticated prose style. This was no simple task, she acknowledged. But while Weichert's production of *Napoleon's oytser* demonstrated an attention to detail that Molodowsky found inspiring, it ultimately failed to fully capture the intricacies of Sholem Aleichem's world. "In general, the production is, in and of itself, very good," she concluded, "but—it is not Sholem Aleichem."[18]

The thrust of her criticism in these reviews of "literary" Yiddish theater productions is striking. Like many other prominent Yiddish writers-turned-theater-critics, Molodowsky paid close attention to how literary texts were adapted onto the Yiddish stage and found ample room for improvement. But unlike most of her literary colleagues, Molodowsky's theater reviews also demonstrated a strong interest in the director's role as the primary interpreter of a dramatic text. In Molodowsky's criticism, the director's task is quite clear. His job is to translate Yiddish literature, in its full complexity, onto the stage, and he alone is fully responsible for the success or failure of any given production. This act of theatrical translation, however, is not merely about strict fidelity to the literary drama, although Molodowsky certainly viewed this as a valuable trait, but also requires the director to have an artistic conception of the stage production that correlates with the literary and stylistic aims of the playwright. In order to get something out of a play, Molodowsky told readers in her review of *The Inspector General*, a director must have a clearly defined artistic concept, as well as a distinct interpretive voice.

Like many of her literary colleagues, Molodowsky also reviewed the decidedly low-brow melodramas known in Yiddish as *shund*. For most other critics, reviewing the *shund* theaters offered a chance to demonstrate one's strongest critical voice in order to heighten the distinction between the literary "art theater" and trashy *shund*. However, Molodowsky's sharp critical tone remained roughly the same, whether she was reviewing would-be artistic productions of literary classics or the much-derided sentimental *shund* dramas. In one such review, Molodowsky refused to even reveal the name of the play that she was reviewing. There is no need to recall the title when it comes to a *shund* play, she told her readers, for they are all essentially the same: "What the 'play' is called matters not. It could be called *Hello, Hello!*; it could also be called *Oy, My Noodles*. Because these are the main pillars upon which the 'play' stands."[19] Even more frustrating, wrote Molodowsky, is the fact that many of the actors are decent and deserve to perform in a much better play. Implicit in the review is a desire for a better dramatic repertoire that would provide talented Yiddish actors and actresses with high quality material.

Molodowsky published theater reviews for only eight months; the review of the Tolstoy production in December 1934 was her last. Still, these reviews indicate the initial development of Molodowsky's professional interest in the theater and offer an early glimpse of her ideological approach to the Yiddish stage. Like many of her peers, Molodowsky, the theater critic, was dedicated to the faithful representation of literary dramas on stage as a means of counteracting the corrupting influence of the *shund* theater. But for Molodowsky, the responsibility for transforming the Yiddish stage depended just as much on the emergence of creative and innovative directors as on the expansion of the repertoire by visionary Yiddish playwrights. It is the job of the director, Molodowsky told readers in her uncompromising reviews, to have a clearly defined and original concept that expands upon its dramatic source. Molodowsky's Yiddish theater criticism is thus doubly unusual: first, as the only Yiddish theater reviews by a woman writing under her own name during this period; and second, as a literary author asserting the director's responsibility for determining the success of any given theatrical production.

Soon after Molodowsky published her last theater review in *Fraynd*, she immigrated to America rather suddenly on the advice of a book publisher who assured her a warm welcome in the American Yiddish literary world.[20] She soon embarked on a cross-country tour of lectures and poetry readings that took her from New York to Philadelphia, Chicago, Detroit, Cleveland, and finally, Montreal. Somewhere between writing theater reviews in Poland in late 1934 and emigrating from Eastern Europe and traveling widely across the United States and Canada in 1935, Molodowsky began to write *Ale fentser tsu der zun*, her first play. Perhaps she included scenes from this play-in-progress as part of her public readings during the tour, though it is impossible to know for certain. Still, shortly after visiting Montreal, the Montreal- and Detroit-based literary journal *Heftn* published a scene from Molodowsky's first draft of the play.

Unlike the book-length version of *Ale fentser tsu der zun* that appeared two years later, there is no indication that this early excerpt was intended to be part of a children's play. The language is poetic and refined, and the content is full of references to troubling current events in Europe. The scene published in *Heftn* opens with the architect Max Grober alone in his workroom gazing at the model of a tower that he has just completed. But this is no ordinary tower; it is a magic tower that has the power to recall historical voices from the past, especially from individuals who have been oppressed or unfairly silenced. The tower lights up and we listen along with Grober as it brings to life voices from key moments throughout history: from major historical moments like Hirsh Lekert's arrest in 1902 Vilna or spy-infiltrated Paris on the eve of the first World War; to the voices of ordinary Jews from the past, from an oppressive and demoralizing *cheder* in a nineteenth-century village to a joyful *shtetl* wedding.

Grober is overjoyed at the sound of these voices, and he quickly instructs his colleague Kon to send out letters announcing his magical invention to the world. In a lengthy scene later cut from the final version in which the two architects discuss which country might welcome them, Molodowsky alerts her American and Canadian readers to the rising danger in Europe:

> KON: Germany. (*Puts down an envelope*)
> GROBER: Hitler—
> They are building prisons there,
> Damp, dark dens,
> They are building prison there,
> And not a playful tower.
> No, no,
> There will be no letter from there.
> KON: Hungary! (*Puts down another envelope*)
> GROBER: Hungary...
> Over there small children
> With their fathers go to the barricades
> And they are shot by the artillery.
> No...[21]

Grober goes on to reject England, the Soviet Union, and France as a proper site for his magical tower. Europe in 1936 is too dire a place to build Grober's tower, with its magical ability to bring to life the voices of the past, and in doing so, remind us of the mistakes of previous generations. In a poetic voice more reminiscent of the sharply political *Dzshike gas* than of Molodowsky's other children's poems and stories, Grober's invention of a magical tower is positioned in opposition to the rapid disintegration of a Europe that seems doomed to repeat its own dark history over and over again. Fantasy and magic, then, serve a political purpose in this play. In the world of *Ale fentser tsu der zun*, the leaders of Europe are leading the world into a darkness that they could avoid altogether were they only to accept the basic principle of Grober's magic tower: one must listen to the past in order to understand the dilemmas of the present. Instead, Grober believes, the rulers of Europe are firmly invested in *not* hearing the voices of the past at all costs, for to truly grasp the mistakes of prior generations would require them to alter their present course.

The rich and the powerful are also unwilling to accept Grober's discovery, and thus, in the world of Molodowsky's play, they are likewise ill-equipped to avert the coming crisis. The final version of the play includes a scene in which Grober and his colleagues invite members of the aristocracy, newspaper moguls, prominent professors, public intellectuals, and the heads of major companies to a demonstration of the tower's abilities. The guests come from far and wide, and at first, they clap politely as the tower begins to speak in the voices of the past. "Truly a sensation, this tower!" cries a gentleman in a top hat during the first scene, in which we hear members of the Catholic Church debating Copernicus' heliocentric theory in 1540.[22] But as the conflict between the voices grows darker, the well-do-to audience becomes increasingly uncomfortable with the tower and all that it implies for their comfortable way of life. It is far easier to go on as one always has, the guests agree. "The tower is a problem, it will stir up too many things," concludes a newspaper mogul. "Why uncover the dust of generations past?" asks another guest of Grober, "What's the point? God has given us forgetfulness, and let us thank him for that gift."[23] Rather than funding Grober's efforts to build a full-size tower open to the public, the guests depart in a hurry and never return. The point is clear: the economic and intellectual establishment is, like the politicians, unwilling to support Grober's project to save the world from disaster. With a blind eye turned to the voices of the past, those who are in power are doomed to repeat the mistakes of previous generations—at the peril of the world.

While the scene detailing the looming political crisis in Europe was ultimately eliminated from the published version of *Ale fentser tsu der zun*, these two scenes, taken together, offer a glimpse into Molodowsky's perspective on developments in European politics in the period immediately following her emigration to the United States. In September of 1935, Germany passed the Nuremberg Laws, which deprived Jews of their German citizenship, including the right to vote, and outlawed marriage between Jews and non–Jews. With her husband still in Warsaw struggling to get an American visa and dozens of other family members and close friends scattered across the continent, the mounting crisis in Europe must have weighed heavily on Molodowsky during her first few years in the United States. These two scenes from the first draft of *Ale fentser tsu der zun* provide insight into Molodowsky's growing anxiety during the first year of her life in America about a Europe that seemed on the verge of repeating the colossal errors of recent history.

Over the next two years, Molodowsky completed and prepared *Ale fentser tsu der zun* for publication in book form. The version that was ultimately published by the press of the prominent Warsaw literary journal *Literarishe bleter* [Literary Pages] incorporated only a scant few lines from the original scene published in *Heftn* in 1936. In this final version of her first play, Molodowsky removed the segment alluding to the political context in Europe entirely and rewrote the rejection of Grober's tower by the establishment in more abstract terms. No longer did Grober debate whether Hitler or Chamberlain would embrace his magic tower; instead, it is unnamed government ministers, well-to-do ladies and gentlemen, and fictional wealthy industrialists who refuse to listen to his message.

Yet Molodowsky's revision of the play went beyond simply abstracting the political context and softening the unambiguous morals of the first draft. In its final published version, *Ale fenster tsu der zun* is both a thoroughly modernist play and a drama for young audiences. Indeed, it is only in this play, and nowhere else in Molodowsky's vast oeuvre, that we see the complete fusion of the two genres that Molodowsky was simultaneously writing during the 1930s. *Ale fentser tsu der zun* fuses together the characteristic daring modernist elements of Molodowsky's renowned poetry with the archetypal characters and plot arc of a children's story.

The play opens as a simple folktale with the protagonist Boom, an imaginative eleven-year-old boy, pretending to build an elaborate train set out of wooden blocks. Immersed in the fantasy world he has created, he pays no heed to his mother, who urges him to get a job so that they will be able to pay their landlord. Boom reluctantly complies with his mother's wishes and is thrust from a world of childhood into the monotonous working life of a tailor's apprentice. His young friends are likewise forced by necessity into various professions: some become carpenter's apprentices, others work for a locksmith, still others cart around heavy wheelbarrows full of sand. Constantly distracted by daydreams and fantasies, Boom makes a poor apprentice and he is soundly fired, to his mother's consternation. Now an adolescent, Boom leaves the tailor's workshop behind and takes to the road hoping to discover a new path for himself.

It is at this point that we are introduced to Max Grober, Boom's second employer, mentor, and future colleague. Grober is an architect by profession, but he also evokes the archetypal folktale figure of the sorcerer or the magician, for it is under his magical influence that the "real" world of drudgery, manual labor, and spirit-crushing elders is transformed into a fantasy world in which the imagination has free reign. Under Grober's influence, the rich interior world of Boom's imagination becomes visible to every other character in the play. In their first encounter, Boom comes upon Grober as he is building a model house and witnesses firsthand the architect's magical ability to transform simple building materials into living objects, by simply putting his imaginings into words. As Grober imagines a man-in-the-moon who converses with his model house, the vision comes to life, to the amazement of young Boom who nearly falls down the stairs in surprise. The more time that Boom spends with Grober, the more skilled he becomes in the architect's craft of turning fantasy into reality. Grober trains Boom as an architect and together they dream of building a better world by creating buildings that will reveal the untold stories of the past. As their playful fantasy world turns real with the invention of a talking tower, the two colleagues dream of the future utopia that they will build with their own hands. "All windows face the sun," imagines Grober as he builds, "All doors open and without locks."[24] Boom too dreams of their tower opening up a future without oppression:

> The robber believes that you can catch a man in the woods, in a cellar, in prison; for wolves are wolves, the trees are deaf, the bricks are deaf, the walls are deaf. [*Hiding his face in his hands.*] But the world's ears are awakening. Every leaf an eye. Every wind a witness, every brick the power to hear. Once everything was hidden—so much grieving, so much screaming, so many tears. Now we will open the world's mouth. Tell us, tell us of the darkness, tell us what is hidden, and we will sift through the winds and recover from them the words of the people.[25]

Grober and Boom's work as imaginative architects is analogous to that of the author who seeks to change the world by expressing the force of his or her imagination. Like the architects with their magical tower, Molodowsky too is using the building materials of her craft to bring unheard voices to life and to sound a warning about the danger that looms ahead.

After the tower fails to impress the wealthy elite of their own society, Grober and Boom turn to the millionaires of Western Europe to fund their tower project. In a comic twist, Sholem Aleichem's instantly recognizable schemer and dreamer Menachem Mendl enters the play and promises to help Grober and Boom by introducing them to the rich millionaire Rotshildovitsch, for a cut of the profits, of course. But Rotshildovich, a thinly veiled Rothschild, is likewise concerned about the political and social implications of a tower that tells stories from the past, and turns the pair away empty-handed.

With their efforts to change the world soundly rejected, Boom and

Grober return home to their *shtetl* in Eastern Europe. Grober is in low spirits, but Boom does not despair. The world will come around one day, he tells his mentor. Suddenly, they hear a voice on the radio inviting them to come and build their tower "in the land where all the windows face the sun."[26] Boom's young working class friends from earlier in the play rush in to join them on their journey to this unnamed better land, and the curtain falls.

Like any folktale, the moral of the story is clear. We must turn to the past in order to learn how to build a better future. Boom and Grober are not only literal architects whose creations bring to life the unheard voices of the past; they are also architects of a new kind of worldview that they hope to bring to the leaders of the world, just as the writer, in bringing characters to life, has the power to create an imaginative new world. Yet as the architects discover, both their local leaders in Eastern Europe and the politicians and millionaires in Western Europe would rather turn a deaf ear to the past so they can continue on their destructive present course. The answer, as the final scene reveals, does not lie in Europe at all, but in an unspecified Somewhere Else, a country where the old ways of thinking have not taken hold and where idealism ("all windows face the sun!") still holds fast. The voice over the radio may come from Israel, where Molodowsky and her husband ultimately moved to in 1949, or from the United States, where Molodowsky was living as she completed the play. But while the precise destination of Boom and Grober is left unspecified at the end of the play, it is clear that neither Eastern nor Western Europe is willing to accept the magically proffered lessons of the past. The utopian vision of Grober and Boom thus cannot and will not be realized on the European continent. If it is indeed to come to pass, it must happen someplace else.

But Molodowsky's modernist leanings are also readily apparent in the play's evocative use of sophisticated poetic language, the complexity of Boom's character, and most prominently, in the counter-realistic motif of juxtaposing the fantastic with ordinary workaday life. Indeed, the play gradually shifts its genre from faux realism, in which Boom's utopia lives only in his child's imagination, to a modernist fantasy in which the imagined interior visions of Boom and Grober are literally realized within the world of the play. This fusion of intensely theatrical modernism and a children's folktale enables the play to be both familiar and groundbreaking at the same time.

The extensive use of visual imagery in *Ale fentser tsu der zun* seems to indicate that Molodowsky wrote it with a stage production in mind. Indeed, the play's effect hinges upon the precise staging of the scenes in which the architects' imaginings are brought to life, and the most evocative scenes are those that rely more heavily upon visual effects then on dialogue. Even in the primarily auditory scenes where the tower brings the voices of the past to life, Molodowsky's stage directions carefully described the use of lighting to achieve maximal visual effect.

In spite of its visually-oriented sensibility and theatrical potential, *Ale fentser tsu der zun* was never produced on the Yiddish stage. We have no record of Molodowsky's reaction to this lack of interest from theater companies and directors, and it is unclear to what extent she tried to promote the play outside of her public readings. Yet the published version of the play also received a surprising lack of attention from Yiddish literary critics. While Molodowsky's poetry and prose publication tended to receive dozens of reviews in prominent papers and journals, her first play received only a single review, a stunning contrast to the more than twenty reviews that appeared after the publication of *Dzshike gas* just five years earlier.

That review, by the children's author and editor Moyshe Taykhman, praised Molodowsky for the originality of her ideas and for her contribution to the burgeoning field of Yiddish children's literature. Taykhman's review recognized the play for introducing an important new genre to Yiddish literature, expressionist children's theater. The review did not shy away from what Taykhman viewed as the play's significant flaws: the sometimes heavy-handed overuse of expressionist tactics, a plot that unfolds too quickly, and underdeveloped minor characters. Ultimately, however, Taykhman concluded that the play represents a major turning point in Yiddish children's literature:

> The language and the articulation of the words is masterful. Many of the scenes are sharp social grotesques. In the hands of a good director it would make a wonderful children's production. The poet deserves our congratulations. Except for the errors indicated above, the play has great value. It will spur our children's literature onward, elevating it to a European level and providing a stimulus to its future development.[27]

*Ale fentser tsu der zun* was, as Taykhman writes, a groundbreaking work in modernist playwriting and children's drama. Yet Molodowsky's first contribution as a playwright was virtually ignored by most of her literary colleagues, in spite of her established reputation as one of the most prominent professional writers in Yiddish literature. Instead, Molodowsky's contributions to interwar Yiddish theater, first as a critic and later as a playwright, were disregarded by the literary establishment, even as her poetry continued to achieve growing international recognition. This lack of interest in Molodowsky's theatrical contributions among her peers reflects a tightly gender-codified literary and cultural system in which interwar Yiddish poetry and prose were acceptable arenas for women's writing; whereas playwriting, theater criticism, and the other "backstage" professions, such as directing, managing, designing, were strictly limited to men. If even Molodowsky, the most famous and renowned female Yiddish writer of her generation, could not surmount this barrier, who else would even try?

## Notes

1. Kadya Molodowsky, "Gogols 'Revizor' in skala teater," *Fraynd*, May 11, 1934, 6.
2. Ibid.
3. Molodowsky's two postwar plays were staged in small productions. *Nokhn got fun midber* (1949) was performed in Chicago and Israel; *A hoyz af grand strit* (1953) was performed in New York. Both productions received little to no attention in the Yiddish press. *Ale fentser tsu der zun* (1938), Molodowsky's single interwar play, was never staged.
4. Admittedly, Zylbercweig's lexicon has several glaring omissions, including the famous comedy team Dzigan and Shumacher. Still, Molodowsky's omission from the lexicon echoes the near-complete silence about her plays from Yiddish theater critics, historians, and directors.
5. Itzik Manger's modernist children's play *Hotsmakh-shpil* [Hotsmakh's Play] caused a sensation when it premiered in Warsaw in 1938. Although Molodowsky's modernist children's play was written before Manger's, it received comparatively little attention and no productions.
6. Upon marrying into the Goldfaden Troupe, Segal changed her name to Sophie Goldstein. Years later in New York, after divorcing Goldstein, she would change her name to Sophie Karp.
7. For biographical information on Kalish, Liptzin, Kaminska, and Adler, see Nahma Sandrow, *Vagabond Stars: A World History of Yiddish Theater* (Syracuse: Syracuse University Press, 1996), 154–156.
8. On actress Paula Dreiblatt's brief stint as head of Vienna's *Jüdisches Künstlerkabarett* in 1930, see Brigitte Dalinger, "Yiddish Theater in Vienna," *Jewish Women: A Comprehensive Historical Encyclopedia*, 20 March 2009, Jewish Women's Archive, accessed January 15, 2012, http://jwa.org/encyclopedia/article/yiddish-theater-in-vienna.
9. Molly Picon, who wrote many of her own songs, is a notable exception. Still in spite of her success as a songwriter, even Picon never tried her hand at playwriting. See Nahma Sandrow, "Yiddish Theater in the United States," *Jewish Women: A Comprehensive Historical Encyclopedia*, 20 March 2009, Jewish Women's Archive, accessed January 15, 2012, http://jwa.org/encyclopedia/article/yiddish-theater-in-united-states.
10. On Klara Segalovitch's directorial career, see Zalmen Zylbercweig, ed., *Leksikon fun yidishn teater*, vol. 5 (Mexico City: Farlag Elisheva, 1967), 4281–4306. On Ida Kaminska, see her memoir *My Life, My Theater*, ed. and trans. Curt Leviant (New York: Macmillan, 1973).
11. See Kathryn Hellerstein, "Introduction," *Paper Bridges: Selected Poems of Kadya Molodowsky* (Detroit: Wayne State University Press, 1999), 21.
12. Molodowsky ultimately published eight book-length collections of her poetry and stories: *Kheshvendike nekht* [Nights of Heshvan] (Vilna, 1927); *Mayselekh* [Tales] (Varshe, 1931); *Dzshike gas* [Dzshike Street] (Varshe, 1933); *Freydke* [Freydke] (Varshe,

1935); *In land fun mayn gebeyn* [In the Country of My Bones] (Shikago, 1937); *Afn barg* [Upon the Mountain] (Nyu york, 1938); *Der meylekh Dovid aleyn iz geblibn* [Only King David Remained] (Nyu york, 1946); and *Likht fun dornboym* (Light from a Thornbush) (Buenos ayres, 1965).

13. *Khesvendike nekht* was reviewed twenty times in the Yiddish press. Molodowsky's subsequent books received an equally significant amount of attention in the Yiddish press, in sharp contrast to her plays, which were rarely reviewed in the Yiddish press. See Hellerstein, "Introduction," 28.

14. Ibid., 23.

15. Review of Molodowsky's *Dzshike gas*, quoted in Hellerstein, "Introduction," 36.

16. Molodowsky, "Gogol's revizor," 6.

17. Kadya Molodowsky, "Teater notitsn," *Fraynd*, December 20, 1934, 4.

18. Kadya Molodowsky, "Sholem Aleichem farn teater," *Fraynd*, August 10, 1934, 6.

19. Kadya Molodowsky, "Tsvey sho af a yarid in teater Eldorado," *Fraynd*, June 29, 1934, 6.

20. Molodowsky immigrated to the United States in 1935, leaving her husband Simche Lev temporarily behind in Warsaw. On Molodowsky's initial reception in America, see Hellerstein, "Introduction," 37.

21. Kadya Molodowsky, "Ale fenster tsu der zun," *Heftn* 1.1 (January-February 1936): 18.

22. Kadya Molodowsky, *Ale fentster tsu der zun* (Varshe: Literarishe bleter, 1938), 45.

23. Ibid., 46.

24. Ibid., 27.

25. Ibid., 35–36.

26. Ibid., 66.

27. Moyshe Taykhman, "Vegn Kadie Molodovskis 'Ale fenster tsu der zun,'" *Literarishe bleter* 15.37 (September 16, 1938): 617.

# Gender and Nation in the 1945 Poems of Kadya Molodowsky and Malka Heifetz Tussman

KATHRYN HELLERSTEIN

In the spring of 1945, two women poets living in the United States each wrote a Yiddish poem addressing the situation of the Yiddish language and the Jewish people after the *khurbm* [the Holocaust].[1] Kadya Molodowsky (1894–1975) in New York, and Malka Heifetz Tussman (1893–1987) in Los Angeles, were colleagues, correspondents, and friends. Both Molodowsky's poem "Eyl khanun" [Merciful God] and Tussman's "Tsu dir miryam" [To You, Miriam] ask how a Jewish poet can continue to write in Yiddish after the speakers of that language have been destroyed. Framing this question with sacred texts, both poets renounce faith in God's authority and call into question the continued existence of the idea of a Jewish nation and its tradition. In the voice of a prophet, speaking for the entire Jewish people, Molodowsky's speaker accuses God directly of having transgressed His own Ten Commandments. In contrast, Tussman's persona addresses the biblical character Miriam, the sister of Moses, as one Jewish woman and poet to another, in order to condemn God.

Between 1941 and 1943, Kadya Molodowsky composed tentative poems that addressed all that she in America could know about the fate of the Jews in Europe through incomplete communication and the impotency of language. In 1945, though, after she learned the extent of the destruction, she was able to write the powerful "Merciful God." Perhaps only full knowledge allowed the poet to take her place so authoritatively in the tradition of response and to speak in the communal voice:

> *Eyl khanun,*
> *klayb oys an ander folk,*
> *derveyl.*
> *mir zaynen mid fun shtarbn un geshtorbn,*
> *mir hobn nit keyn tfiles mer,*
> *klayb oys an ander folk,*
> *derveyl,*
> *mir hobn nit keyn blut mer*
> *af tsu zayn a korbm.*
> *A midbar iz gevorn unzer shtub.*
> *Di erd iz karg fun unz af kvorim,*
> *nishto keyn kines mer far unz,*
> *nishto keyn klog-lid*
> *in di alte sforim.*
>
> *Eyl khanun,*
> *heylik an ander land,*
> *an ander barg.*
> *Mir hobn ale felder shoyn un yedn shteyn*
> *mit ash, mit heylikn bashotn.*
> *Mit skeynim,*
> *un mit yunge,*
> *un mit eyfelekh batsolt*
> *far yedn os fun dayne tsen gebotn.*
>
> [Merciful God,
> Choose another people,
> Elect another.
> We are tired of death and dying,
> We have no more prayers.
> Choose another people,
> Elect another.
> We have no more blood
> To be a sacrifice.
> Our house has become a desert.
> The earth is stingy with our graves,
> No more laments for us,
> No more dirges
> In the old, holy books.
>
> Merciful God,
> Sanctify another country,
> Another mountain.
> We have strewn all the fields and every stone
> With ash, with holy ash.
> With the old,

With the young,
And with little children we have paid
For every letter of your Ten Commandments]² [1–23].

Molodowsky repeats the opening lines, which ask God to choose and elect another people, as a refrain throughout the poem that emphasizes the poet's sense of communal responsibility as she speaks for the people whom God has chosen and then betrayed. In a litany of denial, the speaker negates all the traditional Jewish responses to catastrophe found in "the old holy books," a synecdoche for the written texts of all the prayers, laments, and dirges through which the Jewish people had articulated their ability to survive calamities for millennia.

As she negates the traditional texts of mourning, Molodowsky evokes the imagery of the written Scripture. Such imagery enters even the way the poet addresses God. The Hebrew epithet *eyl khanun* [Merciful God] comes from the penitential prayer "*shlosh-esre middot*" [The Thirteen Attributes of Mercy], recited at several moments in the liturgical calendar, including the *selihot* prayers before Rosh Hashana and at Yom Kippur. This prayer is based on a key biblical verse that, in the prayer, is interpreted as evidence of God's extraordinary compassion.³ That interpretation, however, transposes the meaning of this phrase as it originally appears in the biblical text. In Exodus 34:6–7, just after the episode of the Golden Calf, God, about to rewrite the Ten Commandments on a second set of tablets, tells Moses on Sinai that although He is merciful, God will *not* forgive the Children of Israel their sins nor cleanse them of their guilt. Inverting the context for this biblical verse, the penitential prayer "*shlosh-esre middot*" proclaims that this God *is* a Merciful God who *will* cleanse the penitent sinners who utter the prayer. Repeated in every stanza in Molodowsky's poem, the phrase *eyl khanun*, the epithet that connotes the very writing of the Covenant, reverses the prayer's own reversal of the biblical verse and demands that the Merciful God repent *His* sins and "cleanse" the Jews of their commitment to Him. Because this God of Mercy was not merciful to the Jews during the *khurbm*, Molodowsky's speaker, a post-war Yiddish poet, has no mercy for Him. The unforgiving Yiddish poet, thus, differentiates herself from the liturgical God who ultimately did forgive the Jews. Blasphemously, Molodowsky blames God for choosing the Jewish people: their chosenness has led to their destruction.

At the end of the second stanza, the parody climaxes in an image of fractured script. The poet refers to the covenantal Decalogue not as laws or statements or even words, but as disconnected letters. The murders of the old, of the young, and of the newborn break apart the coherent meanings of the commandments into the elemental symbols in which they are written. Thus fragmented, these letters, the building blocks of the Covenant written down by God, cease to signify anything but their price in human death. Paradoxically, however, these letters reconstitute another meaning in the alphabet in which the poet writes her Yiddish poem.

As the divine laws of the Ten Commandments shatter into letters within Molodowsky's poem, the *folk* [the people, the nation] disintegrate into the ashes strewn across the land and into the list of victims, the old, the young, and the children. Yet the poem provides an answer to the undoing of covenant and of the sacred text on which covenant is based: That answer revises the idea of the Jewish people. The third stanza commands:

> *Eyl khanun*
> *Heyb oyf dayn fayerdike brem,*
> *Un ze di felker fun der velt—*
> *Gib zey di nevues un di yom-noroyim.*
> *In yedn loshn preplt men dayn vort—*
> *Lern di maysim zey,*
> *Di vegn fun nisoyen.*
>
> [Merciful God
> Raise your fiery brow,
> And see the peoples of the world—
> Give them the prophecies and the Days of Awe.
> Your word is babbled in every language—
> Teach them the deeds,
> The ways of temptation][4] [24–30].

Having allowed the Jewish people to be destroyed, God must bestow upon all the other peoples of the world the sacred privileges and obligations that He had once given the Jews. This act would reverse the idea of the Jewish nation and curse all the other nations of the world with what had once been the blessings of God's Chosen People. The Jewish people, no longer "chosen," would then become common:

> *Eyl khanun,*
> *Gib proste bgodim undz,*
> *Fun pastekher far shof,*
> *Fun shmidn bay dem hamer,*
> *Fun vesh-vasher, fun fel-shinder,*
> *Un nokh mer gemeynes.*
> *Un nokh eyn khesed tu tsu undz:*
> *Eyl khanun,*
> *Nem tsu fun undz di shekhine fun gaones.*
>
> [Merciful God,
> Give us simple garments

> Of shepherds with their sheep,
> Blacksmiths at their hammers,
> Laundry-washers, skin-flayers,
> And even the more base.
> And do us one more favor:
> Merciful God,
> Deprive us of the Divine Presence of genius]⁵ [31–39].

Although she speaks in the collective voice in this bitter prayer, Molodowsky's persona undoes the idea of that collectivity, the Jewish nation, and strips the survivors of everything that identifies them as the Jewish people. The enigmatic final line demands the ultimate deprivation, in the phrase *"nem tsu fun undz di shekhine fun gaones"* [Deprive us of the Divine Presence of Genius]. By characterizing the Shekhinah, the emanation of God that follows the Jews in Exile, as the spirit of *gaones*, genius, or Jewish learnedness, Molodowsky demands that God show his "mercy" by taking away the very act of studying the sacred text of the Covenant. The quintessential act of Jewish textual virtue, the male virtue that is, of Torah study, gave the Jews no help during the Holocaust. Molodowsky's pared-down depiction of the survivors as simple artisans and laborers who do not study the written text, cannot help but suggest a different kind of nation, unsanctified, but alive. The speaker in Molodowsky's poem challenges God in a voice resounding with anger and sarcasm that echoes the male biblical prophets who excoriated the errant Jewish people and the medieval Ashkenazic Hebrew poets who complained of God's silence during national crisis.

In contrast to Molodowsky's prophetic voice in "Eyl khanun," Tussman's 1945 poem of Jewish peoplehood insists on its specifically female poetic stance. Instead of challenging God and His Covenant, the speaker of Tussman's "To You, Miriam" addresses Miriam who, in Exodus 15: 20–21, played the role of prophet and poet with her praise song after her brother Moses led the Children of Israel out of slavery and through the divinely parted Red Sea: "And Miriam the prophetess, the sister of Aaron, took a timbrel in her hand; and all the women went out after her with timbrels and with dances. And Miriam sang unto them: Sing ye to the Lord, for He is highly exalted: The horse and his rider hath He thrown into the sea."⁶

With these verses in mind, Tussman's speaker opens the poem by invoking Miriam:

> *Tsu dir, miryam hanovye,*
> *Tsu dayn gezang,*
> *Tsu dayne tantsndike fis vos hobn freydik geblutikt*
> *Af midber-zamd*

*Geyt oys mayn harts in kine*
*Un in benkshaft nokhanand.*

*Du host gezungen in a tsayt*
*Ven got gevezn iz a gerekhter,*
*Iz vunderlekh geven tsu firn in a kidushe-tants*
*Yisroels tekhter.*

[To you, Miriam the prophet,
To your song,
To your feet, joyously bloodied,
Dancing on desert sand,
My heart goes out again
In envy and in longing.

You sang at a time
When God was righteous,
When it was wonderful to lead Israel's daughters
In a sacred dance][7] [1–10].

Tussman's speaker, a Yiddish poet, tells the biblical poet Miriam how she envies her moment in Jewish history. Although in Exodus, Miriam's brief song comes as a postscript, reiteration, or, as some argue, an antiphony of Moses's verses, Tussman's speaker depicts her as prophet and poet at a triumphant moment in the redemption and survival of the Children of Israel. When she sings and leads the women in dancing after the harrowing escape, Miriam's feet bleed on the desert sand. Thus the miraculous rescue of the Children of Israel proves to the poet that, in Miriam's time, "God was righteous" (8). Now, in contrast, the poet blasphemously implies, God is no longer righteous:

*Mit vos zol ikh di froyen fun mayn dor derfreyen*
*Un derhoybn?*
*S'vakht nit mer keyn oyg keyn likhtiks iber undz,*
*Nishto keyn rakhmim oybn.*

*Mit zayn rekhter hant hot got der har*
*Far undz geefnt umkum-thomen.*
*Dokh her un shtoyn, o miryam,*
*Fun tifn opgrunt aroys brekht zikh vi a blits*
*A shvakh zayn libn nomen.*

[How shall I exalt the women of my generation?
How shall I bring them joy?
No longer does a light-filled eye watch over us,
No compassion from above.

With his right hand, God the Master
Has opened abysses of destruction.
Hear and be astonished, oh, Miriam:

> From the deep precipice, like lightning,
> Erupts praise of his beloved Name][8] [11–19].

As Miriam led the women of her time in song and dance, so the speaker wants to uplift her contemporaries. She asks, "With what shall I make happy and exalt/ The women of my generation?" (11–12). Answering this rhetorical question in the negative, the speaker notes that the poet cannot take on this role of spokeswoman for her generation, because God no longer "watches over us" and there is "no compassion above" (13–14). Instead of parting the waters of the Red Sea "With his right hand" (15), as in Miriam's time, God now "has opened the abysses of mass death." The only praise for God is a *shvakh* חבש, a eulogy or praise poem that erupts like lightning" from "the depths of the precipice."

The speaker admits that one form of traditional praise for God does still exist, when women light and bless the candles on the Sabbath eve:

> *Un s'iz nokh faran a shabes-tish in undzer khoyshekh*
> *Nor s'tsankt un lesht zikh shoyn di kedushe.*
> *S'tukn zikh di flemlekh fun di likht*
> *In bushe.*
>
> [And there, in our darkness, a Sabbath table is laid,
> But the sanctity sputters and goes out.
> The candle flames duck
> In shame][9] [20–23].

Although the Sabbath still comes, and women still light the candles, the holiness of the blessing has been destroyed and the flames themselves are ashamed. The metaphor of blessings sputtering out, while the flames themselves burn on, emphasizes how empty tradition is without a righteous God.

The poet blames this unrighteous God for hurting the Jews even more by sending false moralizers who blame the Jews for their victimization:

> *Un shtrofer t'er nokh ongeshikt af undz*
> *Vos musern mit baytshndike tsungen.*
> *Khatoim zukhn zey af undz.*
> *Mir zoln tshuve ton, bafeln undz gots voyle yungen.*
>
> [And he sent men to punish us again.
> They chastise with whipping tongues.
> They find offenses within us.
> God's braggarts command us to repent][10] [24–27].

She excoriates these pundits, *shtrofer*, who, claiming that God has punished the Jews with genocide, speak from a corrupted religious platform that deceitfully echoes the biblical prophets. Unable to respond on behalf of the collective, the speaker will defend herself against such hypocritical accusations:

> *Nor ikh, o dikhterin, mayn shvester, vel zikh vern.*
> *—fargib mayn mut...*
> *Ikh nem gots tsorn mer nit on*
> *Far voyl un gut.*
>
> *Ver bin ikh, vestu fregn.*
> *Ver bin ikh vos zol monen un zikh shteln kegn im?*
> *Nit freg mayn rekht op, miryam.*
> *Mayn yikhes iz a folk martirer un*
> *Ikh hob mayn tseylem elokim.*
>
> [But I, oh, poet, my sister, will defend myself.
> —Forgive my strength...
> I no longer accept God's wrath
> As well and good.
>
> Who am I, you will ask,
> Who am I to make demands and stand against him?
> Do not refute my right, Miriam.
> I stem from a martyr to the people, and
> My image of God sits within me]¹¹ [28–36].

Answering Miriam's anticipated protestations, the speaker rejects the righteousness of God's wrath and defends her rebellious stance (33). She defines herself as one who has the right to "stand against" God, because her "lineage is a nation of martyrs and/ I have my bit of God within me" [35–36].

These Yiddish lines are culturally dense in their connotations and are hard to translate: "*mayn yikhes iz a folk martirer un/ ikh hob mayn tseylem elokim.*" The phrase "*folk martirer*" may be understood to mean either "a nation of martyrs" or "a martyred people." The Hebrew phrase "*tseylem elohim*" means literally "image of God" and comes from Genesis, where God creates man "in His image." In Yiddish idiom, though, the phrase also denotes the godliness in people, the qualities of basic human decency or *mentshlekhkayt*, and a pious Jewish appearance.¹² Writing the phrase "*tseylem elokim*," replacing the "*hey*" with a "*kuf*," Tussman adopts the tone of traditional piety by avoiding one of the actual, sacred names of God; she does this perhaps either to convince the poet Miriam of the poet's own righteousness or to protect herself from God's wrath, even as she challenges Him. This orthographic gesture also emphasizes the several meanings of the phrase "*tseylem elokim*," in a way that is both ironic and profound. At the very moment that she challenges God's authoritative justice, the poet asserts that she does so on the authority of the very qualities within *her* which are God-like and deeply humane.

Possessing such qualities, the poet has the temerity to challenge God in a way that cuts even deeper:

> *Nokh mer—*
> *Ikh tu im nokh farklogn.*
> *Ikh shtel zikh kegn im un klog im on*
> *Tsu zayne tsen gebot.*
>
> [Still more—
> I lodge another complaint.
> I stand up to him and accuse him
> With his own Ten Commandments]¹³ [37–40].

Characteristic of Tussman, the phrasing of the verb "*shteln zikh*" within the Yiddish, "*ikh shtel zikh kegn im un klog im on/ tsu zayne tsen gebot*," emphasizes the contrary stance of the speaker as a poet against the authority of God, the creator and destroyer. The phrase, repeated several times in "To You, Miriam" reflects a central theme in Tussman's poetry; we see it again in another poem from her first book, *Lider*, a poem that questions what she can teach her Yiddish pupils after the Holocaust, "What Shall I Tell Them?," as well as in her 1977 poem "Fargesn" [Forgotten].

More importantly, Tussman's use of the Ten Commandments to accuse God echoes Molodowsky's "Eyl khanun" [Merciful God]: "With the aged,/ With the youthful,/ And with babies, we have paid/ For every letter of your Ten Commandments"¹⁴ (Molodowsky, 20–23). But Tussman evokes this echo to a different effect. Both Molodowsky and Tussman refer to the Ten Commandments with the Germanic Yiddish phrase "*tsen gebotn*," rather than the Hebraic phrase "*aseres-hadibres*," as if to distance their speakers from even the language of those commandments and from the suggestion of religiosity in mentioning them. In lines that descend through the ages of humankind, Molodowsky lists the old, the young, and the infants whose lives comprised the price the Jews paid for every single letter (*os*) that spells out the commandments that God wrote on the tablets, and thus to demand that God reverse the sacred Covenant. In contrast to Molodowsky's attention to the individual letters making up the written text of the law, Tussman's lines address the spirit of the law as her speaker enters a metaphorical courtroom where God is on trial. Acting as a prosecutor, and perhaps echoing I. L. Peretz's famous short story "Bontshe shvayg" [Bontshe the Silent], in which the heavenly prosecutor against the innocent Bontshe wins, she stands in opposition to God in order to accuse him of his crimes against the very laws by which he had commanded the Jewish people to live.

Tussman's poem ends with a statement that negates all hope for the redemption of the Jewish people and also of God himself:

> *Fun undzer vistn hefker hot er farmitn*
> *Zayn barot.*
> *Un nishto inergets nit keyn ondayt,*
> *Inergets nit keyn simen af a goyel.*
>
> *Ikh bashver!*
> *Nit tsindn mer zol letster otem-tsi dem fakl*
> *"shma yisroel"*
> *Shtum, mit gal*
> *Zol zayn*
> *Der letster fal.*
>
> [Abandoning us to destruction, he has put us
> At his mercy.
> And nowhere, anywhere, is any hint,
> Nowhere any sign of a redeemer.
>
> I vow!
> No longer shall a Jew's last breath ignite the torch—
> "Hear, O Israel."
> Mute, with gall,
> Shall be
> The final fall]¹⁵ [41–50].

In the dense phrasing of lines 41–42, the speaker informs Miriam of the extent to which God's disobedience of his own laws has left the Jews without hope: *"fun unzer vistn hefker hot er farmitn/ zayn barot."* Deliberately, Tussman rhymes the word *"barot"* with *"gebot"* two lines above, to emphasize the layered meanings of *"barot."* The lexicographer A. Harkavy defines *"barot"* by itself, as denoting "hazard," but translates the phrase *"af gots barot"* as "at God's mercy," signifying the state of being in God's care or custody.¹⁶ *"Barot"* takes on more treacherous connotations in Weinreich's definition of the phrase *"iberlozn af gots barot,"* which emphasizes the precarious position of such a person, utterly forsaken by human powers and who thus is *"af barot fun got,"* at the mercy of God.¹⁷ Rhyming *"barot"* (hazard, mercy) with *"gebot"* (law, commandment), Tussman's lines depict a people, or a nation, abandoned by humankind and now utterly forsaken in the hands of a God who disobeys his own Ten Commandments. This scofflaw God creates a world without order and negates or stands in the way of any possibility of mercy or any inkling of redemption. Under such arbitrary power, the very word *barot,* "mercy," becomes a cruelly ironic concept. Thus, the poet swears an oath she must keep and prophesies to Miriam, the ancient prophetess. She predicts that Jews will no longer utter, upon dying, the words of the *"shema,"* the watchword of Jewish monotheism given by God to the people of Israel (Deuteronomy 6:4). Rather than address the problem of the poet whom history has silenced,

Tussman depicts how God's betrayal of his own covenant will render every Jew mute.

Writing in 1945, in the wake of the terrible news of the destruction of European Jewry, both Molodowsky and Tussman felt compelled to speak for the Jewish people. Both addressed God's betrayal of the Jews during the Holocaust by invoking the very traditions and texts by which the Jews had defined themselves. Molodowsky shattered the idea of God's covenant with the Jewish people by speaking to God with the collective voice, in the first person plural. This voice subsumes the individual woman within the nation and the modern poet within the prophetic tradition of sacred parody. Molodowsky puts forth the idea of the Jewish nation as *"dos folk"* and *"dos land"* in the poem's opening refrains, *"Klayb oys an ander folk"* (Molodowsky, lines 2, 6) and *"Heylik an ander land"* (Molodowsky, line 16). Throughout, she figures God's betrayal of the Jews in imagery of collectivity and generalizations to convey the enormity of the betrayal and loss.

While Tussman, too, contends with God's treachery and abandonment, she does so through the dramatic persona of one woman poet, the daughter of *"a folk martirer"* (Tussman, line 35), addressing another, the daughter of slaves, across time. If the ancestry of the Jewish poet is a people's martyr, one who sacrificed himself for the sake of the nation, then it is necessary that the poet speak out as an individual who will extend this inherited act of self-sacrifice. In the final stanza, this act turns out to be the speaker's vow of silence. This self-imposed muteness, though, was not a poet's refusal to write, but rather, her refusal, and by extension, that of all Jews, to utter the affirmation of faith at the moment of death.

Molodowsky demands that God erase the learning through which the Jewish nation has known its sacred history, law, and Covenant. Tussman demands that each Jewish person, beginning with herself, silence the statement through which God knows that His people believes in Him. By retracting the Jewish practice of reciting the Shema, the "Watchword" of monotheistic faith, before dying, Tussman deprives God of His authority over human life. Approaching, from opposite rhetorical stances, the subject of the destruction of the Jews in Europe, Molodowsky, speaking in a collective voice that taps into Judaism's classical (and male) tradition, and Tussman, speaking in a particular woman's voice, sever God from his nation.

Whether it is a commonality arising from the historical crisis or a question of one influencing the other, both Molodowsky and Tussman build their poems on the premise that this severance of the Jews from their tradition would make it impossible for a Jew to write at all. At the same time, these poems, both deeply embedded within the tradition, insist on being written. This paradox of a text proclaiming its severance from the same destroyed tradition that it renews through its proclamation derives from the Jewish tradition of subversive prayer or sacred parody, which extends from the biblical Book of Lamentations and the prophets writing after the Destruction of the First Temple in Jerusalem in 586 BCE, through the Hebrew and Yiddish writings in response to the Crusades, the pogroms, and the Holocaust.[18] Throughout the poems in her 1946 book *Der melekh dovid aleyn iz geblibn* [Only King David Remained], Molodowsky invoked this model of the sacred parody, calling forth the tradition that her poems seem to reject in grief and rage, whether or not these poems explicitly address the topic of the Destruction.[19] Tussman, in contrast, emphasized gender as the framework for asking Adorno's famous question—How can one write poetry after the Holocaust? By addressing Miriam and invoking the image of the Sabbath candles, Tussman projected Adorno's general problem with Jews writing poetry after the Holocaust onto the specific situation of a woman poet's responsibility to Jewish tradition.

Although both 1945 poems enact the trope of sacred parody, they differ essentially in the absence or presence of gender. Molodowsky's "Eyl khanun" erases the specifically female poet in order to speak directly to God for the entire Jewish people, recalling the classical Hebrew liturgical tradition in which women's voices were not heard, while the speaker in Tussman's "Tsu dir miryam" alludes to the Yiddish *tkhine* tradition of women's prayers, speaking to God in a particular woman's voice through the intermediary biblical figure of Miriam. The subsuming of gender characterized the general trend of Molodowsky's post–Holocaust poetry, which increasingly addressed the generalized problems of Jewish cultural and national survival. In contrast, as Tussman developed her poetry into a mature oeuvre in the post-war years, she increasingly wrote from an explicitly female perspective, incorporating both gender and sex into the central structure of her poetic voice, as she argued through her own example for the continuity of Yiddish poetry.

## Notes

Kathryn Hellerstein's translation of the Yiddish poem by Malka Heifetz Tussman "Tsu dir miryam" [To You, Miriam] was first published in *Kerem* 12 (2010) and is reprinted with permission of *Kerem* and Kathryn Hellerstein. Kathryn Hellerstein's translation of the Yiddish poem by Kadya Molodowsky "Eyl khanun" [Merciful God] is reprinted from *Paper Bridges: Selected Poems of Kadya Molodowsky*, trans. and ed. Kathryn Hellerstein (1999) with permission of Wayne State University Press.

1. I presented earlier versions of this essay at a conference at Vanderbilt University, "Reflections on Czernowitz 100 Years Later: Yiddish in the 20th Century," March 31,

### Gender and Nation in Molodowsky and Tussman (Hellerstein)   207

2008, and for the Sumpf Lecture at Stanford University, May 4, 2011. I have adapted the discussions of the poems for my book *A Question of Tradition: Women Poets in Yiddish (1586–1987)* (Stanford: Stanford University Press, 2014). SYNPOSIS: In 1945, Molodowsky's poem "Eyl khanun" and Tussman's "Tsu dir miryam" ask how a Jewish poet could continue to write in Yiddish after the speakers of that language had been destroyed. Framing this question with allusions to sacred texts and renouncing faith in God's authority, both poets call into question the continued existence of the idea of a Jewish nation. Yet the gendered terms in which each poet writes raise further questions about the place and power of women as Yiddish poets.

    2. Molodowsky, "Eyl khanun" in *Paper Bridges: Selected Poems of Kadya Molodowsky*, ed. and trans. Kathryn Hellerstein (Detroit: Wayne State University Press, 1999), 352–355. Originally published as "Eyl khanun," in *Der melekh dovid aleyn iz geblibn* (New York: Farlag papirene brik, 1946), 3–4.

    3. *Complete Artscroll Siddur: Weekday, Sabbath, Festival*, 2d ed., 3d impression, trans. with commentary by Rabbi Nosson Scherman, co-ed. Rabbi Meir Zlotowitz (Brooklyn: Mesorah Publications, 1987), notes 434–435 and 817–818.

    4. Molodowsky, "Eyl khanun," in *Paper Bridges*, 352–353.

    5. Ibid., 354–355.

    6. Exodus 15:20–21, in *The Holy Scriptures According to the Masoretic Text*.

    7. Malka Heifetz Tussman, "Tsu dir, miryam," in *Lider* (Los Angeles: Malka Heifetz Tussman bukh komitet, 1949), 6–7. Malka Heifetz Tussman, "To You, Miriam," trans. Kathryn Hellerstein, *Kerem* 12 (2010), 138.

    8. Ibid., 139.

    9. Ibid.

    10. Ibid.

    11. Ibid., 139–140.

    12. Yitskhok Niborski, *Verterbukh fun loshn kodesh-shtamike verter in yidish* (Paris: Bibliotheque Medem, 1997), 251.

    13. Tussman, "Tsu dir, miryam," in *Lider*, 6–7. Malka Heifetz Tussman, "To You, Miriam," trans. Kathryn Hellerstein, *Kerem* 12 (2010), 140.

    14. Molodowsky, "Eyl khanun," in *Paper Bridges*, 352–355.

    15. Tussman, "Tsu dir, miryam," in *Lider*, 6–7. Malka Heifetz Tussman, "To You, Miriam," trans. Kathryn Hellerstein, *Kerem* 12 (2010), 140.

    16. Alexander Harkavy, *Yiddish-English-Hebrew Dictionary*, reprint of the 1928 expanded 2d ed., intro. Dovid Katz (New York: YIVO Institute for Jewish Research and Schocken Books, 1988), 109.

    17. Uriel Weinreich, *Modern English-Yiddish, Yiddish-English Dictionary* (New York: YIVO Institute for Jewish Research and Schocken Books, 1977), 87.

    18. See David G. Roskies, *Against the Apocalypse: Responses to Catastrophe in Modern Jewish Culture* (Cambridge: Harvard University Press, 1984), 15–52; and Alan Mintz, *Hurban: Responses to Catastrophe in Hebrew Literature* (New York: Columbia University Press, 1984), 1–14.

    19. Kathryn Hellerstein, "A Yiddish Poet's Response to the Khurbm: Kadya Molodowsky in America," in *Freedom and Responsibility: Exploring the Dilemmas of Jewish Continuity*, ed. Rela M. Geffen and Marsha B. Edelman (Hoboken: Gratz College and KTAV Publishing House, 1998), 243–260.

# Gendered Experience in Chava Rosenfarb's *The Tree of Life: A Trilogy of Life in the Łódź Ghetto*

JULIE SPERGEL

Soon after completing his long journey home, Turin native Primo Levi felt compelled to record the struggle of his survival in Auschwitz. His famously objective, scientific approach to bearing witness to inhumane circumstances that many others found beyond words eventually leads him to call upon the reader to become an accomplice in his account. He writes, "We now invite the reader to contemplate the possible meaning in the Lager of the words 'good' and 'evil,' 'just' and 'unjust'; let everybody judge [...] how much of our ordinary moral world could survive on this side of the barbed wire."[1] In *The Tree of Life: A Trilogy of Life in the Lodz Ghetto*, Chava Rosenfarb (1923–2011) also addresses how meanings changed as a result of the terror.[2] Her enormous work of fiction, charged with realism and detail, monitors several interconnected individuals' experiences in Łódź from 1938–1944. A survivor of the Łódź ghetto and subsequently Auschwitz, Sasel, and Bergen-Belsen, Chava Rosenfarb doubles as eyewitness and fiction writer, presenting not only men and women who deliberate the meaning of being Jewish in a time of nationalism, but also their attempts to endure a merciless suffering that sometimes forces Jews to turn on one another, transforming them into what Levi once described as "monsters of asociality and insensitivity."[3]

In *The Tree of Life*, her novelistic debut, Rosenfarb takes great pains to depict how the ghetto, in sometimes surprising ways, irreversibly alters the individual inhabitants, making them either monstrous or more human. Similar to Levi's memoir, Rosenfarb's novel relies on its neutral and distant tone more commonly associated with historical texts to make the dramatic point that even a work of fiction this long barely has enough words to describe the horror. By tracing the incremental change of her characters, Rosenfarb calls upon her readers to make their own judgments about individual decisions and ensuing actions. Only when readers begin to draw their own conclusions do the different kinds of suffering in the ghetto begin to take on shape. Requiring such engagement may therefore be considered a deliberate attempt to bridge the gap between public history and private memory; it is an effort to break the silence and convey what was thought to be nearly impossible to express, specifically what life was really like in the Łódź ghetto. In this sense, the novel also becomes a counter-memorial,[4] which is a work of commemoration, created generally for the Holocaust, which resists typical meanings of a monument by marking absence, encouraging participation, and drawing attention to the limits of representation. Rosenfarb's work commemorates the Jews of Łódź by bringing to life a ghetto whose inevitable destruction haunts the entire reading. By bringing these ghosts to the reader's attention, Rosenfarb forces the reader to face the absence that could be the only result of such destruction.

In this time and place marked by suspended morality, there were endless victims and countless ways to suffer. Rosenfarb's novel raises questions about the Łódź ghetto that Levi's chronicle of Auschwitz does not. She asks whether men and women were affected or reacted differently to the traumas of the ghetto. Pairing gender with the Holocaust has been a contentious issue since it was first explored in the early 1980s. The idea continues to shock so many because the Holocaust was undeniably an attack on a group not on individuals. Critics fear that examining the events through the lens of class, gender, age, or nationality could devalue the extent of the catastrophe and consequently undermine the anti–Semitism at its core. However, with the aim of helping others better understand this horrific past, Rosenfarb intentionally uses all of these four variables to describe how life was for all Jews in the ghetto. *The Tree of Life*'s narrative structure contains the reminder that a single story may be told in multiple ways: the novel is peopled with a cross-section of characters who entreat readers to remember the marginal stories, often those belonging to women, which constitute unofficial and official Holocaust history. Moreover, the private and the public version of events compete in the novel and create an irresolvable tension, exposing the rift that exists between actual experience and traditional Holocaust-writing, thereby indicating how memory is constructed to fit into established narrative forms. In this way, too, the novel is a counter-memorial; it questions how accurately official history represents the past. *The Tree of Life* thus stresses the distance between women's untold stories and the more masculine master narrative of official history. Scholar Sara R. Horowitz argues that women's Holocaust experiences were subordinate to men's and that the "evolving master narrative was male" when social historian Emanuel Ringelblum, who headed the *Oneg Shabbes* project in the Warsaw ghetto to collect as much evidence of life there as possible, announced that "[t]he future historian ... dedicate a proper page to the Jewish woman."[5]

Contrasting private memory with public history, Rosenfarb also reveals the dialogic relationship between history and fiction. It may therefore be argued that *The Tree of Life* is a work of historiographic metafiction. While this dialogism helps expose the female heroism and resiliency that have often been ignored in Holocaust writing, Rosenfarb does not do so to the detriment of men's experience. De-privileging men's experience and downplaying their everyday battles does not tell the whole story of the catastrophe. In *The Tree of Life*, unofficial versions of history are revealed to include gender-specific traumas endured by men and women. In turn, this specificity adds a new dimension of understanding to the atrocities of ghetto life.

## *The Łódź Ghetto*

The ghetto was created in the northeast part of the city, in the heart of the slums of Łódź, or Litzmanstadt as it was renamed upon German occupation in November 1939. The ghetto opened officially on February 8, 1940, when starting on that day, 164,000 Jews were forced to resettle and marched uphill towards their new "home," bringing with them, as per order, only what they could carry. The Germans called it the *Übersiedlung*, but a Jewish eyewitness dubbed it "a caravan of poverty."[6] In 1940, the most "comfortable" year in the ghetto, there were 3.2 people per room.[7] The area was small: one could ride the breadth and width of the ghetto in under an hour by coach. Its radius was 4.13 kilometers until 1941, when it was reduced to 3.82. Outside the barbed wire fence that imprisoned the Jews indefinitely as of May 1, 1940 after a few short months of being able to go in and out, hung the sign "*Wohngebiet der Juden. Betreten Verboten*," indicating a residential area and not a ghetto.

The Łódź ghetto was established mostly in the dilapidated Baluty, an area recognized as part of Łódź only since World War I. A small part, however, was located in the *Stare Miasto* [Old Town], the site of the official Jewish ghetto of Łódź until 1861, where the decrepit and overstuffed buildings verified this history. Soon after the creation of the ghetto, the suburban area of Marysin was added, where the orphanage, schools, and *hachsharot*[8] were placed before their original functions were unceremoniously abandoned. Marysin also included the cemeteries and the train station, the *umschlagplatz*, the site of the deportations. Unable to redirect the traffic of the arterial streets Zgierska and Limanowskiego that ran through the ghetto, the Germans were able to keep these busy roads within their territory by connecting Marysin and Baluty with three footbridges. On these bridges, looking down at the trams full of non–Jews going by, for example, was punishable by death. Of the 220,000 Jews who passed through the Łódź ghetto, only 5,000 to 7,000 are estimated to have survived. Hunger, cold, and disease ravaged 21 percent of the population, and the rest were deported to extermination camps or murdered within the ghetto borders. The ghetto was liquidated in 1944.

In *The Tree of Life*, the characters through whose eyes the reader experiences the war in Łódź and who each slowly learn the purpose of the ghetto include the following: the members of the carpenter Itche Mayer's family, whose four sons each belong to a different political party and whose wife longs to return to her *shtetl*; the family members of the wealthy industrialist Samuel Zuckerman, who never succeed in writing a book about the history of the Jews of Łódź; the members of his competitor's family, the Adam Rosenbergs, who foster an unhealthy competition with Zuckerman that follows them into death; the anti–Yiddishist elderly school teacher Miss Diamand, who sees herself as Polish first and foremost; the fiercely proud orphaned red-haired beauty Esther, who finds family in radical communism and various lovers; the young budding poet and fervent Bundist Rachel Eibushitz (a character based loosely on Rosenfarb); Rachel's boyfriend David, whose notebook entries are reproduced as one of the exceptions to the third-person narrator; the vegetarian medical doctor Michal Levine, whose point of view is recorded through unsent letters to his fiancée; the poet Simcha Bunim Berkovitch (a figure based on Simcha Bunim Shayevitsh, Rosenfarb's ghetto mentor and author of the poem "Lekh-Lekho"); and finally, the very real and extremely controversial Mordechai Chaim Rumkowski, a self-perceived second Moses sent by God to protect the Jews, who goes from running an orphanage to becoming the untouchable Eldest of the Jews as the Chairman of the Łódź ghetto. *The Tree of Life* depicts an historical place and describes actual people while infusing the story with a fictional cast. By funnelling ghetto life through the eyes of this varied group of protagonists, readers experience gendered, gradated, and socially diverse individual voices that compete with the perspective of an entire community. This variety of real and fictional voices is one feature that makes *The Tree of Life* a work of historiographic metafiction.

## The Tree of Life *as Historiographic Metafiction*

Though not definitive in its most orthodox sense, *The Tree of Life* may nevertheless be treated as a work of historiographic metafiction. Linda Hutcheon's term, which is outlined in *A Poetics of Postmodernism: History, Theory, Fiction*, identifies a text that blurs the distinctions between public or official history and the more personal, unofficial kind. Rosenfarb's novel admittedly lacks a playfulness in addressing this overlapping of history and fiction, and it does not overtly acknowledge the construction and selection process that emphasizes the fictionality of history. However, *The Tree of Life* tackles the similarities of history and fiction in a rejection of the Enlightenment's view of historiography, thereby throwing into relief the questions of how one may ever know the past and exactly whose past is being told. There is a self-reflexive recognition in *The Tree of Life* that suggests dates and facts do not substantiate the past because official history cannot be reconciled with what individuals actually experienced. The Enlightenment, which rendered obsolete any remaining traces of the fragmented, unreliable powers of history dating back to Herodotus,[9] imposed that thereafter all history would be seen as objective, progressive, and deterministic. In this age of reason, ideas were seen as an immutable force leading only to advancement and improvement, and the collection of "trustworthy" and "accurate" historical facts would reveal the one authentic account of the past. Rosenfarb's need to unearth subversive, controversial, and marginal pasts belonging to the underclass, the politically deviant, or women and to place these stories in contrast to more official versions undermines this view that reigned uncontested until finally met with the challenges of post-modernism. Historiographic metafiction evinces that since the past may only be known through its textualized remains,[10] the past that acts as a basis for identity becomes rooted in impermanent, transitory narratives. With details fed by history and memory, in a style she describes as a "mixture of fantasy, realism, and intuition,"[11] Rosenfarb recreates Jewish life in the Łódź ghetto. She is very clear about the book's status as a work of fiction, and yet its role as an historical account cannot be ignored. *The Tree of Life* is among those novels described by Hutcheon "that admit openly they are fiction, but suggest that fiction is just another means by which we make sense of our world (past and present)."[12]

Rosenfarb heartily accepted the responsibility of bearing witness when she wrote *The Tree of Life*. Although she deems it necessary to reassure readers that the work is a novel, she admits, "I see life through a certain point of view, a prism of a particular kind of colouration of my own individuality. It's not always authentic, true to reality, sometimes my imagination wanders off."[13] This is not an act of divesting herself of the responsibility of correctly remembering. Rather, the weaving of fictional elements into the fabric of history is an effective form of social commentary inherited from Yiddish literature, about which she says, "My tradition comes from Yiddish absolutely."[14] Typically Yiddish literature is full of tales of very bleak social circumstances with humorous or tragic stock figures and characteristics and juxtaposed fiction with fact as a means of criticizing or remarking on the Jewish lot. Stock figures like the sainted fool, such as Toffee Man, or the *kleyne mentshele*, such as Itche Mayer or Krajne Shapsonovitch, both poor but proud, appear more rounded out in the novel.[15] What is interesting, however, is how Rosenfarb takes the tradition a step further. She does not use these manipulations of reality to satirize a situation that was too late to change. The commentary entreats the reader to see what life was really like for the doomed Jews of Łódź. She thus portrays real men and women who existed within the ghetto and who interact with fictional characters drawn so lifelike that they may just as well have been there.

    The imagined witnesses to real events do not provide the only blurring between fact and fiction that occurs within *The Tree of Life*. The map on the inside cover of the Scribe edition, for instance, confuses these distinctions by guiding one not only to the *Kripo* [criminal police], the Zgierska footbridge, or the church, but also to Esther's garret room, Rachel's second dwelling, and Adam's house in Marysin. The function of the fictional markings on an historical map, although presumably meant to enable the reader to visualize the layout of the ghetto and understand the proportions and dimensions of suffering, lends an authenticity to the characters and acts as a constant reminder of the novel's shared role as an historical testament. Rosenfarb employs actual dates and events as a framework to the novel, but the plot is subservient to the characters as well as to the faithful reconstruction of the ghetto world. The multiple competing voices qualifying each other and forbidding dissolution into a single monologic truth supports Rosenfarb's method of combining memory with history. As a result, the meanings of anguish in the Łódź ghetto begin to crystallize. The victims cease being statistics and begin to take on shape, and then finally breathe. In this way, the characters express what it was like in the Łódź ghetto and give the novel "an authority that public history lacks," which further encourages discourse between private and public spheres.[16]

Although more rooted in the Yiddish modern tradition than in postmodernism, the novel demonstrates that fiction may be an authentic vision of the past performed in a manner more true-to-life than non-fiction, thereby exemplifying the tenets of historiographic metafiction.

By translating the novel into English, Rosenfarb revives for contemporary English-speaking audiences what Manuela Costantino and Susanna Egan in their article on auto/biographies call a "pre-historical" place. Pre-historic Poland in this case refers to Poland before it became understood by these modern audiences in its new context with its present borders, allegiances, and "official" history.[17] Rosenfarb resurrects Łódź by "flesh[ing] out the lives" of those in the ghetto, performing a task which museums and monuments with mere artifacts and displays can never achieve. Rosenfarb is able to reproduce the atmosphere of the time and space that her character Rachel fears is unachievable. Rachel muses:

> I wonder whether it is at all possible to write a novel about the ghetto. How can you write without the perspective of time? On the other hand, if you wait for the perspective of time, it will become impossible to recreate the specific atmosphere of this place [895].

Rachel's anxieties test the limits of representation and signify the crisis that the Enlightenment's belief in an objective history underwent when postmodernism began to question whether only documents belonging to a period could be considered authentic. As it turns out, memory and history aid Rosenfarb in commemorating the Łódź ghetto in her literary counter-memorial. The resultant authenticity, though not her primary goal, helped her to achieve the effect that was of utmost importance, specifically to "reproduce the flavor of the place, the flavor of the atmosphere."[18]

Among the most important non-fiction books published about the Łódź ghetto is the anthology compiled and edited by Alan Adelson and Robert Lapides, *Łódź Ghetto: Inside a Community Under Siege*. The volume is pieced together from primary sources in order to give an overview of Jewish Łódź starting with life before the war, covering the formation of the ghetto, and ending with the liquidation in 1944. The work is comprised of German documents, diary entries, official meeting minutes, political leaflets, Rumkowski's speeches, and excerpts from the *Chronicle of the Łódź Ghetto*,[19] an historical document systematically compiled every day by eyewitnesses. Adelson and Lapides's anthology tells the story of the ghetto in the voices of different witnesses. Writing from the point of view of each character in her large cast, Rosenfarb parallels that approach as she attempts to gather "a community's consciousness through the vast written remnants of a society confronting annihilation but struggling to survive."[20] As a result, two hauntingly similar tales are told: one "historical" and one "fictional."

To name one of many examples of narrative parallels between the two works, in the historical text, the poet Bunim's story of his family's deportation is told in a journal entry by Josef Zelkowicz in a straightforward manner.[21] Both Rosenfarb and the eyewitness Zelkowicz recount how Bunim's thirty-three-hour-old baby, along with a sister and mother, who is weakened by childbirth, are taken out of their beds and sent to the camps. To give shape to his suffering, Rosenfarb claims in her novel that the doomed new born baby is a son instead of a daughter. She does so because the first-born male, a man's *kaddish*, is responsible for honoring the memory of and bearing witness to the dead father. Rosenfarb thus turns the loss of his family into what Sara R. Horowitz has called a "gender wounding." First used in a discussion of sexual abuse in the camps, Horowitz describes a gender wounding as a "shattering of something innate and important to [a woman's] sense of her own womanhood."[22] In this case, for Bunim to lose his *kaddish* is also an attack on his sense of manhood; he is being robbed of his family and his legacy, which are, for him, intertwined with his masculinity. Because they are haunted by the same ghosts and their terrifying accounts, *The Tree of Life* and *Lodz Ghetto* may be seen as complementary works.

The similarities between the anthology and the novel are a tribute to Rosenfarb's accomplishment as an observer and storyteller. The detail and precision with which she writes a few decades after the ghetto's liquidation parallels that of the diaries that were written as the events unfolded and were later dug out of the floors, gardens, and other hiding places in 1946 by the Central Jewish Historical Commission in Łódź. To read the diarists' complaints is to hear the analogous cries of suffering in *The Tree of Life*; to read of their shock upon discovering the cruelty of others is to seek out explanation in Rosenfarb's novel. All of their shouts of pain and loss—real or fictional—may be heard simultaneously.

Although there is some argument to show how objective and unmediated eyewitness accounts and diary entries may be, one's language, political sentiments, religious upbringing, fear of discovery, and gender will inevitably shape the texts with a narrative ideology. Along these lines, James E. Young suggests in *Writing and Rewriting the Holocaust: Narrative and the Consequences of Interpretation* that this inescapable "poetics" of diarists' testimony "becomes invaluable to readers, both for understanding how narrative generates interpretation and how interpretations of events as they occurred may have influenced the course they ultimately took."[23] He goes on to conclude that "nothing can be more 'authentic' than the ways in which diarists' interpretations of experiences gathered the weight and force of agency in their lives."[24] He is thus arguing that interpretation *is* the narrative truth, while all evidence is of a constructed nature. Rosenfarb's historiographic metafiction that encompasses her own testimony purposely draws attention to the role of interpretation in the novel as well as to her personal understanding of the interrelation of the factual events. Rosenfarb's story, told by a variety of characters and their divergent points of view, consciously uses the external factors that influence narration, such as gender, politics, age, attitude, and religious beliefs, in order to address the impossibility of paradigm-free accounts. Gender is one tool that Rosenfarb uses to recreate for the reader a real sense of what life was like in the ghetto.

## *Gender Studies and Holocaust Research*

Accounts of sexual assault in the ghettoes or camps began to appear in Holocaust-writing relatively recently. Raped by a German officer, one female survivor of the Theresienstadt ghetto admits in an oral testimony that she consequently never married:

> I never told anyone. I don't want my brother to know. I am so very ashamed. I am seventy and still ashamed. It shouldn't have happened that way ... I never married. I used to like men. Now I tolerate them. I couldn't stand the thought of going to bed with them.[25]

She was never able to recover from the degradation because she could not talk about her rape in connection with her incarceration. Had she been able to realize that one was the result of the other, she may have been able to divest herself of her guilt.

In her seminal article "The Split Between Gender and the Holocaust," Joan Ringelheim describes a survivor who found difficulties in understanding how her sexual assault during the Holocaust fit in with other survivors' accounts:

> Although Pauline recognized her experience as different from men's, she did not know how or where to locate them in the history of the Holocaust. Her memory was split between traditional versions of Holocaust history and her own experience.[26]

Pauline was unable to verbalize her suffering because there was no preceding narrative form to which she could relate. As a result of the master narrative eschewing women's experiences of sexual violation—of favoring the official over the unofficial—she could not have known that if she told her story someone would want to hear it or that others would need to.

Not only has the issue of sexual violation been skirted in Holocaust writing, but the tendency in oral narratives has traditionally been for women to deny their own agency or to feel than any domestic account is unworthy of disclosure and for men to circumvent emotions and family while focusing on tales of heroism in the belief that that is what an audience wants to hear.[27] Regardless of such a stark discrepancy between testimonies, making links between gender and the Holocaust has been controversial ever since it began to gain attention as a result of Ringelheim's pioneering work in the early 1980s.[28] However, as a novel such as *The Tree of Life* further underscores, men and women did experience all aspects of the Holocaust differently. In order to understand the full scope of the trauma, these disparities need to be discussed. As Ringelheim writes:

> Gender-specific experiences are overlooked in Holocaust literature, especially that written by men. The stories told seem to erase or obscure women. In the instance of erasure, the fact that the main person in the story is a woman seems irrelevant to the teller.[29]

In the work of the more enthusiastically received and better-known male writers, she goes on to note that

> women's lives are neutralized into a so-called "human perspective" which, on examination turns out to be a masculine one. [...] It is as if stories about women were being used to tell about the men involved.[30]

Male survivors engaging in life-writing, for instance, would describe a rape scene they witnessed in order to describe their own feelings of powerlessness at being able to do nothing to stop it.[31] The woman's feelings remained unaddressed. In men's Holocaust writing, there is an overarching view of women as victims, incapable of being agents of resistance and who thus exacerbate men's feelings of helplessness. Men's Holocaust writing predominates, explains Sara Horowitz, since women's stories about the Holocaust are atypical; their texts are thus not used in academic research and they eventually fall out of print.[32] It therefore became crucial that an effort was made to hear these stories.

All over Europe, from before the war until after liberation, men and women suffered in distinct ways. Anna Reading cites an example of how before *Kristallnacht* women were more willing to emigrate. By contrast, men attempted to wait out what they thought could surely only be temporary persecution. In the aftermath, men were more likely to flee Germany, while women felt they should stay where needed in order to care for the ill and elderly who could not travel.[33] It would soon be too late for them to get out. While women could sometimes hide behind fake passports, men could never "pass," as their circumcisions made them easily identifiable as Jews. They were also often attacked for their external markings of identity: beards, earlocks, or clothes. Throughout the Nazi terror, Jewish women were viewed as the carriers of the next generation of Jews. Since this was a war against a people, conversion, age, strength, or gender did not matter. In the camps, where pregnancy meant certain death, women were faced with decisions about abortion or infanticide that men were not forced to confront.

Alternatively, in the camps and ghettoes, women alone agonized over whether they would be able to reproduce and raise a family after liberation. As Marlene Heinemann notes:

> Because mothers were especially threatened and because a future for European Jews seemed unlikely to many camp inmates, narratives tend to place a high value on motherhood and fertility. In the context of mass death and compulsory sterility the association of women with reproduction and the preservation of life gives them unique torments and, sometimes, forms of resistance.[34]

Their suffering was heightened when their menses stopped. Amenorrhea was not only a symptom of their persecution, but also what Heinemann sees as "a form of psychological assault on a woman's identity, since most women had no idea whether fertility would return if they survived."[35] At the time, few victims realized that this was the result of malnutrition and duress; many survivors have indicated the widespread belief that the Nazis put a poison in their food that caused the cessation of menstruation. Judith Tydor Baumel suggests the resultant fear is one factor in the population explosion in the DP camps immediately after the war, when "the urge to marry and raise a family as fast as possible was a paramount desire."[36] Women had been so worried that they would not be able to conceive that they tried at once to become pregnant.

Furthermore, in a time that, as Primo Levi suggested, called into question "how much of our ordinary moral world could survive," the distinctions between good and evil disintegrated. Saviours became exploiters when women were used as prostitutes by male resistance fighters or were raped by those hiding them as well as by the Allied liberators who released them from the camps. There were instances of young girls brought to the safety of England in the *Kinderstransport* only to be molested by their host fathers. Alone in a new country, the same men who volunteered to protect them became their tormentors.

## *Women's and Men's Cultures*

Women's stories are decidedly not restricted to traumas of a biological nature. They also include feats of everyday survival, such as protecting children, looking for work, hiding husbands from the *Sperre*,[37] and preparing meals on meager rations. The quotidian is recorded meticulously in Rosenfarb's *The Tree of Life*. The principal difference between Chava Rosenfarb's massive work of historiographic metafiction and the archival *Chronicle of the Łódź Ghetto* is that in the latter, the writers "never report what the victims think and feel about those who caused their tragedy, even when they are being sent to their deaths."[38] In *The Tree of Life*, male and female perspectives alike are examined thoroughly in order to help make sense of the different kinds of torment in the ghetto. Ringelheim argues thus:

> Women's culture (not their biology) provides women with specific and different conditions in which to make moral choices and to act meaningfully. There must be further exploration of these differences between men and women; the assumption that "human" responses are undifferentiable will not stand.[39]

Rosenfarb portrays ashamed women who, while begging for assistance in protecting their fathers or lovers, are required to pay off the intercession with sexual favors, as well as proud mother figures who share the very little food they have with starving neighbors. While Rosenfarb's fiction clearly supports what Ringelheim and her successors have argued, namely that women were often more resilient and adaptable but less likely to survive the Holocaust,[40] she does not allow these stories of moral triumph to outshine the men's. Rosenfarb's novel also calls into question the relevance of such a hypothesis posited by *Women in the Holocaust*, the first anthology on the subject, that men survived through individualism and women through relationships. Although Rosenfarb takes steps to uncover women's issues in the context of the Łódź ghetto, she refuses to privilege their stories over the men's, making it clear that men also suffered from "gender woundings."

Men in the ghetto were also faced with gender-specific troubles, and Rosenfarb is as insistent on confronting these issues as the women's. When David, for example, finds out that his missing father is dead and that, as Michal tells him, "'They were brave, so we must be brave in accepting the truth about their fate'" (779), he decides he must bear this revelation alone. He does not tell his mother or his younger brother about how his father met his end because he feels they cannot face the news with the courage it deserves. This secret, he says "made a man out of me, more than a man, an old man" (779). Later, racked with guilt for his inability to rationalize his way through a hunger that turns him into an "animal," he grasps that his father "was my ideal of a man and thinking about him makes me realise how worthless I am" (990). Just as there is, in Ringelheim's words, a "women's culture" that directs how women make moral choices in immoral times, men, too, were forced to face cultural expectations in the ghetto of how to live meaningfully. Rosenfarb examines how failure to reach these standards added inner torment to an already unbearable physical suffering.

Samuel Zuckerman provides another interesting example of male-centered suffering. Although he provides well for his family in the ghetto, his daughters are ashamed of him:

> "What do you want of me?' he asks apologetically.
> "Am I really such a monster? We ought to count our blessings. People are sent out of the ghetto ... by the thousands. Is it not bad enough as it is?" [759].

In securing a position of power, he is guilty of harming others. He is repulsed by his acts but believes this is what a man must do to protect his family. Shortly after his daughter Junia uncovers his affair with the prostitute Sabinka—from which he also suffers self-disgust—he is sent to the *Kripo*. Ironically, power and sexual prowess seem to emasculate him. Despite his literal castration, after his return from the *Kripo*, Samuel begins to feel more like a man than ever before and refuses to do what Rumkowski demands of him, even though it costs him his job. He later admits to his confidant, the socially inferior Moshe with whom he has developed a deep friendship in the ghetto:

> In the past, it seemed to me that a man carried all of his masculinity between his legs. Now, that I am no longer physically a man ... I am actually beginning to feel like one [790].

The act of torture specifically meted out to render his life a humiliation worse than death verily becomes for him a source of empowerment. When the Carpentry Resort that is the basis of his family's comfort and its insurance against deportation burns to the ground, he almost regrets that he is not responsible. Its destruction purifies him of his complicity and allows him to redefine what it means to be a man in the Łódź ghetto.

In her article, "Absent Fathers, Present Mothers: Images of Parenthood in Holocaust Survivor Narratives," Margarete Myers Feinstein examines survivors' oral testimonies and discovers how they see themselves in gendered terms. Consequently, maternal imagery abounds, while paternal symbolism and terminology are predominately absent. Feinstein reveals that this split is chiefly the result of pre-established gendered narrative forms that stifle new forms of expression and vocabulary, in addition to the crisis of paternal authority that followed the war when many men felt they had failed their families.[41] In the case of the Łódź ghetto, she concludes that male narratives

> give evidence of close relationships dedicated to survival, including the sharing of food and emotional support, contradicting Joan Ringelheim's suggestion that

"men, when they lost their role in the protection of their own families, seemed less able to transform this habit into the protection of others."[42]

Moreover, Feinstein claims that, when probed, male survivors often admitted to seeing themselves in fatherly roles. Rosenfarb's novel corroborates Feinstein's conclusion that even if men do not employ paternal imagery in the telling of their stories, they did not necessarily stop seeing themselves as fathers or that they evaded friendship in preference of a dog-eat-dog approach to survival. In *The Tree of Life*, characters such as Zuckerman, who analyzes his role as father and husband from before the formation of the ghetto until his suicide, provide a key example of behaviours other than those commonly conveyed in many Holocaust representations. Men, too, identified themselves in terms of their relationships and relied on bonds with others for courage and hope.

## Nuancing Holocaust Narratives

Early on, in the interest of recovering women's stories, pioneering scholars in the field of Holocaust and gender studies began amassing and publishing women's untold accounts. As Sara R. Horowitz points out in the article "Gender, Genocide and Jewish Memory," this task has since been accomplished and now the more urgent cause should be dedicated to "nuancing" Holocaust representation:

> When focused exclusively on women, gender analysis runs the risk of viewing women only as objects of a particular subset of genocidal practices connected to their biological functions—for example, pregnancy, motherhood, and sexual violation. While the work of reclamation recovers important facets of the Holocaust, a singular focus on women can unintendedly serve to reinscribe male experience as normative for the development of a master narrative, and relegate women only to the category of mother, or of the sexually abused. And just as Nazi atrocity attacked Jewish women as Jews and as women, it also attacked Jewish men as Jews and as men.[43]

*The Tree of Life* has no feminist agenda. The book neither combines the experiences and wounds of male and female survivors together nor does it explore exclusively female accounts. Neither of these approaches would paint an accurate picture of life during the war. Horowitz suggests that men's stories need to be re-examined in the light of gender studies, alongside the women's, and male and female differences and similarities in each role identified and addressed.[44] Rosenfarb's impartial approach to her fiction gives each of her *ghettoniks* depth and agency and encourages readers to think about what they would do in a similar situation. The following example of Adam and Sabinka's relationship demonstrates how men and women can react to the same situation; their mutually protective/destructive affair is portrayed from both their gendered perspectives.

Like other women afraid for their lives who would attach themselves to powerful men to ward off deportation, Sabinka begins to live with Adam, who would "beat her when he was mad at her, or at himself; he kissed and caressed her when he pitied her, or himself" (1017). Adam, who is planning on escaping the ghetto by dressing up as a woman, is so afraid of losing his masculinity (and thus his sense of self) that he attempts to assert the power his oppressors have taken from him by beating the "humble, the submissive" woman who "gave him strength" because "with her he had learned to master himself" (1021). The prostitute Sabinka is willing to put herself at Adam's mercy and his sexual whims because she wants to live and sees no other means to do so. During the Holocaust, all Jews did not all undergo torment in the same ways. There were as many ways to suffer as there were individuals, but it is nevertheless important to recognize, as Rosenfarb does in her novel, that the persecution was not gender-blind.

However, one risk seen by Horowitz in the telling of sexual abuse suffered in the Holocaust is that a voyeuristic approach may result. In "Gender and Holocaust Representation," she writes that "[m]any scholars fear that bringing sexuality in to the discussion of victims or perpetrators and their respective cultures would be inappropriately titillating or voyeuristic"[45] She asks the question, "But how should [evidence and remembrance of sexual violation] be represented without re-creating the original offense, without again exposing these women to the gaze of strangers?"[46] The threat is that if women's Holocaust stories are reduced to being viewed in terms of sexual violation, it "domesticates the Holocaust, diminishing its horror to something more ordinary and sparing the reader a more disturbing confrontation."[47] This could nuance Holocaust writing in a way that eroticizes women. However, this is where Rosenfarb's objectivity is able to explore life as it really was; instances of rape and abuse unfold as part of the inner workings of the ghetto. Her narrative technique features chapters, or sometimes short sections of chapters, written in an non-intrusive third person, that shift the focus of character for each principal participant, in what linguists would call a standard indirect discourse; it is this technique that admits the reader into the thoughts of the character while remaining aloof. Not only is it a means of showing different viewpoints of the same event, but it also successfully demonstrates that life in the ghetto is not as simple as "good" and "evil" or "just" and "unjust."

One such morally ambiguous act described by Rosenfarb is the choice made by mothers to join their children on the transports out of the ghetto, despite inevitable death, so that their children will not have to die alone. Traditionally, this act has been portrayed as heroic in many Holocaust narratives. However, this approbation may also imply that "women who chose otherwise were unnatural and inferior mothers. Indeed some women rejected their children in an effort to save themselves and earned the scorn of others."[48] With narrative forms of what makes an ideal Jewish woman already in place, where is there room for women who wanted to live? These stories could become hidden in the vaults of memory and excluded from official history, but Rosenfarb's neutrality that commands participation from its audience—if the narrator does not condemn these horrors, who will?—forces readers to make the heartbreaking choice for themselves. By demanding that readers ask, "Would I go along with my child knowing it is also my death sentence?" the work becomes a literary counter-memorial because it never ceases to remind the reader of the void created by the loss of these very lives: those who followed their children into death, as well as "the other women" who refused to give up. Most of the women who survived the deportation of their children, however, would have met a terrible fate at some other time, and once again, the reader is left only with absence.

## *Resiliency in the Ghetto*

Despite the presentation of a great deal of victimhood, Rosenfarb is also able to include many examples of both male and female resiliency. Esther, who loses every person she has ever loved to different dark fates in the ghetto, finds that her vigour can be renewed:

> After every tragedy Esther withered and then came back to life, becoming healthier and stronger than before [...] The tragedies were the yeast in which she matured. They gave her the wisdom to distinguish between what really counted and what was only of momentary importance [1024].

When Esther falls in love with Israel Mayer, the priority of family empowers her: "now when she queued up [for food], it was not to be with people, but for a purpose. She no longer had ample time. She was important. She had family" (954). Rosenfarb further portrays women who tend to the sick at the risk of their own health or who go without their rations so that the ill may recover. Nechama Tec has conducted an analysis of women's heightened adaptability and willingness to make sacrifices on behalf of others in a variety of Holocaust settings. "When the men lost their freedom and with it their ability to discharge their duties as providers and protectors of the family," she claims, "they lost their spirit, became depressed and apathetic. Women's roles changed as well but because these changes placed a higher value on their traditional roles of caring for and helping others, they were not as adversely affected."[49] Feinstein calls into question Tec's assertion that, due to their tendency to form deeper bonds and nurturing relationships, women survived "better" than men. She argues that "many of these conclusions have been reached through literal readings of survivor memoirs, without regard for how gendered memory and narrative construction have emphasized or repressed certain experiences."[50] Again, the need to find a structure to understand one's story becomes as important as the events themselves. Rosenfarb explores men's and women's moral and immoral means of resistance without passing judgment on how ethically men or women survived but describes how they lived through it differently.

Gender becomes an important issue in the ghetto because it exposes the problematic division between public and private memories. To refuse to hear women's stories by arguing that the Holocaust happened to all Jews is to create a gulf between private and public histories. To de-privilege the men's stories in the interest of allowing the women's to be heard will lead to an incomplete version of the past. The gender-inclusive *The Tree of Life*, however, insists that both men's and women's unofficial stories be heard and subsequently "nuanced" in a representative manner.

## Conclusion: Ghost-Stories as Counter-Memorial

The narrative ends with the following chapter headings all appearing on one page: "Chapter Twenty-nine ... Thirty ... Thirty-one ... ad infinitum." Then it bleeds into the only verbal recognition of where the story leads:

AUSCHWITZ. WORDS STOP, UNDRESSED, NAKED, THEIR MEANING, THEIR SENSE SHAVEN OFF. LETTERS EXPIRE IN THE SMOKE OF THE CREMATORIUM'S CHIMNEY ... [1066].

Echoing Adorno's proclamation that no poetry can exist after Auschwitz, six blank pages follow. What is left for the reader is the counter-memorial. Rosenfarb's novel forces the reader to imagine beyond all words what happened to the men and women with whom they have grown exceptionally close.

These ghosts do not want to be silenced, and Rosenfarb gives them a voice in the space where history and memory meet. *The Tree of Life* is an historical account by a writer who willingly shoulders the responsibility of remembering. Her combination of an eyewitness's recollections with a fictional narrative true to history is the method by which she recreates the Łódź ghetto, thus producing an authoritative vision of what life was like in that time and place.

Chava Rosenfarb's interest in unearthing the stories that have slipped through the cracks of history also reveals that there are multiple ways to deal with suffering. Some of the protagonists feel themselves changed for the better. Miss Diamand is even grateful to the ghetto for teaching her to embrace a Jewish identity. Other characters are ashamed of their behavior but are forced by hunger to commit acts they deem despicable. David does not want to steal his mother's bread, nor is he proud of the feeling of relief when she is dead. The reader, who knows each character intimately, who knows each thought that goes through the *ghettoniks*' heads, has the job of deciding whether they can be forgiven or censured for their actions. A work of historiographic metafiction, Rosenfarb's implementation of objectivity, neutrality, and reserved judgment in *The Tree of Life* reveals the dialogic relationship between history and fiction. It is in this forum that the ghosts can be heard; they have the opportunity to tell their stories and explain why they hurt the ones they love. It is their second chance. Margaret Atwood has defined writing as "bringing the dead to life and giving voices to those who lack them so that they may speak for themselves."[51] Rosenfarb has given her characters this breath of life so that the reader is also reminded of the "remedies of the heart" in the ghetto, sprouting despite being overshadowed by darker deeds. These are moments of tenderness and self-sacrifice that cry out for recognition. If their self-imposed deaths or days of hunger are to be judged as noble, the ghosts will know that their actions were not in vain. Readers must decide for themselves and thus engage in the participatory act of commemoration encouraged by the counter-memorial.

In writing that exposes the gulf between public and private spheres and official and unofficial history and that blurs the lines between history and fiction, it is imperative that many voices are given the opportunity to air versions of the past that may be silenced by an established and officially endorsed view of history. While she demonstrates the female heroism and resistance that has often been ignored in Holocaust-writing, as well as the depths of female suffering, Rosenfarb does not neglect the unofficial stories that are a part of men's private experience. Rosenfarb's novel ushers in the next stage of a gender studies approach to Holocaust representation by demonstrating that some of the untold stories were those belonging to men, stories of shame or friendship, not only of heroism or individualism. Men could live meaningfully or they could live selfishly. What is thus gleaned from the novel is that male stories must be re-examined from a gendered perspective, in light of the knowledge that has been gained as the result of recent scholarship. When faced with the injustices and gender woundings of the ghetto, it cannot be uniformly said that women became more human while men became monstrous. In Rosenfarb's *The Tree of Life*, unofficial versions of history include investigations of gender-specific traumas endured by both men and women, which, in the words of Sara R. Horowitz, "[have] the potential to transform our understanding of this terrible past and our own relation to it."[52]

Though firmly rooted in the modern Yiddish tradition, *The Tree of Life* may also be considered a postmodern text because the fate of each character "lies outside the novel's boundaries."[53] The tragic conclusion resides in the space between history and memory, in this same place where meaning in historical testimony is achieved. The deaths of the victims of the Łódź ghetto cannot be compensated or justified, but they can be commemorated by both reader and writer. The narrator's impartial tone in *The Tree of Life* recalls Primo Levi's appeal to readers to decide alone what is "good" or "evil" and "just" or "unjust" in an environment designed to obliterate humanity.

The Yiddish audience, which continued to diminish rapidly after the Holocaust's unfinished attempt to silence all Yiddish voices, is another ghost that haunts the reading of *The Tree of Life*. However, when Rosenfarb decided to translate her novel into an adoptive language, she also embraced a new audience that continues to bear witness to the lives of these Jewish men and women. She is saying *kaddish* for her family, for *yiddishkeit*, and for her home.

## Notes

1. Primo Levi, *Survival in Auschwitz and The Reawakening: Two Memoirs*, trans. Stuart Woolf (New York: Summit Books, 1985), 86.
2. Chava Rosenfarb, *The Tree of Life: A Trilogy About Life in the Lodz Ghetto*, trans. Chava Rosenfarb and Goldie Morgentaler (Melbourne: Scribe, 1985). All subsequent citations are taken from this edition. In 1972, Rosenfarb was awarded the J. I. Segal Prize, and in 1979, the Manger prize—the highest award for Yiddish literature—for this story that was originally published as a trilogy of novels by the Menorah Press in Tel Aviv. It was translated in 1985 by Rosenfarb and her daughter and published under one title by Melbourne's Scribe. In 2004, the work was released by the University of Wisconsin Press as a trilogy.
3. Levi, *Survival in Auschwitz* , 91.
4. Counter-monument or counter-memorial constructions such as Jochen Gerz and Esther Shalev-Gerz's sinking monument or Horst Heisel's negative-form monument are visual counterparts to Rosenfarb's literary counter-memorial. When counter-monuments show voids, it is to underscore the endemic nature of German anti–Semitism and to disprove its teleology. In the example of Daniel Libeskind's extension to the Jewish Museum, Berlin, absence is at the center of the installation because "Libeskind does not want to suggest that this void was imposed on Berlin from without, but was one created

in Berlin from within. It was not the bombing of Berlin which created the void, he says, but the vacuum and inner collapse of moral will that allowed Berlin to void itself of Jews," writes James E. Young in "The Arts of Jewish Memory in a Postmodern Age," in *Modernity, Culture and 'the Jew,'* ed. Bryan Cheyette and Laura Maras (Stanford: Stanford University Press, 1998), 211–225 and 218–219. Compare James E. Young, "Memory and Counter-Memory: The End of the Monument in Germany," *Harvard Design Magazine* 9 (1999): 1–10 and James E. Young, *At Memory's Edge: After-Images of the Holocaust in Contemporary Art and Architecture* (New Haven: Yale University Press, 2000).

5. Sara R. Horowitz, "Gender, Genocide and Jewish Memory," *Prooftexts* 20 1 & 2 (2000): 158–190 and 171.

6. *Übersiedlung* means relocation and is one of those perversely understated and ironic terms used by the Nazis. See Irena Liebman, "Lodz Ghetto Diary," in *Łódź Ghetto: Inside a Community Under Siege,* ed. Alan Adelson, Robert Lapides, and Marek Web (New York: Viking, 1989), 35.

7. Ibid., 88.

8. *Hachsharot* are little plots of land used by Zionist groups to teach agriculture in preparation for developing Eretz Israel.

9. Herodotus, the Greek intellectual commonly accredited with inventing the discipline of history in the fifth century BCE, claims in *The Histories*: "I am obliged to record the things I am told, but I am certainly not obliged to believe them." Herodotus, *The Histories*, ed. and trans. Robin Waterfield (Oxford: Oxford University Press, 1997), 457.

10. Linda Hutcheon, *A Poetics of Postmodernism: History, Theory, Fiction* (New York: Routledge, 1988), 119.

11. Chava Rosenfarb, telephone interview, August 21, 2005.

12. Linda Hutcheon, *The Canadian Postmodern: A Study of Contemporary English-Canadian Fiction* (Oxford: Oxford University Press, 1998), x.

13. Rosenfarb, telephone interview, 2005.

14. Ibid.

15. Michael Greenstein has also made the case that these characters are "Dickensian." See Michael Greenstein, "A Dickensian in the Lodz Ghetto" (review of all three volumes of *The Tree of Life*), *The Globe and Mail*, Book Section (Nov. 18, 2006).

16. Manuela Costantino and Susanna Egan, "Reverse Migrations and Imagined Communities," *Prose Studies: Women's Life Writing and Imagined Communities* 26 1–2 (2003): 105 and 108–134.

17. Ibid., 110.

18. Rosenfarb, telephone interview, 2005.

19. Lucjan Dobroszycki, ed., *The Chronicle of the Łódź Ghetto 1941–1944* (New Haven: Yale University Press, 1984).

20. Adelson and Lapides, *Łódź Ghetto*, xii.

21. Ibid., 345.

22. Sara R. Horowitz, "Mengele, the Gynecologist, and Other Stories of Women's Survival," in *Judaism Since Gender*, ed. Miriam Peskowitz and Laura Levitt (New York: Routledge, 1997), 200–212 and 201.

23. James E. Young, *Writing and Rewriting the* Holocaust: *Narrative and the Consequences of Interpretation* (Bloomington: Indiana University Press, 1988), 36.

24. Ibid.

25. Quoted in Jonathan C. Friedman, *Speaking the Unspeakable: Essays on Sexuality, Gender, and Holocaust Survivor Memory* (Lanham, MD: University Press of America, 2002), 55.

26. Joan Ringelheim, "The Split Between Gender and the Holocaust," in *Women in the Holocaust*, ed. Dalia Ofer and Lenore J. Weitzman (New Haven: Yale University Press, 1998), 340–350 and 346.

27. Margarete Myers Feinstein, "Absent Fathers, Present Mothers: Images of Parenthood in Holocaust Survivor Narratives," *Nashim: A Journal of Jewish Women's Studies* 13 (2007): 155–182, 177, and 179.

28. In 1983, Joan Ringelheim and Esther Katz put together a two-day academic conference on women and the Shoah. As the first of its kind, it attracted a great deal of attention, including some very fervent opposition. For summaries of the debate surrounding a gendered approach to the Shoah and the adversity academics faced in gaining recognition for the discipline, see Judith Tydor Baumel, "'Can Two Walk Together If They Do Not Agree?': Reflections on Holocaust Studies and Gender Studies," *Women: A Cultural Review* 13:2 (2002): 195–206; the introduction to *Women in the Holocaust*, ed. Dalia Ofer and Lenore Weitzmann (New Haven: Yale University Press, 1998), 1–18; and *Experience and Expression: Women, the Nazis and the Holocaust*, ed. Elizabeth R. Baer and Myrna Goldenberg (Detroit: Wayne State University Press, 2003), xiii–xxxv. Also see Horowitz, "Mengele, the Gynecologist, and Other Stories of Women's Survival," in *Judaism Since Gender*, ed. Miriam Peskowitz and Laura Levitt (New York: Routledge, 1997) 200–212, 201; and Horowitz, "Gender, Genocide and Jewish Memory," *Prooftexts* 20:1 & 2 (2000): 158–190 and 171.

29. Joan Ringelheim, "The Unethical and the Unspeakable: Women and the Holocaust," *Museum of Tolerance Online* (1997), Simon Wiesenthal Center Multimedia Learning, 18 June 2008, http://motlc.wiesenthal.com/site/pp.asp?c=gvKVLcMVIuG&b=394977, 3.

30. Ibid.

31. Ringelheim cites Tadeusz Borowski's *This Way to the Gas, Ladies and Gentleman* as an example. See Ringelheim, "The Unethical," 4.

32. Sara R. Horowitz, "Memory and Testimony of Women Survivors of Nazi Genocide," in *Women of the Word: Jewish Women and Jewish Writing*, ed. Judith R. Baskin (Detroit: Wayne State University Press, 1994), 258–282 and 264.

33. Anna Reading, *The Social Inheritance of the Holocaust: Gender, Culture, and Memory* (London: Palgrave Macmillan, 2002), 41.

34. Marlene E. Heinemann, *Gender and Destiny: Women Writers and the Holocaust* (New York: Greenwood Press, 1986), 34.

35. Ibid., 19.

36. Judith Tydor Baumel, *Double Jeopardy: Gender and the Holocaust* (London: Vallentine Mitchell, 1998), 236.

37. *Sperre* literally means curfew, but it became much more in the eight days of its imposition. There was a curfew in place so that the Nazis could round up 15,000 children, women, and infirmed Jews for mass deportation. The term became synonymous with this eight-day period during which ghetto inhabitants completely lost their innocence about what was happening.

38. Dobroszycki, *Chronicle*, xviii.

39. Ringelheim, "The Unethical," 8.

40. "Fewer women than men survived the Holocaust," writes Judith Tydor Baumel in *Double Jeopardy*, "as a result of their lack of physical stamina, the harsher conditions to which it has been suggested that women were subjected, and their automatic selection as mothers" (31).

41. Feinstein, "Absent Fathers, Present Mothers," 168.

42. Ibid., 167.
43. Horowitz, "Gender and Genocide," 177
44. Ibid.
45. Ibid., 113.
46. Horowitz, "Mengele," 210.
47. Ibid.
48. Feinstein, "Absent Fathers, Present Mothers," 176.
49. Nechama Tec, *Resilience and Courage: Women, Men, and the Holocaust* (New Haven: Yale University Press, 2003).
50. Feinstein, "Absent Fathers, Present Mothers," 186.
51. Margaret Atwood, "An End to Audience?" *Second Words: Selected Critical Prose* (Boston: Beacon Press, 1982), 334–457 and 347.
52. Sara R. Horowitz, "Gender and Holocaust Representation," in *Teaching the Representation of the Holocaust*, ed. Marianne Hirsch and Irene Kacandes (New York: Modern Language Association, 2004), 110–122 and 118.
53. Hutcheon, *The Canadian Postmodern*, 79.

# The Earth Hurts Me
## *On the Poetry of Hadasa Rubin*

### Magdalena Ruta

> Walking barefoot on sharp rocks
> The sorrow is great,
> Though no one can see the blood.
> —Hadasa Rubin—*Fun mentsh tsu mentsh*[1]

The poetry of Hadasa Rubin, whom readers of Yiddish literature may consider an obscure author, is noteworthy for a number of reasons. Her literary output is an artistic testimony to the dramatic events of the twentieth-century history of Eastern Europe and the turbulent history of the young Jewish state. It is also a lyrical confession of a woman who reacted with extraordinary sensitivity to the beauty of the world, as well as to the happiness, suffering, and pain of humanity. In 1960, Avrom Sutzkever wrote in the literary quarterly *Di goldene keyt*: "It is with a heartfelt *barukh-habo* [blessing] that we welcome poet Hadasa Rubin upon her arrival in Israel [...] Hadasa Rubin managed to save herself [from the Holocaust and from Communism], as well as her lyrical song. Let both the poet and her oeuvre be blessed."[2] Rubin's poetic oeuvre may be divided into two phases: the Polish period and the Israeli period. In Poland, she made her literary debut in the inter-bellum years by publishing poems in the press, and then went on to publish three books of poetry after the war.[3] In Israel, she published four more volumes of poetry.[4]

Rubin was born in 1906 or 1912 in Yampol near Kremenets, Ukraine.[5] She graduated from a Polish high school. Later on, as a young activist involved in the communist movement, she was imprisoned in Kremenets. During the

1930s she lived in Vilnius, where she commenced her literary career with the publication of her subtle, personal poems[6] and her revolutionary poems. She started writing in Polish[7] and made her debut as a Yiddish writer in 1931 with the poem "Tsum shakhmatist," which was published in the *Vilner tog*.[8] From 1934 on, she was associated with the artistic-literary group *Yung vilne*. Following Germany's invasion of the Soviet Union on June 22, 1941, she escaped to Frunze, Kirghizia. In 1946 or 1947, Rubin and her husband Franciszek Karp returned to Poland and settled in Szczecin, where their daughter Ewa was born. In the years 1948–1952, Rubin chaired the Szczecin branch of the Towarzystwo Społeczno-Kulturalne Żydów w Polsce [Social-Cultural Association of Jews in Poland]. In 1953, she and her family moved to Warsaw, where she worked as an editor in the Jewish press. From 1956–1959, she was a member of the editorial staff of the literary monthly *Yidishe shriftn*. In 1960, she immigrated to Israel and settled in the suburbs of Tel Aviv. She later moved to Haifa, where she continued to live until her death in 2003. In sum, during her lifetime, she published seven volumes of poetry, and her work appeared in many magazines and newspapers, including *Der tog*, *Der fraynt*, *Literarishe bleter*, *Sovetish*, *Letste nayes*, *Di goldene keyt*, *Isroel shtime*, and *Yerusholaimer almanakh*. Her poetry was translated into Polish, Hebrew, and English and earned her several literary prizes, including the Dovid Hofshteyn Prize.[9] Rubin translated Polish poems, such as those of Julian Tuwim's, into Hebrew.[10]

In post-war Poland, Rubin's works were recognized as one of the most interesting phenomena in the field of Yiddish literature,[11] and she continued to receive favorable reviews after her immigration to Israel. Critics emphasized the feminine character[12] and the air of sadness[13] pervading her poems. The typical features of her poetry include the deeply personal tone, the muffled voice, empathy, and the delicate and tender way of speaking about the world. As the only woman in the dominantly male Yiddish literary circle in post-war Poland, she spoke in a distinct, easily recognizable voice, not only due to the use of a unique literary style, but also because she openly manifested her femininity. Her lyric poetry remained an unmistakable phenomenon throughout the Israeli period as well. The metaphorical, and at the same time enigmatic style, the muffled voice, the placid tone, and the ethical sensitivity are present in her personal poetry, in the revolutionary verse, in the poems about the Holocaust, and in those in which the author comes to terms with communism.

## *I Saw That Misery*

Prior to World War II, Rubin's poetry was only published in newspapers, journals, and literary magazines. The poems she was carrying with her during her escape from the Nazi-occupied area were lost in the turmoil of war.[14] Apparently, the number of her publications during the period 1941–1945 must have been very few, because in the first issue of the literary almanac *Yidishe shriftn* published in 1946, David Sfard encouraged her to resume writing.[15] In 1953, her first book *Mayn gas iz in fener* [My Street Is Covered with Banners] was published.[16] The book is a collection of Rubin's pre-war revolutionary and personal, lyric poetry interwoven with poems about the Holocaust and texts written according to the principles of Socialist Realism in the early 1950s. The best and the most interesting are the pre-war poems, mainly the revolutionary ones, in which Rubin depicts her dreams about a better world, reminisces about her prison experience, and declares her vigilance and readiness for struggle upon receiving orders from the party. The cheerfulness of the lyrical subject in these poems results from her sheer delight over the beauty of the world and her very personal, cordial attitude to people.

While pre-war revolutionary verse written by male Jewish authors usually expresses the emotions and expectations of the crowd, Rubin's revolutionary poems are personal in the sense that she reveals the emotions felt upon making decisions.[17] While other revolutionary poets write in order to provoke the reader to fight, Rubin wants to bring joy and offer comfort with her soft words.[18] The writers' intentions are reflected in the tone of their poetry: Rubin's whisper and tender words about individual persons and singular events contrast with other poets' shout intended to rouse anger and hate. In one of the interviews Rubin said, "My way to Communism was not through Marx and Engels, but through Jewish women, [...] I saw that poverty. [...] I saw that misery. [...] That was my Marx and that was my Engels."[19] She wrote about that in the 1935 poem "Undzer bobe" [Our Grandmother].[20] The protagonist of the poem—the grandmother—has resigned herself to her fate and does not even realize that she has the right to aspire to anything more than her humble life has to offer. Her tears are the only response to the overwhelming burden she has to carry. Therefore, it is the young generation who must fight for justice on her behalf.

As Jaff Schatz, a chronicler of the pre-war generation of Jewish communists in Poland wrote, imprisonment was a formative experience for that generation which had given its representatives some heroic feature.[21] Prison turned out to be formative for the young Rubin as well. In her poem "Krates" [The Bars], she writes about the solitude and sorrow that filled the long, prison hours, at the same time expressing her full acceptance of the state of affairs that was the consequence of her deliberate choices.[22] In the poem, the bars are a metaphor of suffering and loneliness. By picturing the transformations that the bars undergo at various times of the day the poet manages to portray the atmosphere of a cramped prison cell with a tiny, barred window at its center in a subtle, and at the same time very evocative way. The metaphorical title opalesces with meanings—during the daytime the woman who is the lyrical subject in this poem interprets the bars as a symbolic instrument of torture, and then in the night she reinterprets their "message," as she realizes that she is not alone in this dire situation. She knows that the eyes of her female comrades who, likewise herself, are in prison and dream about freedom, are fixed on the bars too. The feeling of belonging to a powerful movement enables her to survive her ordeal.

## *I Am Looking for You, My Martyred Ones*

Following Germany's aggression on September 1, 1939 and the Soviet Union's invasion on September 17, 1939, Poland's territory was divided and annexed by its two invaders. Rubin, along with other Jewish artists from Vilnius, found herself on the territory annexed by the Soviets. As fragmentary, yet dramatic news about the tragic fate of the people under German Nazi occupation reached her, Rubin, similar to other Jewish writers, immortalized her concern for her close ones in verse. Her intimate, almost whispery poems reveal her extraordinary empathy with the Jews suffering in the ghettos and in the German Nazi death camps operating in Poland. Typical features of her poetry from that period include the somatization of the victims' distress in the body of the female lyrical subject (who, after all, has not experienced this kind of suffering in person) and the deep sorrow overshadowing her consciousness. One example is the poem "Nakhmu" [Solace] written in 1943.[23] Also, it is notable that the lyrical "I" in Hadasa Rubin's poems about the Holocaust often reveals its female identity, speaking in the voice of a Jewish mother who pleads in "Vesne 1943": "I carry a murdered baby under my heart, / let joy never pass my threshold."[24]

Jewish writers from Poland who spent the war in the U.S.S.R. write about their war wanderings expressing their gratitude to the hospitable Soviet soil. However, those who did not have any affiliations with communism emphasize their homelessness and lack of motherland. For communists, like Hadasa Rubin, it was a time of spiritual revival. "I loved you from the very first day, / you have grown close to me like motherland," she writes in "Farblayb gezunt, mayn ratnfarband."[25] Following the example of Soviet Jewish writers, the communist Jewish writers from Poland try to look at the Jewish fate during the war from two perspectives: not only from the point of view of a victim, but also from the vantage point of a Red Army soldier fighting the enemy. Rubin, too, calls upon the ghettoized Jews to take an active stand against Nazi Germans, at the same time condemning the passive attitude of many Jewish generations who accepted their martyrdom and humiliation without even attempting to fight. In her 1942 poem "Tsum yidishn zelner" [To the Jewish Soldier], she praises the military struggle of Jewish soldiers.[26]

Similar to works by other Jewish survivors in the East, Rubin's poems written immediately after the war express her awareness of the special role to be played by those who managed to survive the extermination of their nation: their task is to keep the memory of the victims alive and carefully revive their Jewish culture. Not unlike other Jewish writers, Rubin responds to the genocide of the six million Polish Jews with anger, mourning, and despair; however, it is noteworthy that she does not call for hatred and revenge. In her 1945 poem "A tfile tsu zikh" [A Prayer to Myself], she says that Jews will need great spiritual power not to succumb to their base sentiments: "To be strong enough to separate / yesterday from today, being from not being."[27] This wise, balanced voice, supported only by the poetic voice of Yeshaye Shpigel,[28] is without precedent in Yiddish poetry in Poland after 1945. Its message is love, a difficult and painful kind of love that gives hope for revival, but does not allow one to forget.

## *My Street Is Covered in Banners*

While referring to the kind of thinking that was typical among Jewish communists from Poland who had had the chance to discover the real image of the Soviet reality during the war, and yet, despite the often painful experiences, remained faithful to their communist ideals, Jaff Schatz coins the term "split thinking."[29] Hadasa Rubin was, to a certain degree, subject to that condition. In 1955, when the era of Stalinism was drawing to an end, Rubin's second book of poetry *Veytik un freyd* [Sorrow and Joy],[30] uneven in terms of artistic quality, was published. The weakest poems in the collection are the ones written according to the principles of Socialist Realism: panegyrics on the communist leaders and the new, "ideal" reality, typical of that period. However, Rubin's placid tone and phraseology—general humanistic, rather than propagandistic—distinguishes her from her contemporaries. Unusual for her times, Rubin speaks in an intimate voice and avoids inciting her readers to hate socialism's enemies. Nevertheless, she is in line with the spirit of her times in using her talent for propaganda purposes to the extent that her lyrical "I" speaks up as a woman and mother. The peculiar use of that role becomes self-evident in Rubin's pacifist poems that expose socialism's enemy who "threatens" the happiness of mothers and children. It is against such enemies that Rubin's female lyrical subject builds a barricade of flowers to protect her family.[31]

At this point it is worth noting that Rubin, unlike her contemporaries, never manipulated the theme of the Jewish Holocaust.[32] The poem "Ikh..." [Me...] in which she protests against the controlling and limiting of the memory of the dead seems to be her response to ideologists' instructions telling writers to put a curb on the Holocaust theme and glorify the new socialist reality instead. In the poem, Rubin speaks on behalf of the small group of survivors who are being forced to forget the Jewish tragedy. As she writes, "You're not my friend if you tell me to forget."[33]

Rubin's second book confirms what was manifest in the first, namely her interest in the human condition, her sensitivity to injustice, her perseverance in shaping the obstructive reality, and her embracing of life, its tragedy and its greatness. The lyrical subject in the title "Veytik un freyd" supports the active stance, rejecting tranquillity and stillness—the first symptoms of spiritual death: "No, I don't want to change anything. / Until I draw my last breath I want to be human. / Mine is the joy and mine is the suffering, / whether it be my blessing or my curse."[34] The consequence of such choice is not only the feeling of fulfilment, but also the inevitability of suffering which, however, does not have to be a curse. Rubin convinces her reader that it is precisely due to suffering that one can recognize happiness and live one's life to the fullest.

## Be a Sign for Me, Oh My Pain, Show Me I'm Alive

The 20th Congress of the Communist Party of the Soviet Union, which took place in February 1956, inaugurated the period of the so-called political thaw. In the course of that congress the crimes committed by the top Soviet leaders were disclosed, and one of the exposed secrets concerned the tragic deaths of prominent Soviet Yiddish writers murdered on August 12, 1952 on the orders of Stalin.[35] Confronting that knowledge was a real shock for communist Jewish writers in Poland.[36] Sharp criticism of the crimes committed by the communists, the liberalization of political life, and a short period of relative freedom of speech constituted another formative experience for members of the generation that Schatz describes, including Rubin herself. It suddenly became clear to them that their most sacred ideals were false and that they had been deceived and deliberately misinformed. As Schatz points out, the most popular reaction was shame, a sense of guilt, condemnation of the crimes, and the need for rehabilitation.³⁷ Yiddish literature joined in the general coming to terms with the Stalinist era and opened itself up to all novelty.³⁸

Rubin's third volume, *Trit in der nakht* [Footsteps in the Night], came out in 1957 and was her last book published in Poland.³⁹ It is considered her most interesting book, the most diverse in terms of choice of topics, and the best in terms of artistic quality. While the majority of poems collected in the volume deal with political responsibility in the light of the 1956 breakthrough,⁴⁰ there are a few poems about the Holocaust. The poems Rubin wrote in 1956 present a particularly broad spectrum of emotions aroused by the revelation of Stalinist crimes: horror, insecurity, the need for honest examination, and the need to settle accounts with the past. In her poem "A kind mit groye hor" [A Child with Grey Hair], she writes that she has lost her sight and, confused as she is, she has to learn how to walk anew. She also writes about her disillusionment in the poem "Vos vestu yarshenen nokh mir, mayn tokhter?" [What Will You Inherit from Me, My Daughter?], admitting that she has theretofore put her faith in false gods whom she perceived as radiant deities. Looking for a diamond for her daughter, she has lost everything and is now standing naked. As she writes, "Only the pain emerged pure from the fire— / I have not lost my heart to the devil. / Desperate, it shrinks and shivers, / but it has not burnt out, it has not grown cold."⁴¹

Indeed, we may even talk about an identity crisis of the lyrical subject in the poems that explore the political responsibility theme. In the poem "Fun a diskusye" [From a Discussion], the poet states, "It is difficult to walk out of one's skin, / to shed it like a worn and torn shirt, / to suddenly turn what used to be my daily bread / into strange abomination."⁴² The poem "Tsu..." [To...] is Rubin's contribution to the public debate on the limits of answerability for the atrocities of Stalinism. The lyrical subject in this poem says that the severest judge is one's own heart, which has remained pure and sensitive despite the evil taking place everywhere around, and the harshest punishment it can take is honest examination of conscience and readiness to face the consequences of the mistakes made unwittingly, while acting in good faith.⁴³ At the same time, in "Vider shoyn" [Once Again], the poet protests against the aversion towards Jewish communists who were increasing in Polish society at that time. Rubin says that this is yet another time in the history of Poland that the Jews are being "condemned for others' sin." For the lyrical subject of Rubin's poetry, the often unfair accusations, combined with the shock evoked by the revelation of Stalinist crimes were a painful ordeal: "Lay down on my chest like a lead-heavy burden, oh my pain / and be a sign for me, show me I'm alive."⁴⁴

Rubin's poems about the Holocaust feature a few motifs typical of the literature written by Polish Jews who had survived the war in the East, specifically the hope for revival symbolized by the image of a young tree blossoming on the ruins, the sense of guilt evoked by the fact of having outlived one's family, and the awareness that the survivor's memory is the only monument commemorating the victims. Rubin's original contribution to the Holocaust poetry written in that period is "A vig-lid" [A Lullaby]. In Holocaust literature, the lullaby as a poetic genre was a deliberate, antithetical reference to the folk model,[45] which made use of irony or parody to achieve an effect that would be the exact opposite of the original usage of this kind of texts.[46] Rubin's "lullaby" was included in her 1957 collection, together with poems dealing with such issues as political and social answerability, as well as Polish anti–Semitism, which suggests that we should consider the message of this poem universal, not limited to the war experiences alone. The author uses her typical voice of the woman and mother here as she writes, "The cradles I've rocked were too few—/ The milk in my breasts is ice frozen now."[47] In this poem, the author uses rhetorical and structural conventions typical of folk lullabies, such as appealing to the baby, mentioning the father's absence, projecting the baby's future, and introducing elements of strangeness and uncanniness. Irony lies at the base of each of these elements, and the convention used here describes a reality that is contrary to the reality of a folk lullaby. The lyrical subject is lulling to sleep babies who are already gone because they fell asleep into eternal sleep. Unlike in the folk tradition, the loneliness of the mother-nanny does not result simply from the absence of her husband, for what she experiences is total, irreversible solitude. The babies' future is also pictured here in reversal and is directly linked with elements of the uncanny because it is strange that the future exists, yet it does not apply to those to whom the poem is addressed. The babies who were supposed to grow up to acquire the wisdom and maturity destined for them are gone. What remains is the time, but there is no one to measure the passing hours, days and years. Stigmatized and condemned to death at the dawn of their life, the babies from Rubin's lullaby find their resting place not on earth, but in the heavenly spaces, and every Jewish mother is destined to live a cursed life, keeping a vigil over the grave that the entire world has turned into.

## The Earth on Which I Learned to Walk Spits Me Out

The question that moved Jewish writers to the core—the problem of anti–Semitism—should be discussed separately.[48] One facet of the communist ideology that attracted so many young Polish Jews to the communist movement in the interwar period was the fight with anti–Semitism. This explains why the anti–Semitic riots that took place in Poland during the events following Stalin's death, persecutions of Jews in the U.S.S.R. and in other Eastern European countries,[49] and finally, the information about the execution of members of the Jewish Anti-Fascist Committee, some of whom were the most prominent Yiddish writers, caused such a shock. The death of the leading Soviet Yiddish authors in particular provided fuel for writers' poetic imagination. In the poem "Azoy zol mer nisht zayn" [It Cannot Be Like This Anymore], Rubin paints a picture of her friends being dragged "down the deaf streets, to the place of shame. / Alive, beheaded, / strangers in their own country," who, upon whispering "Comrades, / heard: 'Jew' in reply."[50]

Rubin reacted in an acutely sensitive way to the anti–Semitic riots in which some Poles blamed the Jewish communists (in Polish *żydokomuna*) for Stalinist crimes. The bitterness palpable in her poem "Vider shoyn…" [Once Again…] results from the gravity of the accusations brought against the Jews.[51] She writes, "Rejected, I became a stranger overnight. / The earth spits me out, the sky does not recognize me."[52] This poem is a harbinger of yet another group of poets getting ready to bid their Polish motherland farewell.

The poem "A nakht" [A Night] broaches a painful and difficult subject that recurred in the poetry written in that period, namely the religious background of the anti–Semitic sentiment displayed by some Poles and the accusations made by the Jewish part who pointed out the hypocrisy that made some Catholics capable of reconciling their belief in Jesus Christ—a Jew born from a Jewish mother—with hate towards Jews in general. Confronting that irreconcilable problem in 1957, Rubin asks with irony, "Was it really me who crucified / the blue-eyed, smooth-faced God? […] / And maybe it's true that I am Shylock / and I collect babies' blood to make *matzah* ?"[53]

For communists like Rubin—disillusioned by the revealed crimes, their Jewish dignity wounded by the hostile Poles—the only option was to leave the country. Thus, the poet heralds her departure in the poem "Oyf di bregn fun vaysl" [On the Banks of the River Vistula].[54] The poem refers to Psalm 137, which has a long inter-textual tradition in Jewish literature. The voice of the lyrical subject in the psalm reminds us about the Exile that is associated with mourning for the lost motherland and calls for the cultivation of its memory and for revenge on those responsible for the nation's loss; whereas the lyrical subject in Rubin's poem bewails a totally different kind of misfortune, as for many generations of Jews Poland meant homeland rather than exile. It was on this soil that they found home, and it was for this land that their Jewish fiddle played. And now, sitting on the bank of the Polish River Vistula, they are bewailing their foster motherland that has betrayed them. While those who mourn the loss of Zion in the psalm are yearning for their homeland and harbouring a hope for return, for Polish Jews it is the time of despair and there is no hope left for them, as they are not going to reunite with their motherland but, rather, say their farewells to it. They are headed for an escape from their cherished land in which they have been derided and rejected, "in which their blood is still putrefying." Rubin's actions were consistent with her words as she left Poland in 1960.

Leaving her homeland behind meant a painful parting with her friends, the land that was so dear to her heart, and the tombs of her Jewish ancestors. Rubin prophesies a difficult kind of longing to herself and other Jewish emigrants as she writes, "In your eyes you shall keep the sadness of my spaces— / that will never leave you. / In the Biblical landscape a white, naked birch tree / shall haunt you in your dreams. / [...] wherever you go, / the longing shall follow."[55] In *Trit in der nakht* from which this poem comes, the reader finds a premonition of loneliness and strangeness that awaits the Jews who are leaving Poland. Indeed, the poet's predictions turned out to be right, as her next book of poetry, *Fun mentsh tsu mentsh* [From Man to Man], published in 1964 in Israel proved.[56]

## *I Call Sorrow by Name*[57]

In *Fun mentsh tsu mentsh,* published four years after her arrival in the new land, Rubin included two series of poems whose titles reveal their contents: "A tfile tsu zikh" [A Prayer to Myself] and "Iberflantsung" [The Replanting]. The former series contains poems written while the author was still living in Warsaw, and the lyrical subject experiences an identity crisis, hurt, and meaningless. This state of mind is probably closely connected with the ideological crisis of the times of political thaw, the news about the death of literary friends the Soviet Yiddish writers, and the anti–Semitic verbal attacks that appeared in the second half of the 1950s. In the poem "Plonter" [Muddle], she says, "I have lost the thread that binds everything together. / It touched me to the core. / My shaded eyes / look but cannot see— / blind."[58] At the same time, in the title poem "A tfile tsu zikh," she reminds her Israeli reader of the values that constituted her credo already in her early youth and in the dreadful era of the Holocaust, namely of courage, honesty, consistency in action, dignity in the hour of solitude, and the ability to share one's joy with others.[59] Her youthful revolutionary poems, too, revising at the very beginning of the collection the moral imperative to protest against man's misery and fight for justice, confirm what the poet declares to be her firm conviction and what has shaped her revolutionary personality.[60]

The latter part of the volume contains poems written after Rubin's settlement in Tel Aviv. The title poem, "Iberflantsung," by referring to the life of a replanted plant, expresses the poet's concern about her successful naturalization in the new environment: "How will you take root, / oh my song, in the soil on which / melody sounds so different?"[61] Echoes of loneliness and the sense of being an outsider in a strange landscape, surrounded by people of strange customs recur in many poems in this collection. However, each poem reveals that the efforts made to domesticate and befriend the new homeland become more and more fruitful. In "Bay nakht in di naftole-berg" [The Naftali Mountains by Night], Rubin says, "Ever so slowly, I learn / to understand the language / of your light / which seems gentle / and dreadful at the same time."[62] In "A bagegenish mit a froy" [A Meeting with a Woman] she progresses to emphasize, "You and me— / we shall not argue. / Only the first smile / did not come easy to us."[63]

While accepting the exotic, breath-taking natural landscape of the new homeland and the autochthons with their disparate customs came easy, accepting the unstable political situation of the young Israeli state was much more of a challenge. In a conversation with local residents who support Israel's robust and brutal policy in its conflict with the Arab countries, the lyrical subject of the poem "Efsher?" [Maybe?] admits that she is not sure whether this is the way it should be. Even if the one who claims that the country "demands our blood" is right, the poet is still dubious about it since her conscience does not accept acts of violence as such, no matter what the cause. So, she replies to her interlocutor that "[her] hands are too week for [his] truth."[64] In the end, however, Israel does become her real motherland/home, not just a place of residence. In "Umru-erd" [Unquiet Earth], she appreciates the meaning of the soil that not so long ago was alien to her, although familiar from ancient Jewish legends. For a nation that has lost six million of its own, the unquiet Israeli ground is something incredibly important. It is a "loud NO without tears"— a sign of protest against Jewish life in the diaspora and a "YES for my nation"— affirmation of its continuity.[65]

An important part of Rubin's next book of poetry, *In tsugvint* [In the Draft] published in Israel in 1981, are the poems expressing affirmation of life, delight in the "little happiness" of everyday life,[66] as well as poems about cheerful passing away and the hope that death is the entrance gate into a "green rainbow," into the "light remembered from melodies and prayers."[67] Some of them are poetic commentaries on the political situation that prevailed in Poland and in East-Central Europe in the late 1960s. And in "Tsu a getodenkmol" [On the Monument to Ghetto Heroes], the poet calls victims of the Holocaust, immortalized in the stone monument dedicated to the heroes of the Warsaw ghetto, to leave the hostile Poland where "anointed madness / may cross the limits of disgrace / ordering you to die once more, / because you are a threat to its country."[68] A similar tone permeates the poem "Shtern" [The Star], in which the author employs scathing irony to comment upon Warsaw Pact forces' invasion of Prague where anti-communist opposition had gained ground. The poet reminisces about her youth when she secretly wore a tiny red star—a symbol of one's membership in the international communist movement—on her chest, whereas "today a gross, fat, red star / haunts me / on the steel sky / of the tanks."[69]

Poems dedicated to the memory of Holocaust victims,[70] as well as an entire series of poems "Mit oysgeshtrekte hent" [With Their Hands Reaching Out] dedicated to the memory of young Israeli soldiers who had given their lives for their country constitute another important group within this collection.[71] The tears shed over the dead bodies of the sons and daughters of Israel do not blot out the sight of the mothers of the soldiers fighting on the other side who are also mourning their dead from the poet's mind. Rubin writes, "[My tears] do not be a thick curtain / concealing the other side, / hostile, speaking a foreign language, / from my sight, / for a tear tastes salty over there as well."[72]

In the next two volumes, *Eydertog* [Daybreak] and *Rays nisht op di blum* [Do Not Pick Up the Flower], published in 1988 and 1995, respectively, Rubin returns to the themes that are so important to her, namely the memory of the Holocaust, memory of the anonymous victims of military conflicts, and protest against bloodshed.[73] She writes about the latter issue in the context of the Israeli-Arab wars, expressing her sharp criticism of the Israeli authorities' policy by the power of which Palestinians were brutally displaced from the occupied areas at the end of 1987 and the beginning of 1988.[74] Apart from that, more and more space in each of these books is dedicated to the issues of passing time, old age, sorrow felt upon the death of one's friends and relatives, as well as waiting for one's own death. What emerges from these poems is a portrait of a person experienced by life, wise with the painful wisdom of someone who has resigned herself to her fate, and yet is always ready to rise against violence, injustice and oblivion. In these two volumes, the lyrical subject looks at the world from a totally different perspective than before; it is the perspective of someone who is about to leave this world, who becomes increasingly concentrated on the shadows populating her memory. However, the tone of melancholy and sadness that recurs throughout Hadasa Rubin's works does not dominate here. While her life is drawing to an end, the poet still finds room for hope, which is reflected in "A naketer boym nokh a sreyfe" [A Naked Tree on the Site of the Fire].[75]

## *To Carry Life Cupped in Two Sentimental Hands*

Communism preached gender equality and Socialist Realism popularized a highly masculinized model of a woman in literature. However, in reality a woman in the world of Socialist Realism was perceived as an intruder and had to fight for her life to keep her position on the ground that was exclusively reserved for men,[76] hence the masculinization of female literary characters that stretched from appointing women to traditionally male jobs to granting "equal rights" in the sexual sphere.[77] At the same time the literature of Socialist Realism eliminated eroticism and love from human life almost completely, replacing it with a new type of erotic relationship that joined man and his/her machine or an individual and his/her collective.[78] Set against the background of Socialist Realism and its literary models, the originality of the feminine lyrical subject created by Rubin throughout her poetic career becomes all the more striking. It combines the typical features of the era in which Rubin lived with some novel elements that seem to contradict the official aesthetic canons. The lyrical "I" reveals its femininity from the very beginning, which clearly defines its relationships with the man or the child; it also refers to the features identified with female nature, such as delicacy, sensitivity, and tenderness. Already in the pre-war poems the reader will notice Rubin's sensitivity to the beauty of nature and of life in general, as well as her intimate knowledge of the child's psyche and her affectionate way of describing those near and dear to her. In the modified variant we also encounter the motif of cross-generational transfer between grandmother / mother and daughter that appears in the works of many Jewish women poets in that period.[79] By lovingly observing her grandmother—poor, silent, and prematurely aged—the female lyrical subject of Rubin's poetry absorbs the legacy of women from the past generations, and the lesson learnt at home transforms into action. In the poetry of Rubin, unlike in the poetry of Kadya Molodowsky or Celia Dropkin, the message is not so much about the fight for women's rights in the more general sense, but, rather, about the fight for social justice. In this way, Rubin transforms into a woman revolutionary who has to demonstrate personality features commonly recognized as male. Thus, she becomes tough, consistent, courageous, and despite her dilemmas, resolute. At the same time, she retains the features and obligations ascribed to women alone—it is her task to bring order into the organizational structure of the world and to take care of its aesthetic dimension. What is also important, she feels comfortable standing by the side of her man and is able to use her femininity to achieve joy and satisfaction. Tough and resolute in action, she softens as she cuddles a baby and becomes submissive in the hands of a man.[80]

In her poem "Ven kh'bin a meydele geven a kleyns" [When I was a Little Girl], Rubin defines her manifesto of femininity. She confesses that as a little girl she yearned to be admitted into men's world, which seemed more interesting to her because men were allowed to ride horses and smoke cigarettes. And now, as an adult, she can do all the things that she used to dream about, and yet her life is tough, so she goes on to ask, "Why is everything so difficult, / even more difficult than it used to be, why do I feel / more and more uncomfortable with my tenderness / that does not want to ripen / and peel off me, hard and dry?"[81] Her hypersensitive senses seem like an open wound exposed to the elements, so she admits to feeling helpless sometimes, especially as she takes on the responsibility for her close ones.[82] Sensitivity of the heart manifests itself in the hypersensitivity of the body and senses as she complains, "I hear with my eyes, I see with my fingers."[83] The woman's contact with the external world is not easy, which perhaps explains why Rubin's lyrical subject has chosen a life of action, conceived as a kind of struggle. This choice, however, does not make a man of her. Men's clothes may disguise the body, but not the heart. In the world created by men, everything is *farbitert-harb*—bitter and hard—for a woman. Thus, the poet comes to this conclusion: "I shall carry my life resolutely, like a man."[84] What really differentiates a woman from a man manifests itself in the mental sphere, not in the world of external attributes, and this inherent difference cannot be negated. Femininity in Rubin's poetry means sensitivity, tenderness, and empathy, which the author accepts as the distinctive features of a woman and not as flaws or weaknesses. In this sense, her entire creative output is feminine to the core: tender, compassionate, focused on the detail, and hopeful despite the sorrow that pervades her, in a word—beautiful and wise the way only a woman may be.

## Notes

A Polish version of this essay entitled "*Ziemia mnie boli. Poezja Hadasy Rubin*" appeared in *Midrasz. Pismo żydowskie* 3 (May-June 2012): 52–60. Permission to reprint the original essay in translation was granted by Katarzyna Jutkiewicz-Kubiak of *Midrasz*, as well as by the translator Maria Piechaczek-Borkowska.

1. Hadasa Rubin, *Fun mentsh tsu mentsh* (Tel Aviv: Farlag Y. L. Peretz, 1964), 25. All quoted poems were translated by Magdalena Ruta.

2. Avrom Sutzkever, "Introduction to a Selection of Poems by Hadasa Rubin," *Goldene keyt* 38 (1960): 35.

3. In Poland, Rubin published *Mayn gas iz in fener* (Varshe: Yidish bukh, 1953); *Veytik un freyd* (Varshe: Yidish bukh, 1955); and *Trit in der nakht* (Varshe: Yidish bukh, 1957).

4. In Israel, Rubin published *Fun mentsh tsu mentsh* (Tel Aviv: Farlag Y. L. Peretz, 1964); *In tsugvint* (Tel Aviv: Farlag Yisroel-bukh, 1981); *Eydertog* (Tel Aviv: Farlag yisroel-bukh, 1988); and *Rays nisht op di blum* (Tel Aviv: Farlag Y. L. Peretz, 1995).

5. See Rava Goldberg, "Rubin Hadasa," in *Leksikon fun der nayer yidisher literatur* 8 (Nyu york: Alveltlekher Yidisher Kultur-Kongres, TSIKO, 1981), 410–411; Arieh Pilovsky, "Rubin Hadassah," in *Encyclopedia Judaica* (CD ROM Edition: 2000), and Dorothee van Tendeloo, "Rubin, Hadasah," in *YIVO Encyclopedia of Jews in Eastern Europe* (November 22, 2010), http://www.yivoencyclopedia.org/article.aspx/Rubin_Hadasah (accessed January 22, 2012). The poet claims 1911 as her date of birth, while pointing out that she is not sure about it. As she says in one of her interviews, even her parents did not remember the exact date. Also see Albert Stankowski's interview with Hadasa Rubin, www.sztetl.org.pl, *1999* (accessed January 22, 2012).

6. See Joanna Lisek, *Jung Wilne—żydowska grupa artystyczna* (Wrocław: Wydawnictwo Uniwersytetu Wrocławskiego, 2005), 72–74.

7. Although page 410 of the *Leksikon fun der nayer yidisher literatur* notes that Rubin made her literary debut in Hebrew, she says that her original literary language was Polish. She switched to Yiddish in a response to the anti–Semitism of a group of Polish students who assaulted her father. See Albert Stankowski's 1999 interview with Hadasa Rubin, www.sztetl.org.pl/ entry Hadasa Rubin (accessed 22 January 2012).

8. Lisek, *Jung Wilne*, 72–74.

9. Van Tendeloo, "Rubin, Hadasah," np.

10. Stankowski, interview, 1999.

11. This opinion was expressed by Moshe Shklar, Hadasa Rubin's colleague from Poland, in an email to Magdalena Ruta. Also see these reviews of Rubin's collections of poems from the Polish period: David Sfard, "Vegn di lider fun hadasa rubin," in *Shtudies un skitsn* (Varshe: Yidish bukh, 1955), 101–105; David Sfard, "Vegn der lider-zamlung veytik un freyd fun hadasa rubin," *Yidishe shriftn* 2 (1956): 4 and 7; and David Sfard, "Trit in der nakht fun hadasa rubin," *Yidishe shriftn* 7 (1958): 2 and 7. For more on Yiddish poetry in postwar Poland, see Magdalena Ruta, *Bez Żydów? Poezja jidysz w PRL o Zagładzie, Polsce i komunizmie* (Kraków-Budapeszt: Austeria 2012). Also, see Magdalena Ruta, ed., *Nie nad rzekami Babilonu. Antologia poezji jidysz w powojennej Polsce / Nisht bay di taykhn fun bovl. Anthologye fun der yidisher poezye in nokhmilkhomedikn poyln/ Nie nad rzekami Babilonu, Antologia poezji jidysz w powojennej Polsce* (Kraków: Księgarnia Akademicka, 2012), a Polish edition with English introduction and footnotes.

12. See Jacob Glatshtein, "Hadasa Rubin," in *Oyf greyte temes* (Tel Aviv: Farlag Y. L. Peretz, 1967), 306–310. Also see David Sfard, "Trit in der nacht fun hadasa rubin."

13. See Efraim Oyerbakh, "Tsvey dikhterins in medinas isroel. Hadasa Rubin," in *Oyf der vogshol*, Vol. I (Tel Aviv: Farlag Y. L. Peretz, 1975), 318–321, and Hirsh Bloshteyn, "A por bamerkungen vegn dem zhurnal Yidishe Shriftn," *Folks-shtime* 31(December 1956): 4. Also see David Sfard's "Vegn di lider fun hadasa rubin," 101–105; "Vegn der lider-zamlung veytik un freyd fun hadasa rubin," 4 and 7; and "Trit in der nacht" fun Hadasa Rubin," 2 and 7.

14. Gitl Meyzil, "Hadasa Rubin," in Gitl Meysil, *Eseyen* (Tel Aviv: Farlag Y. L. Peretz, 1974), 214–221.
15. David Sfard, "Tsum tsurikker fun undzere shrayber," in *Yidishe shrift: a zamlbuch* (Łódź: Fareyn fun yidishe literatn un zhurnalistn in poyln, 1946), 55–59.
16. Sfard, "Vegn di lider fun Hadasa Rubin," 101–105.
17. For examples, see "Krates," in Rubin, *Mayn gas iz in fener*, 6; "A kholem," in Rubin, *Mayn gas iz in fener*, 7; "A zeung," in Rubin, *Mayn gas iz in fener*, 8; "A briv," in Rubin, *Mayn gas iz in fener*, 9; and "Blumen of mayn ganek...," in Rubin, *Mayn gas iz in fener*, 10.
18. See "A lid," in Rubin, *Mayn gas iz in fener*, 11; "Shtiler mayn vort," in Rubin, *Trit in der nakht*, 100; and "Oyb s'ken mayn vort...," in Rubin, *Fun mentsh tsu mentsh*, 68.
19. Stankowski, interview.
20. Rubin, *Mayn gas iz in fener*, 15.
21. Jaff Schatz, *The Generation: The Rise and Fall of the Jewish Communists of Poland* (Berkeley: University of California Press, 1991), 128.
22. Rubin, *Mayn gas iz in fener*, 6.
23. Ibid., 24.
24. Ibid., 23.
25. Ibid., 18.
26. Rubin, *Trit in der nakht*, 9–10
27. Rubin, *Mayn gas iz in fener*, 22.
28. Yeshaye Shpigel, "Tsavoe fun likht," in Yeshaye Shpigel, *Un gevorn iz likht* (Varshe-Łódź: Yidish bukh, 1949), 131.
29. Schatz, *The Generation*, 165, 192 ff.
30. For enthusiastic reviews of the volume, see David Sfard, "Vegn der lider-zamlung veytik un freyd," in *Shtudies un skitsn* (Varshe: Yidish bukh, 1955), 101–105; and Sholem Shtern, "Lider fun veytog un freyd," *Morgn-frayheyt* (15 March 1956): 11.
31. See "Tsu di milkhome untertsinder," in Rubin, *Mayn gas iz in fener*, 27, and "A vig-lid," in Rubin, *Mayn gas iz in fener*, 36. Also, "Mayn blumen-barikade," in Rubin, *Veytik un freyd*, 31.
32. For more on the responses of Yiddish writers in post-war Poland to the Holocaust, see Monika Adamczyk-Garbowska and Magdalena Ruta, "Responses to the Holocaust in Polish and Yiddish Literature," in *The Aftermath of the Holocaust: Poland (1944–2010)*, ed. Feliks Tych and Monika Adamczyk-Garbowska (forthcoming).
33. Rubin, *Veytik un freyd*, 19–20.
34. Ibid., 9.
35. For more about the death of Soviet Yiddish literati, see Joseph Sherman, "Sevenfold Betrayal: The Murder of Soviet Yiddish," *The Mendele Review: Yiddish Literature and Language (A Companion to MENDELE)* 07.009 [Sequential No. 135], 12.08.2003: http://yiddish.haifa.ac.il/tmr/tmr07/tmr07009.htm (accessed on 11 January 2010). About Polish Jews' reaction to the revealed crime, see Gennady Estraikh, *Yiddish in the Cold War* (Oxford: Legenda, 2008), 18–23.
36. Schatz, *The Generation*, 264–281.
37. Ibid., 280–281.
38. For more about the new motifs that appeared in Yiddish literature after the Stalinist era, see Ber Mark, "Tsvishn lebn un toyt. Dos yidishe lebn un di yidishe literatur in poyln in di yorn 1937–1957," *Ikuf-almanakh* (Nyu York: Ikuf farlag, 1961): 60–86. Also see Magdalena Ruta, "Preliminary Remarks on Yiddish Culture in Poland 1945–1968," *Scripta Judaica Cracoviensia* 2 (2004): 61–70.

39. See the review of this volume written by David Sfard, "Trit in der nakht fun Hadasa Rubin."

40. For more about the political responsibility current in the poetry of communist writers from Poland, see Magdalena Ruta, "Yiddish Literature and Communism in Post-War Poland: The Poetry of Kalman Segal, Moshe Shklar and Paltiel Tsibulski," in *Iggud. Selected Essays in Jewish Studies*, Vol. 3, ed. Tamar Alexander, Ziva Amishai-Maisels, Dan Laor, Ora Schwarzwald, and Yosef Tobi (Jerusalem: World Union of Jewish Studies, 2007), 35–57.

41. Rubin, *Trit in der nakht*, 76.

42. Ibid., 45.

43. Ibid., 41.

44. Ibid., 84.

45. For more on folk lullabies, see Ruth Rubin, *Voices of a People: The Story of Yiddish Folksong* (Urbana: University of Illinois Press, 2000), 29–43.

46. About lullabies written during the war, see Frieda W. Aaron, *Bearing the Unbearable: Yiddish and Polish Poetry in the Ghettos and Concentration Camps* (Albany: State University of New York Press, 1990), 117–130.

47. Rubin, *Trit in der nakht*, 77–78.

48. For more on Polish anti-Semitism during the political thaw, see Piotr Machcewicz, "Antisemitism in Poland in 1956," *Polin* 9 (1990): 170–183.

49. About repressions against the Jews in the Communist countries in the early 1950s, see Estraikh, *Yiddish in the Cold War*, 9–37.

50. Rubin, *Trit in der nakht*, 65.

51. Anti-Jewish resentment in Poland was fueled by the fact that Jews held many of the highest positions within the communist party, which after the war enforced the new regime in Poland, a regime that was never accepted by the majority of Polish society.

52. Rubin, *Trit in der nakht*, 83.

53. Ibid., 90. In an interview with Albert Stankowski, the poet reminisces how, in the mid-1950s, she was wrongfully accused of swindling money and contributing to the death of her daughter Ewa's babysitter. The woman died in mysterious circumstances as a result of alcoholism. However, some of her Polish friends bore false witness against Rubin's family. This incident made the poet realize that she did not feel at home in Poland any more. See Stankowski, interview, 1999.

54. Rubin, *Trit in der nakht*, 86.

55. Ibid., 73.

56. See for example, "Iberflantsung," in Rubin, *Fun mentsh tsu mentsh*, 65–66; "Gemeynt," in Rubin, *Fun mentsh tsu mentsh*, 99; "Baym yam hamelekh," in Rubin, *Fun mentsh tsu mentsh*, 102–103; "Midbar," in Rubin, *Fun mentsh tsu mentsh*, 104; and "Efsher t," in Rubin, *Fun mentsh tsu mentsh*, 109. See these reviews of the volume: Jacob Glatshtein, "Hadasa Rubin," in Jacob Glatshtein, *Oyf greyte temes* (Tel Aviv: Farlag Y. L. Peretz, 1967), 306–310; Kadya Molodovski, "Trit iber sherblekh (Vegn lider fun hadasa rubin)," *Svive* No. 19 (1966): 17–19; and Gitl Meyzil, "Hadasa Rubin," in *Eseyen* (Tel Aviv: Farlag Y. L. Peretz, 1974), 214–221.

57. Rubin, *Eydertog*, 76. This words come from Rubin's poem "A dershrokene, shtey ikh farshemt."

58. Rubin, *Fun mentsh tsu mentsh*, 56.

59. Ibid., 7.

60. See "Krates," in Rubin, *Fun mentsh tsu mentsh*, 10 and "Undzer bobe," in Rubin, *Fun mentsh tsu mentsh*, 14.

61. Rubin, *Fun mentsh tsu mentsh*, 65.
62. Ibid., 95.
63. Ibid., 105.
64. Ibid., 109.
65. Ibid., 110–111.
66. See "Vi iber shabes-likht," in Rubin, *In tsugvint*, 14 and "Kleynglik," in Rubin, *In tsugvint*, 103.
67. Rubin, *In tsugvint*, 82.
68. Ibid., 23.
69. Ibid., 24.
70. See "Blondhoriker kholem," in Rubin, *In tsugvint*, 25–26 and "In krayz," in Rubin, *In tsugvint*, 58–60.
71. See "Durkh zeyere," in Rubin, *In tsugvint*, 37; "Vi feldblumen," in Rubin, *In tsugvint*, 39; and "Ikh bin haynt," in Rubin, *In tsugvint*, 46.
72. Rubin, *In tsugvint*, 42.
73. See the review of *Eydertog* written by Shimen Kants, "Hadasa rubin. Eydertog," in Shimen Kants, *Ring nokh ring: eseyen* (Tel Aviv: Yidisher kultur gezelshaft, 1990): 56–61.
74. See "Teg vi shteyner" in Rubin, *Eydertog*, 87 and "Vi lang vel ikh" in Rubin, *Eydertog*, 89.
75. Rubin, *Rays nisht op di blum*, 84.
76. See Magdalena Piechota, "Kobieta w polskim filmie socrealistycznym," in *Socrealizm: Fabuły—Komunikaty—Ikony*, ed. Krzysztof Stępnik and Magdalena Piechota (Lublin: Wydawnictwo Uniwersytetu Marii Curie-Skłodowskiej, 2006), 313.
77. Wojciech Tomasik, "Harmonia ludzi i maszyn. O socrealistycznych obrazach 'nowego' człowieka," in Wojciech Tomasik, *Inżynieria dusz: Literatura realizmu socjalistycznego w planie "propagandy monumentalnej"* (Wrocław: Wydawnictwo Uniwersytetu Wrocławskiego, 1999), 159–162.
78. See Jerzy Smulski, "Obraz kobiety w prozie polskiej pierwszej połowy lat pięćdziesiątych XX wieku. Rekonesans," in *Od Szczecina do ... Października. Studia o literaturze polskiej lat pięćdziesiątych* (Toruń: Wydawnictwo Uniwersytetu Mikołaja Kopernika, 2002), 78.
79. See Celia Dropkin's "Mayn mame," in *Yidishe dikhterins: antologye*, ed. Ezra Korman (Shikago: L. M. Shtayn, 1928), 162; Kadya Molodowsky's "Froyen-lider I," in *Papirene brikn. Geklibene lider fun Kadie Molodovski / Paper Bridges: Selected Poems of Kadya Molodowsky*, trans., ed., and intro. Kathryn Hellerstein (Detroit: Wayne State University Press, 1999), 70; and Miriam Ulinover's "Mayn bobes oytser," in *A grus fun der heym. Lider / Un bonjour du pays natal. Poemes*, intro. and ed. Natalia Krynicka and trans. Batia Baum (Paris: Medem Biblioteque, 2003).
80. Rubin, *Veytik un freyd*, 38–39.
81. Rubin, *Trit in der nakht*, 27.
82. See "Natur-gezets" in Rubin, *Trit in der nakht*, 15, and "Mayn nakht symfonie," in Rubin, *Trit in der nakht*, 29. Also see "First, mame, dos kind bay dem hentl," in Rubin, *Veytik un freyd*, 14.
83. Rubin, *Trit in der nakht*, 29.
84. Ibid., 28.

# Remembering Two of Montreal's Yiddish Women Poets
## Esther Segal and Ida Maza

REBECCA MARGOLIS

During the formative period of Montreal's development as a Yiddish cultural center in the 1920s, the several women poets active in the expanding local literary milieu included Esther Segal (1895–1974) and Ida Maza (Maze/Massey, 1893–1962).[1] Both immigrated to Montreal at a young age during the mass Jewish immigration to Canada from Eastern Europe.[2] Both made their literary debuts in the early 1920s, and both wrote lyrical verse influenced by Yiddish modernist poetry. Both published primarily in literary journals and anthologies, and their writings were well received by their peers, locally and internationally. Yet Segal has fallen into obscurity, while Maza has been widely written about as a poet and activist. Still known in Canadian Yiddish cultural history as *di mame* [the mother], Maza hosted a literary salon where writers, artists, Jewish immigrants, and refugees gathered to share their work and find support. Segal took no public role within the local cultural milieu, and her work has not been translated, nor has she been the subject of academic or popular discourse. In short, how these two poets have been remembered seems to have less to do with their poetry than with the roles they assumed in the local Yiddish cultural milieu.

## Yiddish Poetry in Montreal

For a millennium, the Yiddish language and its culture served as a portable civilization for Ashkenazi Jews in their migrations across Europe, and more recently to Canada and other new centers of settlement. With the emergence in the nineteenth and twentieth centuries of a popular press, theater, educational institutions, and a spectrum of ideological movements, Yiddish culture became an important expression of modern Jewish identity.³ The Ashkenazi masses, who were primarily Yiddish-speaking, encountered Yiddish literature in popular newspapers that had thousands of readers.⁴ In the first half of the twentieth century, Yiddish writers were prominent figures in a wider movement of modern Jewish revitalization; writers allied themselves with political movements and were often closely involved with Jewish institutional life.

The Canadian branch of this transnational Yiddish literary milieu emerged in the teens. The onset of a mass immigration of Jews from Eastern Europe after 1900 had transformed Canada's tiny, anglicized Jewish community into one that was almost entirely Yiddish-speaking. In the 1931 census, over 95 percent of Canada's approximately 157,000 Jews declared Yiddish as their mother tongue. As the country's foremost Jewish immigrant center, Montreal housed a dynamic Yiddish cultural community that supported an array of enduring institutions, notably the daily *Keneder adler* [*Canadian Jewish Eagle*], founded 1907; the *Yidishe folks-biblyotek* [Jewish Public Library], founded 1914; and a system of secular Yiddish schools. Montreal was the hub of a Canadian Yiddish community that forged strong cultural bonds nationally, as well as internationally, through the production, dissemination, and consumption of literature. Across the country, in particular in the cities of Montreal, Toronto, and Winnipeg, a sizable group of Yiddish writers promoted literary activity in newspapers, schools, libraries, and literary clubs. The group, which consisted primarily of recent working-class immigrants who developed their literary careers in their adopted homes in Canada,⁵ understood literature both as artistic expression and as a means of conveying ideology, ranging from leftwing and nationalist movements to religious observance. They contributed to Canada's pioneering journals as well as to international publications, carving out a Canadian tradition of Yiddish letters.

Poetry was the favored means of literary expression among the Yiddish immigrant writers; it required fewer resources than longer fiction and could easily be disseminated and shared in collective settings. Community members banded together to produce journals and other collective volumes dominated by poetry, publishing the verse of scores of writers. Yet, despite this flurry of literary activity, most early Canadian Yiddish poets remained minor figures in the world of Yiddish literature. Poet J. I. Segal (Esther Segal's brother) emerged as Canada's most celebrated Yiddish poet from this early period, and his work has been widely studied, translated and reprinted.⁶ The later arrival of Yiddish cultural figures with established international literary reputations, such as poets Melekh Ravitch and Rokhl Korn, would transform Montreal into a major Yiddish cultural center after the Holocaust.⁷ During the interwar period however, even minor poets were respected cultural figures, as published writers active in the local literary scene. For Esther Segal, Maza, and other writers who found themselves in "New World" centers that lacked a commercial Yiddish book-publishing industry, the periodical press marked their primary site of publication during the interwar period. Virtually all of Canada's Yiddish writers published in the major Yiddish newspapers and in a score of specialty journals. While most of the latter were short-lived, they provided a forum for the development of a Canadian tradition of Yiddish letters. J.I. Segal, a modernist who aligned himself with New York's *Di yunge* [The Young Ones] group of writers, published a series of pioneering Canadian Yiddish literary journals in the 1920s that espoused an "art-for-art's-sake" approach. He encouraged several emerging poets in Montreal to write and publish, and Esther Segal and Ida Maza were among the many who made their literary debuts in his journals.

Published mainly in Montreal and Toronto, the Yiddish journals devoted to literature and culture covered a wide ideological spectrum, from high modernist to proletarian. Beginning with J. I. Segal's journal *Nyuansn* [Nuances] (1921), the publications of the 1920s promoted "high functions" for Yiddish. They featured poetry and prose as art, alongside Yiddish scholarship and discussion and translation of world literature. In the Depression era, the Yiddish community's proletarian tendencies came to the fore in journals that aligned themselves with leftist ideologies, subsuming literature and culture into the struggle of the working class. The advent of World War II marked the end of the proliferation of Canadian Yiddish journals. Esther Segal and Ida Maza typified the patterns of publication for Yiddish authors of their generation, both in Canada and worldwide, by publishing first and foremost in periodicals.

Like so many Yiddish writers of their generation, Segal and Maza staked out their literary careers during the brief period when modern Yiddish culture was a global mass phenomenon. A generation later, secular Yiddish culture— in Canada and abroad—was facing steady attrition in the face of acculturation, the decimation of the Yiddish heartland in Europe in the Nazi Holocaust, the primacy of Hebrew in the newly created State of Israel, and the suppression of Yiddish culture in the Soviet Union. The Canadian census reflects the trend. The Yiddish mother tongue statistic dropped from its high of 95 percent in 1931 to 76 percent in 1941, and, with the linguistic acculturation of Jewish immigrants into English-speaking Canada and a cessation of Yiddish-speaking immigration, to 32 percent in 1961 and 11 percent in 1981.[8] Although Canada absorbed a large number of Yiddish-speaking Holocaust survivors, who bolstered Yiddish cultural activity, the acculturation of Jewish Canada has been overwhelmingly away from Yiddish. A literature about Yiddish Canada and a body of work in translation has emerged in English as well as French, but linguistic fluency outside of ultra–Orthodox Jewish circles has not been maintained.

Segal and Maza form part of a generation of Yiddish speakers for whom Yiddish was their natural literary language. For J. I. Segal and others, writing in Yiddish became associated with commemorating the destruction of European Yiddish civilization in the Holocaust,[9] but neither Esther Segal nor Maza ever appears to have related to Yiddish in a symbolic way. Yiddish was their creative language, the tongue in which they were inspired to express themselves artistically. Most fundamentally, they wrote in Yiddish because it was the dominant Ashkenazi *lingua franca* when they began their literary careers in the 1920s. They were native speakers who emerged in a vibrant Yiddish literary milieu in Montreal, where they had access to a vast infrastructure of fellow Yiddish poets, critics, newspapers, journals, and an international Yiddish readership.

## Esther Segal

Born into a large hasidic family in Slobkovitz, Podolia, in 1895, Esther Segal was educated in a girl's *kheyder*[10] and by private tutors. Her father died when she was young, and she, her mother, and her siblings settled in Montreal in the 1900s and 1910s. Esther herself came to the city in 1909. She worked in a clothing factory and went to school in the evenings, and she also spent some time in New York City attending the Jewish Teacher's Seminary. After her return to Montreal, she began to write and publish Yiddish poetry, while continuing to do factory work and becoming active in leftist political circles. She married fellow poet A. S. Shkolnikov, and they had one daughter.

The Canadian Yiddish literary journals were Segal's primary site of publication, and she published in virtually all of them, gaining the esteem of her peers locally as well as abroad. Her only book of verse, *Lider* [Poems] (1928), was published in Toronto by the "Zerubavel Branch 219" of the labor Zionist *Yidisher natsyonaler arbeter farband* [Jewish National Worker's Union], a leftist organization, and produced and distributed by a group of "young people in

Toronto." This was remarkable in a period when the Yiddish milieu lacked a commercial publishing industry for books, and the publication of most Yiddish volumes in Canada was spearheaded by their authors, with or without the backing of a group of supporters. Moreover, *Lider* received accolades from the international Yiddish literati, including the prominent American literary critics Sh. Niger and Kalman Marmor.[11] In the same year that *Lider* appeared, Segal was included in *Yidishe dikhterins: antologye*, a groundbreaking anthology of Yiddish women's poetry published by the writer Ezra Korman in Chicago.

Segal's poetry falls into two main categories: personal poetry on universal themes such as love, motherhood, and faith, and political poetry on themes that were topical in the late 1920s and 1930s. Segal's personal poems are integral to the history of Canadian verse, even if they have not been included in the canon. As discussed below, the politics of publication, translation, and memory for Yiddish poetry in Canada have often been contingent upon factors that have little to do with the actual literary significance of a given work. This first category includes Segal's debut poems, which appeared in 1922 in *Epokhe* [Epoch], one of Canada's first Yiddish literary journals.[12] The second of her "*Tsvey lider*" [Two Poems] begins with the line "*Oyf dayne tayvedike lipn rut a zater shmeykhl*" [On your lust-filled lips rests a satiated smile]. The poem offers a lighthearted glimpse into a first love. The speaker expresses both the passion of young love, with a "satiated smile" resting on "lust-filled lips," and its playful innocence, with the sun asking "what is a girl doing with a boy" and "wink[ing] saucily at the day."

Segal's poetry shared features with that of many other early twentieth-century Yiddish poets. Like other modernists, Segal wrote lyrical poetry, in regular meter and blank verse, which refracted her own experiences, and she played with both imagery and sound. Much of her early poetry is set at night and explores the liminal state between sleep and wakefulness. For example, "Nakhtklangen" [Night Sounds], which appeared in Montreal's *Royerd* literary journal [Raw Earth] later in 1922,[13] which reads, "*Vos kukt a nakht durkh oysgeloshene fenster / arayn in shlofndike hayzer?*" [What is the night doing peering through darkened windows / into sleeping houses?] draws on poetic devices invented by the New York modernist poet Yankev Glatshteyn (Jacob Glatstein) for his experimental poems of 1921. For example, his poem "Tirtl-toybn" [Turtle Doves] evokes a child's experience of *kheyder* by playing with the language of the *kheyder* in the sound of the word *tirtl-toybn*.[14] Similarly, Segal's "Nakhtklangen" evokes a child's experience of night by breaking up into sounds that onomatopoeically mimic night noises.[15]

Within the vast corpus of twentieth-century Yiddish children's literature, Segal authored poems for and about children that appeared in her *Lider* and in such journals as the New York *Kinder zhurnal* [Children's Journal] and *Kinder tsaytung* [Children's Paper]. Among the poems written about her experiences as a mother is "Hentelekh" [Little Hands], dedicated to her daughter Sheva-Mashele.[16] She writes, "*Mayn tokhterls kleyne hentelekh, / mit lange, tsarte fingerlekh / shpiln oyf di dinste strunes/fun mayn harts.*" [My daughter's little hands, / with their long, soft fingers / pluck the thinnest strings / of my heart.] In the work, Segal's speaker expresses her awe at her child, causing her to alter fundamental perceptions of her world. The existence of her daughter renders the mundane sublime as her "world becomes a rainbow" and her child, "enchanted colors."

Segal's poetry yields insight into her immigrant experience also. Among the poems featured in the *Yidishe dikhterins* is "Mayn prints—der beker" [My Prince, the Baker], which first appeared in *Royerd* in 1927.[17] In the poem, Segal creates a fairytale to portray the dangerous and draining physical conditions in which her husband earned his living, while he agitated for better working conditions as head of the local Baker's Union.[18] To evoke his difficult life, she combines the European figure of the fairytale prince with the biblical Joseph of Jewish tradition, infusing the mundane with heroism by casting her beloved baker-husband as both a prince and a wronged Jewish hero. Her personal struggles in the working class are thereby elevated to the level of an epic combining European and Jewish literary traditions.[19]

A poem from the opening section of *Lider*, "Der mames likht" [My Mother's Candles], offers a glimpse of Segal's identity as a secular Yiddish poet: "*Mayn mames shabes-likht oysgebrent, ... / tsindt mayn shvester likht in ire laykhter.*" [My mother's Sabbath candles have burnt out / so my sister lights candles in her candlesticks.][20] This poem explores the contrast between the speaker and her sister, who has inherited their mother's religious objects—candlesticks and kerchief—as well as her religious practices and beliefs. Although Segal's secular speaker has no such inheritance, she recasts her mother's religiosity into the non-religious terms of her own life. Instead of lighting Sabbath candles, she writes poems. Instead of finding strength and connection to her Jewish tradition in the candle flames, the speaker locates her faith in the "weekdays" that burn with a "blue flame." The poet-speaker transforms her mother's candlesticks and prayers into secular metaphors.[21]

In comparison with Segal's poems on personal/universal themes, the political poetry that drew on her leftist activism seems dated, in large part due to the changes in the historical situation that originally spawned them. Beginning in the late 1920s, Segal became increasingly active in Canadian Jewish leftist circles, which were part of a mass movement within the Yiddish world. In addition to publishing regularly in Toronto's newspaper *Der kamf* [The Struggle], Segal took part in poetry readings organized by the Jewish left, such as a series of Yiddish cultural evenings associated with the Yiddish literary journal *Montreol*.[22] According to her niece Sylvia Lustgarten, Segal participated in a local circle of leftist Jewish women, as well as in communist-oriented Jewish cultural organizations such as the United Jewish People's Order.[23] As an activist in the leftist cultural milieu, Segal wrote about social themes in much of her poetry in the late 1920s and 1930s. But the polemicism of her highly praised poems depicting the hardships of working life and the hazards faced by the worker, such as those published in *Kanade* [Canada] in 1925[24] and in *Royerd* in 1927, does not have the same resonance today. The same may be said of Segal's writing that appeared in leftist-oriented publications, such as the 1928 anthology *Baginen* [Dawn], edited by communist writer Benjamin Katz in Toronto, or the literary journal *Prolit* [Proletarian Literature], where Segal published an epic poem highlighting the role of women in the international battle of the proletariat.[25] The verse, reflecting a combined commitment to women's and leftist struggles that were at the fore when it was published, seems hackneyed now in its use of standard figures of speech and imagery: blood, book, and open hand. While such poems may retain historical value as a reflection of the experiences of Jewish immigrant workers, they retain little in the way of literary value today.

During World War II, which Canada entered in September of 1939, Segal moved away from leftist themes and returned to earlier themes of a lost past. In 1940, Segal's poem "Vayte dermonung" [Distant Memory] appeared in *Kanader zhurnal* [Canadian Journal], the only Canadian Yiddish literary journal produced during the war years.[26] This poem plays on themes of childhood memory and a liminal dream state, where the poet can return to hear her mother's voice. The imagined homecoming may be read as a still-resonant poetic response to impending catastrophe in Nazi Europe. Note the parallel between Segal's poem and a later one by Rokhl Korn, "Fun yener zayt lid" [On the Other Side of the Poem], which opens her 1962 volume of the same name.[27] Both Segal and Korn compose pastoral scenes of the home they can visit only in memory or dream, and both poems end with the speakers' mothers calling them. Segal's bucolic vision of a childhood landscape was written precisely as that landscape was being ravaged by war, its Jewish populations under siege.

The 1940s saw an abrupt decline of both the Yiddish periodicals in which

Segal had published and the political circles in which she had been active. With the decimation of the Yiddish heartland in Europe as well as the general attrition of Yiddish as a vernacular, writers in immigrant centers such as Montreal shifted their efforts away from the publication of the collective journals that had provided inexpensive access to a wide readership and towards books by individual authors. The ranks of the leftist milieu also thinned rapidly in the postwar period, as Jews left the working class and as the Cold War discredited communist-affiliated organizations like the United Jewish People's Order within the mainstream Jewish community. Segal found herself alienated and increasingly withdrew from literary activity. A few poems published in *Montrealer heftn* [Montreal Notebooks], 1955–1958, one of two postwar Yiddish literary publications to appear in Canada, present her fears and hopes for her daughter, Mashe, who had recently settled in Israel, and for her own future. Following her husband's death, she emigrated to Israel in 1965.[28] There she published poetry about the beauty of the land of Israel and its people, but she did not associate with any particular literary milieu. She died in Israel a decade later in a home for the elderly.[29]

Segal's poetry is significant for several reasons beyond its literary value. Her poems provide insight into the creative processes by which a Jewish immigrant woman navigated the Canadian landscape during a period of tremendous vitality and flux. Further, the trajectory of Segal's poetic career spanned the highpoint of Canadian Yiddish literary activity, in particular among the leftist movements. Her story and her poetry have, unfortunately, been buried by neglect, for reasons that had more to do with external factors and the mechanics of communal memory than with her literary talents.

## Ida Maza

Born Ida Zhukovsky in 1893, in Ogli, a village in tsarist Belarus, Maza received a traditional Jewish education. Her family immigrated to the United States in 1907 and settled in Montreal the following year. She married Alexander Massey (an anglicized form of Maza), a traveling salesman, and they had three sons, one of whom died in childhood. In her thirties, she began to devote herself to Yiddish literature, particularly poetry. Like Esther Segal and many other local Yiddish poets, she began to publish in the 1920s with the encouragement of J. I Segal, contributing poems as well as essays and book reviews to literary journals. Maza went on to publish widely; her poetry appeared in a number of literary journals in Montreal, Toronto, New York and Paris, as well as in anthologies, including Korman's *Yidishe dikhterins* and Noah Steinberg's

*Yidish amerike* [Yiddish America].[30] Like Segal's, Maza's poetry earned admiration from the international Yiddish literary community. According to Sholem Shtern, *di yunge* poet Moyshe Leib Halpern eagerly sought her out during a visit to Montreal, after having read her poem "Ikh bin zindik, ikh bin zindik" [I Am Sinful, I Am Sinful] in the *Montreol* literary journal.[31] Her writing was also included in *The Golden Peacock*, a pioneering English-language anthology of Yiddish writing published in England during World War II.[32] Maza also published several books of poetry and prose. Her first, *A mame* [A Mother] (1931), comprised poetry written after the death of her eldest son. It was followed by *Lider far kinder* [Poems for Children] (1938), *Naye lider* [New Poems] (1941), and *Vaksn mayne kinderlekh: Muter un kinder-lider* [My Children Grow: Poems for Mothers and Children] (1954). Her novel *Dineh: Autobiografishe dertseylung* [Dina: An Autobiographical Story] (1970) was published posthumously.

Like Esther Segal, Ida Maza published a body of poetry on universal themes—nature, love, children, and motherhood—that have stood the test of time. Her literary debut in the *Kanade* literary journal in 1925 featured a poem called "Zunen shtral" [Ray of Sun], offering one of the recurring motifs in Maza's writing: a snapshot of nature's beauty. Maza's poems share elements with Segal's. She was influenced by modernist poets, in particular *di yunge* group.[33] Maza's verse refracts her own experiences of natural landscapes, as well as universal themes of love and death, motherhood, and family. She also wrote widely for a readership of children and young adults. A series of her poems on family and motherhood appeared in *Yidishe dikhterins*, among them "Kinder" [Children], which reads, "*Veynen kinder/ durkh di nekht,/un shlofn in frimorgn; / vakhn mames lange nekht, / shlofn nit un zorgn.* [Children cry through the nights / sleeping in the morning; / mothers keep vigil through long nights, worrying, unsleeping.][34] According to Maza's introduction to her 1954 book, *Vaksn mayne kinderlekh* [My Children Grow], "Children are the reason that I started writing. I wrote both my happy and my sad poetry to children." The opening poem, "Vi blimelekh in regn" [Like Little Flowers in the Rain], reads: "*Orim iz mayn shtibele, / mit an altn dakh, / vaksn in im kinderlekh kinderlekh a sakh.*" [Humble is my little house, / its roof is very old, / but my children grow within, children strong and bold.]

Maza's 1941 volume, *Naye lider* [New Songs], contains poems about the poet's inner life as a woman and artist. "A gebet fun a froy" [A Woman's Prayer] explains her interior states.[35] This poem about the loss of a child expresses profound grief in a dialogue with the divine. Because her grief has made it difficult for her to seek solace in poetry, she is on the brink of losing hope.

However, the poem's form is at odds with its content. The rhyme scheme gives a sense of order to a poem that is rooted in a formless despair. The poem expresses the role of poetry in maintaining the speaker's life when she has lost the will to live; she wants "to be far away" and for her eyes to be closed, but she remains tied to the world of the living by the act of writing the poem.

While Maza, like Segal, belonged to Montreal's Jewish working-class immigrant community, she left no body of work motivated by historical realities and political movements that have since faded into the past. Her activism was geared at building literary community rather than promoting leftist ideals. Maza worked with the Jewish Public Library, where she ran a reading group for children as well as adults. It was the *leyen-krayz fun der yiddisher folks biblyotek* [the reading circle of the Jewish Public Library] that published her book *Naye lider*. Local and visiting writers and poets came together at her home in Montreal's Jewish quarter to share their work. Maza rallied on behalf of refugees and Holocaust survivors in Canada, working to help them get settled. She was also instrumental in publishing the work of Yiddish authors, particularly that of the writers who settled in Canada after the Holocaust. In his brief introduction to Maza's autobiographical novel, *Dineh*, Montreal poet M. M. Shaffir writes that Maza had often suggested that the two of them sit down together to go over her manuscript, "but important work always waited for her on behalf of others. She had no time for herself." The book was published posthumously by the "Ida Maza Book Committee."[36]

There is much in common between Maza's literary career and output—in terms of both its themes and how it was received at the time—and Esther Segal's. Nevertheless, the ways in which Ida Maza has been remembered have followed a very different trajectory. She remains among the best known of Canada's Yiddish writers and cultural figures and has been written about widely both in Yiddish and in other languages. This discourse has increasingly focused on her personality over her poetry.

## Esther Segal and Ida Maza in Yiddish Sources

Most major works of Canadian Yiddish-language literary criticism and memoir, penned by Montreal Yiddish writers who were active in the same local literary milieu as Segal and Maza, discuss both of them as significant writers, generally in the context of the broader Yiddish literary milieu.

The Yiddish writing on Esther Segal points both to her talent and to the challenges she faced during her career as a poet, only occasionally touching on her personal circumstances. None of it discusses gender per se, nor do her peers identify the themes in her poetry as peculiar to women. Rather, she is characterized as a lyrical poet with modernist tendencies whose verse addresses universal themes such as nature, love, and social justice. At most, the other writers lament that she failed to publish more.

Thus, H. M. Caiserman's essay on her in his 1934 compendium on Canadian Jewish poets, *Yidishe dikhter in kanade* [Jewish Poets in Canada], opens by calling her "one of the most promising poetesses in Canada" and goes on trace her poetry as it appeared in the literary journals, as well as her book.[37] The entry on Segal in Chaim-Leib Fuks's lexicon *Hundert yor yidishe un hebreishe literatur in kanade* [A Hundred Years of Yiddish and Hebrew Literature in Canada] summarizes her full literary career.[38] Mirl Erdberg-Shatan, a Montreal writer who published in many of the same journals as Segal, authored an obituary for her, in which she noted the difficult economic conditions that kept her from publishing more poetry. Sholem Shtern writes in his memoir, *Shrayber vos ikh hob gekent* [Writers I Have Known],[39] that he first encountered Segal through her book and was impressed by her poetic talent. He describes her impatience to see her poetry recognized in literary reviews, but he also refers to "the indifferent environment that dampened the spirit of the most important woman poet that Canada ever produced."[40] He depicts her growing isolation from the local Yiddish cultural scene after the 1960s; as he writes, she felt alienated after the death of her husband and did not fit into the milieu of the newly arrived post–Holocaust writers. According to Shtern, once in Israel, Segal continued to feel estranged as a leftist in what she perceived as a capitalist society, and as a Yiddish writer in a land where Hebrew dominated. Stern's view is corroborated by a farewell article authored by N. J. Gotlib in the *Keneder adler* upon Segal's departure for Israel in 1965; while referring to her as a "renowned Yiddish poet," he concedes, "It is true: In recent years her poems have appeared but sporadically."[41] As late as 1995, Montreal poet Miriam Krant wrote about Esther Segal in her volume of essays and poetry *Geflekht fun tsvaygn* [Entwined Branches]. The essay, appearing alongside a score of short portraits of Yiddish writers that include half a dozen Montreal women poets,[42] discusses her themes and the positive reception of her *Lider*.

In the Yiddish Canadiana published during her lifetime, Ida Maza is likewise presented first and foremost as a poet. There are, however, inklings of the primary way in which Maza would later be remembered as a community activist. The essay on Maza in Caiserman's *Yidishe dikhter in kanade* opens by saying, "If during all of her years of poetic creativity, Ida Maza had not written a single poem, and had lived, operated, served, helped and encouraged and elevated and enthused at everything associated with humanity and art, her interesting personality alone would have been a wondrous poetic creation." However, Caiserman continues, "luckily, ... there has not been a single anthology, literary collection, or journal that has appeared in the last eight years in Canada, and to a lesser extent in the United States, which Ida Maza's poetry has not graced with her talent."[43] He goes on to discuss her poetry and its motifs. Melekh Ravitch's essay on Maza in *Mayn leksikon* [My Lexicon], originally written in 1942, a year after he settled in Montreal, discusses her poetry and offers a portrait of the poet in which he discusses her longstanding role in the cultural community: "Ida Maza has, for the past decade, been engaging in tireless promotion of the Yiddish language and its crown, its flower, its most heavenly fruit—the Yiddish poem. Thanks to her, books of Yiddish poetry are being sold in Montreal by the hundreds, and Yiddish poetry is being read in Canada, possibly more than anywhere else." He describes her home, using imagery from Jewish tradition: "When one crosses her threshold, it is as if one enters a *yidishn beys-hamidresh* [Jewish house of study] where one studies poetry instead of the Talmud, and where Maza was always prepared to do a favor as needed for her visitors." Like Caiserman, however, Ravitch characterizes Maza first and foremost as a poet and then as a promoter of poetry.[44]

The same is true of Yiddish essays authored by her peers after Maza's death. Although her role as a supporter is always mentioned, and the term "mother" does appear, these are secondary to her poetry. Fuks's lexicon, which provides a detailed overview of her publishing history, offers quotations from critics like Caiserman that repeatedly employ the term "mother," but it does not discuss this aspect of Maza's legacy.[45] Shtern's essay "Dos troyerike lid fun ayde maze" [The Sad Song of Ida Maza] focuses on the sorrow manifest in the poetry Maza wrote in response to the loss of her son. Though he criticizes elements of her verse as predictable and simplistic, he characterizes her "*durkhgetrerte mamelider*" [tear-filled mother-poems] as her highest poetic accomplishment and quotes from them extensively.[46] Miriam Krant's essay introduces Maza's poetry as permeated by the aroma of forests and fields. It refers briefly to Maza as "an institution in her own right," busy with cultural activity and always ready to help others, and discusses her "literary salon." However, the bulk of the essay discusses Maza's poetry and its varied themes, and it is in this context that Maza appears as a "mother": "A gentle motherly feeling [*mame-gefil*] permeates Ida Maza's poetry"; or, as the essay ambiguously concludes, "Ida Maza is the mother of our poetry."

## Esther Segal and Ida Maza in Non-Yiddish Sources

While Esther Segal and Ida Maza appear in most of the same Yiddish-language sources on Canadian Yiddish literature, Segal is virtually absent outside of them, a phenomenon for which there are several possible explanations. She is a minor poet who published widely in literary journals but produced just one slender book, lost amongst the shelves of weighty works authored by her contemporaries. Her brother J. I. Segal, for example, produced a dozen volumes of poetry, and Maza authored four. Esther Segal has unquestionably been overshadowed by her more prominent and prolific brother as well as by her husband, who was actively involved in the literary milieu as an editor. Thus, Gotlib refers to Esther Segal as J. I. Segal's sister and Shkolnikov's wife; and she is introduced as the "sister of J. I. Segal" by Fuks, by the writer Miriam Waddington in an essay on Ida Maza, and by the *Encyclopaedia Judaica*. Needless to say, neither J. I. Segal nor Shkolnikov were identified in relation to Esther Segal.[47] Gender certainly played a role: she is "sister" and "wife," rather than simply "poet." More fundamentally, Segal—as a woman poet—shared the experience of "multiple exile" that Kathryn Hellerstein has described as characterizing women writing modern poetry in Yiddish, both as Jewish émigrés and as women.[48] Finally, Esther Segal did not exert a lasting influence in the Canadian Yiddish cultural world. The leftist milieu towards which she was oriented dissipated to the point that she was left culturally uprooted. She withdrew from her literary milieu later in life and subsequently moved away. Few individuals celebrated her accomplishments after her death, and none called her mentor.

Maza also differs from Segal in her prominent characterization as a "woman writer" in a variety of recent sources. In an essay by Norma Joseph, her name is included in a list of a dozen women writers and artists who "have bestowed their treasures on Canada and the Jewish community."[49] She is also included on a popular website called "A Celebration of Women Writers."[50] Esther Segal does not appear in any of these sources.

If Segal does appear in English- or French-language sources on Yiddish culture in Canada, it is in passing. For example, an article on early Yiddish poets lists both Segal and Maza as poets in Montreal's early group, but only cites poetry by Maza.[51] A short entry on her in the *Encyclopaedia Judaica*, which provides a biographical summary, stands alone.[52] Moreover, her poetry does not appear in contemporary anthologies of Canadian Jewish writing that include Yiddish writing in translation. Works about Yiddish or of Yiddish in translation, which have become the dominant points of popular access to the work of writers such as Maza and Segal, have tended to compact the complexity of the Canadian Yiddish cultural milieu into accessible terms by focusing on central figures and their roles in the infrastructure that supported it. In these discussions in English and, more recently, in French, which often take place at the intersection of scholarship, translation, and memoir, Maza appears as a "mother" who ran a "literary salon" in her home.[53]

The designation "mother"—drawing both on Maza's exploration of the experience of motherhood in her writing and on her community role—became increasingly prominent in the discourse about Maza after her death. If announcements of her death in Anglo-Jewish publications such as the weekly *Canadian Jewish Review* and the *American Jewish Yearbook* identify her as a writer,[54] the announcement that appeared on the front page of the *Keneder adler* refers to her as "renowned poet Ida Maza, who was known in Yiddish literary circles as '*di mame fun der yidisher literature*' [the mother of Yiddish literature] and who was famous for her great deeds on behalf of poor and suffering people."[55] Melekh Ravitch's article "Yiddish Culture in Canada," in the 1963 *Canadian Jewish Reference Book and Directory*, allots Maza the following single line: "Ida Massey (1893–1962), known throughout the Yiddish world as 'Mother of Yiddish Literature in Canada,' was the author of several volumes of lyrics as well as books for children."[56] Here, in contrast to his 1942 Yiddish article focusing on her poetry, the title "Mother," repeated under her photograph, serves as a tagline for Ravitch to encapsulate Maza's importance to a broad readership; similarly, J. I. Segal is tagged as an "Outstanding Contributor to Yiddish Poetry in Canada," and Rokhl Korn as a "Famous Yiddish Poetess." Esther Segal, lacking such a tagline, is not mentioned at all.

This designation for Maza seems to have struck a chord. Seymour Levitan employs it in the opening remarks to his translations of her poems in the magazine *Jewish Dialogue* in 1974,[57] and the term has appeared in virtually every subsequent discussion of Maza in English as well as in Yiddish. In the discourse that has grown up around her, based in her roles as supporter and nurturer, "mother" is a universal concept that easily encapsulates Maza's career, in particular for outsiders to the Yiddish culture in which she functioned. In short, the trope of Maza as mother has rendered her accessible to a non–Yiddish audience. By contrast, Segal remains a product of a particular time and place: a leftist Yiddish literary milieu that has largely disappeared.

Praise of Maza as a maternal figure has come to figure prominently in reminiscences of her in both Yiddish and English. For example, the term "mother" appears frequently in a Yiddish article marking the 45th anniversary of Maza's death, featured in Chana Mlotek's "Pearls of Yiddish Poetry" column in the New York weekly *Forverts* [Forward].[58] Sholem Shtern's memoir stands alone in its lukewarm characterization of Maza's motherly tendencies. He writes how he opted to disengage himself from Maza's home and the many young poets that the *mamedik* [motherly] Maza attracted.[59] In English-language encyclopedia entries on Jewish Canadian writing, Maza is almost invariably presented in motherly terms.[60] The *Encyclopaedia Judaica* article on "Canadian Literature" presents her as "'the mother' of Canadian Yiddish writers," who "conducted a literary salon in Montreal for many years, encouraged other writers, and was instrumental in organizing the publication of their works."[61] A short entry on Maza in the same work underlines the supportive and subordinate aspect of Maza's career.[62]

A similar characterization of Maza appears in "Written Heritage," a virtual exhibit on the website of Montreal's Jewish Public Library.[63] Maza's profile briefly outlines her literary activity before concluding, "Maze will be best remembered, however, for the kind sustaining encouragement she provided at her 'salons.' ... Her approachability and strength shown to other [sic] earned her the name, 'Mother to Yiddish Poets.'" It is noteworthy that there is no male counterpart to Maza as "mother"; the most likely male candidate, J. I. Segal, who mentored so many writers, was not called "father."

Maza's "literary salon" represents another facet of her persona as a supporter and nurturer. This appellation for Maza's apartment appears to have originated in the memoirs of the prominent English-language writer and poet Miriam Waddington, who was a regular guest in Maza's home. Waddington's essay "Mrs. Maza's Salon" describes her family's regular visits from Ottawa in the 1930s, when she was a teenager and budding poet.[64] Waddington describes Maza's walk-up in the heart of the Jewish area and the activity that took place in the dining room, with its expansive "Winnipeg couch." There, a host of writers and painters, both local and visitors from abroad, would gather to hear poetry read aloud, discuss new books or ideas for projects, or gossip. Waddington discusses the central role Maza played in the lives of her visitors:

> To these artists, most of them middle-aged and impecunious, and all of them immigrants, Mrs. Maza was the eternal mother—the foodgiver and nourisher, the listener and solacer, the mediator between them and the world. There she would sit with hands folded in sleeves, her face brooding and meditative, listening intently with her body. As she listened she rocked back and forth, and, as it then seemed to me, she did so in time to the rhythm of the poem being read. She gave herself entirely and attentively to the poem; she fed the spiritual hunger and yearning of these oddly assorted Yiddish writers whenever they needed her; but not only that. She also fed them real food, and not just once a week, but every day.[65]

Studies on Maza by her son Irving Massey, a professor of English, have likewise served to spotlight Maza's community role. In a short study of her literary career accompanied by translations of her poetry, Massey writes: "Ida Maza fulfils the ideals of her community while yet retaining her identity as an individual poet; she is a writer whose work, even at its most private, is subordinate to community. The poetic life that she led was a public life in private."[66] Massey develops this idea in his book *Identity and Community*, where he focuses on Montreal's Yiddish cultural life in the 1930s and offers anecdotes on the atmosphere of Maza's home, from his point of view as a young participant-observer. He refers to her role as "a leader of a literary salon, or perhaps *beys khakhomim* [house of the wise]; entertainer extraordinary for travelling Jewish cultural figures; clearinghouse for information about jobs, visas, sources of funding, contacts, and publishing possibilities; in a word, overseer of a virtual crossroads of Jewish culture."[67]

For Esther Segal, the venture of poetry appears to have entailed a private expression of the poet's inner experiences, even if her writing expressed collective or politicized themes. She read her poetry in community settings and wrote about social issues, but she did not link her art to community building. The literature on Maza points to a different understanding of poetry, as simultaneously a private expression and a means of fostering cultural community. It was something to be written, discussed, and encouraged in others; it was to be published and shared with the wider collective. Poets were to be fed and cared for on all levels, as were members of the broader cultural milieu. This specific cultural role resulted in tributes to Maza in both writing and art; sculptor Bezalel Malchi created a bust of her, and Montreal painter Louis Muhlstock painted her portrait.

Maza's legacy of inspiring and helping others has in many ways superseded her legacy as poet. An essay by the writer Bella Briansky Kalter, who came to Montreal to study nursing, recalls her frequent visits to the Maza home and describes the persuasive quality that enabled Maza to convince doctors, social workers, landlords, and school officials to accommodate those in need. She writes, "A remarkable attribute of Ida Maza's was that she was able to turn the poetry that sustained her into acts of giving, like a sorceress not only turning her own pain into poetry but of the [sic] souls who came to her for advice and help."[68] For Briansky Kalter, Maza was a saintly figure in an imperfect world, "a spiritual mother ... who ... nurtured and sustained the poetry in our lives."[69] Bella's sister, artist Rita Briansky, who drew and painted Maza on a number of occasions, recalled how Maza had helped her find jobs to pay for her art school education.[70] Maza's nephew, pianist, composer, and musicologist Marvin

Duchow, also recalled her as a mentor.[71] In contrast, one of the few English sources to focus on Maza as a poet is "Buffalo Yiddish," a popular website aimed at learners of Yiddish, which presents several of her poems. Its brief biographical entry concludes, "Whereas initially only a few of her poems appeared to have lasting qualities, it now seems that at least a dozen, or possibly two, will enter the classical canon of Yiddish poetry."[72]

Perhaps the best measure of contemporary public memory of Ida Maza was a recent project to designate her home at 4470B Esplanade Avenue in Montreal as a Canadian heritage site.[73] While the Historic Sites and Monuments Board of Canada rejected the nomination on the grounds that the evidence was inconclusive,[74] the project indicates the ways in which Maza is remembered beyond her own Yiddish world.

## *Conclusion*

In the contemporary discourse about Segal and Maza, their relative literary merits appear to have little bearing on how they have been remembered. One determining factor behind this current reality is the fundamental shift in the cultural value placed on Yiddish poetry. With the decline of the language as a *lingua franca*, Yiddish poetry has moved from the center of an immigrant culture to the margins of Jewish cultural life. Another factor has to do with the link between translation and posterity. Segal's increasing isolation and eventual geographic separation from Montreal's literary milieu left her on the periphery of a movement among her peers, notably J. I. Segal, Sholem Shtern, Yaakov Zipper, and Ida Maza, to have their writing translated and thus made accessible to a wider readership. The ongoing recognition of Yiddish writers in Canada has hinged on active lobbying, by them or on their behalf, for their work to be rendered into the country's official languages, English and French. Yiddish prose has largely proven more amenable to translation than poetry. Thus, the 1994 literary anthology *Found Treasures: Stories by Yiddish Women Writers*, which includes an excerpt from Maza's novel *Dineh* along with works by many lesser-known prose authors, does not feature Segal, who was a poet.[75] With fewer individuals able to read these works in the original, and even fewer seeking them out in literary journals, writers such as Segal have been rendered increasingly invisible, their work scattered in obscure periodicals and not translated out of the original Yiddish. Without advocates to push them into the spotlight in a way that is accessible and meaningful to a wide audience—through translation, scholarship, memoirs, or a combination thereof—minor Yiddish poets appear unlikely to be remembered by anyone but a few aficionados.

There is a certain irony to the ways in which Esther Segal and Ida Maza have been remembered. Both were Yiddish poets writing within the same cultural milieu. Esther Segal wrote political poems with the goal of affecting social change in the wider world. However, this leftist poetry did not endure beyond the particular historical moment in which it originated, and she remains one of many lesser-known Yiddish writers whose memory is buried in the pages of obsolete journals.[76] Maza wrote introspective, personal poetry, but she created a communal role for herself, which has resulted in her poetry being remembered.

There is also the additional dimension of what one might call "the Maza allure": her visibility as a nurturer and helper and her characterization as a "mother" have created a persona that extends beyond the corpus of Maza's Yiddish writing. What one might term a "mother mythos," combined with the popular notion of the "Ida Maza literary salon," have helped to propel her memory into the future, particularly for a public that will likely never read her poetry in the original. In contrast, Segal, who did not cultivate a public persona or leave behind a legacy as a beloved and influential nurturer, has been forgotten. Could it be that a Yiddish woman poet requires a "hook"—something above and beyond her actual poetry—to be remembered by? New York City's best-known Yiddish women poets of the 1920s, Anna Margolin and Celia Dropkin, are often remembered for the shock value of their poetry on such themes as sex and death and for their unconventional lives.[77] Neither Esther Segal nor Ida Maza lived radical and tempestuous lives, nor did they write on unconventional themes. However, as "mother," and "salonière," Maza represents a female archetype of a different sort: the nurturer. She remains a quiet but visible remnant of a vanishing Canadian Yiddish cultural scene that has taken Esther Segal and many others along with it.

## Notes

This essay was originally published as Rebecca Margolis, "Remembering Two of Montreal's Yiddish Women Poets: Esther Segal and Ida Maza," *Nashim: A Journal of Jewish Women's Studies & Gender Issues* 19 (Spring 2010): 141–173. Indiana University Press kindly gave permission to reprint the essay. Fair use and other considerations made some editing necessary.

1. Unless otherwise indicated, all translations from the Yiddish are my own. The original Yiddish text is presented in transliteration according to the YIVO system. I would like to thank the editors of *Nashim* and the anonymous reviewers for their feedback on this paper. Special thanks to Kathryn Hellerstein for engaging me in an email dialogue that greatly enriched my readings of the poems.

2. Parts of this study originally appeared in my article, "Ida Maza: Canadian Yiddish Writer and Activist," *Outlook* (September-October 2007): 18–19.

3. See Max Weinreich, *History of the Yiddish Language* (New Haven: Yale University Press, 2008). On Yiddish in the modern period, see Benjamin Harshav, *The Meaning of Yiddish* (Berkeley: University of California Press, 1990).

4. See Nathan Cohen, "The Yiddish Press and Yiddish Literature: A Fertile but Complex Relationship," *Modern Judaism* 28:2 (2008): 149–172.

5. See Adam G. Fuerstenberg, "Faithful to a Dream: The Proletarian Tradition in Canadian Yiddish Poetry," *Yiddish* 6:1 (1985): 84–96. This article includes both Esther Segal and Ida Maza as poets in Montreal's early group and cites poetry by Maza.

6. Studies of J. I. Segal include Adam G. Fuerstenberg, "Transplanting Roots: J. I. Segal's Canadian Perspective," *Yiddish* 4:3 (1981): 63–67; Adam G. Fuerstenberg, "From Yiddish to 'Yiddishkeit': A. M. Klein, J. I. Segal and Montreal's Yiddish Culture," *Journal of Canadian Studies* 19:2 (1984): 66–81; and Shari Cooper, "Between Two Worlds: The Works of J. I. Segal," in *An Everyday Miracle: Yiddish Culture in Montreal*, ed. Ira Robinson, Pierre Anctil, and Mervin Butovsky (Montreal: Véhicule Press, 1990), 115–128. Segal's poetry is featured in *A Treasury of Yiddish Poetry*, ed. Irving Howe and Eliezer Greenberg (New York: Holt, Rinehart and Winston, 1969); *The Penguin Book of Modern Yiddish Verse*, ed. Irving Howe, Ruth R. Wisse, and Khone Shmeruk (New York: Penguin, 1987); *The Spice Box: An Anthology of Jewish Canadian Writing*, ed. Gerri Sinclair and Morris Wolfe (Toronto: Lester & Open Dennys, 1981); and other volumes. It has also been translated into French: J. I. Segal, *Poèmes Yiddish*, trans. Pierre Anctil (Montréal: Édition du Noroît, 1992).

7. See Seymour Levitan, "Canadian Yiddish Writers," in *Identifications: Ethnicity and the Writer in Canada*, ed. Jars Balan (Edmonton: Canadian Institute of Ukrainian Studies, University of Alberta, 1982), 116–134.

8. See Leo Davids, "Yiddish in Canada: Picture and Prospects," in *The Jews in Canada*, ed. Robert J. Brym, William Shaffir, and Morton Weinfeld (Toronto: Oxford University Press, 1993), 153–166.

9. Chava Rosenfarb, "Canadian Yiddish Writers," in *Traduire le Montréal Yiddish / New Readings of Yiddish Montreal*, ed. Pierre Anctil, Norman Ravvin, and Sherry Simon (Ottawa: University of Ottawa Press, 2007), 15.

10. The east European *kheyder* instructed students in the traditional Jewish texts; for girls, this meant in particular the Bible and the prayer book.

11. See Miriam Krant, "Ester Segal," in *Geflekht fun tsvaygn* (Montreal, 1995), 88.

12. Esther Segal, "Tsvey lider" [Two Poems], *Epokhe* (January–April 1922): 85.

13. *Royerd* 2 (December 1922): 30.

14. See Benjamin and Barbara Harshav, eds. and English trans., *American Yiddish Poetry: A Bilingual Anthology* (Berkeley: University of California Press, 1986), 214–215.

15. This reading was developed in an email exchange with Kathryn Hellerstein, December 23, 2009.

16. Esther Segal, *Lider* (Toronto, 1928), 101.

17. See Ezra Korman, ed., *Yidishe dikhterins: antologye* (Shikago: L. M. Shṭayn, 1928), 222.

18. On Shkolnikov's union activities, see Eve Lerner, "Making and Breaking Bread in Jewish Montreal, 1920–1940" (M.A. Thesis, Concordia University, 2002).

19. Kathryn Hellerstein, email exchange with the author, December 17, 2009.

20. Segal, *Lider*, 41.

21. Kathryn Hellerstein, email exchange with the author, December 17, 2009.

22. *Montreol* 6 (January 1934): 20.

23. Author's interview with Sylvia Lustgarten, Toronto, April 14, 2008.
24. *Kanade* (July 1925): 22–23; *Kanade* (October 1925): 14–15.
25. *Prolit* 1:1 (1935): 10.
26. *Kanader zhurnal* (1940): 13.
27. Korn was one of a group of prominent Yiddish writers who immigrated to Montreal after the Holocaust. See Rokhl Korn, "Fun yener zayt lid," in Rokhl Korn, *Fun yener zayt lid* (Montreal, 1962). English translation by Seymour Levitan in Howe, Wisse, and Shmeruk, *Modern Yiddish Verse*, 524. The poem has also been translated by Irena Klepfisz.
28. See Chaim Leib Fuks, "Esther Segal," in Chaim Leib Fuks, *Hundert yor yidishe un hebreyishe literatur in kanade* (Montreal: H. L. Fuks bukh fond komitet, 1980), 180.
29. Interview, Sylvia Lustgarten, 2008.
30. Noah Steinberg, ed., *Yidish amerike: zamlbukh* (Nyu York: Farlag lebn, 1929).
31. Sholem Shtern, "Moyshe-Leyb Halpern," in Sholem Shtern, *Shrayber vos ikh hob gekent* (Montreal, 1982), 19.
32. Joseph Leftwich, ed., *The Golden Peacock: An Anthology of Yiddish Poetry Translated into English Verse* (London: R. Anscombe, 1944), 771–772.
33. Shtern, *Shrayber*, 239 and 292.
34. Korman, *Yidishe dikhterins*, 273.
35. Ida Maza, *Naye lider* (Montreal: Leyen-krayz fun der yiddisher folks biblyotek, 1941), 156; English translation by Seymour Levitan, "Poems by Ida Massey (Ida Maza)," *Jewish Dialogue* (Hanukkah 1974), 25.
36. Ida Maza, *Dineh: autobiografishe dertseylung* (Montreal: Ida Maza Book Committee, 1970), 8.
37. H. M. Caiserman-Wital, *Yidishe dikhter in kanade* (Montreal: Farlag nyuansn, 1934), 59–64.
38. Fuks, "Esther Segal," in *Hundert yor yidishe un hebreyshe literatur*, 180.
39. Shtern, "Di dikhterin Ester Segal," in *Shrayber*, 271–280.
40. Ibid., 275.
41. N. J. Gotlib, "Ester Segal," *Keneder adler* 31 March 1965: 5.
42. Krant, "Ester Segal," 88–92.
43. Caiserman, *Yidishe dikhter in kanade*, 76.
44. Melekh Ravitch, "Ester Segal," in *Mayn leksikon* IV, no. 2 (Tel Aviv: Farlag I. L. Peretz, 1982), 72–74.
45. Fuks, "Ida Maza," in *Hundert yor yidishe un hebreyshe literatur*, 156–157.
46. Shtern, "Dos troyerike lid fun Ayde Maze," *Shrayber*, 290–296.
47. Gotlib, *Keneder adler*, 5; Fuks, *Hundert yor yidishe un hebreyshe literatur*, 180; Miriam Waddington, "Mrs. Maza's Salon," in *Apartment Seven: Essays Selected and New* (Toronto: Oxford University Press, 1989), 5; and Faith Jones, "Segal, Esther," in *Encyclopaedia Judaica* XVIII, 2d ed. (Detroit: Macmillan Reference USA, 2007), 245, *Gale Virtual Reference Library*, Web. 3, June 2014.
48. See Kathryn Hellerstein, "In Exile in the Mother Tongue," in *Borders, Boundaries, and Frames*, ed. Mae Henderson (New York: Routledge, 1994), 64–106.
49. Norma Baumel Joseph, "Jewish Women in Canada: An Evolving Role," in *From Immigration to Integration: The Canadian Jewish Experience—A Millennium Edition*, ed. Ruth Klein and Frank Dimont (Toronto: Institute for International Affairs of B'nai Brith Canada, 2001), 182–195, accessed February 9, 2009, http://www.bnaibrith.ca/institute/millennium/millennium12.html.
50. Mary Mark Ockerbloom, ed., "A Celebration of Women Writers," viewed February 4, 2009, http://digital.library.upenn.edu/women.

51. Fuerstenberg, "Faithful to a Dream," 86.
52. Jones, *Encyclopaedia Judaica*, 245.
53. See, for example, Rebecca Margolis, "Les écrivains yiddish de Montréal et leur ville," *Juifs et Canadiens français dans la société québécoise*, ed. Pierre Anctil, Ira Robinson, and Gérard Bouchard (Sillery, QC: Septendrion, 2000), 97–98; and Chantal Ringuet, "L'engagement littéraire et communautaire d'Ida Maze, la 'mère des écrivains yiddish montréalais,'" (paper delivered at the conference A Celebration of Jewish Studies in Ottawa, Ottawa, October 24, 2007).
54. "Social Notes," *Canadian Jewish Review* (August 10, 1962): 3; "Canada," *American Jewish Yearbook* (1963), 270.
55. The remainder of the article focused on her biography and her poetry. "Ayde Maza, bavuste hige dikhterin geshtorbn: di levaye haynt 1 nokhmitog," *Keneder adler* June 15, 1962: 1.
56. Melech Ravitch, "Yiddish Culture in Canada," in *Canadian Jewish Reference Book and Directory*, ed. Eli Gottesman (Montreal: Central Rabbinical Seminary of Canada, 1963), 80.
57. Levitan, "Poems by Ida Massey," *Jewish Dialogue*, 24.
58. Chana Mlotek, "Ida Maze: a montreoler dikhterin tsu ir 45stn yortsayt," *Forverts*, June 22, 2007, accessed February 9, 2009, http://yiddish.forward.com/node/515.
59. Shtern, "Yosef rolnik," *Shrayber*, 37.
60. An exception is the bilingual English-French *Canadian Encyclopedia*, where Maza is briefly listed alongside other early Yiddish Canadian poets. See Adam G. Fuerstenberg, "Jewish Writing," in *The Canadian Encyclopedia*, Web, viewed February 15, 2009.
61. Michael Greenstein, Pierre Anctil, and Eugene R. Orenstein, "Canadian Literature," in *Encyclopaedia Judaica* IV, 2d ed. (Detroit: Macmillan Reference USA, 2007), 426. Web. Viewed on February 10, 2009).
62. Faith Jones, "Maze, Ida," in *Encyclopaedia Judaica* XIII, 2d ed. (Detroit: Macmillan Reference USA, 2007), 706, Web, viewed February 10, 2009.
63. Jewish Public Library, accessed February 5, 2009, http://www.jewishpubliclibrary.org/archives/heritagevex/heritagemaze.html.
64. Waddington, *Apartment Seven*, 1–8.
65. Ibid., 4.
66. Irving Massey, "Public Lives in Private: Ida Maza and the Montreal Yiddish Renaissance," in Robinson, Anctil, and Botovsky, *An Everyday Miracle*, 156.
67. Irving Massey, *Identity and Community: Reflections on English, Yiddish and French Literature in Canada* (Detroit: Wayne State University Press, 1994), 62.
68. Bella Briansky Kalter, "Ida Maza (A Memoir)," *Canadian Jewish Studies* 6 (1998): 55.
69. Ibid., 61.
70. "An Art for Healing Foundation Initiative: Two Renowned Canadian Artists Unveil Art Donated to the Montreal Children's Hospital," CNW Telbec, October 6, 2008, accessed February 20, 2009, http://www.newswire.ca/en/releases/archive/October2008/06/c3030.html.
71. Alan Belkin, "An Interview with Rebecca Duchow" (2002), accessed February 20, 2009, http://www.musique.umontreal.ca/PERSONNEL/BELKIN/MD.html.
72. "Buffalo Yiddish," accessed February 10, 2009, http://yiddish.bfn.org/maza.html.
73. The site was nominated by Norma Baumel Joseph, Chairperson of the Archives Committee of the Canadian Jewish Congress, which generated a detailed report. See

Dianne Dodd, "Ida Maza (Massey) Salon," Submission Report no. 2007-36, Historical Sites and Monuments Board of Canada, 1–20.

74. Historic Sites and Monuments Board of Canada, Excerpts from the Minutes of December 2007, received by email from Marie-Claude Queenton, Communications Officer, Historic Sites and Monuments Board of Canada, Government of Canada, February 20, 2009.

75. Frieda Forman, Ethel Raicus, Sarah Silberstein Swartz, and Margie Wolf, eds., *Found Treasures: Stories by Yiddish Women Writers* (Toronto: Second Story Press, 1994).

76. This reading was developed in an email exchange with Kathryn Hellerstein, December 23, 2009.

77. See the introductory essay to Anna Margolin, *Drunk from the Bitter Truth: The Poems of Anna Margolin*, ed. and trans. Shirley Kumove (Albany: State University of New York Press, 2005).

# Rajzel Zychlinski's Poetical Trajectories in the Shadow of the Holocaust

ELVIRA GROEZINGER

> In the realm of poetry, four female writers deserve special mention: Miriam Ulinover, Kadia Molodowsky, Rokhl Korn, and Rajzel Zychlinski.
> —Emanuel Goldsmith, *Songs to a Moonstruck Lady*[1]

Unlike Kadya Molodowsky (1894–1975), Malka Heifetz Tussman (1893–1987), or Rokhl Korn (1898–1982),[2] Rajzel Zychlinski, born in the Polish town of Gąbin[3] in 1910 and an American resident from 1951, is still only marginally known.[4] And this is despite receiving the Reuben Ludwig Award from the Yiddish-American journal *Inzikh*[5] for the poem "Der novi un der regn" [The Prophet and the Rain][6] in 1937, after she caught the attention of the American poets in the circle around Yankev Glatshteyn, who was surprised that a young Jewish girl from a small Polish town wrote verses so closely affiliated with Yiddish poetry written in America.[7] Even the fact that in 1975, Zychlinski won the Itzik Manger prize, the most prestigious award in Yiddish literature, generated no significant response. And to date, only a limited circle of Yiddishists recognize her exceptional work.

The reason for Zychlinski's incomprehensible lack of fame may be traced to her life choices. She was not part of the mainstream of Yiddish poets, publishers, and influential people. She did not belong to a leftwing movement like

Dora Teitelboim (1914–1992); she was not religious like Miriam Ulinover (1890–1944); she did not join Jewish literary circles like Celia Dropkin (1887–1956); and she was not a Zionist like Malka Lee (1904–1976). Having no networks to support her career, she remained a lifelong loner and outsider. When Zychlinski died in Concord, California in 2001, she left an oeuvre of seven volumes of Yiddish poetry[8]; some of these poems have been translated into English, French, Hebrew, Polish, and German. Amazingly, she has not been recognized by leading American women scholars yet.

Zychlinski's poems reflect the Eastern European Jewish condition of the twentieth century, mirroring her own tragic destiny as a survivor of the Holocaust after her escape into the Soviet Union, as an émigré, and as an American resident with lifelong guilt about her mother, three siblings and their children who were all murdered in the destruction of her native town. The trajectories in her poetry document imposed rootlessness, turning her like so many other survivors paradoxically into new "wandering Jews," an anti–Jewish figure of the Ahasver.[9] Like the majority of the post–Holocaust Jewish writers, the shadows of the war never left her or her poetry. Even if the American reality had partially replaced nostalgic memories of childhood and the Polish nature, the melancholy, sadness, and permanent feeling of loneliness that emerged early in Zychlinski's works prevail. She has been called "the most authentic and original of the Yiddish female poets,"[10] and "a master of lyrical miniatures of unusual tranquility and deep feeling for the nature."[11] By now, Zychlinski, as the author of striking poems in free verse, with feminine traits, using vivid colors in the earlier, and more gloomy postwar years in a virtuoso manner, should be regarded by scholars and readers as an eminent representative of modern Yiddish literature, along with Avrom Sutzkever and other great American and European Jewish poets of the twentieth century, such as Paul Celan, Rose Auslaender, or Nelly Sachs, with similar personal experience. Indeed, Zychlinski's lyrical imagery has a particularly close affinity to the writings of Avrom Sutzkever and Paul Celan.

## The Motherland

Poland was Zychlinski's home country and Gąbin her native town, but given that her father emigrated to the United States several times during her childhood and youth, the family life revolved around the mother. Thus, the fatherland became a motherland; this had a profound influence on her poetry. Zychlinski wrote a number of poems about her mother, starting with the first volume of lyrics, *Lider*, published in Warsaw in 1936. Rajzel Zychlinski attended a Polish public school from 1916 to 1923 and was educated by private teachers afterwards, since there was no higher school for girls in Gąbin at that time. At home, Polish and Yiddish were spoken. She began to write a diary in Polish at the age of twelve and wrote her first Yiddish poem at the age of seventeen. The Yiddish language remained her poetical tool from then on.

Gąbin was a small town founded in the thirteenth century in which a considerable number of Jews lived for centuries despite repeated persecution and ostracism. Before 1939, Jews comprised about fifty percent of the population. The town was famous for cloth production. It is likely that Rajzel's father, Mordechai Zychlinski, a tanner, originated from the town of Żychlin, only twelve miles from Gąbin. He left the country for the United States three times, the last in 1924 in the company of his two older daughters who were probably from an earlier marriage; he died in Chicago in 1928. Rajzel's mother, the pious Dvoyre, stayed behind and took over the tannery. The rest of the family including Rajzel, her sister Khane, and three brothers, Yankev, Dovid, and Avrom, remained with the mother, who coming from a very learned rabbinical family, did not trust the morals in the strange country, and apart from that had waited for the father's financial success in the *goldene medine*, the promised land, when he finally would earn enough money to guarantee a good education for his children. Rajzel must have had some information about the American way of life, either from the literary works by Jewish immigrants or from their letters. As her father failed to find financial success during his lifetime, Rajzel's family never left Gąbin and so perished in the Holocaust when the Gąbin ghetto was liquidated in 1942. Its 3,030 Jewish inhabitants were deported to the death camps of Chełmno and Treblinka. Since Rajzel lived in Warsaw during the 1930s, she was able to save herself by fleeing from there to the Soviet Union, where she survived the war.

In 1928, when "her short, strikingly different beautiful poems," as the young poet Mates Olitzki (1915–2003?) commented, were printed for the first time in the Warsaw-based Yiddish newspaper *Folkstsaytung*, they were very well received.[12] Zychlinski became a topic of conversation in the literary circles in the Polish capital and was compared to the Jewish poet Else Lasker-Schüler of Berlin. Although deeply rooted in the *shtetl* culture, Zychlinski's miniature-like verses, with their echoes of Expressionism and Surrealism, as well as her readings of Charles Baudelaire, Rainer Maria Rilke, and many other European poets, struck readers as modernistic, avant-garde, and full of subtle humor. No wonder that *Lider*, published by the Yiddish PEN Club in Warsaw in 1936, included an introduction by Itzik Manger (1901–1969). Born in Czernowitz, Manger lived in Warsaw since 1929 and quickly gained fame in the

Jewish scene. Melech Ravitch, the Yiddish poet, essayist, playwright, and literary critic, became Zychlinski's friend and mentor.¹³ He exchanged letters with her in which he advised her to continue to educate herself, which would benefit her poetry.¹⁴ She followed his advice. Later he wrote about Zychlinski:

> I have once visited her in her native Gąbin. Gąbin is a very pretty and arborous shtetl in Poland, it belongs by the way to the places described by Sholem Asch. "Whoever wants to understand the poet should go to his provenience." And only in this ancient wooden house in which Rajzel Zychlinski passed her childhood and youth, did I began really to understand this poetess.¹⁵

Ravitch must have been won over by Zychlinski after he "more antagonistically, in 1927 ... published a vicious group review of books by women poets, whom he coyly refused to identify, attacking them as a homogenous group for not fulfilling his ideal role of women poets as the peacemakers and homebodies of Yiddish literature,"¹⁶ as Kathryn Hellerstein writes. Hellerstein also notes that Ravitch was not the only Jewish male critical of women poets. Another, Shmuel Niger, discerned in the women writers a "feminine disposition" and called their writings "a group poetry, a type of folklore of the female sex."¹⁷ Even Manger had written in the preface to Zychlinski's first book of poems that she was a prisoner of her idyllic home. Given her later homelessness, he may have been right.

Zychlinski's early lyrical subjects were closely connected to the young woman's life and dreams. The distance between the poetical self and the biographical figure is at times obliterated, while only the poetical images and the unspoken hint at her literary license. Zychlinski was reluctant to speak about her personal affairs, even with her biographer, Karina von Tippelskirch, and instead claimed that everything of importance could be found in her poetry. Thus, it is necessary to examine Zychlinski's life in order not to misinterpret her work. The experiences of her early childhood were connected with her parental situation. Her mother, becoming time and again an *agunah*, an undivorced woman whose husband lived far away from home for most of her life, provided a safe haven for the girl who grew up fatherless to show appreciation for other women's plights. Years later, Zychlinski reproached her father for having left them alone, indirectly blaming him for her mother's death in the Holocaust. This may be seen in the poem "Mayn tatns briv" [My Father's Letters], where she writes, "And if my mother was the best / the most beautiful, / why did he run three times to America?"¹⁸ Zychlinski did not write about her absent father in her early lyrical phase. However, later when living in America, she occasionally remembered him. For instance, in the poem "Mayn tatns marshn" [My Father's Marches], she writes, "the Negro parade on a street / suddenly reminded me of my father's long marches."[19] While she associated her father with the foreign and distant land, the mother represented the solid foundation of home, where she, as the Zychlinski poetically recalls, kept the household, did the washing, cleaned up, and pressed linen, often in the presence of a cat, an animal, which was frequently mentioned by Zychlinski in her poems. The cat, a symbol of coziness and warmth, kept her mother company, just as it did with the father during his brief presence at home.

As long as she lived in Poland, Zychlinski felt closely bound to the Polish culture. She had not yet experienced the postwar lack of empathy towards the Jewish survivors of the Holocaust and the deep anti–Semitism of the Christian population leading to pogroms. After the war, those shocked her and caused her to leave her homeland, which was no longer a motherland to her. Zychlinski's poems about her mother reveal this close bond between the intertwined images of home and motherland. The knowledge of folksongs implies a profound acquaintance with the given culture that was not self-evident in case of pre–World War II Polish Jews of whom the majority, especially of women, spoke Yiddish, and Polish, if at all, to a limited degree only. In this respect, Rajzel's mother was different. She sang the songs not only in *mame loshn*, but also in Polish, thus forming a bridge between the two cultures. Like most women in East European Jewish society, she sang the songs to her children while at home, so that the texts and melodies were traditionally passed on to the next generations. But since her siblings were murdered in the war, Zychlinski was the only one able to carry on her mother's cultural heritage. This is expressed in the poem "Mayn mame hot gezungen a poylish lid" [My Mother Sang Me a Polish Song]: "My mother sang me a Polish song: / in everyone's field the rye is greening, / but of my wheat there's not a sign."[20] The song about a love that faded and the longing of a neglected woman for her former lover matched the marital situation of Zychlinski's mother. Raising the children on her own and taking care of the tannery was very demanding for a woman in the prewar town, but she nevertheless seems to have managed very well. However, Zychlinski remembered her mother's overworked "big hands"[21] and "tired eyes."[22] She was grateful for the maternal care that was bestowed on her, and in "Mame" [Mother] writes, "You hear my hair thanking you."[23]

Zychlinski herself transferred this positive, comforting, and warming experience of maternal love received in her childhood to the children in the orphanage in Włocławek, where she worked for a while, and then to her own child who, for his part, gave her comfort and who was a good son. Although she and her husband separated, Zychlinski maintained a strong relationship with her son Marek Kanter, who later translated her poetry and preserves her legacy.

## *From the* Shtetl *to the World*

When Zychlinski left Gąbin at twenty-one years old to become the director of the orphanage in Włocławek, she was starting out as an independent, modern working woman in a bigger town, where the number of Jews was 10,209 or 18.3 percent of the population in 1931.[24] This urge for independence, anticipated in many of Zychlinski's early poems, seems not to have yet been fully satisfied in Włocławek. One of the autumn poems, written by her in Gąbin in 1933, again expresses the wish to "take over the reins"[25] of one's own life.

In Włocławek, she wrote two long poems called "Lider fun yesoymim-hoyz" [Songs from an Orphanage]. The poems realistically portray, almost in the style of the popular Polish nineteenth-century positivist authors like Bolesław Prus[26] or Eliza Orzeszkowa,[27] an orphan inmate, a little skinny girl with shadows under her eyes, called Tobshe. It seems that Tobshe's father, like Zychlinski's father, emigrated and left the family behind. After the mother's death, the child had to be put in the orphanage, seldom a luxurious place, and Zychlinski, identifying with the poor abandoned girl, asks rhetorically, "*Dos viflte vayb hot shoyn Tobshes tate / ergets in der velt?*" [What number wife does Toby's father have by now, / somewhere in the world?].[28] Zychlinski's resentment towards her absent father is evident in these lines.

Critics have noted that Zychlinski's poetry draws upon the Jewish humanist spirit,[29] in which compassion and pity for the suffering—even a dead bird—is a moral and religious imperative. This is especially so when the sufferer is Jewish, because then solidarity is the device, God's commandment, and a passive bystander is a sinner, as one Jew is always responsible for the other: *kol yisrael arevim ze la-ze*. Thus, helping others is a virtue, and Zychlinski, raised traditionally by her mother and a pained individual herself, complied with that commandment. Tobshe stands as *pars pro toto* for the orphaned and wronged children just as beggars, street people, old widows, or even homeless dogs stand in Zychlinski's poems for the wronged of the world. All these figures play an important role in her poetry throughout her life.

In 1936, Zychlinski moved to Warsaw, a goal for most Polish and many Jewish writers. She moved in autumn, a melancholic season, as reflected in her poems written at that time. Warsaw was considerably different from Gąbin, and she worked as a clerk in the bank, earning reasonably well. She spent a lot of her free time in the library and found like-minded people, poet-friends and supporters, though she never joined any particular political movement or any of the predominant literary groups, neither the introspective group *Inzikhists* who discovered her nor the expressionist group *Khalyastre* centered around her friend Ravitch. Nevertheless, this new free and independent existence had a price because it brought a sense of homelessness and longing for her home, for her sister Khane to whom Rajzel was close, and for her mother. She expresses those feelings in "S'iz geven" [It has Been], with these words: "Has there been such a summer day in my life / Yes, there has been one."[30] The reference is to a day spent with her mother.

Zychlinski's second volume of poetry, *Der regn zingt* [The Rain Sings], was published in Warsaw in 1939, in the series of the Library of the Yiddish PEN, shortly before the outbreak of World War II, during which most of the copies were destroyed. These poems are not only full of longing, but of deep sadness. They are, moreover, fearfully anticipatory, even prophetic, of the lurking danger. Zychlinski was not the only Polish intellectual who felt like that at the time, as the political situation in Poland especially for the Jews had been worrisome for a while already. The Polish Marshal József Piłsudski, who came to power after a coup d'état in 1926, had signed the German-Polish Non-Aggression Pact with Nazi Germany in 1934, and after his death one year later, the anti–Semitic Polish Right gained additional influence, thus increasing anti–Semitism in everyday life. Despite the agreement, the apprehension of the German menace grew in Poland in the late 1930s continually, especially after the German annexation of Sudetenland in autumn 1938, when Poland threatened to become Hitler's next target. In spring of 1939, Zychlinski must have also read the Bundists' published warnings about the possible outbreak of war, after Hitler unilaterally cancelled the treaty with Poland and tried to assert his territorial claims to the city of Danzig and a corridor through Polish territory, to which Poland refused to consent.

Hitler's plans for further expansion and his hatred of the Jews were no secret in Poland. Zychlinski was not a political poet, but she sensed the prevailing conditions when the German propaganda fueled anti–Polish resentments and spread rumors about alleged atrocities committed by Poles against the German population. One of Zychlinski's lyrics that seems particularly striking in this respect is "Der regn zingt" [The Rain Sings].[31] The poem refers to the legendary homunculus of the Renaissance, the clay figure of the *golem*, which was brought to life by magical practice and lived as long as the word "*emet*" that was put on his forehead by his creator remained complete, but which lost its life after the first letter of the word "truth," *emet*, the *aleph*, was obliterated and the rest made up the word "dead," *met*.[32] Here is the foreboding of an impending disaster that became a reality shortly after September 1, 1939.

The looming tragedy is also implied in another poem from this immediate prewar period, "Vegn vos hot gezungen der letster yidisher dikhter oyf shpanisher erd?" [What Did the Last Jewish Poet on Spanish Soil Sing About?].[33] Like the nineteenth century German-Jewish poet Heinrich Heine who wrote about Spanish Jewry, Zychlinski also refers, one hundred years later, to the expulsion of the Jews from Spain in 1492 by Isabella the Catholic and Ferdinand of Aragon. This catastrophe for the blooming Spanish-Jewish culture takes a prime place in the pre–Holocaust historiography of Jewish calamities, matched only by the Khmelnytsky massacres of 1648–1657 in Poland and the Ukraine. In her poem, Zychlinski again writes prophetically, although her verses are paired with skepticism of a modern Jewish woman who is thinking in historical categories after she has freed herself from the *shtetl* mentality. Zychlinski questions the naïve hope of Jews in the coming of Messiah who would redeem them and for the Yiddish reader who knows the tragic history of Jakob Frank in the eighteenth century.

The poems that Zychlinski wrote during the war were published in Łódź in 1948 in her first postwar volume *Tsu loytere bregn* [To Clear Shores], after she returned from the Soviet Union to Poland and before she left permanently. The volume includes "Varshe 1939" [Warsaw 1939], the only poem she ever wrote about the last days of prewar Warsaw. It documents the bombed city after its capitulation, brutal destruction, deconstruction of the ways of her world, and an order of things suddenly precipitated into ruin and chaos, shortly before the poet left the city in October 1939.[34] The poem notes that the old times when cats sat in the warm homes are gone; the homes are gone, the cats have been mutilated, and a new era has begun. It was time to get away and save one's own life.

## Behind the River Bug

On September 27, 1939, Warsaw capitulated and was occupied by the Germans who immediately started to persecute the Jewish population. The inhabitants tried to flee to the East, and Zychlinski, with the help and in the company of the writer Salomon Łastik,[35] succeeded in getting out of the city and out of the soon to be German-occupied Poland just in time, unlike her mother, her siblings and their children in Gąbin, situated approximately 100 km west of Warsaw, which became a trap for its Jewish inhabitants. The flight, this crucial experience in Zychlinski's life, saved and changed it decisively. The Soviet Union was in fact safer than Poland despite the effects of the Hitler-Stalin pact,[36] but it was not an absolute haven for Jewish refugees from Poland either. However, it offered a chance to survive for a while, until the Soviet Union became a trap, when Hitler attacked it on June 22, 1941. Zychlinski was lucky to survive this too with the help of the Soviet writer Hershel Polyanker who translated some of her poems so that she could become a privileged member of the Soviet Writers' Union, a *sovetskii pisatel*, a Soviet writer, thus becoming entitled to food ration coupons and recognized as a protected refugee. But the shadows of the Holocaust haunted her ever after, and she never got over it, as she expressed in "If I, Too," from her 1977 volume *Di November-zun* [The November Sun]. She asks, "If I, too, had been 'there'—/ where would the Germans have sent me?"[37]

In a brief curriculum vitae written in a letter to Karina von Tippelskirch on January 2, 1991, Zychlinski reduces her life to the following few details. The fateful escape from the German-occupied Warsaw to the Soviet Union in 1939 on which she dwells most, plays a prominent role:

> Born in Gombin, Poland, daughter of Mordechai and Debora Appel; sister Chana, brothers Jankew, David. My brother Abram lives in Paris. Attended a Polish public school from 1916–1923. There was not a high school in the small town Gombin. I together with another student had a private teacher after the ending of the public school from 1924–1927. Father was a leather worker. He went three time to the United States. His family stayed in Poland. He died in Chicago in 1928. Literary debut in the folkszeitung in 1927 or 1928, a daily Jewish newspaper in Warsaw. Melech Rawitch had there one column each week, under the name "letters to one and to all." Yiddish beginners sent there their poems—and Rawitch answered—to continue to write—or to "break all the pens in the house." I also sent a few poems and his answer in that paper was very encouraging. He was not the redactor. I don't know the name of the redactor. I conducted an orphanage one year, from 1934–1935. I didn't have a special education for the job, but the president of the orphanage in Włocławek read some of my poems in some magazines—and offered me the job. My first book of poems "Lieder" was published by the P.E.N. in Warsaw (The Yiddish pen Club) in 1936. Introduction by Itzik Manger. I was not a teacher in Warsaw. I worked as a clerk in a bank, until the outbreak of the war in 1939. About six weeks after the German army's invasion of the city, I was asked by S. Łastik, if I want to leave Warsaw with him, and two other people in a taxi, which would take us to the river Bug, which has been at this time the border between Poland and Russia. The prize for a place in the taxi was 400 Polish złoties, which was like today 400 dollars. I agreed to it, and was left with almost nothing. The next day we left Warsaw and the taxi brought us to the river. A man with a boat took us across the river, to the other side—and there were Russian soldats. That was not far from the city of Bialystock. And so I escaped from the gas chambers. I lived in Kazan—my son,

Marek Kanter, was born there, on February 15, 1943. He is teaching Math in Universities, included one year in the university of Tel-Aviv. My husband, Isaak Kanter, was a doctor, a psychiatrist, and worked in Russia there in a hospital. He died this year, 1990, in Brooklyn. After I graduated from a high School in New York, I studied in the City College English literature and biology. My name as a student was Rajzel Kanter. In the New School for Social Research, I studied literature and Philosophy.[38]

Behind the Russian border, Zychlinski lived for a couple of months in the Galician town of Lemberg, at the time a meeting place for many refugee writers and artists. From there, she continued to Kolomea, a *shtetl* in Eastern Galicia where her future parents-in-law lived. Isaak Kanter, whom she married in January 1941, also fled from Warsaw and served as a physician in the Red Army. She dedicated the prizewinning poem "Der novi un der regn," printed in her prewar second volume to him. In this poem, the drought comes to an end and the blessed rain comes down as the prayer of the prophet is heard by God. Zychlinski's traditional Jewish learning included the knowledge of the Torah. Although she was not strictly observant anymore, she was nevertheless a believer, putting her trust in God. This trustfulness was shaken to the core by what had followed, and later she argued with God, and reproached Him, just like the biblical Job or Sholom Aleykhem's *Tevye the Milkman*.

The poems, written during the nine years of exile and war, include for the first time the notification of time and place, while following her trajectories from Kolomea to Astrakhan, a petroleum center on the Volga River. During the years in the Soviet Union, the poet's style diverges from the prewar proximity with the avant-garde and moves towards Socialist Realism. The poem, written in Astrakhan in September 1941, is a particularly striking example of this transformation under the influence of the prevailing doctrine in the Stalinist Soviet Union after this official art form was institutionalized in 1934 and became mandatory for the Communist countries worldwide. Zychlinski, then at the mercy of the authorities in a host country and member of the Writers' Union, had no choice but to comply. As the Hungarian-Jewish Marxist philosopher Georg (György) Lukács phrased it, "It is impossible to work out the principles of socialist realism without taking into account the opposition between realism and modernism."[39] Zychlinski set aside the prewar expertise and adopted a new one, helping her to survive under the Stalinist dictatorship. But the traces of her proper penchant and talent shine through the ideological framework imposed on her when she occasionally smuggles in the colors, metaphors, imagery, and sensuality of her former works.

"Eyes" are one of the key words in her poetry, implying, as the case may be, good or bad moods, life or death. The mother had "heaven in her eyes" in the familiar atmosphere of the home, in the poems mourning her, she had "bloodied eyes"; the dead horse had no light in its eyes anymore, and the agile fishermen on the river have eyes as green as the color of life and nature around them, all images expressed the poem "Astrakhaner nekht" [The Nights of Astrakhan].[40]

Understandably Zychlinski, without having been a veteran Communist party member like some of the other refugees, regarded the Red Army in which her husband served at the time as a guarantor of security and a defender against a murderous enemy, and she felt gratitude towards it. When it became a target of German bombing during the offensive on Stalingrad, and after the German army approached in the summer of 1942, Zychlinski could not stay in Astrakhan, and she moved to Kasan, the capital of the Soviet Tatar Republic, where her son was born. There, she wrote "Di partizanke" [The Partisan] about a hanged young partisan girl, Tanya, with a compassion she felt earlier about *di shvindzikhtike poylishe shikses* [the tubercular Polish girls] who "died young in her village." But the decisive cesura in Zychlinski's life and writing came about when she heard, or probably read about in the Yiddish newspaper *Der emes* [The Truth], which printed the information transmitted by refugees from the German-occupied territories of the extermination of the Jewish population of Gąbin, including her own family. Then she began, helpless and desperate, to be haunted by the feelings of guilt and remorse for having forsaken them and to write poetry mourning the murdered people. One of these poems, written in 1943, is called "Fun a volkn" [From a Cloud], indicating a backsliding from Socialist Realism and a turning back towards introspectiveness and subjectivism. Zychlinski reproached herself for having abandoned her mother in time of her biggest need, just as her father had done, for which she rejected him.[41] This feeling never left her.

Several scholars have addressed that point. For example, in "Memory and Testimony of Women Survivors of the Nazi Genocide," Sara R. Horowitz writes that "[r]eflecting on the aftermath of Nazi atrocity, women frequently evoked the murdered mother whose absence concretizes their vast sense of loss."[42] In *Gender and Destiny: Women Writers and the Holocaust*, one of the earliest studies of the impact of concentration camps and ghettos on the writing of the female survivors, Marlene E. Heinemann discusses that because of women's physiques it was even more difficult for them to survive than for men.[43] Zychlinski's flight from one Soviet city to another was hard enough, presaging that her mother and sister must have suffered immensely before they died, and this intensified her feelings of guilt all the more.

Although Zychlinski was lucky to give birth to a healthy boy, and her son was a promise of a happier future, she was unable to seal him off from the trauma that weighed so heavily on her. Psychoanalysts are aware of the transmission of traumas by the victims of the Holocaust to the second or even the third generation; Zychlinski transferred her gloom to the world outside her. To her, the otherwise beautiful month of May is desolate, and the lyrical self finds, other than in the prewar time, no consolation in or from nature anymore. Zychlinski's poems written in Kasan belong to the earliest elegies for the annihilated Jewish world in Poland. She is working within the tradition of *kinnot*, the elegies or lamentations, Jewish religious dirges. These are traditionally sung on the ninth day of the month Av, commemorating the destruction of the two holy Temples in Jerusalem and the beginning of the Jewish suffering in the diaspora, including all the tragic events in the Jewish history, starting with the Book of Lamentations to the Crusades and then the Holocaust. Professional mourning women sing them for the dead. Zychlinski's first postwar volume of poetry, *Tsu loytere bregn* [To Clear Shores], includes the elegy "Vayt, vayt iz dos shtetl" [Far, Far Away is the Shtetl], written in Kasan in 1943.[44] The word "snow" as found in the poem is another code often used by the poet. The word has both positive and negative connotations with the winter season, turning from blanketing coziness when being watched from a warm home to the menacing cold if someone or an animal is homeless and finally to stillness of death, overspreading and hiding the traces of crime (blood). Zychlinski's use of the code "snow" is similar to Paul Celan's, whose mother had also been murdered in the Ukraine—the snowy Ukraine, as he poetically described it.

With the German army in full retreat, Zychlinski moved from Kasan to Mariupol in East Ukraine, where she lived to see the capitulation of Nazi Germany. It was the happy moment of liberation that was bestowed on her, as she felt it, by the "Red Star" under Stalin's leadership. On May 9, on the day of Russian victory, she wrote "Der tost" [The Toast], again with strong elements of Socialist Realism. It is evident that political poetry was not Zychlinski's forte. At that point, she could not have known that the death toll of World War II might have reached sixty million, including approximately six million Jews and thirty million citizens of the Soviet Union. Zychlinski felt that she, who was able to have kept her own little son near her, was more fortunate than many other mothers who were waiting in vain for their sons to come home from the front, but she also always kept in mind that her own individual survival was overshadowed by her dead loved ones. As the war came to an end, it was time for her to end the wanderings and return home to Poland, her motherland.

## At the Jewish Cemetery

The erstwhile trusted land of the mother, however, had in the meantime turned into a land where the mother was dead and a wicked stepmother ruled. In 1945, the surviving Jews began to return to Poland. On July 4, 1946, in the Polish town of Kielce, there was a pogrom against the Jewish community. The mob consisting of normal citizens and officials killed around forty Jews, including women and children, all of them survivors of the Holocaust, following an accusation of alleged blood libel, just as in the Middle Ages. This was not the only one,[45] but was the bloodiest outbreak of violence in postwar Poland and shocked the Jewish community at home and abroad. It put an end to the illusion that Poland could again become a home for the Jewish repatriates and a mass emigration of panicked Polish Jews followed. Among the approximate forty thousand Jews who decided once more to flee, besides Zychlinski with family, were the Yiddish writers Rokhl Korn, Nokhem Bomze, Khayim Grade, Avrom Sutzkever, and others. Sutzkever, who founded the Yiddish literary journal *Di goldene keyt* [The Golden Chain] in Tel Aviv in 1949, later published a number of Zychlinski's poems.

The postwar Poland, the site of Auschwitz and other Nazi camps, had become a Jewish cemetery for the repatriates, with only traces of the life of three and a half million Polish Jews. In 1947, the well-known Polish-Jewish poet Antoni Słonimski, wrote the "Elegy for the Jewish Villages," which was set to music by the Polish-Jewish composer Shimon Laks (1901–1983), a survivor from Auschwitz. The poet sums up the situation with these words: "Gone now are those little towns where the wind joined / Biblical songs with Polish tunes and Slavic rue."[46] There is almost nothing left of the pre-war life.

The volume *Tsu loytere bregn* is dedicated to "The blessed memory of my mother Dvoyre, my sister Khane, my brothers Yankev and Dovid, and their children, my mother's grandchildren—victims of Chełmno and Treblinka." In the preface, Zychlinski writes:

> 1939, shortly before the war, my second book of poems was published, *Der regn zingt*. A bloody stream had washed away my book, my readers, and uprooted my home. My home—my first poetical vision—has been erased like all our homes. Emptiness, endless emptiness. Almost ten years later I come back. In this book I shall not speak only about the destruction, not only about wandering and exile, but also show a glimmer of hope, which I have brought along from the hospitable Russian soil and which is rising at the shores of the promised land.[47]

When Zychlinski came back to the "promised land," Poland, the glimmer of hope could not fan into a fire. She first lived in a displaced persons camp in Lower Silesia, the ex–German territory, now called the "Regained Territories," where the majority of the Jewish repatriates had been settled by the Polish authorities after the German population had been expelled. Zychlinski was aware of what is called ethnic cleansing today, but she did not feel pity for the deported Germans, regarded by her as enemies and murderers, who lived well while Jews were exterminated, as described in her poem of 1946, "Do hobn daytshn gelebt..." [Here Germans Have Lived...]. From Silesia, Zychlinski's family moved to Łódź, a prewar home to 230,000 Jews and afterwards to approximately 30,000.[48] Her husband worked in a neurological hospital there. The survivors tried to reorganize their lives after the city was liberated in January 1945, and for a while, Jewish political parties, organizations, and cultural activities were active. Zychlinski's book *Tsu loytere bregn* was also printed there in 1948. By 1950, though, half of the Jewish inhabitants of Łódź had left the country.

Reading Holocaust poetry is thus like reading from the ashes.[49] Survivors like Zychlinski attempted to live a life after the survival,[50] more dead than alive themselves, identifying with the murdered victims, as proclaimed in "Mir lebn vayter" [We Go on Living].[51] The poem is written with a feeling of despair, not proud and defiant like the famous Yiddish song "Mir lebn eybik" [We Live Eternally] by the poet Leyb Rosenthal (1916–1944) for the revue *Moyshe halt zikh* in the Vilna Ghetto in 1943, which became an anthem of the Jewish fighters in this and other ghettos. Rosenthal himself was shot, but his song lives as a historical document of the Jewish spirit of resistance. By contrast, Zychlinski's poem is full of resignation; she is alive but never able to be joyous again. Although she is full of love for her son who needs her, she cannot be casual and carefree anymore. This is reminiscent of the refrain in "Death Fugue" by Paul Celan: "Black milk of daybreak we drink it at nightfall / we drink it at noon in the morning we drink it at night / drink it and drink it we are digging a grave in the sky it is ample to lie there [...]." Additionally, Celan writes, "this Death is *ein Meister aus Deutschland* [a master from Germany], his eye it is blue."[52] In Zychlinski's poem, death is omnipresent. Green trees turn to white, the color of death. The Jewish eyes are not blue; they are dark, the color of sadness and mourning.

Zychlinski's poem "Mayne yidishe oygn" [My Jewish Eyes], written in Łódź after her return to Poland in 1947, corroborates this feeling of inconsolable mournfulness and inner numbness.[53] The "curse" in the poem implies the imagined but deeply felt guiltiness towards the victims and is an allusion to the figure of the wandering Jew, having to bear life eternally, although it often seems unbearable.

In the aftermath of the Holocaust, Jewish intellectuals had to re-direct themselves. The German-Jewish philosopher Theodor W. Adorno (1903–1969), who emigrated to the United States in 1938 and worked at the Institute for Social Research, claimed after his return to Germany in 1949 in the essay "Kulturkritik und Gesellschaft," published in 1951, that "writing poetry after Auschwitz is barbaric." This dictum was very controversial, and Adorno later modified it several times, among others in his *Negative Dialektik*, recognizing the fact that "Perennial suffering has as much right to expression as a tortured man has to scream." Zychlinski did scream, silently but unmistakably, and unceasingly, and finding no consolation, she now dissociated herself from God. She did not become an atheist, but lost her traditional faith like many other Jews in the Holocaust, not being able to grasp how God could have allowed such crimes towards His chosen people and had left them alone at the mercy of the merciless. Zychlinski's most famous poem written at this time, "Got hot bahaltn zayn ponem" [God Hid His Face], an elegy, with elaborate stylistic means of refrain-like repetitions, which have an insistent effect on the reader, is also one of the most unequivocal poems in the post–Holocaust literature. The poem starts with the lines, "All the roads lead to death, / all the roads."[54] She deliberately uses the litany, a traditional form of prayer, which is on one hand a lamentation in view of God's absence, but on the other a shocking indictment of what the poet experiences as betrayal on His part for having forsaken the martyred. In a world full of sorrow from which God is absent, in which even the mountains have remained silent while the Jewish inhabitants in their midst were murdered, is a world in which gravestones prevail, and where humans are petrified, too, as in Zychlinski's poem "In mitn der velt" [In the Middle of the World] written in Silesia upon her return. Hoping in vain to find some surviving relatives, she soon traveled to Gąbin, where she wrote the long elegiac poem "Lider fun mayn heym" [Songs from My Home], (Gombin, October 1946), dedicated to "The 3030 holy victims in my home village, Gombin, who died in the gas chambers of Chełmno, in Poland, in April 1942."[55] It is a cry, angry and at the same time desperate. Not only was also the beloved familiar nature indifferent to the suffering of the innocent Jewish victims, but so were the Polish neighbors, who it seems have stolen all the usable parts of the house. As indicated in the bitterly sarcastic poem "Tayere shkheynim" [Dear Neighbors], Zychlinski tried to get rid of this house before she departed, fled, from Gąbin forever in 1948. She writes, "Buy, buy dear neighbors, / buy this piece of earth. / Cheap!"[56] Not only the shocking visits to Gąbin and the pogrom of Kielce, but numerous unpleasant experiences made the family ready for emigration from Poland. In 1948, they departed for Paris, as Zychlinski's only surviving brother Avrom was living there.

## In a Strange Land

For the next three years, before they were permitted to enter the United States, their final destination, in 1951, the Kanters lived in Paris. Isaak Kanter's medical diploma was not recognized in France. He had no work permit, and the family was supported by Jewish organizations. Paris, normally a place of longing for Polish citizens, was a disappointing way station for Jewish moneyless Holocaust survivors. Zychlinski, feeling humiliated by the insecure and dependent situation, was compassionate as ever, and even identified with the prostitutes in the Parisian streets, as she writes in her 1951 poem "Shteyn azoy mayne shvester?" [Are Those My Sisters Standing There?].[57] This poem echoes the popular Yiddish song "Dray shvester" by Morris Winchevsky, which is about three impoverished Jewish sisters who live in the English city of Leicester; one of whom "trades in herself." America, where Zychlinski's father searched for luck in the past, became the place she headed for with her family, "Tsu vayte hafns" [To Distant Harbors].[58] Although Zychlinski was not able to shed her emotional burden and had to carry it with her overseas where it would always accompany her, in the sight of the Statue of Liberty, her material situation was about to get incomparably better. In 1937, as a winner of the Reuben Ludwig Award from the American *Inzikhistn*, Zychlinski was warmly welcomed by Yiddish writers in New York. While her husband had to complete medical courses in order to validate his diploma and work as a psychiatrist, Zychlinski was employed in a tie factory and pursued her own education in a strange country, in a new language. With admirable energy, she graduated from high school and later from the City College of New York, where she took classes in biology and English literature. Finally she attended classes at the famous New School for Social Research in New York. This school, founded in 1919 by pacifist progressive thinkers, functioned as a university in exile from 1933 and as a haven for the refugee intellectuals from Europe under the Nazi threat. No wonder that Zychlinski who went there for classes in literature and philosophy considered this period among open minded people as the happiest in her life. But it was not completely happy either. In the 1950s, she and her husband separated, and her son was raised by his father. Following that, under her maiden name, Zychlinski published four books of poetry: *Shvaygndike tirn* [The Silent Doors] in 1962; *Harbstike skvern* [Autumn Squares] in 1969; *Di november-zun* [The November Sun] in 1977; and *Naye lider* [New Poems] in 1993. In 1975, she was awarded the Itzik Manger prize in Israel, thus attaining a place in the Yiddish literary word. After she "had been driven away from so many homes," as she complained in "Fun vifl heymen," Zychlinski hoped that the United States would become her new and permanent home, as she expressed in "In der heym" [At Home].[59] But unfortunately, Zychlinski was unable to feel at home anywhere. She was a stranger since she left her home in Gąbin and felt *in der fremd*, a stranger everywhere, like she had felt in Warsaw in 1938, when she prophetically wrote, "In a strange land, I pray / to a strange God."[60] Now, living in a strange country, alienated from most layers of the society, and writing in a language on the margins, the poet could not have felt completely *heymish* there either. Moreover, her mental situation remained as unstable as ever, and her frequent mentions of sleepless nights in the poems indicate insomnia, one of the symptoms of depression. She moved frequently from one apartment to another and regularly strolled through the streets of New York City.

Compassionate as she was, Zychlinski must have condemned social injustice and racial discrimination towards the black people who were visible in the streets. Although her poems do not transmit an explicit political message, she wrote sympathetically about them in these poems: "A neger iz ayngeshlofn" [A Negro Fell Asleep], "Groye negers" [Gray Negroes], and "Kh'vil zayn a negerin" [I Want to be a Negro Woman]. In the same spirit, she wrote about other matters and people who were intriguing and apparently appealing, such as the poor Jews from the Delancey Street on the Lower East Side and "the homeless people" on the Bowery. At that time, the Bowery was a slum and gang area, with "flop houses" for the homeless, mostly alcoholics, who were called the "Bowery bums." These were the years when the racist Ku Klux Klan fought against the human rights movement and desegregation through terror and murders, and when, in 1955, Rosa Parks from Montgomery, Alabama, refused to obey a bus driver who ordered her to make room for a white passenger.

These incidents could not have left Zychlinski indifferent. When she arrived, the United States was not a peaceful country in which she, an immigrant from Eastern Europe now behind the Iron Curtain, could relax. The Korean War was fought from 1950 to 1953, and the Cold War and the McCarthy era were burdensome. In a climate of mass hysteria, thousands of Americans and European immigrants, including actors such as Charlie Chaplin, writers such as Bertolt Brecht, and scientists such as J. Robert Oppenheimer, were accused of sympathizing with Communism and investigated. As Zychlinski and her husband had lived in the Soviet Union and were associated with the Red Army, they must have been under special surveillance, although there is nothing about it in Zychlinski's poems. This shows that she was very discrete about her previous life and anxious not to arouse any suspicion, but she must have lived in permanent fear. Natural phenomena, before the earthquakes later made her panicky, also appeared menacing to her, like the eclipse of the moon in 1964. In the same-titled poem, the shadow is like "God's sword" and the moon is "wrapped in the smoke / of burning Jews."[61] This God is not absent, but cruel, menacing, and not merciful anymore, and the poet is left alone at the mercy of her associations and the ghosts of the past, with nothing and nobody to reassure her.

Another frequent motif in Zychlinski's poetry is loneliness and mortality, her own and that of others. And as she grew older, she wrote about the loneliness of elderly women and men. The expressionistic poem "Oyfn taymsskver" [On Times Square] reminds one at first glance of the inter-war poetry, full of energy and élan-vital, and of the Polish-Jewish Julian Tuwim and many of his contemporaries, with whom Zychlinski was acquainted. In it, she conveys her feeling of being at lost in modern times. The poem starts like this: "All the clocks in Times Square / ring the message of death."[62] While the Vietnam War is mentioned in the poem, there are no allusions to the upheavals caused by student revolts, hippies, and other events or social phenomena of the late twentieth century. The poet seems to be detached from these things, wrapped or enshrouded in the "fog" that she dragged with her in the above mentioned "sacks" from overseas. The lyrical self is evoked again in the same-titled miniature poem "Neplen" [Fog]: "Fog within me, / fog around me, / there is no longer a road— / the city is a cloud, / the lamps are dim, / I can hardly see."[63] The only indication of permanent tension under which Zychlinski lived is that she was fearful and easily startled. Life in the big city was full of dangers of all sorts daunting her, and the poet tended to lock herself more and more in her internal microcosm, excluding the global macrocosm from her poetry, like in "Gey ikh farbay" [When I Pass].[64] In the poem, Zychlinski makes a reference to Raskolnikov, the protagonist of Dostoyevsky's *Crime and Punishment* who murdered a pawnbroker. Extremely impoverished and hungry himself, Raskolnikov wanted to use the money he hoped to find for a good cause. Raskolnikov's poverty and illogical good intentions may be the cause for his gradually growing madness. In the poem, Zychlinski sense of justice is ambiguous. Open questions remain: does she sympathize with Raskolnikov who is perhaps lurking for the rich landlord? Does she condemn and fear him, at the same feeling guilty herself? Or does she refer to her own possible borderline personality disorder? Although Holocaust-related poems became rare in Zychlinski's later poetry, her unvoiced incessant feeling of guilt as a survivor plays an important role—even if it is only implicit, just like in the poem about banal objects such as vacuum cleaners. Indeed, the poem "Der shtoybsoyger" [The Vacuum Cleaner] is one more example of the seemingly irrational anguishes tormenting Zychlinski in her everyday life, with similar ambiguity. She writes that like the vacuum cleaner "I will suck you in too."[65] The ordinary objects, however, are very disturbing. In "A vekzeyger klingt" [An Alarm Clock Rings], they take unexpected turns and reach disturbing dimensions. For example, Zychlinski writes that the ringing of the clock "will awaken the dead!"[66] Other than in the suburbs, where in her view, life was calmer and more pleasant, the city that today would have "no-go areas" had streets that, in the poet's view, were not safe. She warns about that in the poem "Yene gas" [The Street] with an apocalyptic vision like in *The Plague* by Alfred Camus: "Don't go to live on that street! / The rats are more numerous there / than people."[67]

Zychlinski's resorting to the modernistic, expressionistic, even surrealistic elements of her earlier lyrics is apparent in many of her New York poems. The angle from which the lyrical self-glances at the world is one of a critically observing outsider, but lacking the attitude of a *flâneur*. Her dilemma of being haunted by shadows from the past, doomed to restlessness, and urged to roam, is articulated in the poem "Farbaygeyer" [Passerby], dated 1961.[68] The city was definitely not comforting to her and not home like Gąbin, so she moved restlessly to Florida, California, and Canada. However, she regarded the United States as her home. In a letter to von Tippelskirch, written on October 1991, the poet wrote, "About Exil [sic]: I don't feel that I live here being exiled from Poland. I never intended to return there, and I never will. I live here already half of my life and here is my home."[69] But actually, since her native home in the old world was shattered, the rest of the world remained out of joint forever. She never managed to completely restore the lost order inside or outside of her. Then a heavy earthquake occurred on October 17, 1989 in Northern California, destroying buildings and killing and wounding many people. Zychlinski panicked again and fled back to New York. The reaction shows that she was very thin-skinned, and at the same time, she had an astoundingly strong will to survive. Like the flight from the burning city of Warsaw in 1939, now, exactly fifty years later, it is a similar escape from what the poet perceives as a lethal danger, fearing the repetition of an inferno, as had hit San Francisco in 1906. She described this natural disaster in a poem printed in her last volume, *Naye lider*, called "Di erd-ziternish in yor 1989" [The Earthquake of 1989]: "The walls of my home shook / and I with them."[70] "Di erd-ziternish in yor 1989" also refers to the poem "October," which Zychlinski wrote in Gąbin in 1930, a pre-deluge piece of poetry, when dreams were still promising, ripe and not withered yet. In that poem, she writes, "In October people speak /

softly. / The water is heavier, / the pitcher—larger. / The old tree / drinks up its shadow. / The well draws us into its depths, / me and you—ripe dream."⁷¹

Seven short stories by Zychlinski are included the 1977 volume *Di November-zun*; these are her only works of prose. Loneliness appears as a prevalent theme in the stories too. "The Old Woman and the Sea," "Without a Crown," "Through the Backdoor," and "The Empty House" are about old age and loneliness. "The Orphan" is about the loneliness of orphans and of immigrants. "The Woman from Union Square" is about poverty, loneliness, and madness. "Someone Came" is a reminiscence of the immediate postwar Stalinist life in the impoverished Ukraine.

Twenty years after the publication of *Di November-zun*, when old age and loneliness began to considerably bother her, Zychlinski decided to move from Brooklyn to California, where her son lived. There, the homeless wanderer found a last shelter in Concord, near Berkeley. Once more Zychlinski could compare herself with the figures of her poems. For instance in "Di akhtzikyorike" [The Eighty-Year-Old Woman], she writes that "The spring sun / doesn't like an eighty-year-old woman—/ it wrinkles on her face."⁷² Zychlinski had come a long way. People of her age generally lived in old-age homes. She expressed her feelings about that in "Dos hoyz fun di alte" [The Old-Age Home], when she writes that grief is "deeply hidden amid the bricks."⁷³

## Epilogue

Rajzel Zychlinski died on June 13, 2001. According to her request, her ashes were spread over the sea on July 27, which would her been her ninety-first birthday.⁷⁴ Thus, she remained as homeless in her death as in her life. Her long and difficult journey of life could be summed up by the poem she wrote as early as 1937 in Warsaw, "Fun ale vegn, or vayl" [Of All the Ways]: "Of all the ways, / I have chosen / my way— / Let me rest here."⁷⁵

## Notes

1. Barnett Zumoff, *Songs to a Moonstruck Lady: Women in Yiddish Poetry* (Toronto: TSAR Publication in association with the Dora Teitelboim Center for Yiddish Culture, 2005), xiii.
2. The details concerning these dates of birth vary. According to Carol Cosman, Joan Keefe, and Kathleen Weaver, *The Penguin Book of Women Poets* (Harmondsworth: Penguin, 1978), Kadya Molodowsky was born in 1893 and Malka Heifetz Tussman in 1896, whereas according to Sorrel Kerbel, Muriel Emanuel, and Laura Phillips, *Jewish Writers of the Twentieth Century* (New York: Fitzroy Dearborn, 2003), Tussman's birth date was given as 1893 with a question mark and Molodowsky's as 1894. Some of the discrepancies may be due to differences between the Jewish and the Christian calendars.

3. In Yiddish, Gombin.

4. Karina von Tippelskirch published the first and so far the only monograph on Rajzel Zychlinski, *Also das Alphabet vergessen? Die jiddische Dichterin Rajzel Zychlinski*, Ph.D. diss. (Marburg: Tectum, 2000). This monograph is the basis of the quoted biographical details about the poet whose name is written in different ways. In the YIVO system of transliteration, it would be Rayzel Zhikhlinski. In Polish, it is Rajzla Żychlińska; she called herself Rajzel Zychlinska, but usually her name is spelled Rajzel Zychlinski, and I follow that latter spelling.

5. The *Inzikh* journal was founded in 1920 by the Jewish American Modernists introspective poets Yankev Glatshteyn and Aaron Glanz-Leyeles. Celia Dropkin became affiliated with the introspective poets in 1922. The group also influenced Yiddish poets outside the United States.

6. *"Der novi un der regn"* is a modernist poem with biblical references that Zychlinski dedicated to her husband, I. Kanter.

7. Yankev Glatshteyn, "Rajzel Zychlinski," in *In tokh genumen: eseyen* (New York: Matones, 1956), 335–341. Quoted in von Tippelskirch, *Also das Alphabet vergessen?*, 39.

8. The volumes are *Lider* (Warsaw, 1936); *Der regn zingt* (Warsaw, 1939); *Tsu loytere bregn* (Lodz, 1948); *Shvaygndike tirn* (New York, 1962); *Harbstike skvern* (New York, 1969); *Di november-zun* (Paris, 1977); and *Naye lider* (Tel Aviv, 1993).

9. The thirteenth-century legend is about a Jew who was doomed to roam the earth until the end of the days for having taunted Jesus on his way to Golgotha. It is a curse to live eternally without the solace of death, and this tragic destiny inspired writers in many countries, of whom many dissociated with the anti–Semitic origin and connotation of the legend.

10. Zumoff, *Songs to a Moonstruck Lady*, xiv.

11. Zew Szeps, *Antologia poezji żydowskiej: (1868–1968)* (Londyn: Oficyna poetów i malarzy, 1980), 303.

12. Nathan Cohen, "Olitski Brothers," in *YIVO Encyclopedia of Jews in Eastern Europe*, accessed November 26, 2011, http://www.yivoencyclopedia.org/article.aspx/Olitski_Brothers. Mates Olitski's first poems were published in *Literarishe bleter* in 1935.

13. Pseudonym of Zekharye-Khone Bergner (1893–1976). In 1921, Melech Ravitch settled in Warsaw, where for a brief and intense period of time he became very close to Perets Markish and Uri Tsvi Grinberg and founded the poet group known as *Di khalyastre* [The Gang]. Between 1924 and 1934, Ravitch served as executive secretary of the *Fareyn fun yidishe literatn un zhurnalistn in varshe* [Association of Jewish Writers and Journalists in Warsaw], the central address for Yiddish literature in Poland and one of the symbols of secular Yiddish culture in general. Along with Israel Joshua Singer, Perets Markish, and Nakhmen Mayzel, Ravitch was a cofounder of the main literary journal in interwar Poland, *Literarishe bleter*, which he also coedited from 1924 to 1926. Later, he edited the literature page of the Bundist daily *Folks-tsaytung*, using his position to encourage young Yiddish writers and writing numerous reviews of Yiddish books. See Abraham Novershtern, "Ravitch, Melech," in *YIVO Encyclopedia of Jews in Eastern Europe*, accessed November 26, 2011, http://www.yivoencyclopedia.org/article.aspx/Ravitch_Melech.

14. Nathan Cohen, *Books, Writers and Newspapers: The Jewish Cultural Center in Warsaw, 1918–1942* (Jerusalem: The Hebrew University Magnes Press, 2003), 219, footnote 22.

15. Von Tippelskirch, *Also das Alphabet vergessen?*, 29. All translations are mine unless noted otherwise.

16. Kathryn Hellerstein, "From 'ikh' to 'zikh': A Journey from 'I' to 'Self' in Yiddish Poems by Women," in *Gender and Text in Modern Hebrew and Yiddish Literature*, ed. Naomi B. Sokoloff, Anne Lapidus Lerner, and Anita Norich (Cambridge: Harvard University Press, 1992), 116.

17. Ibid. Kathryn Hellerstein also points out that "Melekh Ravitsh referred regretfully to the sudden silence of Fradl Shtok, the poet from Galicia, whom he accused of being more woman than poet in his review of the anonymous women poets in 1927." See Kathryn Hellerstein, "Canon and Gender: Women Poets in Two Modern Yiddish Anthologies," in *Women of the Word: Jewish Women and Jewish Writing*, ed. Judith R. Baskin (Detroit: Wayne State University Press, 1994), 151, note 24.

18. Rajzel Zychlinsky and Emanuel S. Goldsmith, *God Hid His Face: Selected Poems of Rajzel Zychlinsky*, trans. from the Yiddish by Barnett Zumoff, Aaron Kramer, Marek Kanter, and others (Santa Rosa, CA: Word & Quill Press, 1997), 18.

19. Ibid., 126.

20. Ibid., 69; and Zumoff, *Songs to a Moonstruck Lady*, 34.

21. "Dos alte lid" [The Old Song—The Cat Is Washing Herself] written in 1935 appears in Zychlinsky, *God Hid His Face*, 196.

22. "My Mother's Shoes," Zychlinsky, *God Hid His Face*, 85; and translation by Marc Kaminsky in *Voices Within the Ark: The Modern Jewish Poets*, ed. Howard Schwartz and Anthony Rudolf (New York: Avon, 1980), 375.

23. Zychlinsky, *God Hid His Face*, 177.

24. Marcin Wodziński, "Włocławek," in *YIVO Encyclopedia of Jews in Eastern Europe*, accessed November 26, 2011, http://www.yivoencyclopedia.org/article.aspx/Włocławek.

25. Rajzel Zychlinsky, *Die lider 1928–1991. Die Gedichte Jiddisch und deutsch*. Edited and translated by Hubert Witt (Frankfurt am Main: Zweitausendeins, 2003), 110; von Tippelskirch, *Also das Alphabet vergessen?*, 25.

26. Pen name of Aleksander Głowacki (1847–1912) who supported charitable institutions for the benefit of children and the poor.

27. The writer, 1841–1910, nominated in 1905 for the Nobel Prize, criticized the bad social conditions at the time in her occupied homeland.

28. Zychlinsky, *God Hid His Face*, 200.

29. Shloyme Bikl, "Rajzel Zychlinski," in *Shrayber fun mayn dor*, volume 2 (Tel Aviv: Farlag Y. L. Peretz, 1965), 136.

30. Dated Warsaw 1937, this poem appears in Rajzel Zychlinski, *Der regn zingt* (Warsaw: Bibliotek fun yidishn P.E.N. klub, 1939), 34.

31. Dated Gąbin 1937, this poem appears in Zychlinski, *Der regn zing*, 14; it is reprinted in Rajzel Zychlinski, *Shvaygndike tirn* (Nyu york: Yidishn PEN klub, 1962), 147.

32. This is the most popular version of Rabbi Loew's golem legend.

33. Zychlinsky, *God Hid His Face*, 54. This poem is also called "Ibn Dagan of Andalusia." The translation is a free adaptation. I therefore chose to translate it more literally myself.

34. Ibid., 53.

35. Łastik survived in Kazakhstan, returned to Poland after in 1949, and together with the poet Arnold Słucki, co-edited and annotated an anthology of Jewish poetry that was published posthumously many years later as *Antologia poezji żydowskiej* (Warszawa: Państwowy Instytut Wydawniczy, 1983), with six poems by Rajzel Żychlinski. Łastik died in 1968, the year Słucki was forced to emigrate. Słucki died in 1972.

36. Polish history with the tragedy of Katyń is closely connected to this treaty, also

called the Molotov-Ribbentrop Pact, officially titled the Treaty of Non-Aggression between Germany and the Soviet Union and was signed in Moscow a week before Hitler's invasion of Poland and the beginning of World War II on September 1, 1939. On September 17, the annexation of Eastern territories of Poland, among others in Lithuania, White Russia, and Ukraine (North Bukovina) by the Soviet Union followed. Hitler's invasion of the Soviet Union in June 1941 put an end to the treaty. See Marek Gałęzowski, Adam Dziurok, Łukasz Kamiński, and Filip Musiał, *Od niepodległości do niepodległości. Historia Polski 1918–1989*, 2nd revised ed. (Warszawa: Instytut Pamięci Narodowej, 2011).

37. Zychlinsky, *God Hid His Face*, 46.

38. Von Tippelskirch, *Also das Alphabet vergessen?*, 14–15. The style and orthography are as quoted there.

39. Georg Lukács, "Critical Realism and Socialist Realism," in *The Meaning of Contemporary Realism* (London: Merlin Press, 1963). The historical insights in these writers' works and the methods they used to achieve these insights are vital to an understanding of the forces shaping the present and the future. They may help us to understand the struggle between the forces of progress and reaction, life and decay, in the modern world. To ignore all this is to throw away a most important weapon in our fight against the decadent literature of antirealism (http://ecmd.nju.edu.cn/UploadFile/17/8075/socrealism.doc [1.12.11]).

40. Rajzel Zychlinski, *Tsu loytere bregn* (Łódź: Farlag Yidish-bukh, 1948), 32.

41. Zychlinsky, *God Hid His Face*, 25. Reprinted as "My Mother Looks at Me."

42. Baskin, *Women of the Word*, 278.

43. See Marlene E. Heinemann, *Gender and Destiny: Women Writers and the Holocaust* (New York: Greenwood Press, 1986).

44. Zychlinski, *Tsu loytere bregn*, 15; also reprinted in Zychlinski, *Shvaygndike tirn*, 131.

45. The public anti–Jewish excesses were usually enticed by the spread of false blood libel accusations against Jews, nourished by both the Catholic Church and politically motivated perpetrators in many Polish villages and towns, among these Kraków, Kielce, Bytom, Białystok, Bielawa, Częstochowa, Legnica, Otwock, Rzeszów, Sosnowiec, Szczecin, and Tarnów, totaling to 327 murders between 1945 and 1946. Cf. inter alia Bożena Szaynok, "The Role of Antisemitism in Postwar Polish-Jewish Relations," in *Antisemitism and Its Opponents in Modern Poland*, ed. Robert Blobaum (Ithaca: Cornell University Press, 2005).

46. My translation. Cf. Antoni Słonimski, *Wybór poezji* (Warszawa: Czytelnik, 1983), 84.

47. My translation. Cf. von Tippelskirch, *Also das Alphabet vergessen?*, 80.

48. See Shimon Redlich, *Life in Transit: Jews in Postwar, Lodz 1945–1950* (Brighton, Massachusetts: Academic Studies Press, 2010).

49. This term was coined by the Polish writer Jerzy Ficowski (1924–2006) in his anthology of Holocaust poems *Odczytanie popiołów*, first published in 1980 in the Polish underground press.

50. Cf. title of a 1982 documentary film by the German-Jewish journalist and director Erwin Leiser (Berlin 1923–Zurich 1996).

51. Zychlinsky, *God Hid His Face*, 13. This poem is also included in Zychlinski, *Shvaygndike tirn*. It is one of Rajzel's few poems that rhymes.

52. The Jewish poet Paul Celan (Antschel) from Czernovitz (1920–Paris 1970) wrote in German. He survived, but his parents who were deported in 1942 did not. Celan,

who never got over this loss, suffered from depression and committed suicide by jumping into the Seine. This translation is by John Felstiner. See http://mason.gmu.edu/~lsmith g/deathfugue.html (November 23, 2011).

53. Zychlinski, *Tsu loytere bregn*, 5.
54. Zychlinsky, *God Hid His Face*, 7.
55. Ibid., 39–41. Published under the title "I Want to Walk Here Once More."
56. Also titled "A shtikl erd," in Zychlinski, *Tsu loytere bregn*, 21. Reprinted in Zychlinski, *Shvaygndike tirn*, 119.
57. From Zychlinski, *Svaygndike tirn*. Also in *God Hid His Face*, 179.
58. Zychlinsky, *God Hid His Face*, 213.
59. Ibid., 60.
60. Ibid., 182.
61. Ibid., 24.
62. Ibid., 98.
63. Ibid., 136. In the Yiddish original, the poem has the rhyme scheme: aabccd, and it is not a "cloud" but "*vate*" [cotton wool], which rhymes with "*mate*" [dim].
64. Ibid., 109.
65. Ibid., 135.
66. Ibid., 134.
67. Ibid., 168.
68. Ibid., 164.
69. Von Tippelskirch, *Also das Alphabet vergessen?*, 22. Spelling as in the original.
70. Zychlinsky, *God Hid His Face*, 26. The thirty one poems in this volume were all published by Avrom Sutzkever in *Di goldene keyt*. Whereas Zychlinsky's first volume was called *Lider*, her last title *Naye lider* indicates that her work has come full circle, not merely because she returned to the memories of her childhood and her mother. She stopped writing poems after that and wrote to von Tippelskirch in a letter of February 12, 1993: "I don't write any more poems. Enough is enough" as quoted in von Tippelskirch, *Also das Alphabet vergessen?*, 280.
71. Zychlinsky, *God Hid His Face*, 67.
72. Ibid., 197.
73. Ibid., 145.
74. Karina von Tippelskirch, "Rajzel Zychlinski," in *Jewish Women: A Comprehensive Historical Encyclopedia*, 1 March 2009, *Jewish Women's Archive*, accessed December 1, 2011, http://jwa.org/encyclopedia/article/zychlinski-rajzel.
75. Zychlinsky, *God Hid His Face*, 66.

# Bibliography

Aaron, Frieda W. *Bearing the Unbearable: Yiddish and Polish Poetry in the Ghettos and Concentration Camps*. Albany: State University of New York Press, 1990.
Adelson, Alan, Robert Lapides, and Marek Web. *Lodz Ghetto: Inside a Community Under Siege*. New York: Viking, 1989.
Adler, Ruth. *Women of the Shtetl—Through the Eyes of Y. L. Peretz*. Cranbury, NJ: Associated University Presses, 1980.
Akhmatova, Anna, and D. M. Thomas. *Anna Akhmatova: Selected Poems*. New York: Penguin Classics, 1995.
Atwood, Margaret. "An End to Audience?" *Second Words: Selected Critical Prose*. Boston: Beacon Press, 1982.
Bark, Sandra. *Beautiful as the Moon, Radiant as the Stars: Jewish Women in Yiddish Stories: An Anthology*. New York: Warner Books, 2003.
Baskin, Judith R. *Jewish Women in Historical Perspective*. Detroit: Wayne State University Press, 1991.
Baskin, Judith R. *Women of the Word: Jewish Women and Jewish Writing*. Detroit: Wayne State University Press, 1994.
Bassin, Morris. *500 yor yidishe poezye*. Volume 2. Nyu york: Dos bukh, 1917.
Baumel, Judith Tydor. "'Can Two Walk Together If They Do Not Agree?': Reflections on Holocaust Studies and Gender Studies." *Women: A Cultural Review* 13:2 (2002): 195–206.
Baumel, Judith Tydor. *Double Jeopardy: Gender and the Holocaust*. London: Vallentine Mitchell, 1998.
Baumgarten, Jean, and Jerold C. Frakes. *Introduction to Old Yiddish Literature*. Oxford: Oxford University Press, 2005.
Bellow, Saul. *Great Jewish Short Stories*. New York: Dell, 1963.
Bergelson, Dovid. *Nokh alemen*. Vilna: Kletzkin, 1913.
Beyder, Chaim. *Этюды о еврейских писателях*. Kiev: Izdat of "Spirit i litera," 2003.
Beyder, Chaim, and Gennedy Estraikh. *Leksikon fun yidishe shrayber in ratn-farband*. Nyu york: Alyeltlekhn yidishn kultur-kongres, 2011.
Biale, Rachel. *Women and Jewish Law: The Essential Texts, Their History, & Their Relevance for Today*. New York: Schocken Books, 1984.
Bikl, Shloyme. "Rajzel Zychlinski." In *Shrayber fun mayn dor*. Vol. 2. Tel Aviv: Farlag Y. L. Peretz, 1965.
Binyamin, H. "Tsili shel Gnesin." *Siman kria* 12–13 (February 1981): 240–241.
Bloch, Anna. *Poezye fun a litvisher meydl in afrike*. Johannesburg, 1921.
Brenner, Naomi. "Slippery Selves: Rachel Bluvstein and Anna Margolin in Poetry and in

Public." *Nashim: A Journal of Jewish Women's Studies & Gender Studies* 19 (2010): 100–133.
Brinkman, Bartholomew. "Making Modern Poetry: Format, Genre and the Invention of Imagism(e)." *Journal of Modern Language* 32:2 (2009): 20–40.
Burstin, Hinde Ena. "Culture, Meaning and Translation." In *Voices and Spaces: Indigenous and Multicultural Writers in Dialogue*, edited by Jennifer Martiniello, 94–98. Canberra: Kennarre Arts, 2006.
Burstin, Hinde Ena. "Female Fantasies from the Other Side of the Wall: Twentieth Century Lesbo-Sensuous Yiddish Poetry." In *Jews and Sex*, edited by Nathan Abrams, 38–51. Nottingham: Five Leaves, 2008.
Burstin, Hinde Ena. "Finding My *Vey*: Dilemmas of a Feminist Yiddishist Translator." *Bridges: A Jewish Feminist Journal* 14:2 (Autumn 2009): 44–55.
Caiserman-Wital, H. M. *Yidishe dikhter in kanade*. Montreal: Farlag nyuansn, 1934.
Calder, Angus, and Lizbeth Goodman. "Gender and Poetry." In *Literature and Gender*, edited by Lizbeth Goodman, 41–70. London: Routledge in Association with the Open University, 1996.
Chametzky, Jules. *Jewish American Literature: A Norton Anthology*. New York: Norton, 2001.
Chapman, Abraham. *Jewish-American Literature: An Anthology of Fiction, Poetry, Autobiography, and Criticism*. New York: New American Library, 1974.
Cohen, Nathan. *Books, Writers and Newspapers: The Jewish Cultural Center in Varshe, 1918–1942*. Jerusalem: Hebrew University Magnes Press, 2003.
Cohen, Nathan. "The Yiddish Press and Yiddish Literature: A Fertile but Complex Relationship." *Modern Judaism* 28:2 (2008):149–172.
Comini, Alessandra. *The Fantastic Art of Vienna*. New York: Knopf, 1978.
Cooper, Adrienne. "Making Music with Anna Margolin: Creating 'Shake My Heart Like a Copper Bell': A Poet, a Composer, an Interpreter—Three Lives in Yiddish Art." *Bridges: A Jewish Feminist Journal* 15: 2 (Autumn 2010): 39–49.
Cooper, Shari. "Between Two Worlds: The Works of J. I. Segal." In *An Everyday Miracle: Yiddish in Montreal*, edited by Ira Robinson, Pierre Anctil, and Mervin Butovsky, 115–128. Montreal: Véhicule Press, 1990.
Cosman, Carol, Joan Keefe, and Kathleen Weaver. *The Penguin Book of Women Poets*. Harmondsworth: Penguin, 1978.
Costantino, Manuela, and Susanna Egan. "Reverse Migrations and Imagined Communities." *Prose Studies* 26, no. 1–2 (2003): 96–111.
David, Anthony. *The Patron: A Life of Salman Schocken, 1877–1959*. New York: Metropolitan Books, 2003.
Davids, Leo. "Yiddish in Canada: Picture and Prospects." In *The Jews in Canada*, edited by Robert J. Brym, William Shaffir, and Morton Weinfeld, 153–166. Toronto: Oxford University Press, 1993.
Dobroszycki, Lucjan. *The Chronicle of the Łódź Ghetto, 1941–1944*. New Haven: Yale University Press, 1984.
Dobrushin, Yekhezkl. "Undz Tsushteyer [vegn Khane Levins lider-buch]." *Di royte velt* 11–12 (1929): 181–189.
Dropkin, Celia. *In heysn vint*. Nyu york: [J. Dropkin], 1959.
Dropkin, Celia. *In heysn vint: lider*. Nyu york: Tsilye Drapkin, 1935.
Dropkin, Celia. *The Acrobat: The Selected Poems of Celia Dropkin*. Translated from the Yiddish by Faith Jones, Jennifer Kronovet, and Samuel Solomon. Huntington Beach, CA: Tebot Bach, 2014.
Even-Zohar, Itamar. "Polysystem Theory." *Poetics Today* 1 (1979): 287–310.
Even-Zohar, Itamar. "The Position of Translated Literature Within the Literary Polysystem." In *Literature and Translation: New Perspectives in Literary Studies,* edited by James Holmes, Jose Lambert, and Raymond van den Broeck, 117–127. Leuven: ACCO, 1978.

Faygenberg, Rokhl. *A pinkes fun a toyter shtot: khurbn-dubova.* Varshe: Farlag gezelshaft, 1927.
Faygenberg, Rokhl. *Strange Ways.* Jerusalem: Gefen, 2007.
Fein, Richard J., and Seth L. Wolitz. *With Everything We've Got: A Personal Anthology of Yiddish Poetry.* New York: Host Publications, 2008.
Feinstein, Margarete Myers. "Absent Fathers, Present Mothers: Images of Parenthood in Holocaust Survivor Narratives." *Nashim: A Journal of Jewish Women's Studies* 13:1 (2007): 155–182.
Fishman, David. *The Rise of Modern Yiddish Culture.* Pittsburgh: University of Pittsburgh Press, 2005.
Forman, Frieda, and Sam Blatt. *The Exile Book of Yiddish Women Writers.* Holstein, Ontario: Exile Editions, 2013.
Forman, Frieda, Ethel Raicus, Sarah Silberstein Swartz, and Margie Wolf. *Found Treasures: Stories by Yiddish Women Writers.* Toronto: Second Story Press, 1994.
Frank, Helena. *Yiddish Tales.* Philadelphia: Jewish Publication Society of America, 1912.
Frieden, Ken. *Classic Yiddish Fiction: Abramovitsh, Sholem Aleichem, and Peretz.* Albany: State University of New York Press, 1995.
Friedman, Jonathan C. *Speaking the Unspeakable: Essays on Sexuality, Gender, and Holocaust Survivor Memory.* Lanham, MD: University Press of America, 2002.
Fuerstenberg, Adam G. "Faithful to a Dream: The Proletarian Tradition in Canadian Yiddish Poetry." *Yiddish* 6:1 (1985): 84–96.
Fuerstenberg, Adam G. "From Yiddish to 'Yiddishkeit': A. M. Klein, J. I. Segal and Montreal's Yiddish Culture." *Journal of Canadian Studies* 19:2 (1984): 66–81.
Fuerstenberg, Adam G. "Transplanting Roots: J. I. Segal's Canadian Perspective." *Yiddish* 4:3 (1981): 63–76.
Fuks, Chaim Leib. *Hundert yor yidishe un hebreyishe literatur in kanade.* Monṭreal: H. L. Fuḳs bukh fond ḳomiṭeṭ, 1980.
Gałęzowski, Marek, Adam Dziurok, Łukasz Kamiński, and Filip Musiał. *Od niepodległości do niepodległości. Historia Polski 1918–1989,* 2d rev. ed. Warszawa: Instytut Pamięci Narodowej, 2011.
Garai, Jana. *The Book of Symbols.* New York: Simon & Schuster, 1973.
Garland, Tony W. "Brothers in Paradox: Swinburne, Baudelaire, and the Paradox of Sin." *Victorian Poetry* 47:4 (Winter 2009): 633–645.
Gennady, Estraikh. *In Harness: Yiddish Writers' Romance with Communism.* Syracuse: Syracuse University Press, 2005.
Gennady, Estraikh. "The Kharkiv Yiddish Literary World, 1920s–mid-1930s." *East European Jewish Affairs* 32, no. 2 (2002): 70–88.
Gennady, Estraikh. *Yiddish in the Cold War.* London: Legenda, 2008.
Ginzburg, Shaul M., and Pesach S. Marek. *Еврейскія народныя пѣсни въ Россіи.* Saint Petersburg: Voskhod, 1901.
Glaser, Amelia, David Weintraub, and Dana Craft. *Proletpen: America's Rebel Yiddish Poets.* Madison: University of Wisconsin Press, 2005.
Glasser-Andrews, Ida [Edith]. *In halb-shotn.* Nyu york: Kultur, 1922.
Glatshteyn, Yankev. *In tokh genumen: eseyen.* Nyu york: Matoneś, 1956.
Glatshteyn, Yankev. *Oyf greyṭe ṭemes.* Tel-Aviv: Farlag Y. L. Peretz, 1967.
Glatstein, Jacob, Israel Knox, and Samuel Margoshes. *Anthology of Holocaust Literature.* Philadelphia: Jewish Publication Society of America, 1969.
Glenn, Susan A. *Daughters of the Shtetl: Life and Labor in the Immigrant Generation.* Ithaca: Cornell University Press, 1990.
Glueckel. *The Memoirs of Glückel of Hameln.* Translated by Marvin Lowenthal. New York: Schocken Books, 1977.
Gluzman, Michael. "The Exclusion of Women from Hebrew Literary History." *Prooftexts* 11: 3 (September 1991): 259–278.

Goldberg, Isaac. *Great Yiddish Poetry*. Girard, KS: Haldeman-Julius, 1923.
Goldberg, Isaac. *Yiddish Short Stories*. Girard, KS: Haldeman-Julius, 1923.
Goldsmith, Emanuel S., and Barnett Zumoff. *Yiddish Literature in America, 1870–2000*. Jersey City: KTAV, 2009.
Goodman, Henry. *The New Country: Stories from the Yiddish About Life in America*. New York: YKUF, 1961.
Gorshman, Shira. *Bli marah: siporim, rishomin, zikronot*. Hebrew translation of *On a gal*. Tel Aviv: Ḥalunot, 2003.
Gorshman, Shira. *Ikh hob lib arumforn*. Moskva: Sovetskii Pisateli, 1981.
Gorshman, Shira. *In di shpurn fun gdud ha-avodah*. Tel Aviv: Yisroel-bukh, 1998.
Gorshman, Shira. *Khanes shof un rinder*. Tel Aviv: Yisroel-bukh, 1995.
Gorshman, Shira. *Der koyekh fun lebn*. Moskva: Der emes, 1948.
Gorshman, Shira. *Lebn un likht*. Moskva: Sovetskii Pisateli, 1974.
Gorshman, Shira. *On a gal*. Tel Aviv: Yisroel-bukh, 1996.
Gorshman, Shira. *Oysdoyer*. Tel-Aviv: Farlag Y. L. Peretz, 1992.
Gorshman, Shira. *33 noveln*. Warsaw: Yidish bukh, 1961.
Gorshman, Shira. *Tret'e pokolenie: novelly i rasskazy*. Russian translation of *33 noveln*. Moskva: Sovetskii Pisateli, 1963.
Gorshman, Shira. *Vi tsum ershtn mol*. Tel Aviv: Yisroel-bukh, 1995.
Gorshman, Shira. *Yontef in mitn vokh*. Moskva: Sovetskii Pisateli, 1984.
Gorshman, Shira. *Zhizn' i svet: rasskazy, povest.'* Russian translation of *Lebn un likht*. Moskva: Sovetskii Pisateli, 1979.
Great Books Foundation. *The Soul of the Text: An Anthology of Jewish Literature*. Chicago: Great Books Foundation, 2000.
Greenberg, Eliezer, and Irving Howe. *A Treasury of Yiddish Poetry*. New York: Schocken Books, 1974.
Grin, Ber. "Yidishe dikhterins." *Yidishe kultur* (December 1973): 31.
Grupińska, Anka. *Najtrudniej jest spotkać Lilit*. Kraków: Wydawn Austeria, 2008.
Gutman, Rosa. *Far gor dem noenstn: lider*. Berlin: Farlag Renesans, 1925.
Hadda, Janet. "The Eyes Have It: Celia Dropkin's Love Poetry." In *Gender and Text in Modern Hebrew and Yiddish Literature*, edited by Naomi B. Sokoloff, Anne Lapidus Lerner, and Anita Norich, 93–112. New York: Jewish Theological Seminary of America, 1992.
Hadda, Janet. *Isaac Bashevis Singer: A Life*. New York: Oxford University Press, 1997.
Halpern, Ben, and Jehuda Reinharz. *Zionism and the Creation of a New Society*. New York: Oxford University Press, 1998.
Harkavy, Alexander. *Yiddish-English-Hebrew Dictionary*. Reprint of the 1928 expanded 2d ed. New York: YIVO Institute for Jewish Research and Schocken Books, 1988.
Harshav, Benjamin. *The Meaning of Yiddish*. Berkeley: University of California Press, 1990.
Harshav, Benjamin, and Barbara Harshav. *American Yiddish Poetry: A Bilingual Anthology*. Berkeley: University of California Press, 1986.
Harshav, Benjamin, and Barbara Harshav. *American Yiddish Poetry: A Bilingual Anthology*. Stanford: Stanford University Press, 2007.
Heinemann, Marlene E. *Gender and Destiny: Women Writers and the Holocaust*. New York: Greenwood Press, 1986.
Hellerstein, Kathryn. "Canon and Gender: Women Poets in Two Modern Yiddish Anthologies." In *Women of the Word: Jewish Women and Jewish Writing*, edited by Judith R. Baskin, 136–152. Detroit: Wayne State University Press, 1994.
Hellerstein, Kathryn. "From 'ikh' to 'zikh': A Journey from 'I' to 'Self' in Yiddish Poems by Women." In *Gender and Text in Modern Hebrew and Yiddish Literature*, edited by Naomi B. Sokoloff, Anne Lapidus Lerner, and Anita Norich, 113–143. New York: Jewish Theological Seminary of America, 1992.

Hellerstein, Kathryn. "In Exile in the Mother Tongue." In *Borders, Boundaries, and Frames*, edited by Mae Henderson, 64–106. New York: Routledge, 1994.
Hellerstein, Kathryn. "Gender and the Anthological Tradition in Modern Yiddish Poetry." In *The Anthology in Jewish Literature*, edited by David Stern, 259–280. New York: Oxford University Press, 2004.
Hellerstein, Kathryn. "The Metamorphosis of the Matriarchs in Modern Yiddish Poetry." In *Yiddish Language and Culture Then & Now*, edited by Leonard Jay Greenspoon, 201–23. Omaha: Creighton University Press, 1998.
Hellerstein, Kathryn. "A Question of Tradition: Women Poets in Yiddish." In *Handbook of American Jewish Literature: An Analytical Guide to Topics, Themes, and Sources*, edited by Lewis Fried, Gene Brown, Jules Chametzky, and Louis Harap, 195–237. New York: Greenwood Press, 1988.
Hellerstein, Kathryn. *A Question of Tradition: Women Poets in Yiddish (1586–1987)*. Stanford: Stanford University Press, 2014.
Hellerstein, Kathryn. "Translating as a Feminist: Reconceiving Anna Margolin." *Prooftexts* 20: 1 & 2 (Winter/Spring 2000): 191–208.
Hellerstein, Kathryn. "A Yiddish Poet's Response to the Khurbm: Kadya Molodowsky in America." In *Freedom and Responsibility: Exploring the Dilemmas of Jewish Continuity*, edited by Rela M. Geffen and Marsha B. Edelman, 243–260. Hoboken: Gratz College and KTAV Publishing House, 1998.
Herodotus. *The Histories*. Edited and translated by Robin Waterfield. Oxford: Oxford University Press, 1997.
Hershfeld, Pesi. *Koraln*. Shikago: Yidishn froyen kunst-klub, 1926.
Hoffman, Leah K. *In kinder-land*. Nyu york: Kultur, 1921.
Horowitz, Sara R. "Gender and Holocaust Representation." In *Teaching the Representation of the Holocaust*, edited by Marianne Hirsch and Irene Kacandes, 110–122. New York: Modern Language Association, 2004.
Horowitz, Sara R. "Gender, Genocide and Jewish Memory." *Prooftexts* 20 1 & 2 (2000): 158–190.
Horowitz, Sara R. "Memory and Testimony of Women Survivors of Nazi Genocide." In *Women of the Word: Jewish Women and Jewish Writing*, edited by Judith R. Baskin, 258–282. Detroit: Wayne State University Press, 1994.
Horowitz, Sara R. "Mengele, the Gynecologist, and Other Stories of Women's Survival." In *Judaism Since Gender*, edited by Miriam Peskowitz and Laura Levitt, 200–212. New York: Routledge, 1997.
Howe, Irving. *Jewish-American Stories*. New York: New American Library, 1977.
Howe, Irving, and Eliezer Greenberg. *Ashes Out of Hope: Fiction by Soviet-Yiddish Writers*. New York: Schocken Books, 1977.
Howe, Irving, and Eliezer Greenberg. *A Treasury of Yiddish Poetry*. New York: Holt, Rinehart and Winston, 1969.
Howe, Irving, and Eliezer Greenberg. *A Treasury of Yiddish Stories*. New York: Viking Press, 1954.
Howe, Irving, and Eliezer Greenberg. *Voices from the Yiddish: Essays, Memoirs, Diaries*. Ann Arbor: University of Michigan Press, 1972.
Howe, Irving, Ruth R. Wisse, and Khone Shmeruk. *The Penguin Book of Modern Yiddish Verse*. New York: Viking, 1987.
Howe, Irving, Ruth R. Wisse, and Khone Shmeruk. *The Penguin Book of Yiddish Verse*. New York: Penguin, 1988.
Hulme, T. E. *Speculations: Essays on Humanism and the Philosophy of Art*. Edited by Herbert Read. New York: Routledge, 2014.
Hutcheon, Linda. *A Poetics of Postmodernism: History, Theory, Fiction*. New York: Routledge, 1988.

Hutcheon, Linda. *The Canadian Postmodern: A Study of Contemporary English-Canadian Fiction.* Oxford: Oxford University Press, 1998.

Hyman, Paula E. "Discovering Puah Rakovsky." *Nashim: A Journal of Jewish Women's Studies and Gender Issues* 7 (2004): 97–115.

Hyman, Paula E. "Gender and the Immigrant Jewish Experience in the United States." In *Jewish Women in Historical Perspective*, edited by Judith R. Baskin, 312–336. Detroit: Wayne State University Press, 1991.

Jones, Faith. "Criticizing Women." *Bridges: A Jewish Feminist Journal* 13: 1 (2008): 76–81.

Jones, Faith. "Esther Kreitman: Renewed Recognition of Her Writing." *Canadian Jewish Outlook* 38:2 (March/April 2000): 17–18.

Joseph, Norma Baumel. "Jewish Women in Canada: An Evolving Role." In *From Immigration to Integration: The Canadian Jewish Experience—A Millennium Edition*, edited by Ruth Klein and Frank Dimont, 182–195. Toronto: Institute for International Affairs of B'nai Brith Canada, 2001.

Kagan, Berl. *Leksikon fun yidishe shraybers.* Nyu york: Ra'aya Elman-Cohen, 1986.

Kalechofsky, Robert, and Roberta Kalechofsky. *The Global Anthology of Jewish Women Writers.* Marblehead, MA: Micah Publications, 1990.

Kalter, Bella Briansky. "Ida Maza (A Memoir)." *Canadian Jewish Studies* 6 (1998): 55–63.

Kaminska, Ida. *My Life, My Theater.* Edited and translated by Curt Leviant. New York: Macmillan, 1973.

Kants, Shimen. *Ring nokh ring.* Tel Aviv: Yidisher kultur gezelshaft, 1990.

Katz, Dovid. "The Days of Proletpen in American Yiddish Poetry." In *Proletpen: America's Rebel Yiddish Poets*, edited by Amelia Glaser and David Weintraub, 3–25. Madison: University of Wisconsin Press, 2005.

Kaye/Kantrowitz, Melanie, and Irena Klepfisz. *The Tribe of Dina: A Jewish Women's Anthology.* Montpelier, VT: Sinister Wisdom, 1986.

Kaye/Kantrowitz, Melanie, Irena Klepfisz, and Esther F. Hyneman. *The Tribe of Dina: A Jewish Women's Anthology.* Rev. and ex. ed. Boston: Beacon Press, 1989.

Keel, Othmar, and Bolesław Mrozewicz. *Pieśń nad Pieśniami: biblijna pieśń o miłości.* Poznań: Zysk i S-ka, 1997.

Kerbel, Sorrel, Muriel Emanuel, and Laura Phillips. *Jewish Writers of the Twentieth Century.* New York: Fitzroy Dearborn, 2003.

Klepfisz, Irena. "*Di mames, dos loshn*/The Mothers, the Language: Feminism, Yidishkayt, and the Politics of Memory." *Bridges* 4:1 (Winter-Summer 1994/5754): 12–47.

Klepfisz, Irena. "Queens of Contradiction: A Feminist Introduction to Yiddish Women Writers." In *Found Treasures: Stories by Yiddish Women Writers*, edited by Frieda Forman, Ethel Raicus, Sarah Silberstein Swartz, and Margie Wolfe, 21–62. Toronto: Second Story Press, 1994.

Klevan, Andrew. *Disclosure of the Everyday: Undramatic Achievement in Narrative Film.* Trowbridge, Wiltshire: Flicks Books, 2000.

Kolodny, Annette. "Some Notes on Defining a 'Feminist Literary Criticism.'" *Critical Inquiry* (Autumn 1975): 75–92.

Kope, Rivke. *Intim mitn bukh: mekhabrim, bikher, meynungen.* Paris: Drukeray Edison Poliglot, 1973.

Korman, Ezra. *Yidishe dikhterins: antologye.* Shikago: L. M. Shṭayn, 1928.

Korn, Rokhl. *Dorf.* Vilna: Kletskin farlag, 1928.

Korn, Rokhl. *Fun yener zayṭ lid.* Tel Aviv: Farlag Y. L. Peretz, 1962.

Korn, Rachel, and Seymour Levitan. *Paper Roses: Selected Poems of Rachel Korn.* Toronto: Aya Press, 1985.

Kramer, Aaron, and Saul Lishinsky. *The Last Lullaby: Poetry from the Holocaust.* Syracuse: Syracuse University Press, 1998.

Krant, Miriam. *Geflekhṭ fun tsyaygn: eseyen un lider.* Monṭreal: [o. fg.], 1995.

Kreitman, Esther. *Brilyantn*. London: W. & G. Foyle, 1944.
Kreitman, Esther. *Deborah*. New York: Feminist Press at the City University of New York, 2004.
Kreitman, Esther. *Diamonds*. London: David Paul, 2010.
Kreitman, Esther. *Der sheydim-tants [Danse macabre]*. Warše: Farlag Bzšoza, 1936.
Kreitman, Esther. *Yikhes*. London: Narod Press, 1949.
Kreitman, Esther, and Maurice Carr. *Deborah*. London: Virago, 1946.
Kumove, Shirley. "Drunk from the Bitter Truth: The Life, Times and Poetry of Anna Margolin." In *From Memory to Transformation: Jewish Women's Voices*, edited by Sarah Silberstein Swartz and Margie Wolfe, 35–48. Toronto: Second Story Press, 1998.
Landau, Zishe. *Antologye: di yidishe dikhtung in amerike biz yor 1919*. Nyu york: Farlag yidish, 1919.
Lapidus, Rina. *Jewish Women Writers in the Soviet Union*. New York: Routledge, 2012.
Lefevere, Andre. *Rewriting, Manipulation of Literary Fame*. London: Routledge, 1992.
Leftwich, Joseph. *An Anthology of Modern Yiddish Literature*. The Hague: Mouton, 1974.
Leftwich, Joseph. *The Golden Peacock: An Anthology of Yiddish Poetry*. Cambridge, MA: Sciart, 1939.
Leftwich, Joseph. *The Golden Peacock: An Anthology of Yiddish Poetry Translated into English Verse*. London: R. Anscombe, 1944.
Leftwich, Joseph. *The Golden Peacock: A Worldwide Treasury of Yiddish Poetry*. New York: Thomas Yoseloff, 1961.
Leftwich, Joseph. *Great Yiddish Writers of the Twentieth Century*. Northvale, NJ: J. Aronson, 1969.
Legutko, Agnieszka. "Cyrkowa dama– poezja Celii Dropkin czytana z perspektywy genderowej." In *Nieme dusze?: Kobiety w kulturze* jidysz, edited by Joanna Lisek, 207–242. Wrocław: Wudawnictwo Uniwersytetu Wrocławskiego, 2010.
Lempel, Blume. *Balade fun a kholem*. Tel Aviv: Farlag I. L. Peretz, 1981.
Lempel, Blume. "The Fate of the Yiddish Writer." *Yidishe kultur* 48 (November-December 1986).
Lempel, Blume. "Pastorale." *Di tsukunft* 95:4 (Nov./Dec. 1990).
Lempel, Blume. *Rege fun emes*. Tel Aviv: Farlag yisroel-bukh, 1986.
Lempel, Blume. "Widowhood." *Di tsukunft* 93:1–2 (Jan./Feb. 1987).
Lerner, Eve. "Making and Breaking Bread in Jewish Montreal, 1920–1940." M.A. Thesis, Concordia University, 2002.
Levi, Primo. *Survival in Auschwitz and the Reawakening: Two Memoirs*. Translated by Stuart Woolf. New York: Summit Books, 1985.
Levin, Khane. *Eygns*. Kiev: Melukhe-farlag, 1941.
Levin, Khane. *Tsushteyer*. Ukraine: Melukhe-farlag fun Ukraine, 1929.
Levitan, Seymour. "Canadian Yiddish Writers." In *Identifications: Ethnicity and the Writer in Canada*, edited by Jars Balan, 116–134. Edmonton: Canadian Institute of Ukrainian Studies, University of Alberta, 1982.
Lifshits, Yeḥezkel, and Mordechai Altshuler. *Briv fun yidishe soveṭishe shraybers*. Jerusalem: Hebrew University, 1979.
Liptzin, Sol. *A History of Yiddish Literature*. New York: Jonathan David, 1972.
Lisek, Joanna. "Jidisze mame—ciało i mit." *Tsvishn* 3 (2010): 4–11.
Lisek, Joanna. *Jung Wilne—żydowska grupa artystyczna*. Wrocław: Wydawnictwo Uniwersytetu Wrocławskiego, 2005.
Lisek, Joanna. "Peruka, chodaki i jedwab. Poetyckie sukienki w jidyszowej szafie." *RitaBaum* 17 (2011): 18–23.
Lukács, György. *The Meaning of Contemporary Realism*. London: Merlin Press, 1963.
Lurye, Noyekh. "Der koyekh fun lebn." *Heymland* 6 (1948): 137.
Machcewicz, Piotr. "Antisemitism in Poland in 1956." *Polin* 9 (1990): 170–183.

Mann, Barbara. "Picturing the Poetry of Anna Margolin." *MLQ: Modern Language Quarterly* 63:4 (2002): 501–536.
Margolin, Anna, and Shirley Kumove. *Drunk from the Bitter Truth: The Poems of Anna Margolin*. Albany: State University of New York Press, 2005.
Margolis, Rebecca. "Les écrivains yiddish de Montréal et leur ville." In *Juifs et Canadiens français dans la société québécoise*, edited by Pierre Anctil, Ira Robinson, and Gérard Bouchard, 85–106. Sillery, QC: Editions du Septendrion, 2000.
Mark, Ber. "Tsvishn lebn un toyt. Dos yidishe lebn un di yidishe literatur in poyln in di yorn 1937–1957." *Ikuf-almanakh*. Nyu york: Ikuf farlag, 1961: 60–86.
Massey, Irving. *Identity and Community: Reflections on English, Yiddish, and French Literature in Canada*. Detroit: Wayne State University Press, 1994.
Massey, Irving. "Public Lives in Private: Ida Maza and the Montreal Yiddish Renaissance." In *An Everyday Miracle: Yiddish Culture in Montreal*, edited by Ira Robinson, Pierre Anctil, and Mervin Butovsky, 129–157. Montreal: Véhicule Press, 1990.
Mayzel, Nakhman. *Dos yidishe shafn un der yidisher shrayber in sovetnfarband*. Nyu york: Ikuf farlag, 1959.
Maza, Ida. *Dineh: autobiografishe dertseylung*. Montreal: Ida Maza Book Committee, 1970.
Maza, Ida. *Naye lider*. Montreal: Leyen-krayz fun der yiddisher folks-biblyotek, 1941.
Medem, Gina. *Di froy in der heym, in fabrik, in gezelshaftlekhn lebn*. Nyu york: Kooperativer folks-farlag fun internatsyonaln arbeter ordn, 1937.
Meyzil, Gitl. *Eseyen*. Tel Aviv: Farlag Y. L. Peretz, 1974.
Migrant Women Writers' Group. *Here We Are: An Anthology*. Upper Ferntree Gully, Victoria, Australia: Migrant Women Writers' Group, 1989.
Miller, Marc. *Representing the Immigrant Experience: Morris Rosenfeld and the Emergence of Yiddish Literature in America*. Syracuse: Syracuse University Press, 2007.
Mintz, Alan. *Hurban: Responses to Catastrophe in Hebrew Literature*. New York: Columbia University Press, 1984.
Miron, Dan. "Why Was There No Women's Poetry in Hebrew Before 1920." In *Gender and Text in Modern Hebrew and Yiddish Literature*, edited by Naomi B. Sokoloff, Anne Lapidus Lerner, and Anita Norich, 65–91. New York: Jewish Theological Seminary of America, 1992.
Molodowsky, Kadya. *Afn barg*. Nyu york: "Yungvarg" bibliotek bam kooperatiyn folks-farlag fun internatsyonaln arbeter ordn., 1938.
Molodowsky, Kadya. *Ale fentster tsu der zun*. Varshe: Literarishe bleter, 1938.
Molodowsky, Kadya. *Dzshike gas*. Varshe: Aroysgegebn durkh dem literatur fond baym literatn-farayn un durkh di literarishe bleter, 1933.
Molodowsky, Kadya. *Freydke*. Varshe: Literarishe bleter, 1935.
Molodowsky, Kadya. *In land fun mayn gebeyn*. Shikago: L. M. Shṭayn, 1937.
Molodowsky, Kadya. *Kheshvendike nekht*. Vilna: B. Ḳletsḳin, 1927.
Molodowsky, Kadya. *Likht fun dornboym lider*. Buenos ayres: Ḳiem, 1965.
Molodowsky, Kadya. *Mayselekh*. Varshe: Yidisher shul-organizatsye in poyln, 1931.
Molodowsky, Kadya. *Der melekh dovid aleyn iz geblibn*. Nyu york: Farlag papirene brik, 1946.
Molodowsky, Kadya, and Kathryn Hellerstein. *Paper Bridges: Selected Poems of Kadya Molodowsky*. Detroit: Wayne State University Press, 1999.
Mordell, Albert. *The World of Haldeman—Julius*. New York: Twayne, 1960.
Morgenstern, John. "The 'Center of Intensity': T. S. Eliot's Reassessment of Baudelaire in 1910–1911 Paris." *Religion and Literature* 44:1 (Spring 2012): 159–167.
Muraskin, Bennett. *The Association of Jewish Libraries Guide to Yiddish Short Stories*. Teaneck, NJ: Ben Yehuda Press, 2011.
Neugroschel, Joachim. *No Star Too Beautiful: Yiddish Stories from 1382 to the Present*. New York: Norton, 2002.

Newman, Zelda Kahn. "The Correspondence Between Kadya Molodowsky and Rokhl Korn." *Women in Judaism: A Multidisciplinary Journal* 8:1 (Spring 2011): 1–26.
Niborski, Yitskhok. *Verterbukh fun loshn kodesh-shtamike verter in yidish*. Paris: Bibliotheque Medem, 1997.
Niditch, Susan. "Portrayals of Women in the Hebrew Bible." In *Jewish Women in Historical Perspective*, edited by Judith R. Baskin, 25–45. Detroit: Wayne State University Press, 1991.
Niger, Samuel. *Leksikon fun der nayer yidisher literatur 5*. Band 5. Nyu york: Alyetlekher yidisher kultur-kongres, 1963.
Niger, Samuel. *Leksikon fun der nayer yidisher literatur 6*. Band 6. Nyu york: Alyetlekher yidisher kultur-kongres, 1965.
Niger, Samuel. *Leksikon fun der nayer yidisher literatur 8*. Band 8. Nyu york: Alyetlekher yidisher kultur-kongres, 1981.
Niger, Samuel. "New Trends in Post-War Yiddish Literature." *Jewish Social Studies* 1:3 (July 1939): 337–358.
Niger, Samuel. *Yidishe shrayber in soyet-rusland*. Nyu york: Aroysgegebn fun Sh. Niger bukh-komitet baym alyeltlekhn yidisher kultur-kongres, 1958.
Niger, Samuel, and Jacob Shatzky. *Leksikon fun der nayer yidisher literatur*. Nyu york: Alyeltlekhn yidishn kultur-kongres, 1956.
Norich, Anita. "The Family Singer and Autobiographical Imagination." *Prooftexts* 10:1 (Jan. 1990): 97–107
Novershtern, Abraham. "'Who Would Have Believed That a Bronze Statue Can Weep': The Poetry of Anna Margolin." *Prooftexts* 10:3 (1990): 435–467.
Ofer, Dalia, and Lenore J. Weitzman. *Women in the Holocaust*. New Haven: Yale University Press, 1998.
Olsen, Tillie. *Silences*. New York: Delacourt Press, 1962.
Opotov, Leonard, Naftoli Gross, Eliezer Greenberg, Abraham Sutzkever, Riesel Zhichlinsky, and Jacob Glantz. *Five Yiddish Poets: Gross, Greenberg, Sutzkever, Zichlinsky, Glantz*. Chicago: Midwest Poetry Chapbooks, 1962.
Oyerbakh, Efraim. "Tsvey dikhterins in medinas isroel. Hadasa Rubin." In *Oyf der vogshol*. Vol. I, 318–321. Tel Aviv: Farlag Y. L. Peretz, 1975,
Parush, Iris. "Women Readers as Agents of Social Change Among Eastern European Jews in the Late Nineteenth Century." *Gender and History* 9:1 (April 1997): 60–82.
Pratt, Norma Fain. "Anna Margolin's *Lider*: A Study in Women's History, Autobiography, and Poetry." *Studies in American Jewish Literature* 3 (1983):11–25.
Pratt, Norma Fain. "Culture and Radical Politics: Yiddish Women Writers, 1890–1940." *American Jewish History* 70:1 (September 1980): 68–90.
Pratt, Norma Fain. "Culture and Radical Politics: Yiddish Women Writers in America, 1890–1940." In *Women of the Word: Jewish Women and Jewish Writing*, edited by Judith R. Baskin, 111–135. Detroit: Wayne State University Press, 1994.
Pratt, Norma Fain. "Transitions in Judaism: The Jewish American Woman Through the 1930s." *American Quarterly* 30:5 (Winter 1978): 688–689.
Rabinovich, Israel. *Froyen: literarishe zamlung*. Moskve: Tsentraler felker-farlag fun F.S.S.R., 1928.
Raicus, Ethel. "Women's Voices in the Stories of Yiddish Writer Rokhl Brokhes." In *From Memory to Transformation: Jewish Women's Voices*, edited by Sarah Silberstein Swartz and Margie Wolfe, 25–34. Toronto: Second Story Press, 1998.
Rakovsky, Puah, Paula E. Hyman, and Barbara S. Harshav. *My Life as a Radical Jewish Woman: Memoirs of a Zionist Feminist in Poland*. Bloomington: Indiana University Press, 2002.
Ravitch, Melekh. "Ester Segal." In *Mayn leksikon* IV, no. 2, 72–74. Tel Aviv: Farlag I. L. Peretz, 1982.
Ravitch, Melekh. "Yiddish Culture in Canada." In *Canadian Jewish Reference Book and Directory*, edited by Eli Gottesman. Montreal: Central Rabbinical Seminary of Canada, 1963.

Reading, Anna. *The Social Inheritance of the Holocaust: Gender, Culture, and Memory.* New York: Palgrave Macmillan, 2002.
Redlich, Shimon. *Life in Transit: Jews in Postwar, Lodz 1945–1950.* Brighton, MA: Academic Studies Press, 2010.
Reisen, Sarah. *Lider.* Vilna: Farein fun yidishe shriftshteler un zhurnalistn, 1924.
Rejzn, Zalman. *Leksikon fun der yidisher literatur, prese un filologye. Band 1.* Vilna: Kletskin farlag, 1928.
Rich, Adrienne. *On Lies, Secrets and Silence: Selected Prose 1966–1978.* New York: Norton, 1979.
Ringelheim, Joan Miriam. "The Split Between Gender and the Holocaust." In *Women in the Holocaust*, edited by Dalia Ofer and Lenore J. Weitzman, 340–350. New Haven: Yale University Press, 1998.
Rosenfarb, Chava. "Canadian Yiddish Writers." In *Traduire le Montréal Yiddish / New Readings of Yiddish Montreal*, edited by Pierre Anctil, Norman Ravvin, and Sherry Simon, 11–18. Ottawa: University of Ottawa Press, 2007.
Rosenfarb, Chava. "Feminism and Yiddish Literature: A Personal Approach." In *Gender and Text in Modern Hebrew and Yiddish Literature*, edited by Naomi B. Sokoloff, Anne Lapidus Lerner, and Anita Norich, 217–226. New York: Jewish Theological Seminary of America, 1992.
Rosenfarb, Chava. *The Tree of Life: A Trilogy About Life in the Lodz Ghetto,* translated by Chava Rosenfarb and Goldie Morgentaler. Melbourne: Scribe, 1985.
Rosenfeld, Max, and Sholem Asch. *Pushcarts and Dreamers: Stories of Jewish Life in America.* South Brunswick, NJ: Thomas Yoseloff, 1967.
Roskies, David. *Against the Apocalypse: Responses to Catastrophe in Modern Jewish Culture.* Cambridge: Harvard University Press, 1984.
Roskies, David. "The Treasures of Howe and Greenberg." *Prooftexts* 3 (January 1983): 109–114.
Rothenberg, Joshua. *Fun a mol un fun haynt: zikhroynes un eseyen.* Tel Aviv: Farlag Y. L. Peretz, 1990.
Rozhanski, Shmuel. *Di froy in der yidisher poezye: antologye.* Buenos ayres: Yosef Lifshitsfond fun der literaturgezelshaft baym yivo in argentine, 1966.
Rubin, Hadasa. *Eydertog.* Tel Aviv: Farlag Yisroel-bukh, 1988.
Rubin, Hadasa. *Fun mentsh tsu mentsh.* Tel Aviv: Farlag Y. L. Peretz, 1964.
Rubin, Hadasa. *In tsugvint.* Tel Aviv: Farlag Yisroel-bukh, 1981.
Rubin, Hadasa. *Mayn gas iz in fener.* Varshe: Yidish bukh, 1953.
Rubin, Hadasa. *Rayst nisht op di blum.* Tel Aviv: Farlag Y. L. Peretz, 1995.
Rubin, Hadasa. *Trit in der nakht.* Varshe: Yidish bukh, 1957.
Rubin, Hadasa. *Veytik un freyd.* Varshe: Yidish bukh, 1955.
Rubin, Ruth. *Voices of a People: The Story of Yiddish Folksong.* Urbana: University of Illinois Press, 2000.
Ruskino, Elaine. "Russian Acmeism and Anglo-American Imagism." *Ulbandus Review* 1:2 (Spring 1978): 37–49.
Russ, Joanna. *How to Suppress Women's Writing.* London: Women's Press, 1984.
Ruta, Magdalena. *Bez Żydów? Poezja jidysz w PRL o Zagładzie, Polsce i komunizmie.* Kraków-Budapeszt: Austeria 2012.
Ruta, Magdalena. *Nie nad rzekami Babilonu. Antologia poezji jidysz w powojennej Polsce / Nisht bay di taykhn fun bovl. Anthologye fun der yidisher poezye in nokhmilkhomedikn poyln/ Nie nad rzekami Babilonu, Antologia poezji jidysz w powojennej Polsce.* Kraków: Księgarnia Akademicka, 2012.
Ruta, Magdalena. "Preliminary Remarks on Yiddish Culture in Poland 1945–1968." *Scripta Judaica Cracoviensia* 2 (2004): 61–70.
Ruta, Magdalena. "Yiddish Literature and Communism in Post-War Poland: The Poetry of

Kalman Segal, Moshe Shklar and Paltiel Tsibulski." In *Iggud. Selected Essays in Jewish Studies*, Vol. 3, edited by Tamar Alexader, Ziva Amishai-Maisels, Dan Laor, Ora Schwarzwald, and Yosef Tobi, 35–57. Jerusalem: World Union of Jewish Studies, 2007.

Sandrow, Nahma. *Vagabond Stars: A World History of Yiddish Theater*. Syracuse: Syracuse University Press, 1996.

Schachter, Allison. "Modernist Indexicality: The Language of Gender, Race, and Domesticity in Hebrew and Yiddish Modernism." *Modern Language Quarterly* 72:4 (December 2011): 493–520.

Schatz, Jaff. *The Generation: The Rise and Fall of the Jewish Communists of Poland*. Berkeley: University of California Press, 1991.

Scherman, Nosson. *The Complete ArtScroll Siddur: Weekday, Sabbath, Festival*. Brooklyn: Mesorah Publications, 1987.

Schulman, Elias. *Leksikon fun forverts shrayber: zint 1897*. New York: Forward Association, 1987.

Schulman, Elias. "*Sovietish Heimland:* Lone Voices, Stifled Creators." *Judaism* 14, no. 1 (1965): 64–65.

Schwartz, Howard, and Anthony Rudolf. *Voices Within the Ark: The Modern Jewish Poets*. New York: Avon, 1980.

Schwarz, Leo W. *A Golden Treasury of Jewish Literature*. Philadelphia: Jewish Publication Society of America, 1937.

Schwarz, Leo W. *The Jewish Caravan: Great Stories of Twenty-Five Centuries*. New York: Rinehart, 1935.

Segal, Esther. *Lider*. Toronto: Aroysgegebn fun zerubavel brentsh 219, I.N.A.P., 1928.

Shandler, Jeffrey. "Anthologizing the Vernacular: Collections of Yiddish Literature in English Translation." In *The Anthology in Jewish Literature*, edited by David Stern, 304–323. New York: Oxford University Press, 2004.

Shener, Mordechai. *Sefer zikaron le-ḳehilat Pintṣ'ev: in Pinṭshev ṭogṭ shoyn nishṭ*. Tel Aviv: Irgun Yots'e Pinṭshev be–Yiśra'el uba-tefutsot, 1970.

Shere, Jeremy. "Collective Portraits: The Anthological Imagination of Leo W. Schwarz." *Shofar: An Interdisciplinary Journal of Jewish Studies* 23:3 (Spring 2005): 25–47.

Sherman, Joseph. *Writers in Yiddish*. Detroit: Thomson Gale, 2007.

Shmeruk, Khone, Benjamin Harshav, Abraham Sutzkever, and Mendel Piekarz. *A shpigl af a shteyn*. Tel Aviv: Goldene keyt, 1964.

Shpigel, Yeshaye. *Un gevorn iz likht: lider*. Varshe-Łódź: Yidish bukh, 1949.

Shtern, Sholem. *Shrayber vos ikh hob geḳenṭ: memuarn un eseyen*. Monṭreal: Shalom Shṭern bukh fond ḳomiṭeṭ, 1982.

Sinclair, Clive. *The Brothers Singer*. London: Allison and Busby, 1983.

Sinclair, Gerri, and Morris Wolfe. *The Spice Box: An Anthology of Jewish Canadian Writing*. Toronto: Lester & Orpen Dennys, 1981.

Singer, Isaac Bashevis. *In My Father's Court*. New York: Farrar, Straus and Giroux, 1962.

Singer, Israel Joshua. *Di brider ashkenazi*. Varshe: Brzoza, 1936.

Singer, Israel Joshua. *Di brider ashkenazi*. Nyu york: Maks N. Mayzil, 1937.

Singer, Israel Joshua. *Di mishpokhe karnovski*. Nyu york: Matones, 1943.

Singer, Israel Joshua. *Fun a velt vos iz nito mer*. Nyu york: Matones, 1946.

Smulski, Jerzy. "Obraz kobiety w prozie polskiej pierwszej połowy lat pięćdziesiątych XX wieku. Rekonesans." In *Od Szczecina do ... Października. Studia o literaturze polskiej lat pięćdziesiątych*. Toruń: Wydawnictwo Uniwersytetu Mikołaja Kopernika, 2002.

Sokoloff, Naomi B., Anne Lapidus Lerner, and Anita Norich. *Gender and Text in Modern Hebrew and Yiddish Literature*. New York: Jewish Theological Seminary of America, 1992.

Stavans, Ilan. *The Oxford Book of Jewish Stories*. New York: Oxford University Press, 1998.

Steinberg, Noah. *Yidish amerike: zamlbukh*. Nyu york: Farlag lebn, 1929.

Stępnik, Krzysztof, and Magdalena Piechota. *Socrealizm: fabuły-komunikaty-ikony*. Lublin: Wydawnictwo Uniwersytetu Marii Curie-Skłodowskiej, 2006.
Stern, David. *The Anthology in Jewish Literature*. New York: Oxford University Press, 2004.
Swartz, Sarah Silberstein, and Margie Wolfe. *From Memory to Transformation: Jewish Women's Voices*. Toronto: Second Story Press, 1998.
Symons, Arthur. *The Symbolist Movement in Literature*. New York: E. P. Dutton, 1919.
Szaynok, Bożena. "The Role of Antisemitism in Postwar Polish-Jewish Relations." In *Antisemitism and Its Opponents in Modern Poland*, edited by Robert Blobaum, 265–283. Ithaca: Cornell University Press, 2005.
Szeps, Zew. *Antologia poezji żydowskiej: 1868–1968*. Londyn: Oficyna poetów i malarzy, 1980.
Taitz, Emily, Sondra Henry, and Cheryl Tallan. *The JPS Guide to Jewish Women: 600 B.C.E.– 1900 C.E.* Philadelphia: Jewish Publication Society, 2003.
Tec, Nechama. *Resilience and Courage: Women, Men, and the Holocaust*. New Haven: Yale University Press, 2003.
Tomasik, Wojciech. "Harmonia ludzi i maszyn. O socrealistycznych obrazach 'nowego' człowieka." In *Inżynieria dusz. Literatura realizmu socjalistycznego w planie "propagandy monumentalnej*," edited by Wojciech Tomasik, 159–162. Wrocław: Wydawnictwo Uniwersytetu Wrocławskiego, 1999.
Tregebov, Rhea. *Arguing with the Storm: Stories by Yiddish Women Writers*. New York: Feminist Press at the City University of New York, 2008.
Tsitron, Sh. L. [S. L. Zitron]. *Barimte yidishe froyen*. Varshe: Farlag gezelshaft, 1927.
Tussman, Malka Heifetz. *Lider*. Los Angeles: Malka Heifetz Tussman bukh komitet, 1949.
Tussman, Malka Heifetz, and Marcia Falk. *With Teeth in the Earth: Selected Poems of Malka Heifetz Tussman*. Detroit: Wayne State University Press, 1992.
Ulinover, Miriam. *Der bobes oytser*. Varshe: Khayim Levin Epshteyn, 1921.
Ulinover, Miriam. *A grus fun der alter heym. Lider / Un bonjour du pays natal. Poemes*. Introduced and edited by Natalia Krynicka and translated by Batia Baum. Paris: Medem Biblioteque, 2003.
Veprinski, Rashel. *Ruf fun fligl*. Nyu york: [s.n.], 1926.
Vinogradskaya, Eda. "Поэты моего детства." *Вестник народного университета еврейской культуры* 6 (2000): 181.
Von Tippelskirch, Katrina. "Also das Alphabet vergessen? Die jiddische Dichterin Rajzel Zychlinski." Ph.D. diss. Marburg: Tectum, 2000.
Vurtsel, Khane. *Hundert lider*. Nyu york, 1927.
Waddington, Miriam. *Apartment Seven: Essays Selected and New*. Toronto: Oxford University Press, 1989.
Waldinger, Albert. *Shining and Shadow: An Anthology of Early Yiddish Stories from the Lower East Side*. Selingsgrove, PA: Susquehanna University Press, 2006.
Weinreich, Max. *History of the Yiddish Language*. New Haven: Yale University Press, 2008.
Weinreich, Uriel. *Modern English-Yiddish, Yiddish-English Dictionary*. New York: YIVO Institute for Jewish Research, 1968.
Weinreich, Uriel. *Modern English-Yiddish, Yiddish-English Dictionary*. New York: YIVO Institute for Jewish Research and Schocken Books, 1977.
Weinstein, Miriam. *Prophets & Dreamers: A Selection of Great Yiddish Literature*. South Royalton, VT: Steerforth Press, 2002.
Weissler, Chava. "Prayers in Yiddish and the Religious World of Ashkenazic Women." In *Jewish Women in Historical Perspective*, edited by Judith R. Baskin, 169–192. Detroit: Wayne State University Press, 1991.
Whitman, Ruth. *An Anthology of Modern Yiddish Poetry*. New York: Workman's Circle Education Department, 1979.
Wineberger, Eliot. "The Vortex." *Chicago Review* 51, no. 4–52, no.1 (Spring 2006): 186–202.

Wisse, Ruth R. "*Di Yunge* and the Problem of Jewish Aestheticism." *Jewish Social Studies* 38, no. 3 & 4 (Summer-Autumn 1976): 265–276.
Wisse, Ruth R. *The Modern Jewish Canon: A Journey Through Language and Culture*. New York: Free Press, 2000.
Yakubovitsh, Rosa. *Mayne gezangen*. Varshe: [s.n.], 1924.
Young, James E. *At Memory's Edge: After-Images of the Holocaust in Contemporary Art and Architecture*. New Haven: Yale University Press, 2000.
Young, James E. "The Arts of Jewish Memory in a Postmodern Age." In *Modernity, Culture and 'the Jew*,' edited by Bryan Cheyette and Laura Maras, 211–225. Stanford, CA: Stanford University Press, 1998.
Young, James E. "Memory and Counter-Memory: The End of the Monument in Germany." *Harvard Design Magazine* 9 (1999): 1–10.
Young, James E. *Writing and Rewriting the Holocaust: Narrative and the Consequences of Interpretation*. Bloomington: Indiana University Press, 1988.
Yudika [Judith Tsik]. *Naye yugnt*. Kovna: Likht, 1923.
Zalcberg, Sima. "'Grace Is Deceitful and Beauty Is Vain': How Hassidic Women Cope with the Requirement of Shaving One's Head and Wearing a Black Kerchief." *Gender Issues* 24:4 (September 2007): 13–34.
Zeitlin, Arn, and Yekhiel Yeshaye Trunk. *Antologye fun der yidisher proze in poyln tvishn beyde velt-milkhomes*. Nyu york: CYCO, 1946.
Zinger, Sh. D. "Ven du vest dem toyt in libe derkenen." *Tsukunft* (October 1956): 374–375.
Zumoff, Barnett. *Songs to a Moonstruck Lady: Women in Yiddish Poetry*. Toronto: TSAR Publication in Association with the Dora Teitelboim Center for Yiddish Culture, 2005.
Zychlinski, Rajzel. *Harbstike skvern*. Nyu york: CYCO, 1969.
Zychlinski, Rajzel. *Lider*. Varshe, 1936.
Zychlinski, Rajzel. *Naye lider*. Tel Aviv: Farlag yisroel-bukh, 1993.
Zychlinski, Rajzel. *Di november-zun*. Paris: IMPR. IMPO, 1977.
Zychlinski, Rajzel. *Der regn zingt*. Varshe: Bibliotek fun yidishn PEN klub, 1939.
Zychlinski, Rajzel. *Shvaygndike tirn*. Nyu york: Hammeḥabbēr, 1962.
Zychlinski, Rajzel. *Tsu loytere bregn*. Łódź: Farlag yidish-bukh, 1948.
Zychlinski, Rajzel, and Hubert Witt. *Di lider: 1928–1991. Die Gedichte: jiddisch und deutsch*. Frankfurt am Main: Zweitausendeins, 2003.
Zychlinsky, Rajzel, Barnett Zumoff, Aaron Kramer, and Marek Kanter. *God Hid His Face*. Santa Rosa, CA: Word & Quill Press, 1997.
Zylbercweig, Zalmen. *Leksikon fun yidishn teater*. Vol. 5. Mexico City: Farlag Elisheva, 1967.

# About the Contributors

Hinde Ena **Burstin** is a native Yiddish speaker and a Yiddishist. She has published widely on Yiddish women writers, presented at invited lectures on four continents, and is the coordinator of the Jacob Kronhill Program in Yiddish language and culture at the Australian Centre for Jewish Civilisation, Monash University, where she is also a lecturer of Yiddish language, literature, and culture. Recent research interests include 1920s Yiddish poetry by women.

Debra **Caplan** is an assistant professor of theatre at Baruch College, City University of New York. She received a Ph.D. in Yiddish from Harvard University in 2013 and was the founding executive director of Harvard's Mellon School of Theater and Performance Research. Her research focuses on Yiddish theater and theatrical travel, and her work has appeared in *Comparative Drama* and *New England Theatre Journal*. An area of particular interest is Jewish theater artists and the aesthetics of itinerancy.

Ellen **Cassedy** is the author of the award-winning volume *We Are Here: Memories of the Lithuanian Holocaust*. Along with Yermiyahu Ahron Taub, she is the winner of the 2012 Translation Prize awarded by the Yiddish Book Center in Amherst, Massachusetts. Her translations appear in the anthology *Beautiful as the Moon, Radiant as the Stars: Jewish Women in Yiddish Stories*, as well as in *Pakn Treger*, the magazine of the National Yiddish Book Center.

Dafna **Clifford** has taught at the Oxford Institute for Yiddish Studies and lectured in Yiddish, modern European Jewish, and Israeli literature. She is the author of *Unifying Elements in European Jewish Fiction 1890–1945: Between Disillusion and Destruction* She has contributed to numerous publications, including Dov-Ber Kerler's *Politics of Yiddish Studies in Language, Literature, and Society* and Gennady Estraikh and Dovid Katz's *Intensive Yiddish*.

Elvira **Groezinger** is the author of many scholarly articles and books in Polish, German, Yiddish, French, English, and Hebrew. Her books include *Die jiddische Kultur im Schatten der Diktaturen*; *Heinrich Heine*; and *Unser Rebbe unser Stalin ... Jiddische Volkslieder aus den St. Petersburger Sammlungen von Moishe Beregowski (1892–1961) und Sofia Magid (1892–1954)*.

Paula **Hayes** is a professor of English at Strayer University. She holds a doctorate in textual studies and English from the University of Memphis and a master of arts in philosophy and religious studies from the University of Tennessee. Her most recent publication is *Robert Lowell and the Confessional Voice*. Her poetry and articles have been featured in publications such as *Hispanic Culture Review*, *Phati'tude Literary Journal*, and *Black Magnolias*.

Kathryn **Hellerstein** is an associate professor of Germanic literatures and languages at the University of Pennsylvania. Her books include a translation and study of Moyshe-Leyb Halpern's poems, *In New York: A Selection*; *Paper Bridges: Selected Poems of Kadya Molodowsky*; and *Jewish American Literature: A Norton Anthology*, of which she is co-editor. She is also a recipient of grants from the National Endowment for the Arts, the National Endowment for the Humanities, and the Guggenheim Foundation. Her latest work is *A Question of Tradition: Women Poets in Yiddish, 1586–1987*.

Rosemary **Horowitz** is a professor of English at Appalachian State University. Her research interests are in literacy studies, with a particular focus on writing in the Jewish community. In addition to writing numerous articles and authoring *Literacy and Cultural Transmission in the Reading, Writing, Rewriting Jewish Memorial Books*, she is the editor of the collections *Elie Wiesel and the Art of Storytelling* and *The Memorial Books of Eastern European Jewry*.

Faith **Jones** has worked as a librarian for many years in the United States and in Canada. In addition to her numerous articles, presentation, and translations, she has been active in organizations dedicated to feminism, peace and justice, and Yiddish. She won the 2007 RUSA ABC-CLIO Online History award for her work digitizing the *yizker* book collection at the New York Public Library.

Irena **Klepfisz** is a poet, short story writer, Yiddish translator, and scholar of Eastern European Yiddish women writers and activists. She is the author of *A Few Words in the Mother Tongue* (poetry) and *Dreams of an Insomniac* (essays), as well as a recipient of a National Endowment for the Arts in poetry. She teaches courses on Jewish women's history, literature and culture in the Women's Gender and Sexuality Studies Department at Barnard College.

Joanna **Lisek** is a lecturer in Jewish literature, culture, and Yiddish language at the Department of Jewish Studies in the University of Wrocław in Poland. Her interests include Jewish poetry, women's activism, and Yiddish culture. In 2005, she published the book *Yung Vilne—the Jewish Artistic*. In 2010, her edited volume *Mute Souls? Women in Yiddish Culture* was published. Recent research includes a study on women's Yiddish poetry from the beginning of the century until the Holocaust.

Rebecca **Margolis** is an associate professor with cross-appointments in the Department of Modern Languages and Literatures, the Institute of Canadian Studies, and the Department of Classics and Religious Studies at the University of Ottawa. Her fields of interest are Yiddish language and culture in the modern period and in Canada, Canadian Jewish studies, and Holocaust studies. Along with her many articles, presentations, and translations, she is the author of *Jewish Roots, Canadian Soil: Yiddish Culture in Montreal, 1905–45*.

Magdalena **Ruta** is an associate professor at the Institute of Jewish Studies at the Jagiellonian University, where she teaches Yiddish language and literature. She has translated prose works from Yiddish into Polish and has published numerous articles on modern Yiddish literature. She is the editor of *Nusech Pojln* and a trilingual (Yiddish-Polish-English) anthology, *Nisht bay di taykhn fun Bovl: Antologye fun der yidisher poezye in nokhmilkhomedikn Poyln*. Her monographs include *Pomiędzy dwoma światami: O Kalmanie Segalu* and *Bez Żydów? Literatura jidysz w PRL o Zagładzie, Polsce i komunizmie*.

Julie **Spergel** is a Canadian scholar with a doctorate in English philology from the University of Regensburg in Germany. Her award-nominated dissertation is entitled "Canada's 'Second History': The Fiction of Jewish Canadian Women Writers." She has published extensively on women's writing, as well as Canadian and American literatures.

Yermiyahu Ahron **Taub** is the author of four books of poetry: *Prayers of a Heretic/ Tfiles fun an apikoyres*, *Uncle Feygele*, *What Stillness Illuminated/Vos shtilkayt hot baloykhtn*, and *The Insatiable Psalm*. He was named by the Museum of Jewish Heritage one of New York's best emerging Jewish artists. With Ellen Cassedy, he won the Yiddish Book Center's 2012 Translation Prize. Taub has been nominated twice for a Pushcart Prize and twice for a Best of the Net award.

Sheva **Zucker** is the executive director of the League for Yiddish and the editor of its magazine *Afn Shvel*. She is the author of the textbooks *Yiddish: An Introduction to the Language* and *Literature & Culture*, Volumes I and II. She teaches Yiddish and Yiddish literature in the Uriel Weinreich Summer Program in Yiddish Language, Literature, and Culture under the auspices of Bard College and the YIVO Institute for Jewish Research. Her research and translations focus on women in Yiddish literature.

# Index

*Ale fenster tsu der zun*  181, 189
*American Yiddish Poetry*  21, 54
anthologies  1, 6, 9, 11–12, 15, 17, 19–20, 22–23, 74, 122, 248, 255, 260
*The Anthology of Holocaust Literature*  6
anti–Semitism  77, 209, 237, 238, 274, 276
*Antologye: di yidishe dikhtung in amerike biz yor 1919*  32
*Arguing with the Storm*  1, 6, 18–19, 122
*Ashes Out of Hope*  16
Azyland, Reuven  164, 168

*Balade fun a kholem*  107, 121, 124
Bassin, Morris  31
*Beautiful as the Moon*  6, 20, 122
Bes, Lily  8, 26–27, 29, 35
*Brilyantn*  92, 96–101
Bund  23

Canada  8, 18, 184, 246–250, 252–253, 255–259, 262, 286
Communism  94, 213, 233, 235

*Deborah*  1, 14, 90–94, 96
*Diamonds*  1, 89
*Dineh*  256–257, 264
*Dray un draysik noveln*  78
Dropkin, Celia  2, 7–8, 14–15, 18, 20–22, 32, 51–64, 126, 151, 242, 265, 271
*Drunk from the Bitter Truth*  1, 157, 165

erotic  51, 53, 56, 60, 64, 115, 141, 145, 240
*Exile Book of Yiddish Women Writers*  1, 6, 18–19, 122
*Eydertog*  241
*Eygns*  128, 183
"Eyl khanun"  195–196, 198–199, 203, 206

fathers  20–21, 92, 132, 187, 218, 220, 222
Faygenberg, Rokhl  1, 30

*Five Yiddish Poets*  16
*Found Treasures*  1, 6, 18–19, 122, 264
*Di frayhayt*  6, 27, 32, 33, 37
friends  30, 32–33, 76, 82, 103, 109–110, 121, 233, 271, 274
"Froyen lider"  42, 183–184
"Fun eynge vent"  26–27, 38, 42–45
*Fun mentsh tsu mentsh*  230, 239

Glantz-Leyeles, Aaron  159, 172
Glatshein, Jacob (Yankov Glatshteyn)  16, 98, 142, 159, 182, 252
*God Hid His Face*  1, 284
Goldberg, Isaac  13
*The Golden Peacock*  7, 14, 256
*A Golden Treasury of Jewish Literature*  13
*Di goldene keyt*  109, 115, 119, 230–231, 282
Goldsmith, Emanuel  21–22, 270
Goodman, Henry  16
Gorshman, Shira  7, 16, 18–19, 70–83
*Great Jewish Short Stories*  16
*Great Yiddish Poetry*  13
*Great Yiddish Writers of the Twentieth Century*  14
Greenberg, Eliezer  15, 16, 17, 23

Hadda, Janet  2, 53, 58, 62, 89
Haldeman-Julius, Emanuel  13, 23
*Harbstike skvern*  286
Harshav, Barbara  21, 54, 159
Harshav, Benjamin  21, 54, 159
Hellerstein, Kathryn  2, 12, 19, 22, 34, 195, 260, 273
Holtman, Rachel  27, 28, 29, 33
Horowitz, Sara R.  6, 11, 210, 215, 217, 221–222, 226, 280
Howe, Irving  15–17, 21, 23

*Ikh hob lib*  77
Imagism  157–158, 165–166, 171

*In heysn vint* 51, 54, 56, 60
*In tsugvint* 240
*Inzikhistn* 54, 158–160, 162, 164, 168, 172, 173, 286
Israel 8, 14, 16, 35, 57, 70, 79–80, 83, 90, 92, 104, 120–121, 189, 195, 197–198, 202, 221, 228–229, 237–239, 248, 253, 256, 283

Jewish American Literature 16, 22
*Jewish Caravan* 13
Jewish Publication Society 12–13
Jones, Faith 35, 70

kaddish 112, 215, 226
*Khanes shof un rinder* 80
*Kheshvendike nekht* 30, 183
Klepfisz, Irena 5, 17–18, 32
Korman, Ezra 1, 30–33, 127, 252, 255
Korn, Rokhl 1, 2, 5, 7, 14–15, 18–22, 30, 250, 254, 261, 270, 282
*Der koyekh fun lebn* 74, 77
Kreitman, Esther 1, 18, 88–100

*The Last Lullaby* 21
*Lebn un likht* 77
Leftwich, Joseph 7, 14–15, 17
Lempel, Blume 7, 18–20, 103–104, 106–122
Levin, Chana 7, 14, 126–133, 135, 137–145, 147–148, 150–153
lover 56, 60–62, 112, 125, 138–139, 145, 164, 174, 272

Manger, Itzik 181, 270, 272–273, 278, 285
Mann, Barbara 2, 165
Margolin, Anna 1, 7–8, 14–15, 18, 21–22, 126, 151, 157–176, 265
Mary Poems 169
*Mayn gas iz in fener* 232
*Mayselekh* 183
Maza, Ida 8, 14, 248, 250–251, 255–265
modernism 157–168, 171, 173, 175, 181, 191, 279
modesty 41, 59, 136, 139, 176
Molodowsky, Kadya 2, 5–8, 14–15, 17–18, 21–22, 30, 34, 42, 57, 128, 151, 180–199, 203, 205–206, 242, 270
*Morgn frayhayt* 107
motherhood 28, 52, 129, 131, 140, 166–167, 216, 219, 250, 254, 259

*Naye lider* 256–257, 285, 288
Neugroschel, Joachim 20
*The New Country* 16
newspapers 13, 26, 51, 76, 96, 105, 107, 165, 183, 189, 255, 273, 279, 281
Niger, Shmuel 1, 32–34, 51–52, 54, 252, 273

*No Star Too Beautiful* 20
*Di November-zun* 279
Novershtern, Abraham 2, 156, 166, 171, 288

*The Oxford Book of Jewish Stories* 20

Palestine 14, 70–75, 79, 81–83, 106, 163, 168
*The Penguin Book of Modern Yiddish Verse* 21
Peretz, I. L. 12–14, 20, 104, 120, 122, 127, 203
Polish Jews, 234, 237–239, 274, 282
post-modernism 212, 214
Pratt, Norma Fain 2, 17, 27, 29, 54
*Proletpen* 21
*Pushcarts and Dreamers* 16

Ravitch, Melech 32, 34, 250, 259, 261, 273, 276
*Rays nisht op di blum* 241
"The Red Flower" 51–52, 64
*A rege fun emes* 104, 115, 119
Rich, Adrienne 15, 157
Rosenfarb, Chava 1, 7–8, 18–22, 29, 37, 116–117, 121, 208–226
Rubin, Hadash 8, 230–242

Schocken Books 15–16
Schwarz, Leo 13–14
Segal, Ester 8, 30, 120, 182, 248–265
Serdatsky, Yente 12, 18, 22
sexual 41, 53–54, 56, 58–60, 62–63, 95, 115, 133, 135, 137–138, 141–144, 146, 213–215, 217–220, 240
*Shining and Shadow* 20
Shtok, Fradel 13–14, 17–18, 20–22, 31–32, 35, 41
*Shvaygndike tirn* 285
Socialist Realism 232, 234, 242, 279–281
*Songs to a Moonstruck Lady* 21, 270
*The Soul of the Text* 20
*Sovetish heymland* 77, 79
Soviet writers 79
Sutzkever, Avrom 16, 21, 115, 118–120, 230, 271, 282

theater 181, 182, 185
*tkhine* 204
*Der tog* 35, 51, 107, 164, 231
*A Treasury of Yiddish Poetry* 15
*A Treasury of Yiddish Stories* 15
*The Tree of Life* 1, 208–226
*The Tribe of Dina* 6, 17–18
*Trit in der nakht* 236, 239
"Tsu a kolege" 26–27, 32, 36–38, 45
"Tsu dir miryam" 195, 206
*Tsushteyer* 128, 141, 151

Tussman, Malka Heifetz  1, 8, 21–22, 103, 116, 121, 195, 270

Ulinover, Miriam  14, 21, 30, 270–271

*Veytik un freyd*  234–235
*Voices from the Yiddish*  16
*Voices Within the Ark*  21

Wisse, Ruth  21, 159–161
*With Everything We've Got*  21
women's journals  30

*Yiddish Literature in America, 1870–2000*  21
*Yiddish Tales*  12–13
*Yidishe dikhterins*  30–32, 127, 252–253, 255–256
YIVO  99
*Di yunge*  14, 55, 157–164, 167, 171–173, 250

Zhitlowsky, Chaim  120, 163
Zucker, Sheva  2, 51, 115, 253
Zumoff, Barnett  21–22
Zychlinski, Rayzel  1, 7, 14–15, 21–22, 270–289

www.ingramcontent.com/pod-product-compliance
Lightning Source LLC
Chambersburg PA
CBHW070300240426
43661CB00057B/2606